Screen Genealogies

MediaMatters

MediaMatters is an international book series published by Amsterdam University Press on current debates about media technology and its extended practices (cultural, social, political, spatial, aesthetic, artistic). The series focuses on critical analysis and theory, exploring the entanglements of materiality and performativity in 'old' and 'new' media and seeks contributions that engage with today's (digital) media culture.

For more information about the series see: www.aup.nl

Screen Genealogies

From Optical Device to Environmental Medium

Edited by
Craig Buckley, Rüdiger Campe, and Francesco Casetti

Amsterdam University Press

The publication of this book is made possible by award from the Andrew W. Mellon Foundation, and from Yale University's Frederick W. Hilles Fund.

Cover illustration: Thomas Wilfred, *Opus 161* (1966). Digital still image of an analog time-based Lumia work. Photo: Rebecca Vera-Martinez. Carol and Eugene Epstein Collection.

Cover design: Suzan Beijer
Lay-out: Crius Group, Hulshout

ISBN	978 94 6372 900 0
E-ISBN	978 90 4854 395 3
DOI	10.5117/9789463729000
NUR	670

Every effort has been made to obtain permission to use all copyrighted illustrations reproduced in this book. Nonetheless, whosoever believes to have rights to this material is advised to contact the publisher.

Printed and bound by CPI Group (UK) Ltd, Croydon, CR0 4YY

Table of Contents

6

Formats

Introduction

Craig Buckley, Rüdiger Campe, and Francesco Casetti

A flourishing of screens increasingly defines our contemporary lifeworld. Screens have become more numerous and more protean, changing in size, position, and dimension as well as thickness, shape, and material. But with this increase in number and variety, the screen's functions have also mutated. No longer solely surfaces for the display of representations, they are central to mobile, multi-directional communication. They are surfaces for writing and aggregating messages; they also serve as interfaces for the storage, sharing, and filtering of information. As their uses expand, screens also reshape the most public as well as the most intimate of experiences, obliterating many of the boundaries through which these spheres were formerly distinguished. We should not mistake the screen's immediate visual impact as proffering transparent or universal access. The explosion of screens also depends on and produces new invisibilities, divisions, and enclosures. As more and more aspects of production, consumption, leisure, and communication rely on interactions with screens, so fears grow of the risks and dangers associated with screen exposure—fears that increasingly issue from the very technologists who design and program screens.[1]

The present surfeit of the screen puts pressure on the familiar assumption that screens are primarily optical devices. Against the grain of the burgeoning literature on screens, this book argues that their present superabundance cannot be understood as an expansion and multiplication of the screen that found its epitome in cinema: the screen as a surface that plays host to impermanent images and readily disappears under these images. Rather, screens continually exceed the optical histories in which they are most commonly inscribed.[2] As contemporary screens become increasingly dis-

1   See, for instance, articles by Bowles 2018; and Manjoo, 2018.
2   This insight was the point of departure for the Yale University Sawyer Seminar in the Humanities, sponsored by the Andrew W. Mellon Foundation during 2017-2018. The initial text to which speakers were invited to respond was Francesco Casetti's 'Notes on a Genealogy of the Excessive Screen', 2016.

Buckley, C., R. Campe, F. Casetti (eds.), Screen Genealogies. From Optical Device to Environmental Medium. Amsterdam: Amsterdam University Press, 2019
doi 10.5117/9789463729000_intro

persed in a distributed field of technologically interconnected surfaces and interfaces, we more readily recognize the deeper spatial and environmental interventions that screens have always performed.

For screens have long been something more and other than optical devices. Let's take the English word *screen*—but the same can be said for the Italian *schermo,* the French *écran,* and the German *schirm*. The classical edition of the Oxford English Dictionary (OED), edited by James A.H. Murray at the turn of the century, offered the following main definitions of the word: '1. A contrivance for warding off the heat of a fire or a draught of air. [...] 2. A partition of wood or stone, pierced by one or more doors, dividing a room or building in two parts', and in this sense also '2c. A wall thrown out in front of a building and masking the façade'. The word *screen* could also be '3. Applied to any object, natural or artificial, that affords shelter from heat or wind'. Correlatively, a *screen* could be defined as '3b. Something interposed as to conceal from view [...] 3c. A small body of men detached to cover the movement of an army. [...] 4. A means of securing from attack, punishment, or censure. [...] 5. An apparatus used in the sifting of grain, coal, etc'. Finally, the word *screen* was also '6. Applied to various portions of optical, electrical, and other instruments, serving to intercept light, heat, electricity, etc'.[3] These definitions focus on functions other than supporting a representation: functions of separating, filtering, masking, or protecting, mostly in space and sometimes in time. It is only in the early nineteenth century that the word *screen* was bound to the optical, in connection with the emergence of spectacles like the phantasmagoria.[4] And yet it appears that the screen's optical connotations penetrated the dictionary very slowly. The aforementioned edition of the OED mentioned the optical screen almost incidentally, in a sense derived from other uses.[5] What mattered were the word's older meanings.

So, for most of its history, a screen was a filter, a divide, a shelter, or a form of camouflage. These functions indicate the screen's environmental character. A screen was a barrier or a mobile device; it was an object that marked a significant threshold and that could be placed anywhere; it was an object always shaping and shaped by the space in which it was located.

---

3   *A New English Dictionary*, VIII, 272-273.
4   The inaugural occurrence of the word's optical meaning can be located in two notices referring to the patent granted to Paul De Philipsthal on 26 January 1802, respectively published in the *Cobbett's Political Register* II (p. 1053) and in *The Monthly Magazine* (p. 488). See in particular note 20 in Casetti's contribution in this volume.
5   'A contrivance in the form of a screen [sense 1a], for affording an upright surface for the display of objects for exhibition; a flat vertical surface prepared for the reception of images from a magic lantern or like.' *A New English Dictionary*, VIII, p. 272.

When definitions such as 2c or 3c imply the screen's visuality, they do so in terms related to concealment, deception, and distraction more than display or projection. Only the advent of cinema—and later of television—attached to the screen its now widely accepted identity as a surface supporting a changing representation.

Though intertwined with the movies and the TV, the current explosion of screens quite paradoxically favours the reappearance of these older meanings. New media expand the screen's function beyond the optical. Surveillance cameras provide protection and defence from the outside as much as they reveal or display. In retrieving information, computers sift through vast reservoirs of data, combining a user's query with a search engine's secret algorithms. Hand-held devices enable users to create existential bubbles in which they can find intimacy and refuge, even in public. Global Positioning Systems parse territory and identify potential escape routes. Interfaces create or emphasize separations between worlds and maintain control over the passages between them. Illuminated digital façades promise to make buildings more conspicuous and responsive while also hiding their underlying structures. Screens have again become filters, shelters, divides, and means of camouflage. They remain surfaces that display images and data, yet their opticality has been deeply affected by their reference to, connection with, and impact upon the various spaces they inhabit.

The current debates on the nature of the screen—which we will retrace shortly—either ignore the opposition between the screen's environmental and optical connotations or treat the screen's transformation from spatial to optical device as a complete and decisive break. Against this background, we contend that historians and theorists of the screen must recognize and further explore the paradoxical coexistence of its two connotations as environmental medium and as optical device. Such an exploration is a necessary step towards grasping the complexity of the screen's modernity. The essays in *Screen Genealogies* trace alternative histories of the screen that depart from the well-travelled paths in screen studies. These histories revise, reverse, and reframe the still largely dominant optical conception of the screen. To stress the environmental aspect of the screen is to reconsider the historically contingent and conjunctural role that screens have played as mediators between interior and exterior, protection and exposure, visibility and invisibility. To borrow a concept from the philosopher and historian of science Ian Hacking, we might say that screens today are not only devices for *representing* but are even more so devices for *intervening* in the world.[6]

6   See Hacking, 1983.

Screen Genealogies aims to rediscover the history of screens in places where we don't expect to find them; it also seeks to comprehend the ways in which an optical understanding of the screen came to dominate other historical possibilities. It means to insist that screens always have more than one side.

Screen archaeologies

Recent years have seen a blossoming of efforts to theorize the changing functions and histories of screens.[7] These have been written not only from the perspective of film and media studies but also by historians of art, communications, music, science, and architecture. Rather than seek to summarize the entire history of this burgeoning scholarly field, we will highlight two significant vectors. First, there is the effort to consider the screen's role in the 'post-cinematic' transition from analogue film to digital media; second, the effort to question—and sometimes to multiply—the historical lineages of contemporary screens.

The movement of film into the art gallery since the 1990s has raised significant questions about the screen's mediality and historical mutability. The long history of the screen has become an increasingly important rubric for theorizing the difference between such gallery-based moving image exhibitions and the theatrical exhibition form that had characterized much twentieth-century cinema. Curators have played a key role in this process, as Okwui Enwezor, Chrissie Iles, Phillipe-Alain Michaud, Mark Nash, and Jean-Cristophe Royoux, among others, have proposed the emergence of new genres of multiscreen work specific to the art gallery and to other non-theatrical exhibition spaces.[8] The revision of the historical and theoretical notion of the *dispositif*, or apparatus, developed in film theory has been important to critics and historians as different as Raymond Bellour, Erika Balsom, Francesco Casetti, and Noam M. Elcott. These and other scholars have re-engaged the notion of the apparatus less as a framework for ideological critique than as a means of thinking about the difference between the dominant theatrical mode of cinematic reception and the current reconfiguration of screens in a range of spectatorial contexts, including, but not limited to, those of contemporary art.[9] Historians such as Beatriz Colomina, Orit

7   McQuire, Meredith Martin, and Sabine Niederer, 2009; Tamara Todd, 2011; and Dominique Chateau and José Moure, 2016 have all collected important recent contributions.
8   See Enwezor, 2001; Royoux, 1999; Iles, 2001 and 2017; Michaud, 2006; and Nash, 2001.
9   See Bellour, 2009; Balsom, 2014; Casetti, 2015; and Elcott, 2016.

Halpern, Branden W. Joseph, Liz Kotz, Janine Marchessault, Kate Mondloch, Fred Turner, and Andrew Uroskie have excavated and theorized the varied para-cinematic roles assumed by screens during the mid- and late twentieth century.[10] From the context of world's fairs to the rise of video installation, and from expanded cinema to happenings, these studies have highlighted just how important a multiple and variable array of screens was to both the cultural ambitions of states and corporations and to a range of counter-cultural artists and movements. Rethinking the screen has been also been key to recent work on film that has sought to trouble the privileged place of vision in film criticism. Informed by phenomenology and affect theory, Laura U. Marks's *The Skin of Film: Intercultural Cinema, Embodiment, and the Senses* (2000) influentially theorized the screen as a site of 'haptic vision'. As the qualities of film or video images become blurred, shallow, unfocused, and textured, they intermingle with the qualities of the screens on which they are perceived, yielding an embodied, multi-sensual response that Marks argues is central to intercultural and diasporic cinema.[11] Giuliana Bruno's *Surface: Matters of Aesthetics, Materiality, and Media* (2014) argued that the screen was central to an interdisciplinary investigation of the fate of materiality in our contemporary 'age of virtuality'. Drawing on practices from contemporary architecture, art, and film, Bruno highlights the haptic qualities of contemporary façades, installations, and moving image works to examine their physical composition and experiential qualities, emphasizing the screen as a host of changing optical representations and as a 'space of material relations'.[12] In parallel, yet not directly in dialogue, with these appraisals of the post-cinematic screen are recent efforts to document and re-interpret the meaning and function of pre-modern screens, including choir screens in the Gothic cathedrals of Western Europe, folding screens in China and Japan, and iconostases in Byzantine and Eastern Orthodox churches.[13]

Alongside efforts to engage the variable practices, effects, and ma-terialities of the screen in a post-cinematic age are important efforts to reconsider the historicity of the screen under the broad umbrella of 'media archaeology'.[14] An early effort to outline a genealogy of the screen

10   See Colomina, 2001; Halpern, 2015; Joseph, 2002; Marchessault and Lord, 2007; Kotz, 2004; Turner, 2013; Uroskie 2014.

11   Marks, 2000.

12   Bruno, 2014.

13   On Gothic choir screens, see Jung, 2012. On religious screens more broadly, see Gerstel, 2006.

14   On the challenge of defining 'media archaeology' as an approach, see Huhtamo and Parikka, 2011.

appeared in Lev Manovich's *The Language of New Media* (2001), which postulated three screen types linked to different historical phases. The classical screen, Manovich argued, was a fixed frame for fixed representation and was epitomized by Alberti's metaphor of linear perspective as a view from an 'open window'. The second type, the dynamic screen, was a fixed frame that contained moving images and was epitomized by technologies such as the cinema, television, and video. Finally, the computer screen characteristic of new media, he argued, was a dynamic frame with the capacity to control a range of media—from moving and still images to texts and graphics—by means of multiple windows that could be activated simultaneously. Manovich's genealogy charted a teleological development of the screen across media ruptures; the screen was progressively reconfigured to absorb more and more types of media into multiple frames, while at the same time becoming ever more expansive and immersive.[15] In 2004, writing from the perspective of 'the new film history', Thomas Elsaesser welcomed debates over the impact of the digital screen on conceptions of film history—yet he proposed a method of media archaeology that stood in direct contrast to Manovich's teleological narrative. Elsaesser agreed with Manovich's assertion that digital screen technologies marked a profound rupture in media history, yet he argued that this rupture itself compels us to break with genealogical and chronological models of history, calling for an archaeological approach that understands the screens of the past not as steps leading toward the present but as fragments, comprehensible only as pieces of lost totalities: 'irrecoverably other'.[16] Anne Friedberg's *The Virtual Window: From Alberti to Microsoft* (2006) revisited the historical terrain noted by Manovich while making a profoundly different historical argument. Rather than a development from static frames toward more dynamic, multiple, and immersive screens, Friedberg argued that the conventions of 'windowing' within digital interfaces paradoxically installed the window as the dominant metaphor for the computer screen.[17] In a more general move, W.J.T. Mitchell explored the closeness of the concepts of screen, grid, wall, sheet, and window, tracing the diverse operations and subject positions that each of these surfaces implies.[18] Finally, Erkki Huhtamo, who, together

15   Manovich, pp. 95-100.
16   Elsaesser, 2004, pp. 98-100.
17   Friedberg also noted that this metaphoric reinscription of a new technology in an old form took place at a time when the function of architectural windows were increasingly being transformed by the operations of the virtual screen to which they were likened. Friedberg, pp. 10-12.
18   See Mitchell, 2015.

with Jussi Parikka, has been a leading voice in defining the project of media archaeology for Anglophone audiences, has proposed 'screenology' as its own branch of media studies.[19] Concerned with a deeper history of screens as 'information surfaces', Huhtamo's screenology searches previous eras for patterns and schemata that anticipate contemporary screen technologies, formats, and practices, with a particular emphasis on nineteenth-century popular culture. Thus nineteenth-century panoramas, shadow theatres, peepshows, billboards, and optical furniture are highlighted as historical media that are examined for their anticipatory relationship to the present.

A genealogical approach

This archaeological fervour quite often relies on a teleological vision of history, in which what matters is a lineage—or a set of anticipations or resonances—based on likeness and causality. When Foucault resumed archaeology and then genealogy as key concepts for retracing the history of ideas, he insisted on a non-linear, non-causal, and non-mimetic approach. His inclination was to identify moments of discontinuity and dispersion rather than narrate linear evolution; he wanted to emphasize the role of contingent elements in historical emergence rather than trace a development based on necessity.[20] Hence our second contention, heralded by the title of this collection: while directly referring to a genealogy of the screen, we try to capture the forces and events through which a technique or practice is absorbed into a 'system of purposes'—to use a phrase from Nietzsche— foreign to its own origin.[21] Indeed, the specific screen objects and screen phenomena assembled in this book pinpoint such events, stressing the ways in which screens are neither pre-existing objects nor inventions but rather a diverse and contingent range of surfaces that *become* screens. A surface becomes a screen through an arrangement of apparatus and by virtue of a struggle between forces and practices. A screen always enlists an ensemble of elements—an assemblage—characterized by certain dispositions and

19   See, for instance, their comparative overview, Huhtamo and Parikka, 2011. On Screenology, see Huhtamo, 2004 and 2013.
20   A central reflection on genealogy as historical approach is Foucault's 'Nietzsche, Genealogy, History', 1977.
21   'For history of every kind there is no more important proposition than that one which is gained with such effort but also really *ought to be gained*—namely, that the cause of the genesis of a thing and its final usefulness, its actual employment and integration into a system of purposes, lie *toto coelo* apart.' Nietzsche, 1998, p. 50.

sustaining certain types of operations.[22] Genealogies of the screen thus emphasize processes of transformational descent and emergence rather than moments of invention or historical culmination.[23]

A genealogical emphasis requires us to rethink some of the most influential premises of recent media studies, such as the claim that the languages of new screen media originate in those developed for the cinema screen.[24] A perspective stressing transformational descent rather than origins and roots emphasizes that the understanding of the screen as an optical surface, while crucial to cinema, was but one instance in a larger set of intersecting and competing definitions of the screen. The screen's beginnings, moreover, cannot be traced to a single technology or moment; rather, multiple emergences of the screen have crystallized amid the dispersed range of entities that the word 'screen' has served to name. Rather than accumulation and growth, descent implies a process of dispersal and consolidation across different and conflicting currents. Thus the gradually increasing dominance of visuality in the nineteenth century should be seen as neither inevitable nor irreversible, as the increasing entanglement of the screen with the management of ecologies, environments, and spaces in the twentieth and twenty-first centuries serves to highlight. Far from telling a simple story about objects and technologies, an emphasis on descent can illuminate the screen's relationship to bodies which are, in Foucault's words, 'imprinted by history' and to nervous systems whose potentials and pathologies are defined by multiple inheritances.[25]

For Foucauldian genealogy, descent was defined less by lines of continuity than it was by moments of sudden emergence. Such emergence cannot be understood as the appearance of a new object within a pre-existing field but rather as an event. The event of emergence or absorption in a pre-existing field is always unpredictable and singular, defined by the conflict of forces that seek to determine the configuration, direction, and purpose of entities with the capacity to change the shape of the historical field. The event of an emergence, Foucault noted, designated a *non-lieu*, or 'non-place', precisely

22   As Deleuze and Guattari use the term in *A Thousand Plateaus*, 'assemblage' indicates heterogeneous elements that enter into a new relation, forming a coherent but mutable unity. For the utility of the concept in film studies in an age of excessive screens, see Casetti, 2015, pp. 67-98.
23   The centrality of 'descent' and 'emergence' to Foucaudian genealogy descend (as it were) from his reading of Nietzsche, for whom *Entstehung* ('emergence') and *Herkunft* ('descent') 'are more exact than *Ursprung* ('origin') in recording the true objective of genealogy'. Foucault, 145.
24   This argument was central to Manovich, 2001.
25   Foucault, p. 148.

because adversaries 'do not belong to a common space'.[26] Put another way, the conflict that impels something to emerge is itself a conflict between incommensurate organizations of space. Unfolding from interstices and sites of instability, an emergence redefines the relation of places to non-places. The spatial vocabulary latent within genealogy is worth emphasizing in considering the long historical descent of the screen. Continually defined and redefined by virtue of its between-ness, the screen might be recognized as a crucial element for thinking about such interstices and 'non-places'—a category that has become central to a contemporary ethnography of the sites of transit, consumption, and leisure within contemporary globalization.[27] For this very reason, a genealogical account of the screen's various emergences cannot remain at the level of narrating the history of the changing technologies that host visual representations. The struggle over such interstices has always concerned not just representations but also *interventions*, efforts to control and experiment with the environments and sites where screens and screening operate. Yet the concept of *intervention* does not displace or replace the importance of representation. Rather, interventions are precisely what link representations to other actions: the means by which images can filter external elements, shelter components, divide spaces, and camouflage appearances.

The plan of this book

The contributions to this book bring together a broad range of screen events that highlight the accidents, deferrals, reversals, appropriations, and deviations that characterize screen emergence. In addition to the familiar screens that one would expect to find in such a book—cinematic, televisual, and digital screens—the contributions reflect on a range of entities that radically stretch the boundaries of what has been considered a screen. Along with the phantasmagoria, the movie screen, smart phones, and virtual reality headsets, the reader will encounter shields, mirrors, hunting blinds, canvases, mechanical scenery, technical standards, hypnotic gestures, curtains, legal

26 Foucault, p. 150.
27 Foundational in this respect is the work of the ethnographer Marc Augé, who developed the concept of '*non-lieux*' (non-places) to analyze airports, shopping malls, toll-booths and other spaces characteristic of what he termed 'supermodernity'. Like that of Foucault two decades earlier, Augé's use of '*non-lieu*' depended on a neologism. Advanced as a term for thinking about space, '*non-lieu*' was distinguished from its established juridical sense, which designated a lack of grounds for prosecution, the dropping of a charge for want of evidence. Augé, 1995.

concepts, stereoscope viewers, façades, murals, atomic blasts, artificial fog and clouds, and many others. To understand many more things as screens (and as things that effect different kinds of screening) does not mean that genealogy extends the concept of the screen indefinitely; we do not mean to propose that anything or everything could be considered a screen. By extending the notion of the screen beyond its optical use we mean to introduce a different focus. Instead of fixating the identity of the screen on an object with one particular function the effort is rather to the grasp the struggles and conjunctures that characterize the emergence of different screen functions. Drawing on examples from antiquity to the present, the contributions mark out a temporal framework at odds with the dominant periodizations of screen studies, which have tended to unfold from the late eighteenth and early nineteenth century into the twentieth century. The unorthodox temporality of *Screen Genealogies* contains a provocative suggestion: that the screens associated with literary, artistic, and cinematic modernism may well represent a period of relative stability and calm rather than an epoch of rupture and turbulence, as is often assumed – if we look at it in the context of a longer and more varied history.

The essays are brought together in four sections that engage questions central to a media genealogy of the screen in such a wider history: 'Becoming Screen', 'Spaces', 'Atmospheres', and 'Formats'. The initial section, 'Becoming Screen', explores the process through which the screen as a technical device emerges as a component of a media *dispositive* or, better, a media *assemblage*. The individual screen types and screen artifacts encountered in this book may appear 'new', yet from the genealogical perspective their discrete ontogenesis can be seen to emerge from the complexities and struggles characteristic of a larger technical, social, and practical phylogenetic process. In his opening essay 'Primal Screens', Francesco Casetti explores the process of becoming-screen challenging the traditional screen archaeologies. In contrast to arguments that draw a teleological arc between contemporary screens and a first (or primal) screen, Casetti argues that these origin myths are just that—myths, which tell us little about the historical circumstances of the screen's emergence. Instead, these 'prefigurations' reveal many of our present-day assumptions and priorities. To test this assertion, Casetti playfully stages three 'primal scenes', each of which offers a potential origin point: Athena's shield, which Perseus converted into an optical tool of warfare; Butades's wall, on which his daughter fixed her lover's shadow; and Alberti's window, which the artist transforms into an abstract mathematical tool for visualization. No one of these situations represents an 'ancestor' of our screens; yet, once critically re-read, these primal scenes reveal the ground from which screens emerge. The screen only ever comes into being thanks to a recurring set of operations, which integrate the most diverse material objects into their mode of working, give their components new functions and roles, and assign a new orientation to the whole. It is against this backdrop that we can capture the process of becoming a screen, the persistence of an environmental aspect within the prevalent screens' optical connotation, and finally the great variety of screens within an enveloping 'screenscape.'

For his account of the screen's becoming a screen, Rüdiger Campe's "*Schutz und Schirm*": Screening in German During Early Modern Times' takes its departure from the distinction between the two main German terms for screen: *Bildschirm* and *Filmleinwand*. While *Filmleinwand* (film canvas/screen) denotes a movie screen, *Bildschirm* (image screen) remains specific to electronic and digital displays, such as radar, TV, and computer screens. Such a neologism, Campe argues, should be understood via a return to the semantic field of the term *Schirm* in early modernity. Screens in early modern German did not denote surfaces for image projection but rather such things as elaborate *Jayd-Schirme,* or hunting blinds, which were complex means of visual concealment that also configured deadly forms of projection. The meaning of *Schirm* was further located in the legal sphere, notably in the principle of '*Schutz und Schirm*', a provision for exceptional administrative and military protection that also allowed for the projection of a legal entity that would otherwise not exist within the ordinary structures of power and politics. Given that there was nothing optical about the combined sense of protection and projection in the early modern *Schirm*, how should one comprehend the return of the term within the language of electronic display? Campe elucidates Friedrich Kittler's notion of 'implementation' as a concept for how such early modern practices of the screen—and the closed technical systems that characterize the modern media history of the optical screen—can be seen as discontinuous in one respect and continuous in another. 'Implementation', in this reading, means to identify certain functions—such as protection and projection—for possible technical development but also to construct autonomous technological—in this case optical—systems that resume such functions.

The following three sections—'Spaces', 'Atmospheres', and 'Formats'—each highlight shared problems central to emerging work on screen genealogies. The essays in 'Spaces' underscore how a screen's optical functions have been shaped by questions of location, configuration, and orientation. Whereas the spatiality of the screen has often been considered in relation to the auditorium of the movie theatre, these essays highlight the operations of screens as a function of a broader range of architectural, urban, and virtual spaces.

Craig Buckley's 'Face and Screen: Toward a Genealogy of the Media Façade' questions the tendency to see the multi-media façade as paradigmatic of recent developments in illumination and display technologies in the twentieth and twenty-first centuries. Instead, Buckley reconsiders the conflicting urban roles in which façades, like screens, have been cast. Through the course of the nineteenth century, façades underwent an optical redefinition parallel to that which defined the transformation of the screen. An eighteenth-century physiognomic conception of the building's exterior as a representation of its inner identity and purpose was displaced by an idea of the façade as an over-wrought and deceptive screen, dangerously independent from the structure to which it was attached. The extensively glazed building envelopes of the early twentieth century set themselves in contrast to such false faces—yet, confronted with increasingly congested commercial environments, they were also caught up in a conflict over visibility in the metropolis. Through an unexpected twist, buildings that sought to do away with a classical conception of the façade emerged as key sites of experimentation with illuminated screening technologies. In designs for storefronts, cinemas, newspaper offices, union headquarters, and information centres, the media façade emerged as an environmental agent defined by its capacity to operate on and intervene in its surroundings rather than express an interior.

Nanna Verhoeff's 'Sensing Screens: From Surface to Situation' considers recent screen-based public art installations that extend from their architectural site into surrounding urban space in order to engage techniques of 'remote sensing', interactivity, and public display. In these installations, Verhoeff identifies a genre of artwork that aims to raise awareness of urban social issues by visualizing and making 'present' otherwise invisible crises relating to the meeting of the social and the environmental. These installations compel one to look past the *surface* of the screen to its surrounding *situation*. Drawing on a range of contemporary examples, Verhoeff conceptualizes an approach to screens as site-specific boundaries that produce various ways for the subject to *interface* with his/her immediate, as well as remote, surroundings. Verhoeff thus reorients cinematic concepts of the *dispositif* towards a broader spectatorial territory, one with a porous and permeable boundary that opens onto other spaces. Fundamentally performative, the spectatorial territories Verhoeff identifies are defined by their building-scaled interfaces that reach beyond their local situation to remake, create, and influence surrounding space by sensibly linking it to other, more distant spaces.

Ariel Rogers's 'Taking the Plunge: The New Immersive Screens' addresses the contemporary experience of virtual reality (VR) technology and its long and volatile relationship to ideas of immersion. The multiplication and pervasion of screens has often been viewed as a break from previously dominant forms of screen engagement. Whereas viewers' encounters with the twentieth-century cinema screen (conceived as singular and static) has typically been framed as an experience of centred space, marked by fixity and transfixion, the experience of enclosure in multiple-screen environments has often been conceptualized via concepts of spatial fragmentation and information flow. Contemporary VR sets confound this distinction: not only are they 'immersive' and centring, they are also unanchored, breaking the tight identification of frame and screen that has dominated much of cinema's history. With VR technologies, the 'frame' appears to move when the screen moves, an effect most notable and problematic in the search for effects oriented to vertical spatial movement within many VR films. Insofar as Virtual Reality technologies mark the emergence of a new kind of screen assemblage, they are oriented, Rogers argues, less towards representation than to emergent forms of spatial penetration.

The next section, 'Atmospheres', gathers together contributions that consider the screen less as a technical surface and more in terms of the qualities and functions associated with its surrounding atmosphere. The essays in this section pinpoint intersections in which the idea of the screen was redefined by virtue of struggles over how to comprehend diffuse phenomena in which the natural and the technological were not distinctly separable. Antonio Somaini's 'Atmospheric Screens, Atmospheric Media' highlights one salient point of intersection in the veils, mists, and fogs that appear in the late canvases of J.M.W. Turner. Reading Turner's canvases in relation to the starkly opposed accounts offered by William Hazlitt and John Ruskin, Somaini brings to light the canvas's status as an 'atmospheric screen'. Drawing on the etymology of the term 'medium', Somaini probes the reemergence of an environmental media concept in relation to the rediscovery of the environmental nature of the screen. Their parallel genealogies, he suggests, intersect in Romantic landscape painting and in nineteenth-century German *Naturphilosophie* and Romantic literature, each of which might be situated within a line of transformational descendence running from Aristotle's notions of *metaxy* in *De Anima* to mediaeval theories of *media diaphana*. The controversy over Turner's canvas—its status as an atmospheric screen and an immersive environment—is a potent reminder of the unsettled status of the atmosphere at a moment when the optical conception of the screen was not yet dominant.

Yuriko Furuhata's 'The Fog Medium as Environmental Screen' explores the fog sculptures of artist Nakaya Fujiko. Nakaya's deployment of fog and smoke recalls other expanded cinema practitioners and environmental artists in the postwar period, including Matsumoto Toshio, Anthony McCall, and the art and engineering collective E.A.T. Yet her experiments take on a different significance when seen not as a descendant of the phantasmagoria but as part of an assemblage linked to the development of smoke screens for aerial warfare. Paying particular attention to the dual function of fog screens—which obfuscate visibility yet also make visible such qualities as temperature, humidity, and wind—Furuhata historicizes the epistemological and political conditions behind the turn to fog and smoke within expanded cinema and the environmental arts during the Cold War. In so doing, Furuhata provides a geopolitically nuanced analysis of what the philosopher Peter Sloterdijk has called the process of 'atmospheric-explication', which he regards as a universally modern relationship to the environment—adding a different twist to the recent interest in 'atmospheric media' and 'elemental media'.

John Durham Peters, whose *The Marvellous Clouds: Towards a Philosophy of Elemental Media* (2015) helped lay the groundwork for theorizing atmospheric and elemental media, extends this investigation in 'The Charge of a Light Barricade: Optics and Ballistics in the Ambiguous Being of Screens'. The essay invites us to rethink the optical and environmental duality of the screen by examining media practices that link projection to protection and showing to shielding. The ontological ambiguity of the screen—at once a site for the representation of a world and a real element embedded in the world—enables one to think of media as a key part of what Peters calls 'infrastructures of being'. The intertwined history of optics and ballistics are crucial to the conflicted character of this infrastructure, whose work enables aggressive destruction and essential forms of protection. Outlining the historical convergences between cultural practices of targeting and visualizing in Western history, Peters weaves together a rich and unexpected set of voices from the onset of the 'atomic age'—from James Joyce and Vladimir Nabokov to Harold Edgerton and Norbert Wiener—illuminating the imbrications of detonation and image-making across photographic, filmic, televisual, and celestial screens.

The final section, 'Formats', comprises essays that examine the roles played by screen formats and standards in the domains of opera, early cinema, and contemporary art respectively. Engaging the concept of format rather than atmospheres or spaces, these essays take seriously the manner in which overlooked technical and epistemological conditions can function environmentally only to the extent that they are embedded in ratios, staging practices, or gestures.

Gundula Kreuzer's 'Flat Bayreuth: A Genealogy of Opera as Screened' challenges assumptions about the 'screenification' of contemporary opera productions by reconsidering the historical formats of screening techniques within staged opera. Beginning with the Baroque picture-frame stage, she highlights the emergence of a key 'spatial dilemma' in which a desire for visual illusion on stage came into conflict with the increasingly complicated array of equipment, scenery, and props required to produce such elaborate scenes. Retracing the architectural, scenic, lighting, and compositional strategies tested out at Wagner's Festspielhaus at Bayreuth, she argues that the theatre's curtain line came to operate as an invisible screen, a flat plane of illusion with the capacity to organize the depth of the stage together with the visual and acoustic environment of the auditorium. Rather than a device of manipulation or a part of the telos of modernist painting, she highlights this flattened planar format as the outcome of technical and aesthetic conflict, whose unsettled and enduring legacy proves highly relevant to contemporary experiments with opera staging today.

Ruggero Eugeni's 'The Imaginary Screen: Hypnotism and the Dispositives of Early Cinema' argues for a deep congruence between the medium of film and the medium of hypnosis through an examination of the iconography of hypnotic induction in early cinema. From the nineteenth to the twentieth century, hypnotism was itself a shifting format. In early depictions, hypnotists pointed their fingers at the subject in order to hit him or her with a shot of magnetic fluid. By the early twentieth century, subjects were induced into a hypnotic state when the hypnotist's hand was waved repeatedly in front of the eyes. In this period, many films staged the setting of hypnosis as a metaphor for the cinematic dispositive itself; the gestural format of hypnosis in these movies mirrored and shaped in imaginary terms the film's screening conditions and the viewer's experience. At a moment when a nascent cinema might have been defined in a number of ways, the anachronistic figure of the hypnotist's hand worked to establish the screen—rather than the film or the projector—as the essential element of an emerging assemblage.

Noam Elcott's 'Material. Human. Divine. Notes on the Vertical Screen' takes cues from architecture, painting, and experimental cinema to map three distinct paradigms for the format of the vertical screen. Portraiture—the erect human figure or face—may be understood as the eponymous and paradigmatic form of this vertical format. Vertical screens also align with the celluloid strips that run vertically through nearly all projectors, thus hinting at film's otherwise invisible material support, whose properties were interrogated by postwar avant-gardes and have taken on renewed urgency in light of celluloid's impending obsolescence. Finally, the luminous verticality of stained glass windows helped define the Gothic order, which provided a model for avant-garde experiments in light and space for a century or more, and which have suddenly returned to centre stage in contemporary art. Elcott's three distinct paradigms—material, human, and divine—map a centuries-long encounter with vertical screens that resonate unexpectedly yet unambiguously in the present.

By emphasizing questions of space, atmosphere, and format, these essays provide alternative avenues for examining the processes of 'becoming screen' that emerged and consolidated during the nineteenth and twentieth centuries. The present volume seeks to further a diachronic, interdisciplinary conversation around the questions raised by screens by recognizing the distinct environmental and optical histories of the screen and by better understanding the historical interrelations between these two modalities. The multiplication of contemporary screens—their differing arrangements and environmental entanglements—demand a renewed attention to the historically shifting ways in which cultural production, technologies, infrastructures, and bodies form functioning relationships, together with the range of effects these produce. In this sense, screens never simply stand between a spectator and his or her visual object; they also fundamentally intervene in the world. Screens are increasingly essential to life. The effects of their different configurations raise questions that are not strictly about particular media, like film or television. Firstly, these effects cannot be understood as specifically geared towards human consciousness. As elements that form distinctions between interior and exterior, protection and exposure, visibility and invisibility, screens enact a deeper and more primary structuring of the lifeworld in which perception, orientation, and representation take place. Secondly, many of the essays in this volume demand a recognition that screens exceed conventional oppositions between technology and nature and belong more fundamentally to both at the same time.

It is for the same reasons that the emergent manifestations of the screen belong to no discipline in particular. Screens have become an object of concern across the humanities more broadly, even if this has only recently begun to be recognized. No longer a topic solely for Film and Media Studies, it speaks to disciplines such as the History of Art and Architecture, Literature, Communication Studies, Theatre, and the History of Science, to name only a few. Far from exhausting the capacious task implied by a genealogy of the screen, this volume highlights a domain whose faults, fissures, and layers will, we hope, continue to be debated, elaborated, and explored by others. In fundamentally rethinking the descent of the screen, we think again about what the screen might become.

Works Cited

Augé, Marc. *Non-Places: Introduction to an Anthropology of Supermodernity*. Translated by John Howe. New York: Verso Books, 1995.

Balsom, Erika. *Exhibiting Cinema in Contemporary Art*. Amsterdam: Amsterdam University Press, 2013.

Bellour, Raymond. *La querelle des dispositifs: Cinéma, installations, expositions*. Montreal: Librarie Gallimard, 2016.

Bowles, Nellie. 'A Dark Consensus About Screens and Kids Begins to Emerge in Silicon Valley.' *The New York Times*, 26 October 2018.

Bruno, Giuliana. *Surface: Matters of Aesthetics, Materiality, and Media*. Chicago: University of Chicago Press, 2014.

The Century Dictionary and Cyclopedia. New York: The Century Company, 1911.

Casetti, Francesco. *The Lumière Galaxy: Seven Key Words for the Cinema to Come*. New York: Columbia University Press, 2015.

———. 'Notes on a Genealogy of the Excessive Screen.' In *SCREENS: Genealogies of the Excessive Screen, A Mellon Sawyer Seminar at Yale*. New Haven: Department of Film and Media Studies, 2017. http://dev.screens.yale.edu/sites/default/files/files/Screens_Booklet.pdf. Accessed 21 January 2019.

Chateau, Dominique and José Moure, eds. *Screens: From Materiality to Spectatorship*. Amsterdam: Amsterdam University Press, 2016.

Colomina, Beatriz. 'Enclosed by Images: The Eameses' Multimedia Architecture.' *Grey Room* No. 2 (Winter 2001): 5-29.

Deleuze, Gilles and Felix Guattari. *A Thousand Plateaus: Capitalism and Schizophrenia*. Translated by Brian Massumi. Minneapolis: University of Minnesota Press, 1987.

Enwezor, Okwui. 'Black Box,' in *Documenta 11, Platform 5: Exh. Cat.* Kassel, Germany: Documenta and Museum Friedrichanium Veranstaltungs, 2002.

Elcott, Noam. M. *Artificial Darkness: An Obscure History of Modern Art and Media*. Chicago: University of Chicago Press, 2016.

Elsaesser, Thomas. 'The New Film History as Media Archaeology.' *Cinémas: Revue d'études cinématographiques / Journal of Film Studies* 14.2-3 (2004): 75-117.

Foucault, Michel. 'Nietzsche, Genealogy, History.' In *Language, Counter-Memory, Practice: Selected Essays and Interviews*, edited by D.F. Bouchard, pp. 139-164. Ithaca: Cornell University Press, 1977.

Friedberg, Anne. *The Virtual Window: From Alberti to Microsoft*. Cambridge, MA: MIT Press, 2006.

Gerstel, Sharon E.J., ed. *Thresholds of the Sacred: Architectural, Art, Historical, Liturgical, and Theological Perspectives on Religious Screens, East and West*. Washington: Dumbarton Oaks, 2006.

Hacking, Ian. *Representing and Intervening: Introductory Topics in the Philosophy of Natural Science*. Cambridge, UK: Cambridge University Press, 1983.

Halpern, Orit. *Beautiful Data: A History of Vision and Reason Since 1945*. Durham, NC: Duke University Press, 2015.

Huhtamo, Erkki. *Illusions in Motion: Media Archaeology of the Moving Panorama and Related Spectacles*. Cambridge, MA: MIT Press, 2013.

—— and Jussi Parikka, eds. *Media Archaeology: Approaches, Applications, and Implications*. Berkeley: University of California Press, 2011.

Iles, Chrissy. *Into the Light: The Projected Image in American Art, 1964-1977*. Exhibition catalogue. New York: Whitney Museum of American Art, 2001.

——. *Dreamlands: Immersive Cinema and Art 1905-2016*. Exhibition catalogue. New York: Whitney Museum of American Art, 2016.

Joseph, Branden. '"My Mind Split Open": Andy Warhol's Exploding Plastic Inevitable.' *Grey Room*, No. 8 (Summer 2002): 80-107.

Jung, Jacqueline. *The Gothic Screen: Space, Sculpture, and Community in the Cathedrals of France and Germany, ca. 1200-1400*. Cambridge, UK: Cambridge University Press, 2012.

Kotz, Liz. 'Disciplining Expanded Cinema.' In *X-Screen: Film Installation and Actions in the 1960s and 1970s*. Edited by Matthias Michalka. Vienna: Museum Moderner Kunst Siftung Ludwig Wien, 2003.

Manjoo, Farhad. 'We Have Reached Peak Screen. Now Revolution Is in the Air.' *The New York Times*, 27 June 2018.

Manovich, Lev. *The Language of New Media*. Cambridge, MA: MIT Press, 2001.

Marchessault, Janine and Susan Lord, *Fluid Screens, Expanded Cinema*. Toronto: University of Toronto Press, 2007.

Mitchell, W.J.T. 'Screening nature (and the nature of the screen).' *New Review of Film and Television Studies*, Vol. 13, No. 3 (2015): 231-246.

Mondloch, Kate. *Screens: Viewing Media Installation Art*. Minneapolis: University of Minnesota Press, 2010.

Nash, Mark. 'Art and Cinema: Some Critical Reflections.' in *Documenta 11, Platform 5*. Exhibition catalogue.

A New English Dictionary on Historical Principles. Edited by James A.H. Murray. Oxford: Clarendon Press, 1914.

Nietzsche, Friedrich, *On the Genealogy of Morality: A Polemic*. Translated by Maudemarie Clark and Alan J. Swenson. Indianapolis and Cambridge: Hackett Publishing Company, 1998.

The Oxford English Dictionary. Second Edition. Prepared by J.A. Simpson and E.S.C. Weiner. Oxford: Clarendon Press, 1989.

Philipsthal, Paul, 'Patent for the invention of the Phantasmagoria.' In *Cobbett's Political Register*, Vol. 2. London: Cox and Baylis, 1802.

———. 'Patent for the invention of the Phantasmagoria.' *The Monthly Magazine*, Vol. 87, June 1802.

Royoux, Jean-Christophe, 'Remaking Cinema.' In *Cinema, Cinema: Contemporary Art and the Cinematic Experience*. Rotterdam: NAi Publishers, 1999.

Todd, Tamara, ed. *Screen/Space: The Projected Image in Contemporary Art*. Manchester: Manchester University Press, 2011.

Turner, Fred. *The Democratic Surround: Multimedia and American Liberalism from World War II to the Psychedelic Sixties*. Chicago: University of Chicago Press, 2013.

Uroskie, Andrew. *Between the Black Box and the White Cube: Expanded Cinema and Postwar Art*. Chicago: University of Chicago Press, 2014.

About the Authors

Craig Buckley is an assistant professor of modern and contemporary architecture in the Department of the History of Art at Yale University. His research interests include the intersections of modern architecture with avant-garde movements; the entanglement of architectural design with the poetics, technics, and politics of media; and the historiography of modern architecture in the nineteenth and twentieth centuries. His essays and criticism have appeared in *Grey Room, Log, October,* and *Texte zur Kunst.* He is the author of *Graphic Assembly: Montage, Media and Experimental Architecture in the 1960s*, published by University of Minnesota Press (2019) as well as a number of edited collections including *After the Manifesto: Writing, Architecture, and Media in a New Century* (2015), *Utopie: Texts and Projects 1967-1978* (with Jean-Louis Violeau, 2011), and *Clip/Stamp/Fold: The Radical Architecture of Little Magazines* (with Beatriz Colomina, 2010).

Rüdiger Campe is the Alfred C. and Martha F. Mohr Professor of Germanic Languages & Literatures at Yale University. Before joining the Yale faculty, he taught at Johns Hopkins and Essen University, and has held visiting professorships at NYU, Konstanz, Siegen, European University at Frankfurt/Oder, and other institutions. He is author of *Game of Probability. Literature and Calculation from Pascal to Kleist* (2012; German, 2002) and co-editor with Julia Weber of *Rethinking Emotion. Interiority and Exteriority in Pre-Modern, Modern, and Contemporary Thought* (2014). Further book publications include *Baumgarten-Studien* (with Anselm Haverkamp and Christoph Menke, 2014), *Affekt und Ausdruck* (1990), and *Penthesileas Versprechen* (2008). He has published on science and literature, literature and law, rhetoric, media theory and history, and the theory of communication.

Francesco Casetti is the Thomas E. Donnelly Professor of Humanities and Film and Media Studies at Yale University. He has previously taught in Italy where he served as president of the scholarly society of Film and Media Studies. He has also been visiting professor at Paris 3 La Sorbonne Nouvelle, at the University of Iowa, and at Harvard. His books include *Inside the Gaze, Theories of Cinema, 1945-1995, Eye of the Century: Film, Experience, Modernity,* and *The Lumière Galaxy. Seven Key Words for the Cinema to Come,* a study on the reconfiguration of cinema in a post-medium epoch. His current research focuses on two topics: the early film theories, especially the role of cinephobia; and a genealogy of screen that underlines its environmental aspects and the ways in which it becomes a component of our current 'mediascapes'.

1.   Primal Screens

Francesco Casetti

Abstract

In a polemical stance against current media archaeologies, Francesco Casetti re-reads what film theories consider 'proto-screens'—respectively Athena's shield, which Perseus converted to a tool of warfare; Boutades's wall, on which his daughter fixed her lover's shadow; and Alberti's window, which the artist transforms into a perspectival matrix. While these narratives are just that—narratives—they reveal many of our present-day assumptions and priorities. In particular, they uncover how screens do not exist as such. A screen *becomes a screen* thanks to an assemblage of elements and within a set of operations in which it can perform specific functions. Furthermore, screens are not only optical devices; they are *environmental media*. The dispositives illustrated by the three narratives heavily imply space: while exploiting environmental components, they address hands, legs, distances, and alignments as much as they move eyes and sights.

Keywords: Assemblage, Media Archaeology, *Dispositif,* Myth

Prefigurations

Media studies often falls prey to a strange fascination. The more frantic the transformations of the media landscape, the more theorists feel the need to cast a retrospective look at the media past. This historical view is expected to capture not only the story of a single medium but also its place in a longer lineage: its origins and previous instantiations. Hence the current boom of media archaeology, whose tasks and methods have been voiced especially by Erkki Huhtamo and Jussi Parikka—and in a more critical mode, by

Buckley, C., R. Campe, F. Casetti (eds.), *Screen Genealogies. From Optical Device to Environmental Medium.* Amsterdam: Amsterdam University Press, 2019
DOI 10.5117/9789463729000_CH01

Thomas Elsaesser.[1] Beyond offering readers the pleasure of its historical reconstructions, media archaeology is symptomatic of the desire to find roots and continuity in an age of breathless change.

This fascination with ancestry is not new: early film theory experienced it extensively. In an attempt to understand film's amazing success, many commentators argued for the medium's ancient pedigree. It suffices to mention the Czech critic Václav Tille, who in 1908 opened his foundational essay 'Kinema' by writing about shadow theatre; the American poet Vachel Lindsay, who in 1915 devoted a famous chapter of his *The Art of the Moving Picture* to hieroglyphics; and the Italian musicologist Sebastiano Arturo Luciani, who in 1916 connected the new art with the Roman pantomime.[2] As in many recent media archaeologies, early film scholars appealed to a principle of likeness ('what is similar belongs to the same family') and a principle of causality ('what comes first is the source of what comes later') in order to find how film was foreshadowed.[3]

The psychological need for prefiguration is not without reasons: at the very least, it confers the prestige usually granted by a 'myth of origin'.[4] Yet, if we go back to the Foucauldian idea of archaeology, and even more to his reinterpretation of Nietzche's genealogy,[5] the idea of prefiguration is simply nonsensical. Genealogy looks at the way a dispositive emerges: at the breaks and rearrangements that its emergence implies and the peculiarities that characterize every emergence. In this framework, according to Foucault,

> ...to follow the complex course of descent is to maintain passing events in their appropriate dispersion; it is to identify the accidents, the minute deviations—or conversely, the complete reversals—the errors, the false appraisals, and the faulty calculation that gave birth to those things that continue to exist and have value for us.[6]

*   This contribution has been developed in the framework of my ongoing conversation with Bernard Geoghegan aimed at a systematic exploration of what we call 'screenscapes'. An early version of this essay was discussed at the ICI-Berlin: my thanks to Christoph Holzhey and Manuele Gragnolati. For substantive feedback on early drafts, thanks to Mal Ahern. This essay is dedicated to Gary Tomlinson.
1   See Huhtamo and Parikka, 2011; Parikka, 2012; Elsaesser.
2   Tille, pp. 71-91; Lindsay, pp. 75-76; Luciani, pp. 1-2.
3   An indicative example of recent screen archaeology using the principle of likeness—in a volume that is nevertheless a very useful collection—can be found in Moure, 2016.
4   Frederic Jameson speaks of the 'prestige of a "myth of origins"'. Jameson, p. 174.
5   See Foucault, 1972, 1997.
6   Foucault, 1977, p. 146.

We are not dealing here with a family tree; on the contrary, we must cope with a composite landscape, a field characterized by discontinuity, singularity, and divergence.[7] Ancestors do not have much room on this field.

The only way of conceiving of a prefiguration, then, is to admit that it is an account of origins that emerges only after the historical fact of that emergence has taken place. A prefiguration is a retrospective fantasy: it is something that we identify because a dispositive already exists, and it is something we use as an explanation for that dispositive's emergence. It is a reconstructed 'pre-' that we project onto an asserted 'post-'.

Why, then, give space to prefigurations? Because their paradoxical status can be a resource. A prefiguration highlights what *we* perceive as crucial in a dispositive—so crucial that we feel we must search the history and pre-history of that dispositive for the original occurrence of its defining characteristics. A prefiguration makes material and perceptible our own concerns about a medium, and consequently it uncovers that medium's often-implicit social meaning. In this sense, the idea of a medium's pre-history can help us gain a self-reflexive vision. At the same time, a prefiguration is an emergence in its own turn; as such, it is always marked by a singularity. Yet, once we assume—at least tentatively—that it is a *pre*-figuration, its singularity no longer coincides with a simple uniqueness. Occurrences become re-occurrences, in which an event recurs while keeping its nature of event and at the same time establishing connections that go beyond formal likeness or historical causality. In this sense, the idea of an anteriority can help us gain a perspective that, while refusing easy shortcuts like family trees, nevertheless preserves the idea of a certain communality.

In the next pages, I will tackle three examples of the screen's prefiguration, testing them as potential resources in the genealogy of the screen. Often considered 'primal scenes' in a long history of cinema, these three examples have satisfied film theorists' appetite for origins and archetypes. Here, I will analyze them instead in their distinctiveness, underscoring the ways in which each of them deals with dispositives that we can recognize *ex post facto* as connected with screens. As a consequence, the three examples reveal the contexts, the sets of operations, and the basic conditions that allow a screen—whatever its materiality and substance—to perform *as a screen*. Seen within the framework of a non-causal, non-linear, and non-teleological history, these prefigurations do not tell us anything about the screen's actual

7   '[Genealogy] must recall the singularity of events outside of any monotonous finality; [...] it must be sensitive to their recurrence, not in order to trace the gradual curve of their evolution, but to isolate the different scenes where they engaged in different roles.' Foucault, 1977, pp. 139-140.

lineages; instead, they suggest the *playground* on which screens emerge. They do not delineate the screen's ideal typology; instead, they enumerate the screen's *affordances*. They do not define the screen's essence but illustrate its process of *becoming-screen*.

Athena's shield

Perseus's myth enjoyed widespread circulation in the classical world: it is present in Homer and Hesiod, but it found its most complete and best-known version in Ovid's *Metamorphoses*.[8] More recently, Jean Pierre Vernant has offered an expanded version of the myth that includes its multiple variants.[9]

In short, the story is the following. Sent by King Polydectes, Perseus travels in search of Medusa—one of the three Gorgons, the only one who is mortal but also the most terrible of all. Her hair is made of serpents; her gaze transforms everybody who meets it into stone. Perseus must kill Medusa and behead her: this is the deed assigned to him. On his way, Perseus avoids the threat posed by the three Graeae, stealing the one eye they share between them. He meets the Nymphae who give him winged sandals that let him fly, a mask that makes him invisible, and a sack in which he will hide the Gorgon's head once severed, so as to cover her murderous eyes. He adds these objects to a shield that Athena lent him and to a scythe that he received from Hermes.

When Perseus finally reaches Medusa, he approaches her while she sleeps. He does not look at her directly but gazes at her reflection on the polished surface of the Athena's shield.

> In the mirror of his polish'd shield
> Reflected saw Medusa slumbers take
> And not one serpent by good chance awake.[10]

Thanks to this ruse, Perseus avoids being stoned by Medusa; he comes upon her and he beheads her with the Hermes's scythe, thus fulfilling King Polydectes's request. And yet Medusa's head preserves its nefarious power: back in Polydectes's court, when Perseus lifts the disembodied head out of

---

8   See Hesiod, lines 274-286; Ovid, IV, lines 735-803.
9   Vernant, 2001, pp. 173-184.
10 Ovid, IV, lines 782-784.

the sack, he petrifies the king and the courtiers.Why did Medusa become a monster? She had once been a beautiful woman with golden ringlets, but after Neptune seduced her in a temple dedicated to Athena, the angry Goddess transformed her golden hair into snakes. Perseus bestows Medusa's head upon Athena in recognition of her help: eventually, the severed head adorns the Goddess's breastplate, as a sign of power and as admonition to her enemies.[11]

Most of the interpretations of Perseus's myth revolve around Medusa's paralyzing gaze. Explications abound. The Gorgon is the symbol of castration that terrifies the little boy when he looks at female genitals for the first time and realizes that the possession of his penis cannot be taken for granted.[12] She recalls the animals that reproduce on their skins images of eyes in order to scare and deceive their attackers.[13] She is a hint of the source of the evil-eye superstition that we meet in so many cultures.[14] She is the absolute otherness that we are unable to incorporate into our world.[15] It was the film theorist Siegfried Kracauer who shifted his attention from Medusa's face to Athena's shield. In the last pages of his *Theory of Film*, he claims that the shield is a direct ancestor of the movie screen. Kracauer writes:

> The moral of the myth is, of course, that we do not, and cannot, see actual horrors because they paralyze us with blinding fear; and that we shall know what they look like only by watching images of them which reproduce their true appearance [...] Now of all the existing media the cinema alone holds up a mirror to nature. Hence our dependence on it for the reflection of happenings which would petrify us were we to encounter them in real life. The film screen is Athena's polished shield.[16]

Kracauer's interpretation is undoubtedly compelling. Yet how can a polished shield become a screen? What allows us to assign it this function and this

11 'Yet above all, her length of hair, they own, /In golden ringlets wav'd, and graceful shone. /Her Neptune saw, and with such beauties fir'd, /Resolv'd to compass, what his soul desir'd. / In chaste Minerva's fane, he, lustful, stay'd, /And seiz'd, and rifled the young, blushing maid. / The bashful Goddess turn'd her eyes away, /Nor durst such bold impurity survey; /But on the ravish'd virgin vengeance takes, /Her shining hair is chang'd to hissing snakes. /These in her Aegis Pallas joys to bear, /The hissing snakes her foes more sure ensnare, /Than they did lovers once, when shining hair.' Ovid, IV, p. 139.
12 Freud, 1993, pp. 212-213.
13 See Caillois, 1960.
14 See Siebers, 1983.
15 See Vernant, 1985.
16 Kracauer, 1960, p. 305.

status? And what are the consequences of doing so? I will re-read the myth of Perseus with the screen in mind, focusing my attention on the key elements at stake.

First, Athena's shield is part of a collection of objects (including a scythe, a sack, a mask, and winged sandals) that Perseus brings with him and which orient his actions. They are gifts he received from gods or demi-gods, but they were not specifically conceived for a duel with the Gorgon. Under the pressure of events, Perseus *converts* them into tools that serve a new purpose. The shield becomes a mirror in the same way that the scythe becomes a sword, and a bag is transformed from a container into a disguise. In this way, these objects enter a sort of complex that allow Perseus to face the situation. They congregate and interact: they form a *dispositive*—or, better, an *assemblage*, to borrow the term Deleuze used to describe a coalescence and interplay of components.[17]

The emergence of an assemblage responds to what is happening, and it arises from what is available. Perseus's condition presents some threats and some opportunities: the hero must reckon with the former and use the latter. He must organize what is at hand and transform these objects into weapons, and so accomplish his task and survive. From this point of view, an assemblage relies on contingency and at the same time on conjuncture. It takes shape and gives shape to its components according to the chances and the affordances offered by a situation. Yet, once established, an assemblage provides a persistent framework within which one can cope with reality and reflexively recognize events. In short, it becomes a *recognized space of mediation*.

In this overall picture, the conversion of Athena's shield merits further explanation. The shield is typically a barrier behind which soldiers seek safety. Here, it changes its primary function: it is no longer supposed to intercept the enemies' blows; on the contrary, it has to provide a new kind of sight—indirect, yet capable of orienting the bearer in the battlefield. It no longer hides; it shows. It is still a technology of warfare more than it is a mirror in a conventional sense—in ancient Greek culture, mirrors were feminine and feminizing tools—nevertheless, it shifts from being a rejecting surface to a reflecting surface.[18] It protects not because it keeps

17   The term *assemblage* is the English translation of the original French term *agencement*, yet it fully recovers the meaning of the original word. See Deleuze. For a discussion on the appropriateness of the English term, in contrast with the term *apparatus*, see Casetti, 2015, pp. 78-81

18   For a discussion of the mirror as feminine tool—and a tool that feminizes men who use it—see Frontisi-Ducroux and Vernant, 1997, p. 53; for Athena's shield as an improper mirror, and as an arm, see ibid., p. 70.

the world separated, beyond the barrier, but because it replicates the world and consequently provides for its user a visual control of the situation. It grants a safe look, as Kracauer appropriately highlights.

But the conversion of the shield into an optical device is not without cost. From now on, Perseus's victory depends on what his eyes are able to capture as much as on what his arm is able to reach. It is not just the primacy of the sight that is established; it is a new confidence in visual data. Such a dependence on visual data recalls the process of 'visualization' that, according to Bruno Latour, so deeply transformed Western culture from the sixteenth century onward.[19] It is at the climax of this process that the word 'screen' changed its main connotation. From denoting a protection against fire or air, or a divide that splits a room, or a filter that sieves grain, the term 'screen' begins to designate in the early nineteenth century, in connection with the emergence of the Phantasmagoria, a surface that hosts impermanent images.[20] If there is a possible similarity between Athena's shield and the screen, it rests on such a conversion more than on some physical or functional similarity: Athena's shield also shifts from one connotation to another in the framework of an assemblage.

What kind of sight does the polished shield provide? Not only an indirect view but also a fragmentary one. Perseus barely has a whole and stable picture of the scene, even though the convex surface of the shield can provide enlarged visions. Moving forward, he must explore his surroundings, focus on the different elements within them, and then connect these in his mind. This is the only way he can get an idea of his context and therefore perform his action. Ovid offers insight into this behavior when he describes Perseus first approaching his target, then discovering Medusa asleep, and then finally checking the snakes on

19   See Latour, 1986.
20   I found two early occurrences of the word's new meaning in two notices referring to the Phantasmagoria's patent granted to Paul De Philipsthal on 26 January 1802, respectively published in the *Cobbett's Political Register* (p. 1053) and in *The Monthly Magazine* (p. 488). The two notices read 'transparent screen', while, quite curiously, the text of the patent published a few months before in *The Repertory of Arts and Manufactures* (p. 303-305) reads 'transparent body'. The substitution of the old term with the new—authorized by the fact that in the Phantasmagoria the screen had to hide the projector, before hosting the projected images—allows us to detect the time and context in which the visual connotations of screen emerged. The OED signals two later occurrences of the word, dated 1810 and 1846, respectively referred to as the Phantasmagoria and magic lantern. See *The Oxford English Dictionary*, XIV, p. 722.

her head.[21] The shield gives back the world bit by bit, and Perseus must literally reconstruct it from these fragments. This kind of sight prompts two consequences. First, a direct encounter with Medusa would elicit not only the terror tied to an absolute threat but also the awe tied to a radical otherness. It would provide the freezing experience of the sublime. By using a screen as a tool for the progressive reconstruction of a situation, Perseus eliminates this possibility. The shield transforms perceptual awe into a set of operations aimed at appropriating the object; it turns the sublime into a spectacle at hand. Second, while Athena's shield details the surrounding reality, it never reflects Perseus's face. Unlike Narcissus, our hero does not have access to his own image. A look that progressively reconstructs a situation offers an answer to such a lack: Perseus can see his reflection through his own deeds. He can identify himself in the ongoing position that he occupies on the battlefield and in the ongoing effects of his action.

The myth does not end with Perseus's victory. There is a sort of coda that sees another assemblage emerge—and another conversion occur. Medusa's head becomes the adornment of Athena's breastplate. Consequently, the reflection on the surface of the shield is transformed and substituted by an emblem tied to another material support: a corset. Instead of a temporary mirrored image, we have now a permanently retained icon. And instead of a war machine, we have a piece of ceremonial regalia. Athena's statue, sculpted by Phidias, and which long stood on the Parthenon in Athens, epitomizes this last instantiation: the statue included both the shield and the head, and they represented a meaningful 'memento' of the goddess's deeds.[22]

At this point, the lesson imparted by Athena's shield is quite clear. No element, including a screen, is given as such: it becomes what it is through a process that often implies the conversion of an object into a specific tool. This process of becoming-screen always takes place in the context of a dispositive—or better, of an assemblage—whose constitution responds to both the contingencies and the conjunctures of a situation. Assemblages

---

21 'What wasteful havock dire Medusa made. /Here, stood still breathing statues, men before; /There, rampant lions seem'd in stone to roar. /Nor did he, yet affrighted, quit the field, /But in the mirror of his polish'd shield /Reflected saw Medusa slumbers take, /And not one serpent by good chance awake. /Then backward an unerring blow he sped, /And from her body lop'd at once her head.' Ovid, IV, p. 138.

22 'The statue of Athena is upright, with a tunic reaching to the feet, and on her breast the head of Medusa is worked in ivory. She holds a statue of Victory that is approximately four cubits high, and in the other hand a spear; at her feet lies a shield and near the spear is a serpent.' Pausanias, p. 125.

offer a framework for perceiving a situation and performing an action; optical assemblages do so through the production and circulation of visual data. Finally, an assemblage is always ready to yield room to another assemblage: its components can be re-drawn and re-defined—they can undergo another 'becoming'.

Butades's wall

The legend is seemingly simple and undoubtedly seductive. Pliny the Elder tells it in the Book 35 of his *Natural History*.

> Butades, a potter of Sicyon, was the first who invented, at Corinth, the art of modelling portraits in the earth which he used in his trade. It was through his daughter that he made the discovery; who, being deeply in love with a young man about to depart on a long journey, traced the profile of his face, as thrown upon the wall by the light of the lamp. Upon seeing this, her father filled in the outline, by compressing clay upon the surface, and so made a face in relief, which he then hardened by fire along with other articles of pottery. This model, it is said, was preserved in the Nymphæum at Corinth, until the destruction of that city by Mummius.[23]

Mixing nighttime desire, a sexual encounter, and a father's intervention, Pliny depicts an intense primal scene.[24] It is not by chance that the legend has exerted a persistent seduction on writers, art historians, painters, and photographers.[25] As Maurizio Bettini claims, it is an archetype for the recurring narratives about love portrayed—and, accordingly, about our love for portraits.[26] In his *Brief History of the Shadow*, Victor Stoichita describes the daughter's attempt to 'capture' the image of her lover in order to both rehearse his death and keep him 'upright' and 'alive' in a sort of erotic exorcism and propitiatory practice. Once the young man falls on the battlefield, the portrait that the father molds provides a 'duplicate' that, differently from the 'specter' on the wall, preserves in some way both a

---

23 Pliny the Elder, 35: 43.

24 It is not the first time that Pliny mentions the projected shadows. See in particular Pliny the Elder, 35:5, where at stake there is the origin of painting. Here the narrative moves to the origin of portraiture, and it regards not only the figurative arts but also the plastic arts.

25 Jacques Derrida 1993 refers to paintings on the topic by Joseph Benoit Suvee and Jean-Baptist Reignault.

26 See Bettini, 1999.

body and a soul.[27] Despite the wealth of components in the story, its core is the projected shadow—hence its link with film theories. Though film scholars barely mention the legend, there is a repeated tendency to trace the origin of cinema to a fascination with projected shadows. It is what Václav Tille states in his 1908 essay.[28] In 1956, the French sociologist Edgar Morin resumes the argument in a brilliant analysis of film's anthropological roots.[29] Pliny's legend thus offers a background to film theory.

Yet is not just the shadow that matters. Once again, we must look at the assemblage of tools, practices, and environment in which the shadow emerges. It is in this framework that we can understand how the shadow becomes present and why this tale of the origin of portraiture can elucidate the way in which screens emerge and work.

Looking at the scene, the first elements that come to the fore are the lamp from which the light emanates, the lover's face that intercepts the light, and the wall on which the lover's silhouette is outlined. The shadow exists because of them: literally, it is the product of a source of light, an obstacle that halts the light, and a surface that makes the shadow visible. Such a complex of elements implies a cogent *spatial arrangement*. Indeed, in order to produce a shadow and to cast it on a surface, the lamp, the face, and the wall have not only to coexist in the same space; they must also be positioned each in connection with each other, aligned on the same axis. The dispositive, or the assemblage, becomes spatial: in a word, it becomes an *installation*.

Within this spatial assemblage, we can recognize a set of operations that, quite paradoxically, work in pairs. On the one hand, there is an act of *casting*: the lamp casts a light, while the lover's face casts a shadow. The two actions have a different cogency. The lamp can be substituted with other sources, including the sun: not by chance, Quintilian's version of the legend stages the scene in broad daylight,[30] and some of the most famous

27 Stoichita, 1997, pp. 16-20. Stoichita also compares Pliny's story with consonant narratives by Atenagoras, Quintilian, and especially Plato.
28 'The shadow is, of course, a very brittle and ephemeral material to use for artistic creation, yet its very versatility, volatility, swiftness, and malleability allow for the extraordinary powerful flowering of human fantasy, and the intricate and complex preparation required by the material creates a space for the boldest of compositions.' Tille, 2008, p. 89.
29 'There remains, in our childhood development, a stage of fascination with shadows, and our parents' hands do their best to represent wolves and rabbits on our walls. There remains the charm of shadow theaters, known to the Far East. There remain the terror and anguish that the shadow can arouse—and that the cinema has admirably been able to exploit, in the same way it has been able to make good use of the charm of the mirror.' Morin, p. 29.
30 Quintilian, X:ii, 7.

paintings inspired by Pliny's story do the same.[31] Conversely, the lover's face is unique: it is precisely his silhouette, and nobody else's, that will ignite the next steps of the story. On the other hand, there is the act of *intercepting*: the lover's face intercepts the light, while the wall intercepts the shadow. Once again, the paired actions are similar, yet different. The face halts what is intercepted; the wall retains it. The former filters, the latter hosts. Playing with the polysemy of the word 'screen', we can say that the face is a screen that obstructs, while the wall is a screen that retains. Butades's legend states that the two aspects can be synchronized: an obstruction coexists and interacts with a retention.[32]

This complex set of correlations reveals the assemblage's orientation: in Pliny's story, the situation aims not simply at reflecting images but moreover at projecting them. A *reflection*, like the one we met in Athena's shield, requires just a surface that accommodates preformed images. A *projection*, instead, entails the facts of aiming towards a target, determining what is to be thrown, and throwing it towards the target: it implies a sophisticated form of ballistics. The connection between casting, filtering, and retaining satisfies these conditions. The wall (the screen) aggregates a set of practices. That said, reflection and projection tend to overlap: both are considered attributes of a screen. Not by chance, and from the very beginning, the screen has been identified in both of these ways, and recursively: as both a projective and a reflexive tool.[33] Kept in reserve, the difference nevertheless resounds.

Let's go back to Pliny's legend: the projection has a spectator. Butades's daughter looks at the shadow on the wall, then at her lover, again at the wall. She intervenes. She draws on the wall the outlines of her lover's profile. Her gesture is elicited by a desire but also by a fear: she is afraid the young man is going away. Hence the lines on the wall: they will amend a loss by granting a permanence, even though in effigy. This attempt at retaining the object of love—and at protracting, symbolically, an act of (carnal)

---

31   See, for example, Jean-Baptiste Regnault, *The Origin of Painting* (1785) or Karl Friedrich Schinkel, *Origin of Painting* (1830).

32   Mauro Carbone has insisted on the idea that any screen, in the sense of surface that retains images, needs a counter-screen, which filters these images. To him, these two screens form the basic structure of what he calls the arche-screen, i.e. the ideal object that exemplifies the conditions of possibility of a screen. See Carbone, 2016b.

33   Many early film theorists use the 'mirror' metaphor to designate the screen. See this example from 1907: 'Sitting before the white screen in a motion picture theatre we have the impression that we are watching true events, as if we were watching through a mirror following the action hurtling through space.' Papini, p. 48.

possession—implies the passage to a new kind of action: what comes to the fore is a form of *notation*. The daughter draws a representation that retains what is otherwise temporary: thanks to the few lines that she jots down, she provides a substitute for her lover but also a record of his presence. This action triggers a change in the whole assemblage. With a new player (the young woman) comes a new orientation (towards permanence).

Indeed, the lines traced on the wall transform an extremely variable image into a defined profile. The shadow—like a cloud—is character-ized by an extreme capriciousness: it can recall anything and everything. Notations, conversely, create steadiness: they capture one instant in a flow and eternalize it. Thanks to these lines, the wall also finds a stability as an element in this assemblage. It is no longer a fortuitous support; it becomes a stable fixture. Only an intentional erasure of the sketch drawn by the young girl could bring the wall back to its pristine status.

A notation does not imply that the image on the wall now pertains to the order of painting. The sketch is no longer a mobile and changing image as it was the shadow on the wall; nor is it yet an autonomous image whose meaning can be captured independently from its situation. What is drawn is a portrait but a portrait unable to detach itself from the portrayed. This is why Stoichita attributes to the image on the wall the quality of a ghost: it is something between two worlds.[34] The same can be said of the wall: no longer an accidental support, it is not yet a dedicated space for one single and unique representation. It retains, but it does not secure. This fact can explain the difference between the screen and the canvas. The latter is a surface on which stability and permanence are granted; the former is a surface where a retention fights with a flow. The screen is a transitional object: like the young woman's sketch, it lies between two worlds.

This is when Butades, the father and the potter, makes his entrance. He takes some clay and following the lines on the wall he shapes a human form. He complements the sketch with more details, a relief, and colours.[35] Then he detaches the mold from the wall and fires it with other pieces of pottery. Later, when his work is finished, he puts it in a temple. His action, which according Pliny marks the birth of portraiture, is deeply ambiguous.

34 'The silhouette traced by the young woman was only an *eidolon*, an image without substance, the intangible immaterial double of the one who was leaving', as opposed to the *colossus*, the statue which celebrated something which was "durable and alive"'. Stoichita, 1997, p. 20.
35 'Butades first invented the method of colouring plastic compositions, by adding red earth to the material, or else modelling them in red chalk'. Pliny the Elder, 35: 43.

As father, Butades brings the portrait of the daughter's lover to its end, and in this way he fulfills his daughter's desire. At the same time, he truncates his daughter's romance: using the young man's profile for one of his works, he dismisses him as a lover and transforms him into a model. As a potter, Butades goes even further. Molding a statuette, he transforms a precarious drawing into a solid and "professional" work. In doing so, he creates an object that is no longer tied to a singular and personal situation but that can freely circulate, either as a commodity to be sold or as a relic to be revered. Not by chance the lover's portrait ends in a temple. The outcome of Butade's action is in a certain sense dramatic. The wall now is empty: it ceases to host either a shadow or a draft. Without traces, it is no longer a support. We have reached the end of the game.

What does Pliny's legend add to the basic elements that we have learned from Perseus's myth? Again, we follow the becoming-screen of a screen: it 'happens' that the wall is converted into a host for images. This becoming-screen takes place within an assemblage: the wall needs a number of other elements and actors in place if it is to work as a screen. The coordination of elements within this assemblage and their position in a particular spatial arrangement are the only means through which to produce and project a shadow on the wall. This shadow can also be the object of a notation. Yet this notation, in turn, elicits a change in the assemblage and the set of operations that it performs. Finally, the assemblage can collapse. When a notation becomes an independent object, it no longer needs a source or a support.

Alberti's window

'Let me tell you what I do when I'm painting. First of all, on the surface on which I'm going to paint, I draw a rectangle of whatever size I want, which I regard as an open window through which the subject to be painted is seen.'[36] The third scene I want to analyze is set in 1435, when Leon Battista Alberti famously describes the system of perspective in his *De Pictura*.[37] The window metaphor would enjoy a broad appeal and apply not only to painting but also to narrative and finally to film—to say nothing of the

36   Alberti, p. 55.
37   The first version of the book is in Italian and is entitled *Della Pittura*; an expanded Latin version is dated 1439-41.

present-day desktop of a computer operating system.[38] Connected with the idea of the screen, Alberti's dispositive would highlight the propensity of a surface not only to host reflected or projected images, as Athena's shield and Butades's wall do, but also to *frame* an image, containing it within a border and organizing it in a composition.[39]

In this vein, it is worthwhile to retrace how far Alberti goes with his metaphor. First, he recommends filling the rectangle with a number of lines that extend transversally, longitudinally, and backwards, all connected to a centric point.[40] In this way, the window becomes a gridded space that can coherently map the scene that the painter intends to depict. Second, Alberti suggests the possibility of using a physical veil attached to a rectangular frame in order to simulate the presence of a window.[41] The veil has to be gridded, this time with parallel squares, and the painter must look through it in order to locate individual objects within the field of vision as a whole, to define their mutual connections and to reduce their volume to flatness. He can then transfer the scene onto a similarly gridded sheet of paper or a canvas.[42] Finally, Alberti states that a good painter does not need a physical

38   Émile Zola describes storytelling as a look through a window—on a screen!—in his 'Lettre à Antony Valabrègue,' pp. 373-381. The metaphorical description of cinema as a window is especially developed by André Bazin in his essay, 'Theater and Cinema'. An early occurrence is in Italian film theories: '[At the cinema] what matters is feeling calmly as if one is an indifferent spectator, as if at the window, of whom neither intelligence of judgment, nor the exertion of observation, nor the nuisance of investigation is required.' Panteo. The continuity of the metaphor from Alberti to the computer culture is underscored in Friedberg.

39   It is in this capacity that the window would identify the screen as such, as in Friedberg 2006.

40   'I decide how large I wish the human figures in the painting to be. I divide the height of this man into three parts, which will be proportional to the measure commonly called a braccio. [...] With this measure I divide the bottom line of my rectangle into as many parts as it will hold; and this bottom line of the rectangle is for me proportional to the next transverse equidistant quantity seen on the pavement. Then I establish a point in the rectangle wherever I wish; and as it occupies the place where the centric ray strikes, I shall call this the centric point. [...] Having placed the centric point, I draw straight lines from it to each of the divisions on the base line.' Alberti, p. 55.

41   'A veil loosely woven of fine thread, dyed whatever colour you please, divided up by thicker threads into as many parallel square sections as you like, and stretched on a frame. I set this up between the eye and the object to be represented, so that the visual pyramid passes through the loose weave of the veil.' Alberti, p. 69.

42   'This intersection of the veil has many advantages, first of all because [...] the object seen will always keep the same appearance. A further advantage is that the position of the outlines and the boundaries of the surface can easily be established accurately on the painting panel; for just as you see the forehead in one parallel, the nose in the next, the cheeks in another, the chin in one below, and everything else in its particular place, so you can situate precisely all the features on the panel or wall which you have similarly divided into appropriate parallels. Lastly, this veil affords the greatest assistance in executing your picture, since you can see any object that is round and in relief, represented on the flat surface of the veil.' Alberti, p. 69.

veil; it suffices that he imagines one in his field of vision, and then he can execute the painting according to it.[43]

Alberti's three steps are all aimed at improving the process of *notation*.[44] Architectural windows are not neutral objects: they always mediate our view of the world. Alberti's window makes room for a more sophisticated mediation or, if you like, for a remediation of previous ways of looking: it elicits a sight indissolubly tied to the production of paintings that reiterate the same spatial organization of the world and that consequently acquire the nature of reliable visual data.

To embrace a process of notation to this extent has a consequence. What at first appearance was just a metaphor becomes a very precise set of tools. The window becomes a gridded rectangle, then a stretched and gridded veil, and finally a template that helps an artist perform the correct distribution of elements within the depicted scene. These tools are functional: they are purpose-built devices that respond to a precise task in an unequivocal and specific way. They are interchangeable: the painter can switch from one tool to another and combine them in a more effective complex. They impart precise instructions: they entail coordinated manual, optical and mental actions. Finally, these tools are replicable and improvable: the painter can easily find a veil or draft a rectangle or imagine a grid; and he can build a square wooden frame and add to it an eyepiece set from which to watch the scene at a fixed distance in a more accurate and uniform way. In other words, these tools are technical devices in a proper sense, inserted in a process of production and able to perform a range of tasks and generate a range of objects.

Alberti's metaphor and its avatars showcase their potentialities even better if we look at them against the backdrop of what is the true inaugural moment of perspective. I am referring here to Brunelleschi, the dedicatee of Alberti's *De Pictura*, who had a few years earlier offered a complementary experiment. He created a panel painted with the exterior of Florence's Baptistery as seen on a mirror placed three *braccia* inside the main entrance of the Cathedral. 'He painted it with such care and delicacy and with such great precision in the black and white colours of the marble that no miniaturist could have done it better.'[45] The only part he did not paint was

43 'Should they [some painters] wish to try their talents without the veil, they should imitate this system of parallels with the eye, so that they always imagine a horizontal line cut by another perpendicular at the point where they establish in the picture the edge of the object they observe.' Alberti, p. 69.
44 See Panofsky and Baxandall.
45 Manetti, p. 44.

the sky: the panel contained instead a burnished silver, 'so that the real air and atmosphere were reflected in it, and thus the clouds seen in the silver are carried along by the wind as it blows'. The panel was pierced at the centre with a peephole, placed in coincidence with the point of view from which the Baptistery was seen by the painter. Whoever wanted to test the experiment had to stand at the same point on which the panel was painted, to look through the hole on the back of the panel, and to hold a flat mirror with the other hand in such a way that the painting would be reflected on it. The panel and the mirror had to cover the real Baptistery in such a way that the observer was just seeing the reflected panel. 'With the aforementioned elements of the burnished silver, the piazza, the viewpoint, etc., the spectator felt he saw the actual scene when he looked at the painting.'[46]

Brunelleschi's device is quite convoluted. It assembles a pierced panel containing a depiction of an iconic Florentine building, a burnished surface, and a mirror designed to reflect both the panel and the reflection created by the burnished silver. It combines some of the elements that we have already encountered: it includes sources that 'cast' light and images—the sky, the panel—and a target that 'reflects' what hits it—the mirror. It requires users to perform a very precise action: they must keep the panel and the mirror aligned against the depicted building. It is also site-specific: whoever wants to enjoy the experiment is asked to stand on an exact point and to orient the panel and the mirror towards the real San Giovanni, hiding the building with the two devices in such a way that the image depicted on the panel and reflected on the mirror can substitute the building as actually seen.[47] Finally, the purpose of Brunelleschi's device is a twofold amazement. On the one hand, spectators can appreciate the force of images so well designed that they look like reality. They can enjoy the substitution of reality with its representation.[48] On the other hand, if Brunelleschi's spectators keep their eye on the hole but remove the mirror and look at the real Baptistery, they can enjoy a game of peekaboo with the world.

---

46   Ibid. Brunelleschi's experiment raised many varying interpretations. Among them, Samuel Y. Edgerton offers a religious reading, tied to St. Paul's epistle to Corinthians, in *The Mirror, The Window, and the Telescope*, pp. 34-35 and 52-53. On the contrary, Friedrich Teja Bach finds a Platonic background in 'Filippo Brunelleschi and the Fat Woodcarver'.

47   The site-specificity is strongly suggested by Edgerton, 2006, pp. 51-52.

48   It is a pleasure that modern optical media would extensively exploit. Edgar Morin correctly recalls the fact that early spectators were flocking into temporary movie theaters not because they were anxious to know new pieces of the world but because they were astonished by the reduction of the world to image. See Morin.

Compared with Brunelleschi's device, Alberti's window and its avatars retain the characteristics of an assemblage of tools and practices and at the same time enjoy huge advantages. First, they are lighter. Alberti's dispositive meets a decisive simplification: it becomes a gridded surface that organizes the painting's composition, whatever its form—the ethereal surface of the window, a gridded paper or canvas, a transparent veil, a mere template, or all these things together. Second, Alberti's dispositive frees itself from the constraints of site-specificity. The window and the veil can be mounted anywhere, and they are ready to intercept any kind of reality. Third, and more radically, Alberti's dispositive is subjected to a process of internalization: the window and the veil can become a mental template and work 'inside the mind' of the painter, so to speak. The dispositive still assembles physical and virtual objects, practices, and situations: yet the assemblage is condensed and made ubiquitous in order to become more and more effective.

Lightness, ubiquity, and internalization are the ultimate characteristics that distinguish Alberti's window not only from Brunelleschi's experiment—which is its immediate reference—but also from Athena's shield and Butades's wall. These characteristics make Alberti's dispositive or assemblage a 'technical object' that has reached a more advanced stage in the process of individuation, to use Gilbert Simondon's term.[49] In other words, Alberti's assemblage is a 'machine' able to fully express its mode of working, to the point that its individual components can be replaced and the whole can still operate, and in different situations. This does not mean that the previous devices did not possess their own identity—a detectable 'technical essence', again in Simondon's words. Rather, they were simply far from the phase of consolidation that Alberti's window fulfilled.

Becoming-screen

Not one of the primal scenes that I discussed is an ancestor of contemporary dispositives in a strict sense. There is no direct lineage between these prefigurations and our current screens: if we call the three episodes 'primal scenes', it happens in the framework of a preposterous temporality in which a 'pre-' surfaces as an effect of a 'post-'. Yet these primal scenes—and others that I could have added, including Plato's cave and prehistoric cave paintings, both of which are frequently associated with cinema—offer some useful

49 See Simondon.

suggestions.[50] This is not because they 'are like', 'caused', or 'led to' the definition of a screen today but because they problematize it.

In particular, these stories teach us that we cannot delineate a screen 'as such', as if it were a freestanding and self-contained device existing independently of its context. A screen always materializes as part of a dispositive; it *becomes* a screen in the framework of an *assemblage* of objects, needs, practices, actors, and circumstances that produce it as a screen. Habitual exposure to a screen may well have a naturalizing effect, causing the process underpinning its production to withdraw from perception. Yet what is always at stake is a convergence of elements that make it literally emerge. This emergence does not result from a straightforward historical causality but rather responds to contingencies and conjunctures. It does not follow a well-defined path but a route marked by digressions, impasses, and intersections. Once an assemblage is established, it can define its elements' functions and roles—a screen can become 'a' screen and 'this' screen. It can even simply 'be' a screen before the situation in which it operates reactivates the process of *becoming-screen* as its basic condition of existence.

In this process of becoming-screen, our stories underscore some recurring steps. First, the emergence of screen is always a *conversion*. There are objects (a shield, a wall, and a piece of paper or a canvas) that exploit some of their characteristics in order to acquire a new aptitude. This new propensity, which comes to the fore under the pressure of circumstances (in our stories, respectively, these pressures are a deadly gaze, an impending goodbye, and a desire to record visual data), elicits a re-arrangement of the elements at hand and, at the same time, it finds a decisive support in the assemblage that takes shape in the new situation. Everything within this field of emergence—including elements borrowed from outside—converge toward, and become functional to, the presence of the screen.[51]

Second, the consolidation of the assemblage discloses a complex *ecology of operations* that underpin the screen's existence.[52] This ecology includes

50   On Plato's cave as a model for cinema, see Lapierre. The parallel became a pivotal issue in Jean Louis Baudry's essay '*Le Dispositif*'. For a discussion on caves' paintings, see a recent and comprehensive discussion in Cometa.

51   On the components' transfer from one dispositive to another, see Simondon. The process of transference recalls here the concept of de- and re-territorialization in Deleuze and Guattari. See also the concept of re-location and the coincidence of persistence and difference that it allows in Casetti.

52   The concept of 'ecology of operation', an elaboration of Harun Farocki's idea of 'operational images', was first developed by Bernard Geoghegan in his 'Vision, Territory, Attention: the Birth of Digital Screens from Radar,' forthcoming.

several spheres of action: it simultaneously invests technological tools, human behaviors, environmental elements, material objects, normative discourses, interpersonal exchanges, and forms of imaginations. The ways in which the different domains are addressed and interconnected vary: in Perseus's myth, the operations have to do with the tools and tactics of a warrior; in Boutades's legend, they involve the desires and ruses of a lover; in Alberti's account, they invest the skills and performances of a professional painter. Whatever the field of application, these operations define the range and extension of the assemblage of which the screen is part—whether it is contained or expanded, temporary or permanent. Through their performances, these operations also expose the assemblage's way of working—including its orientations and propensities. Finally, the variety of these operations can reveal the presence of internal conflicts or misalignments, with the emergence of points of contradictions. The screen is the pivotal elements that keep together the whole set of operations.

Third, our three examples uncover a recurring tendency to convert the screen into an *optical* dispositive. Surfaces that previously were aimed at other purposes—in particular, at shielding a warrior, at sheltering a couple of lovers, and at filtering the external world—become either the receptacle of reflected images (Athena's shield), the target of projection (Boutades's wall), or the set of tools that will generate and frame representations (Alberti's canvas and veil). Such a tendency recalls the transformation of the meaning of screen between the eighteenth and nineteenth centuries: what was first identified as a device for warding off the heat of a fire or a draft of air, or for dividing a room, or for hiding an object became a surface that addressed the eye and implied visual data. Rudiger Campe, in his essay included in this book, explores at length how, in early modern German culture, the word *schirm* moved from the idea of protection to the idea of display. We can detect the same tendency in the English *screen*, the French *écran*, or the Italian *schermo*. Our three examples underscore how the optical connotation of the term 'screen' is not a historical universal. Instead, it is an option that stems from a set of contingent needs, which in turn reflect a cultural orientation (the role of visuality either in the Classical or the Modern). The assemblage embodies this option, reorienting its components and its operations—even when they primarily imply hands and legs and not eyes, as in Perseus's myth.

Fourth, visuality is not uncontaminated. On the contrary, it still resonates with screen's previous functions. Athena's shield keeps protecting Perseus also when it becomes a reflecting surface. The wall on which the boy's shadow is projected preserves some physical intimacy to the two lovers.

The veil through which the painter looks at the world continues to be a filter that sieves reality. The screen associates the looking-at-ness to other, older orientations. Moreover, the optical dimension is always connected with a *space*. Athena's shield guides Perseus's footsteps towards his target; Boutades's wall requires that the lamp and the lover be well aligned in order to produce shadows; Alberti's window, while transforming a landscape into a notation, defines the observer's vantage point. Screens are also spatial devices. In particular, they define the way in which the visible is *distributed*, to use Jacques Rancière's felicitous term.[53] In doing so, screens create points of access and blind spots, spaces of communality and seclusion; they coordinate the element at stake in order to either enhance or to dissipate visibility; and, finally, they define their own allocation. In short, they build the terrain—a playground or a battlefield, depending on the situation—upon which any action, including the act of seeing, becomes possible. In this sense, a screen is always part of a *screenscape*—a physical site innervated and catalyzed by the presence of a surface that hosts impermanent images, aimed at offering a mediation with the world and the others thanks to both the images that it hosts and its very nature of site.

A conversion, an assemblage, an ecology of operations, an optical dimension, and an environment. Despite their persistence and recursiveness, these steps do not fulfill all the conditions of the existence of screens—which in their entirety become apparent only at the moment of each screen's emergence, in connections with the contingencies and conjunctures that make that emergence possible. In the same vein, these steps do not sketch a unique model of the screen, as it were an object characterized by a well-established set of features. What these steps do is to unearth some of the key passages that every screen develops in its own way—a chain of procedures and occurrences that do not have the cogence of a formal syntax and that nevertheless disclose the backdrop from which a screen emerges and consolidates. In other words, the characteristics here envisioned, more than providing a 'definition' of what a screen is and must be, depict the 'ground' from which a screen surfaces—a 'ground' ready to give way to a specific 'form' but where forms are still in formation.[54] Borrowing again Simondon's terms, these characteristics are sparks of a 'technical essence' that each screen would develop along different stages of individuation and often along alternative paths, on a playground that nevertheless is perceived as largely common to all screens.

---

53   See Rancière.
54   On the interplay of figure and ground against which technical inventions emerge, see the illuminating passage by Simondon, pp. 59-62.

In this sense, and only in this sense, the steps that we met in all our stories can illuminate how a screen becomes a screen—whatever its substance, from a bank of fog to the hypnotist's hand, from a building's façade to a painter's canvas.[55] They also explain why and how we can envision a general idea of screen that encompasses screens' different instantiations—an *arche-screen*, to use Mauro Carbone's term, to be taken more as a matrix than as a model.[56] Finally, these steps can illuminate how the idea of a screen can suddenly change—as happened at the very beginning of the nineteenth century, when the screen assumed its current dominant optical connotation at the expense of previous meanings focused on the capacity of filtering, sheltering, or hiding an external element, and as is happening now, when touch screens or immersive screens move our sensorium away from the mere sight.

This is why our primal scenes are significant. They show, retrospectively, how, where, and when screens can make an entrance. Indeed, their common nature is to stage a drama—whether through a myth, a legend, or a treatise. All together, they do not display a coherent and linear plot; on the contrary, they preserve differences, cracks, dissonances. In doing so, they suggest to us the means by which we can capture connections without obligations, developments without finality, and, moreover, histories without lineages. Simple stories, yet telling and exemplary: this is why they matter.

Works Cited

Alberti, Leon Battista. *On Painting and On Sculpture*. Edited by Cecil Grayson. London: Phaidon, 1972.

Baudry, Jean Louis. 'The Apparatus: Metapsychological Approaches to the Impression of Reality in the Cinema.' *Camera Obscura* 1 (Fall 1976): 104-26.

Baxandall, Michael. *Painting and Experience in Fifteenth Century Italy*. Oxford: Clarendon Press, 1972.

Bazin, André. 'Theater and Cinema.' In *What is Cinema?*, vol. 1, edited and translated by Hugh Gray, pp. 76-124. Berkeley: University of California Press, 1967.

Bettini, Maurizio. *The Portrait of the Lover*. Berkeley: University of California Press, 1999.

Caillois, Roger. *Meduse et Cie*. Paris: Gallimard, 1960.

Carbone, Mauro. *Filosofia-schermi*. Milano: Cortina, 2016.

---

55   See in this collection the essays respectively by Furuhata, Eugeni, Buckley, and Somaini.
56   See Carbone 2016a and 2016b.

———. 'Thematizing the *arche-screen* through its variations.' In *Screens*, edited by Dominique Chateau and José Moure, pp. 62-69. Amsterdam: Amsterdam University Press, 2016.

Casetti, Francesco. *The Lumiére Galaxy: Seven Keywords for the Cinema to Come.* New York: Columbia University Press, 2015.

Cometa, Michele. 'Surfaces profondes. Au-delà de l'écran dans les cultures visuelles paléolitiques.' In *Des pouvoirs des écrans*, edited by Mauro Carbone, Anna Caterina Dalmasso, and Jacopo Bodini, pp. 35-52. Milan: Mimésis, 2018.

Deleuze, Gilles. "What is a *Dispositif?*" In *Two Regimes of Madness: Texts and Interviews 1975-1995*, pp. 338-348. New York: Semiotext(e), 2006. Originally "Qu'est-ce qu'un dispositif?" In *Deux régimes de fous: textes et entretiens 1975-1995*, pp. 316-325. Paris: Éditions de Minuit, 2003.

——— and Felix Guattari. *Anti-Oedipus: Capitalism and Schizophrenia.* Translated by Robert Hurley, Mark Seem, and Helen R. Lane. New York: Viking Press, 1977.

Derrida, Jacques. *Memoirs of the Blind: The Self-Portrait and Other Ruins.* Translated by Pascale-Anne Brault and Michael Naas. Chicago: University of Chicago Press, 1993.

Edgerton, Samuel Y. *The Mirror, The Window, and the Telescope.* Ithaca: Cornell University Press, 2009.

Elsaesser, Thomas. *Film History as Media Archaeology: Tracking Digital Cinema.* Amsterdam: Amsterdam University Press, 2016.

Foucault, Michel. *The Archaeology of Knowledge*, Translated by A.M. Sheridan Smith. New York: Pantheon Books, 1972.

———. 'Nietzsche, Genealogy, History.' In *Language, Counter-Memory, Practice: Selected Essays and Interviews*, edited by D.F. Bouchard, pp. 139-164. Ithaca: Cornell University Press, 1977.

Freud, Sigmund. 'Medusa's Head.' In *Sexuality and the Psychology of Love*, edited by Philip Rieff, pp. 202-203. New York: Collier Books, 1993.

Friedberg, Anne. *The Virtual Window: From Alberti to Microsoft.* Cambridge, MA: The MIT Press, 2006.

Frontisi-Ducroux, Françoise and Jean-Pierre Vernant. *Dans l'oeil du miroir.* Paris: Odil Jacob, 1997.

Hesiod. *Theogony. Works and Days. Testimonia.* Edited and translated by Glenn W. Most. Loeb Classical Library 57. Cambridge, MA: Harvard University Press, 2007.

Huhtamo, Erkki and Jussi Parikka, eds. *Media Archaeology: Approaches, Applications, and Implications.* Berkeley: University of California Press, 2011.

Jameson, Frederic. *The Prison-House of Language.* Princeton: Princeton University Press, 1972.

Kracauer, Siegfried. *Theory of Film: The Redemption of Physical Reality*. New York: Oxford University Press, 1960.

Lapierre, Marcel. *Le cent visage du cinema*. Paris: Grasset, 1948.

Latour, Bruno. 'Visualization and Cognition: Thinking with Eyes and Hands.' *Knowledge and Society* 6 (1986): 1-40.

Lindsay, Vachel. *The Art of the Moving Picture*. 2nd ed. New York: Macmillan, 1922.

Luciani, Sebastiano Arturo. 'The Poetics of cinema.' In *Early Film Theories in Italy: 1896-1922*, edited by Francesco Casetti, Silvio Alovisio, and Luca Mazzei, pp. 329-332. Amsterdam: Amsterdam University Press, 2017.

Manetti, Antonio di Tuccio. *The Life of Brunelleschi*. Edited and translated by Howard Saalman. University Park and London: The Pennsylvania State University Press, 1970.

The Monthly Magazine 87, June 1802.

Morin, Edgar. *The Cinema, or, the Imaginary Man*. Translated by Lorraine Mortimer. Minneapolis: University of Minnesota Press, 2005.

Moure, José. 'Archaic paradigms of the screen and its images.' In *Screens: From Materiality to Spectatorship*, edited by Dominique Chateau and José Moure, pp. 42-61. Amsterdam: Amsterdam University Press, 2016.

Ovid, *Metamorphoses in Fifteen Books. Translated by the most eminent hands. Adorn'd with sculptures*. London: Jacob Tonson, 1917. Available online through Eighteenth Century Collections Online. Ann Arbor: University of Michigan Library, 2007. http://name.umdl.umich.edu/004871123.0001.000. Accessed July 2018.

The Oxford English Dictionary. Second Edition. Prepared by J.A. Simpson and E.S.C. Weiner. Oxford: Clarendon Press, 1989.

Panofsky, Erwin. *Perspective as Symbolic Form*. Translated by Christopher S. Wood. New York: Zone Books, 1991.

Panteo, Tullio, 'Il cinematografo,' *La scena illustrata* 19, no. 1 (October 1908).

Papini, Giovanni. 'The Philosophy of Cinematograph.' In *Early Film Theories in Italy: 1896-1922*, edited by Francesco Casetti, Silvio Alovisio, and Luca Mazzei, pp. 47-50. Amsterdam: Amsterdam University Press, 2017.

Parikka, Jussi. *What is Media Archaeology?* Cambridge, UK and Malden, MA: Polity Press, 2012.

Pausanias. *Description of Greece*. Translated by W.H.S. Jones. New York: G.P. Putnam Sons, 1918.

Pliny the Elder. *The Natural History*. Translated by John Bostock. London: Taylor and Francis, 1855.

Rancière, Jacques. *The Politics of Aesthetics*. New York: Continuum, 2006.

The Repertory of Arts and Manufactures, vol. 16. London: Nichols and Son, 1802.

Siebers, Tobin. *The Mirror of Medusa*. Berkeley: University of California Press, 1983.

Simondon, Gilbert. *On the Mode of Existence of Technical Objects*. Translated by
    Cécile Malaspina and John Rogove. Minneapolis: Univocal, 2017.
Stoichita, Victor I. *A Short History of the Shadow*. Translated by Anne-Marie
    Glasheen. London: Reaktion Books, 1997.
Teja Bach, Friedrich. 'Filippo Brunelleschi and the Fat Woodcarver.' *Res: Anthropol-
    ogy and Aesthetics*, 51 (Spring 2007): 157-174.
Tille, Václav. 'Kinéma.' In *Cinema All the Time: An Anthology of Czech Film Theory
    and Criticism, 1908-1939*, edited by Jaroslav Anděl and Petr Szczepanik, pp. 71-91.
    Prague: National Film Archive, 2008.
Tomlinson, Gary. *Culture and the Course of Human Evolution*. Chicago: Chicago
    University Press, 2018.
Vernant, Jean Pierre. *The Universe, the Gods, and Men*. Translated by Linda Asher.
    New York: Harper Collins, 2001. Originally published as *L'univers, les dieux, les
    homes*. Paris: Seuil, 1999.
——. *La mort dans les yeux*. Paris: Hachette, 1985.
Zola, Émile. 'Lettre à Antony Valabrègue.' In *Correspondance*, pp. 373-381. Paris:
    Éditions du CNRS, 1978.

About the Author

Francesco Casetti is the Thomas E. Donnelly Professor of Humanities and
Film and Media Studies at Yale University. He has previously taught in Italy
where he served as president of the scholarly society of Film and Media
Studies. He has also been visiting professor at Paris 3 La Sorbonne Nouvelle,
at the University of Iowa, and at Harvard. His books include *Inside the Gaze*,
Theories of Cinema, 1945-1995, *Eye of the Century: Film, Experience, Modernity*,
and *The Lumière Galaxy. Seven Key Words for the Cinema to Come*, a study
on the reconfiguration of cinema in a post-medium epoch. His current
research focuses on two topics: the early film theories, especially the role
of cinephobia; and a genealogy of screen that underlines its environmental
aspects and the ways in which it becomes a component of our current
'mediascapes'.

2.   'Schutz und Schirm': Screening in German During Early Modern Times[1]

Rüdiger Campe

Abstract

Rüdiger Campe analyzes the term *Schirm* (screen) and its various fields of application in early modernity before it designates the optical device called screen in the new media. If *Jagd-Schirme,* or hunting blinds, were complex means of visual concealment that also configured deadly forms of projection, *Schirm* was also located in the legal sphere, where it designated an exceptional administrative and military protection that also allowed for the projection of a legal entity that would otherwise not exist within the ordinary structures of power. How can one comprehend the return of the term within the language of electronic display? Campe elucidates Friedrich Kittler's notion of 'implementation' as a concept for how such early modern practices of the screen can be seen as discontinuous with the modern history of the optical screen in one respect and continuous in another. 'Implementation' means to identify certain functions—such as protection and projection—for possible technical development but also to construct autonomous technological systems capable of assuming such functions.

Keywords: Early Modernity, Protection, Law, Implementation, Friedrich Kittler

Ever since the advent of electronic and digital projection, looking at screens or displays in German amounts to gazing at *Schirme*: screens or displays. More precisely, in German you look at *Bildschirme*: screens intended for

1   I am grateful to Francesco Casetti, Craig Buckley, Bernard Geoghegan, and the other participants in the Yale Mellon Seminar on the *Genealogies of the Excessive Screen* for providing me with inspiration, critique, and help. I wish to thank Sophie Duvernoy and Mal Ahern for comments, suggestions, and editing.

Buckley, C., R. Campe, F. Casetti (eds.), *Screen Genealogies. From Optical Device to Environmental Medium.* Amsterdam: Amsterdam University Press, 2019

DOI 10.5117/9789463729000_CH02

the display of images. By contrast, the projection surface in a movie theatre never came to be known as a *Bildschirm* but instead as a *Filmleinwand*, or 'movie canvas', in a nod to the semantic regime of painting. Only radar, TV, computer displays, and other devices whose projection techniques do not reproduce images analogically acquired the status of *Bildschirm*, or screen, rather than *Leinwand*, or canvas.[2]

By adopting the word *(Bild)Schirm* (screen) for such advanced projection processes, the German language returned, as it were, to the origins of modern optical theory. This is the time when René Descartes and Isaac Newton undertook their investigations of optics and Athanasius Kircher and Christiaan Huygens developed the projection technique of the magic lantern.[3] In this period—approximately between the second half of the seventeenth and the first decades of the eighteenth centuries—*Schirm* (screen) had a broad range of meanings referring to important social and political practices. The word covered an extended semantic field of partitioned spaces and channels of power. It referred to an array of legal and administrative concepts (such as *Schutz und Schirm*, meaning protection and safeguard) and it was at the same time a term used in aristocratic pastimes such as hunting (e.g, the *Jagd-Schirm*, a blind that allows hunters to hide from their prey). In the early modern period, the concept of *Schutz und Schirm* organized the constitution of statehood—first in the territorial states of northern Italy and France, then the Holy Roman Empire of German Nations—by means of two fundamental gestures. The first concerns the emergence of the monopoly of violence within the modern state (protection and safeguard); the second refers to the basic configuration of nature and culture, animals and humans, within the states' territories (the hunting blind).[4] In all of these cases, *Schutz und Schirm* may be considered as designating certain social practices. These legal concepts not only permeated many forms of social interaction, they also provided techniques and material means that became part of the larger *dispositifs* of social organization.[5] Finally, operating on the margins

2   See Huhtamo, 'Elements of Screenology'.

3   Smith, *From Sight to Light*, Chapters 8 and 9, pp. 323-416; Mannoni, *The Great Art of Light and Shadow*, Chapters 2-5, pp. 28-135; and Grosser, 'Kircher and the Laterna Magica'.

4   Grimm, 'Das staatliche Gewaltmonopol'; Corvol, *Histoire de chasse*, Part I, pp. 15-146.

5   *Dispositif* is used here and in what follows according to Michel Foucault. The term designates an ensemble of strategies, discursive and material devices within an institutional framework; see Foucault, 'The Confession of the Flesh' (1977); cf. Agamben, *What is an Apparatus?*, pp. 1-24 (Agamben reconstructs a theological background for Foucault's 'dispositif' in the 'oikonomia' or God's governance of the world and expands 'dispositif' into the realm of technology). In this essay, the term 'apparatus' is not meant as a synonym for 'dispositif' but stands exclusively for technological configurations of machines in functionally closed systems. Occasionally,

of legal practices associated with the *Schirm*, the optical meaning of the term 'screen' imposed itself as the material object that, in the twentieth century, resurfaced as the *Bildschirm* of the radar display, the TV screen, and the laptop.

As material objects of many sorts and fabrics, *Schirme* in this latter sense were readily at hand in seventeenth-century everyday life, primarily among the ruling and upper classes, and to a lesser degree among servants, peasants, farmhands, and manufactory workers. There were screens for windows, ovens, rain, heat, and light: the *Fensterschirm* was a shutter; the *Feuerschirm* was a screen used with the stove; and of course, the upper classes could shield themselves from the elements with a *Parasol* (sun shade) and *Regenschirm* (umbrella). These objects, then, could incidentally hold decorative presentations on their surfaces. Umbrellas and parasols were covered with images, as was the painted or translucent shade called a 'window screen' and the peculiar room partition called the *Bettschirm* (bed screen). The image-bearing *Schirm* is an ornamental addendum to the material object called *Schirm* or screen and is only marginally related to the complex screening practices that constitute the core of *Schutz und Schirm* in early modernity.

Studying the cultural-technical field of the *Schirm* is thus a twofold task.[6] It is important to explore how the social practices surrounding the concept of the *Schirm* give shape and meaning to the screen as a material object and how they inform the function of this object's image-bearing surface. This means we must study how the optical screen relates to the early modern social practices of *Schutz und Schirm*. However, we cannot consider the emergence of the *Schirm* as an optical device and a presentational surface to be the inevitable *telos* or semantic centre of *Schirm*. Rather, the optical device called *Schirm* was a marginal apparition among the meanings and practices surrounding *Schutz und Schirm*. This then means we must describe the origins of the history of optical screens as both continuous and discontinuous with broader social practices of *Schutz und Schirm*.

In what follows, the semantics of *Schutz und Schirm* between the seventeenth century and the first half of the eighteenth century will be investigated within the *Great Universal Lexicon of All Sciences and Arts*, which

'assemblage', a term forged by Gilles Deleuze, is used to emphasize the interplay between strategies or technologies on the one side and their users' affects and social attitudes on the other (Deleuze, Guattari, *Kafka*, pp. 81-88).

6   Here and in what follows, methodical considerations were inspired by and developed in discussion with Casetti, the author of 'Primal Screens', in this volume; see also Casetti, 'What is a Screen Nowadays?'.

was edited and published by the bookseller and printer Johann Heinrich Zedler from 1731 to 1745.[7] Zedler's encyclopedic dictionary forms an ideal venue for this investigation. In spirit and organization, it harks back to the humanists' epistemological principle of the *res* and *verba* as a double access to knowledge. In this vein, the *Great Universal Lexicon*'s form professes faith in a certain ontological order contained within the treasury of words and narratives. Zedler completed the publication of the encyclopedia's 68 volumes in 1745, the same year in which a first, short *Prospectus* for d'Alembert and Diderot's *Encyclopédie* appeared in print (publication of the actual volumes began in 1751). In the case of the French *Encyclopédie*, the totality of knowledge was accounted for from the principal assumption of a systematic order of the world mirrored in the fields of human knowledge. For Zedler, on the other hand, the form of the dictionary was a compromise; its form conceded that human understanding was unable to accurately express the ideal systematic unity of knowledge in a direct way.[8] Positioned halfway between the Erasmian, humanist universality of the *copia rerum et verborum* and Diderot's sceptical view of the unity of sciences and knowledge, Zedler's *Great Universal Lexicon* evokes a network of meanings and practices rather than a systematic unity of knowledge. Dense cross-references connect various entries to each other and link together different areas of knowledge and action. The reader learns just as much about the juridical definition of *Schutz und Schirm-Gerechtigkeit* (the rights of seeking and granting protection) as he does about how to build a hunting shelter. Advice on painting shutters and constructing parasols is adjacent to brief theological treatises on the protection offered by God and the Saints to faithful believers. The modern optical screen appears only at the margins of the complex network of meanings and techniques inherent to the *Schirm*. Reconstructing this semantic and pragmatic network provides an ideal window into techniques of culture and the culture of techniques prior to the advent of the modern *Bildschirm*, which inaugurates the history of media proper.

Two vastly different examples can sketch out the semantics around *Schirm* in the seventeenth and eighteenth centuries. The first illustrates the spiritual resonances of the word *Schirm* in Lutheran Germany. It occurs at the beginning of Psalm 91: 'He that dwelleth in the secret place of the most High shall abide under the Shadow of the Almighty. I will say of the LORD, He is my refuge

---

7   Zedler, *Grosses vollständiges Real-Lexikon aller Wissenschaften und Künste*.
8   This view is most succinctly expressed in Denis Diderot's elaborate 1750 *Prospectus* (different from the short 1745 announcement) and incorporated in the 1751 *Preliminary Discourse*; see Diderot, *Preliminary Discourse*.

and my fortress: my God; in him I will trust.' Luther translates the 'secret place' as *Schirm*: '*Wer unter dem Schirm des Höchsten sitzt.*'[9] This particular sense of *Schirm* is present in many Protestant hymns and in Protestant (Silesian) baroque poetry throughout the seventeenth century, including the music of Johann Sebastian Bach, his sons, and others composers in the Lutheran tradition. Psalm 91 characterizes the protection granted by God in the 'secret place' as a defence from physical danger and persecution: the secret place provides shelter to the animal chased by the hunter, the warrior fleeing from the enemy, or the ordinary human seeking refuge from the horrors of the night and the dangers of pestilence in the heat of day. Beyond instances of physical danger, the *Schirm* also provides protection against political danger. God's 'truth' is the *Schirm und Schild* (protection and shield) that protects his people from its enemies just as a bird hides her offspring under her wings.[10]

Rather than providing shelter from persecution, the *Schirme* found in domestic life are structuring elements of everyday needs and desires. The *Bettschirm,* or bed screen, is a standout among the many *Schirme* that protect from light, heat, rain, and cold. A long, painstaking article in the *Great Universal Lexicon* details its use and gives instructions for how to build it. Like other domestic *Schirme*, the *Bettschirm* grants physical protection from cold and light, but its main function is that of a room divider, protecting a person from the gaze of others.[11] Certainly, the *Bettschirm* safeguards one's physical existence—but rather than shielding it from violence, it shields the physical integrity of the nude body, hiding its sexual and erotic nature. It partitions the space of the being-with-others (to use Heidegger's term), a function underlined by its own structural proliferation of smaller screens within a larger screen. Small movable frames functioning as doors can be integrated into the main screen of the *Bettschirm*. These doors emphasize the partition's ability to separate the private from the public parts of the house. The screen-within-the-screen forms a door one does not even have to use in order to reach the other side. The door within a separating device that may simply be circumvented underlines the symbolic essence of the door: its very *doorness*, one might say.

Arguably, the *Schirm*'s move from the divine guarantee of physical integrity to the invasion of the everyday—its provision of relative privacy in a home still far removed from the nineteenth-century *intérieur*—is made

9   Psalm 91, verse 1-2. For the German see Luther, *Werke*, 3.10; for the English the *King James Version*.
10   Psalm 91, verse 4.
11   Zedler, art. 'Schirm (Bett-)', XXXIV, col. 1614f.

possible by means of its deep entrenchment in the popular imagination. The *Schutzmantelmadonna* or Virgin of Mercy (literally, the Sheltering-Cloak Madonna) was a popular facet of *Schutz und Schirm* in the Christian tradition disseminated from the fifteenth to the seventeenth centuries. Many altarpieces from the Middle Ages onward, particularly in the Franciscan tradition, depict the Virgin Mary clad in a large, usually blue mantle.[12] Mary opens her mantle—often on both sides, sometimes only on one—like a framing curtain, which envelops groups of small human figures. A famous example of these womb-like representations of the open mantle is Piero della Francesca's 'Madonna of Misericordia', which is paradigmatic for its depiction of the Virgin of Mercy.[13] The human figures enveloped within the Virgin's mantle are not in imminent physical danger but rather represent disciplined worshippers and supplicants. Their bodies are arranged in a hierarchical order. They may express certain passions, but those passions are devotion and humility rather than fear or shame. They are not hiding in Mary's mantle as much as occupying a privileged place in which to properly adore her. They each have their place within the sheltering cloak, enjoying a well-regulated relationship with each other, the Virgin Mary, and further intermediaries between the supplicants and the saint. In short, the *Schutz und Schirm* provided by Mary's cloak reveals an already disciplined, hierarchically and emotionally ordered body politic performing the ritual of requesting protection. The worshippers and the saint are both already part of the church of Christ. Together they form the image of an institution of protection. The idea of this institution had been delineated in famous verses in the Gospel of Saint John. This apostle had forged the notion of Christ or the Holy Spirit as the *paraclete* (helper or comforter), developing the Roman institution of patron and client into a relationship between Christ or the Holy Spirit and the congregation of believers. The Virgin of Mercy's *Schirm* no longer implements the protection or partitioning of social space in our being-with-others in *actu* but rather expresses and confirms an already achieved state of protection. The images of the *Schutzmadonna* thus celebrate the *Schirm* as an institution.

Jagd-Schirm: The hunting blind

Two concepts stand out among the various practices and meanings attributed to the *Schirm* in Zedler's *Great Universal Lexicon* that bring far-reaching

12   Van Asperen, 'The Sheltering Cloak'.
13   Ahl, 'The Misericordia *Polytych*'.

social and political consequences into play. The first is the *Jagd-Schirm*, or hunting blind, which is a 'secret place'—to use the language of Psalm 91—in which hunters can lie in wait for game. (As will become evident, the *Jagd-Schirm* is, however, a more complex device than the English term 'hunting blind' would suggest, so that in what follows I will refer to it as a 'hunting shelter', a translation closer to the term's German wording.) The second concept I wish to discuss is the juridical and political institution of *Schutz und Schirm*: the right to special protection within the lands of the Holy Roman Empire of German Nations. *Schutz- und Schirmgerechtigkeit* (the right to protection and safeguard) is an important legal construction that partakes in the early modern development of the state's monopoly on violence. Although these two instances of the *Schirm* seem far removed from the screen within media history, they both contribute functionally to the broader arrangement—the dispositive, in the Foucauldian sense of the term—in which optical display and representation can take place.

The *Jagd-Schirm* is a mobile construction that hides hunters from their prey.[14] It does not protect vulnerable bodies, as in the Psalms. Rather, it was meant to distract the prey's attention and thus render it more vulnerable. Protecting the human hunter strategically increased the exposure of the hunted animal. The size of the *Schirm*—its length and height—was thus chosen with respect to the so-called *Lauff-Platz* (running space): a cleared, unprotected area in which the game appeared (or ran) in front of the hidden hunters. In mild weather, the *Schirm* could be a simple hiding place of grass and branches, made by gardeners. In that case, it could (and indeed had to be) constructed anew each time. In its narrower sense, however, the *Jagd-Schirm* was a more elaborate wooden construction: a transportable summer house of sorts used by aristocrats in the seventeenth and eighteenth centuries. The *Schirm*, which was erected on columns on a fixed wooden bottom, was both solid and transportable. This dual character of mobility and material stability is, in Bruno Latour's analysis, precisely what turns a thing into a media device.[15]

Zedler's description of the *Jagd-Schirm* specifies that 'everything which belongs to such matters must be loaded up on vehicles and preserved in the armoury for further usage'.[16] In order to be taken apart, stored away, and made available 'for further usage', the various parts of the *Schirm* were numbered and connected with screws. The *Jagd-Schirm* thus combined a stable house,

---

14   Zedler, art. 'Jad-Zelt, Jagd-Schirm', XIV, p. 158f.
15   See Latour.
16   Zedler, XIV, p. 159.

or a fixed place of cultural settlement, with a transportable machine or technical apparatus. The *Schirm* was the movable house of early modern times, providing the material manifestation of a certain strategic context.

Through its relation to the aristocratic pastime of hunting, the *Schirm* was also part of the culture of feudal representation and involves the self-contained public sphere of the court.[17] The *Jagd-Schirm* was, in Zedler's words,

> the sort of container in which the lord who is keen on hunting, together with ladies and cavaliers, lies in wait during the chasing on the *Lauff-Platz* (running space), with exquisite pleasure, for the game to be driven forward and chased into the open.[18]

The container provided a space for the exquisite pleasure of the lord's company, beginning with hunting and killing, and ending with eating the animal. For this purpose, its interior was decorated in the style of a banquet hall for grand dining. It thus served as a stage for two closely related moments of aesthetic pleasure—the pleasure of seeing the game appearing and the pleasure of eating its meat—which are linked and interrupted by the act of killing. In the first case, the *Schirm* is a divider that separates inside from outside; in the second, it creates an inclusive interior that houses the social ritual of the shared meal.

In the case of the *Jagd-Schirm*, the screen does not provide protection from danger but is instead a device that organizes a field of exposure that can be used to observe, surveil, and target game. The term used for this field, *Lauff-Platz* (running place), evokes a significant word in German poetics of the time: the *Schau-Platz*, which was the scene or site of the theatre as well as a term used in legal discourse to designate the scene of a crime or the site of a skirmish or battle in warfare. The concepts of *Lauff-Platz* and *Schau-Platz* exhibit similar structures. In both, a space is sealed off, emptied out, and turned into an open field with no visual obstructions to the human gaze. The site or scene of the *Schau-Platz* (literally, showing place) enacts a double showing: it is shown as an empty space to the onlooker so that something can show itself on it.[19] The concept of the *Lauff-Platz* exhibits

---

17   Fontin, *Amusemens de la chasse et de la peche*; German translation: *Adelicher Zeit-Ver-treiber / Oder Neu-Erfundene Jagdergötzungen*; see also Tänzer, *Der Dianen Hohe und Niedere Jagd-Geheimnüß*.

18   Zedler, XIV, p. 158.

19   Benjamin, *Origin of the German Mourning Play*, pp. 115-117 and 140-144. On Benjamin's concept of the stage, see Weber, 'Storming the Work: Allegory and Theatricality in Benjamin's Origin

this dialectical relationship even more readily. The 'running place' was a clearing in the woods prepared for the game by the removal of obstacles that was strewn with fodder to entice the game to appear in clear view and range of the hunters.

The *Lauff-Platz* is thus even more intimately related to a space of projection than the theatrical *Schau-Platz*. Certainly, the baroque theatre transformed the three-dimensional space into a two-dimensional perspectival construction through the use of backdrops. With its columns, trees, and buildings, the early modern stage simulated a vanishing point for its onlookers. In other words, the baroque stage made three-dimensional modifications to a site in order to map it as a two-dimensional representation of itself. For the *Lauff-Platz*, by contrast, projection was not implemented in a supplemental manner but took place in an utterly literal sense: hunters hurled deadly projectiles at the animals on the open field. Paraphrasing the *Schirm* as a specific element within the larger *dispositif* of hunting, one might reverse Jean-Paul Sartre's famous formula according to which seeing means to be seen, or to see the gaze of others.[20] In the *Lauff-Platz*, the *Schirm* is a proto-projection mechanism that makes the opposite happen. The screen protects the hunters from being seen so that they can see the game. It could be argued that this is the functional—not the material—basis for screens of projection in the media-historical sense. It is, however, important to note that the hunting screen is rather a material component of a larger strategy than an apparatus in its own right. More importantly, the *Jagd-Schirm* can only perform its function in the context of other material and strategic arrangements. It is a moment in the process—the *dispositif*—of hunting, rather than a thing in and of itself.

Schirm-Recht and *Schirm-Gewalt*: Screening (safeguard) as right and power

While the hunting screen epitomizes the *Schirm* within the context of a strategic operation, the term *Schutz und Schirm* (protection and safeguard) is primarily used within the legal sphere.[21] It designates a right that can be obtained following a negotiation between two parties. In Hans Jakob

---

of the Mourning Play,' in: Weber, *Theatricality as Medium*, pp. 160-180; also Weber, 'Technics, Theatricality, Installation,' ibid., pp. 54-96.

20   Sartre, *Being and Nothingness*, pp. 340-400.

21   Zedler, art. 'Schutz, Schirm, Schirm-Vogtey, Schutz und Schirm, Schutz-Gerechtigkeit oder Schutz- und Schirm-Recht', XXXV, col. 1710f.

Christoffel von Grimmelshausen's 1668 picaresque novel *Simplicius Sim-
plicissismus,* the protagonist, who is serving in the army of the Emperor,
is captured and held prisoner by Swedish troops. Simplicius negotiates an
agreement with the Swedish commandant according to which he regains
his physical freedom without having to renounce his oath to the Catholic
Emperor as long as he does not return to war against the Protestant party.
As long as Simplicius remains in the Swedish garrison, the commandant
grants him '*Schutz / und Schirm / und alle Freyheit* (shelter, protection,
and every freedom)', so long as Simplicius promises to refrain from any
hostility against the Swedish. Instead, he must swear to '*deren Nutzen und
Frommen fördern / und ihren Schaden nach Müglichkeit wenden* (promote
the benefits and appurtenances of the town, do my utmost to avert harm
thereto)'.[22] No sovereign authority is presupposed in this situation; rather, two
quasi-autonomous entities enter into a contractual relationship with each
other. Simplicius accepts the offer of protection from the commandant and
directs his best intentions towards the Swedish, while the Swedish obtain
and assume the right of protection. This mutual agreement depends on
Simplicius remaining under military authority and hence within the jurisdic-
tion of the Swedish officer. The protection sought and granted involves a
particular relationship of rights and power. It establishes a relationship
between stronger and weaker actors, and it establishes rights—the right
to claim authority and the right to ask for active help and support—that
were not in existence before the agreement.

   The Grimmelshausen episode is an exceptional case given the circumstances of the Thirty Years' War. During the war, the lands of the Holy Roman
Empire turned into a vast battlefield, and issues of *Schutz und Schirm* were
the subject of interminable, ever-shifting negotiations between parties.
During these decades, the sovereign guarantee of protection in the Empire as
well as in its principalities was often weak or even missing. In this context, the
temporary character of a *Schutz und Schirm* contract, without reference to an
overarching sovereignty, is a suggestive episode. Yet beyond such particular
circumstances, *Schutz and Schirm* was a powerful concept throughout the
Empire's history. It referred to various situations in which rights and power
could be demanded and provided in the manner of a particular, exceptional
institution. The *Great Universal Lexicon*'s article on *Schutz, Schirm* declares:

---

22   Grimmelshausen, *Simplicissimus Teutsch,* Book 3, Ch. 15, *Werke* 1, p. 307; *Adventures of
Simplicius Simplicissimus,* p. 253.

Ordinary protection or safeguard is provided by the ordinary government to its subjects; however, the *Schirm-Recht*, which is at issue here
is a right that originates in the free act of one party subjecting itself,
and the acceptance of such self-subjection by another party. By these
acts, neither the status of a subject (*Untertänigkeit*) nor of governmental
authority (*Obrigkeit*) are established, and the one granting protection
(the *Schirmer*) is not allowed to claim rights other than those specified
and conveyed to him.[23]

In the words of the mnemonic rhyme cited by Zedler: '*Schutz- und Schirm-
Gerechtigkeit, giebt keine Obrigkeit* (the right of protection and safeguard
does not result in governmental authority)'.[24] Famously, Carl Schmitt, Walter
Benjamin, and more recently Giorgio Agamben have described the early
modern sovereignty of the territorial state in terms of the exception as the
normative instance for distributing and implementing rights and power.[25]
Regardless of the descriptive and analytic adequacy of their hypothesis,
Zedler's article on *Schutz, Schirm* comes strikingly close to such a legal
construction of institutional power. *Schirm-Gerechtigkeit* details a situation
in which the request and the provision of protection occur in a state of
exception from ordinary structures of authority and subjection. A relationship centred on or reduced to surveillance and protection is thus delimited
within the framework of the Empire. The provision, however, is that such a
relationship does not create the ordinary bond of authority and obedience
and that it must not be extended beyond the assignments of the agreement.

　　The model for these reduced relationships or states within the state during
the times the Empire was the steward or lord protector (*Vogt* in German).
The lord protector exercised administrative and military power typically
on behalf of a cloister or other properties and institutions of the Church
that did not exercise governmental functions themselves. In this sense,
the Emperor can be called in a general sense the *Schirmer* (lord protector)
of the Church in the Holy Roman Empire, whereas *Vögte* (lord protectors)
of abbeys and cloisters are *Schirmer* in the narrower and more practical
sense. If we agree with Schmitt's affirmative and Benjamin and Agamben's
critical observation that the modern territorial state has its defining origin

---

23　Zedler, XXXV, col. 1710.
24　Ibid.
25　Schmitt, *Concept of the Political*, p. 35f.; Benjamin, *German Mourning Play*, p. 48-50; Agamben,
State of Exception, pp. 1-40. For recent developments, see Krahmann, *States, Citizens and the
Privatization of Security*.

in protection (or biopolitics), then we might venture the thesis that it is the special right of *Schirm-Gerechtigkeit* that has forged such a government and state within the old, medieval Empire. As we have seen, it is exactly the legal specificity of *Schirm-Gerechtigkeit* that does not create authority by itself but operates instead without reference to the ordinary authority of law and government in the Empire.

If we now conceive of *Schirm-Gerechtigkeit* as a model for modern statehood, Benjamin and Agamben's critical point would indeed be supported.[26] The modern territorial state, if seen as following the example of *Schutz und Schirm*, would in fact turn out to be a regime of protection and surveillance outside of the ordinary relationship of government and obedience, law and citizenship. It would make permanent (in the form of the state) what is in the legal instrument of *Schutz und Schirm* in fact a private, temporary contract.

In every article on *Schirm*, *Schutz*, and *Schirm-Gerechtigkeit*, Zedler's *Great Universal Lexicon* makes reference to the article on *advocatio*.[27] *Advocatio*, it could be argued, is the historical model and the conceptual backing of *Schutz und Schirm*.[28] It would be too far from the task at hand to pursue its origins within Roman law, social organization, and legal rhetoric. However, it is important to note that the relationship between the party asking for protection and the party providing it is formulated in terms of the Roman relation between client and patron. This relation was, in turn, the model for the relation between a person seeking legal representation in court and the advocate or orator providing such support.[29] The importance is only heightened by the fact that legal commentators in the seventeenth and eighteenth centuries knew well that the Roman understanding of patronage and advocacy no longer applied to the written investigation and trial procedures practiced in early modern times. This circumstance underlines the conceptual importance of advocacy as a model for the construction of right and power in *Schutz und Schirm*. *Schutz und Schirm* is structurally analogous to the manner in which the orator advocates before the judge on behalf of his client. The client acquires the status of a legal person only through this act of advocacy. To put it differently, the orator speaking before the judge on his client's behalf creates an image of the defendant, his world, and his deeds for

26 See for Agamben also: 'The Messiah and the Sovereign. The Problem of Law in Walter Benjamin'.

27 Zedler, art. 'Advocat, Advocatus, Avocat', 1, col. 590-592; art. 'Advocatia', 1, col. 592; 'Advocatus Eglesiae', 1, col. 592-595.

28 See Mager von Schönberg, *De advocatia armata*.

29 On the rhetorical-legal concept of advocacy and representation, see R. Campe, 'Outline for a Critical History of *Fürsprache*'.

the court. This is yet another facet of projection which, in the media-historical sense, is accomplished on a screen. By acting in defence and protection of his client, the orator brings his client before the court and before the law. The advocate gives his client shape, contour, and a voice that can reach the ears of the judges. In an analogous fashion, the early modern lord protector not only defended his client against a dangerous and hostile environment but also granted administrative and legal stature to an institutional complex that could not otherwise take part in the administrative world of powers and rights. This type of legal and administrative *screening*, which provided protection against danger in the outside world, always involved an act of projection in which an entity with no place in the realm of politics and power was given presence and a voice in it.

Paries (the wall), or the optical screen to come

In early modern law and politics, these mechanisms of screening and protection were worked out with great precision. Subtle semantic distinctions can be found in this context that determine the practices of protection as a specialized skill or a specific right. During the same centuries, screening was also relevant in practices of surveillance and targeting. Scenes of screening involving hunting blinds span from farm and village life to the aristocracy and the court. The legal construction of protection on the one side, and the example of the hunters' screening devices on the other, disclose the complex practices and strategies that surrounded these scenes. And yet, outside such complex dispositives of screening, there were also the simple surfaces called screens, and these screens were as ubiquitously present in everyday life then as they are today. The *Bettschirm* (bed screen) described above can stand in many respects as the epitome of these lampshades and shutters, door panes and umbrellas—which are all called *Schirme* in German.

These screening devices interpose themselves in the natural media of air or light, and they channel or defend against heat or cold, light or air, sun or rain. These simple *Schirm* devices filter, limit, and modulate the flow of natural (and sometimes social) media in space and time. They do so without further refining the concept of projection. Yet a considerable number of these simple screens, interposed between human bodies and their environment, also took on secondary, decorative uses. Umbrellas and parasols were decorated with all kinds of visual motifs, while painted window and bed screens made from transparent materials produced illuminative effects. The surprisingly detailed articles on these objects in Zedler refer the users of the encyclopedia time and again to Johann Melchior Cröker's *Wohl anführende Mahler* (The Well Instructing Painter), which promised to teach its readers how to decorate their doors, windows, and other facets of their domestic space with oil painting and related skills.[30]

With such interposed *Schirme*, translucent panes and other transparent surfaces come into play. In particular, this applies to the *Fensterschirme*, or window screens. Illuminated images projected through translucent surfaces (parchment, paper, glass) resurrect an old fascination that goes back as far as the medieval times. In terms related to the modern understandings of the terms 'projection' and 'screen', we might consider these transparent surfaces as accidental lantern slides. The transparent surface called the screen can, in other words, be seen as a slide in the *laterna magica*. What makes the magic lantern a unique seventeenth-century invention is, however, not this deployment of the 'screen' in the early modern sense of the word. Rather, it is the manipulation of mirrors and lenses around it. It is only through their construction and configuration that the core apparatus of the magic lantern is defined and developed beyond the visual effects on the translucent surface. Only through the devices of optical projection technology does the magic lantern become a technical media. The technization of the projection mechanism via lenses and mirrors is, we might say, the first step towards reinventing the practices and meaning of protection—of transforming the screen from its early modern function to one that serves as an element in an optical technology.

However, in order to technically implement the traditional cultural meaning of 'screening', another step is required, one that was never fully taken in the seventeenth century. The apparatus of the magic lantern only hints at it. Only this second and final step would bring about the full integration of what we call the 'screen' from the time of the cinema on (and in the German language even only with the display of the radar and related technology). In the seventeenth-century magic lantern, the 'screen' on which visual representations appear is largely ignored as part of the apparatus proper. Only the 'through-screen', the slide through which the projection is beamed, is considered part of the technical set-up. The 'on-screen' remains at the margins of the apparatus. Yet nothing would appear without the 'on-screen'.[31]

The magic lantern does not form a closed optical system of projection as long as it does not acknowledge the display as an integral technical part

---

30 Cröker, *Der wohl anführende Mahler.*
31 For a discussion of on-screen and through-screen, see Mitchell, 'Screening Nature (and the Nature of the Screen)'.

of its own apparatus. This step is only taken when the 'screen' becomes a fully developed element of the optical system. Neither the Jesuit Athanasius Kircher's diagrammatic images nor the striking illustrative plates depicting Jan van Musschenbroek's and other magic lanterns in Willem 's Gravesande's *Physices Elementa Mathematica* pay any attention to the display surface.[32] They focus instead on a technical construction produced by concave mirrors (which collect and intensify a beam of light) or by lenses that project the light through slides. The surface of display—which in the cinematic configuration would become the screen—is often simply omitted from the construction diagrams or is an afterthought in them. It is just the bare wall of a room. There is even a considerable number of seventeenth-century illustrations of the magic lantern in which the projected image appears to be part of the optical pyramid shining forth from the apparatus rather than being displayed on any surface.

The optical screen thus remains beyond the apparatus and its technical and optical mode of being. The projected image either appears virtually within the conic diagram of the optical reconstruction or is produced by a non-technical effect in which a surface happens by chance to be in the path of light rays. A notable exception to this rule is Christiaan Huygens's 1694 sketch of a magic lantern, completed almost forty years after his first work on the device.[33] Huygens provides the following handwritten legend for the elements of the apparatus: *speculum cavum* (concave mirror), *lucerna* (oil lamp), *lens vitrea* (lens), *pictura pellucida* (translucent picture), *lens altera* (second lens), *paries* (wall).[34] In this diagrammatic representation, which is both analytic and instructional, the 'screen' makes its first appearance, even if only under the name of a wall. It is schematically represented as a straight line, indicating a simple surface without any further specification. Marginal as it is, the line labelled *paries* (wall) represents the advent of what later would be called the 'screen'. In Huygens's sketch, the *paries* may not

32   See Kircher, *Ars magna lucis et umbrae*, vol. 2, pp. 907-915 on transmitting messages by the prototype of a magic lantern (steganographia). Kircher sketches out a series of possible realizations, from transmitting letters to drawings to coloured and moving images and from mechanisms based on sunlight to those based on artificial light. See in particular table XXXIV, p. 912, and the description on p. 910. Willem Jacob 's Gravesande, *Mathematical Elements of Natural Science,* Plate XIV, Fig. 1, p. 104; see the description, p. 101f. in which the surface receiving the images figures under the name of 'white plane'.

33   Huygens, *Œuvres complètes*, XXII, p. 197, "Pour des representations par le moyen de verres convexes à la lampe," dated 1658.

34   Huygens, *Œuvres complètes*, XIII, p. 786. The sketch – dated 1694, a year before the author's death – is added to the first supplement of the *Dioptrica* manuscript. Huygens had been working on the *Dioptrica* since 1653.

materially signify anything other than the coincidental wall of the room that happens to intercept the light rays. And yet, in its constructive vein, the diagram renders the *paries* a part of the technical set-up which, as such, has the same status as the lenses and the mirrors, the slide and the lamp. In its function, the *paries* becomes a technical object, and it is from this moment on that its further elaboration as a technical object develops. This moment makes the *paries* a screen to come. It may be said that it bears even further significance. With the *paries* becoming screen, not only the image-bearing wall but the whole set-up of the magic lantern severs its ties with the natural and social environment from which it has emerged. In that very moment, the cultural functions of proto-technical screens like the bed screen and the window screen—which first and foremost serve the twin functions of protection and projection—give way to the new intrinsic cultural meaning of the optical—and technical—apparatus.[35] In its quality of a closed system of technical objects, the optical apparatus is able to reintegrate the more complex cultural and social meanings of protection and hiding one's own gaze within the optical technology. The screen's technical and optical implementation, however, was to reach its full technical embodiment only later within the phantasmagoria, the panorama, and then the cinema. Regarded even more strictly, one could argue that the screen comes about only with the emergence of the radar monitor and other integrated display devices. In these devices, the screen ceases to resemble the wall or canvas or window shade in any respect. As an electronic display element, its technization is complete. The radar screen is thus the culmination of a process beginning in the *paries* becoming screen.[36]

This narrower understanding of the *Schirm* is reflected in its usage in German. As noted before, the word *Bildschirm* (image screen) resurfaces in German only with the radar screen and comparable monitoring devices following the development of Karl Ferdinand Braun's cathode-ray tube in the 1930s. The vacuum tube's use of an electron gun and a phosphorescent receiving device models the modern technology of display for monitoring purposes. As Joachim Heinrich Campe's *Dictionary of the German Language* shows, *Schirm* had, however, been defined in a similar way as 'screen' in English and '*écran*' in French ever since the eighteenth century. One might

35   For the notion of cultural techniques and its further development of Kittlerian media studies, see Siegert, pp. 1-17.
36   For the understanding of the radar as a closed integrated system and the technical importance of the screen, I am indebted to Geoghegan, 'An Ecology of Operations: Fire-Control, Vigilance, and the Birth of the Digital Screen', manuscript.

say that since then, the German *Schirm* was ready to become the optical screen or *écran*. As Campe explains, each instrument

> is called a *Schirm* (screen) that is made out of canvas or silk and suspended in quadrangular or round frames on legs or pedestals or that is suspended through several poles with one major pole in the middle in order to protect oneself against too much heat of the fire, too much light for the eyes, or against sun and rain.[37]

And yet Germans continue to use the word *Leinwand* (canvas) in the case of film, as if to preserve the proximity between the painted and the projected image. *Bildschirm* is used only in the vocabulary of optical (and acoustic) technology after the invention of Braun's cathode-ray tube and its integrated projection technology. This late, limited use of *Bildschirm* then evokes the complex early modern meanings of projection, as exemplified by the hunting screen and the 'rights of protection and safeguard'. In these cases, the screen's protection and projection mechanisms are more complex than a mere filtering of natural media. Protection and projection are mutually linked, such as when one protects one's gaze in order to see an object or when a protector allows a client to become a legal person or an administrative entity in the first place. In these complex cases, it becomes evident that *projection is based on and defined by the very act of protection*. The *Filmleinwand* (film canvas) is a case in which projection is an exclusively optical and technical process (though a sophisticated theoretical account of cinema might read projection differently). Monitoring screens such as the radar screen make the mutual relation between protection and projection far more explicit than the movie screen. They bring to life the forgotten dispositives of screening in the early modern era, which German word usage reflects.

Neither the practices and semantics nor the technical and legal concepts nor the theological aura of *Schutz und Schirm* are part of the screen's media history in any proper sense. Rather, these concepts provide the background for this volume's examination of the optical and technical implementation of the screen. This background does not reveal an alternative history, since every history (and even every prehistory) presupposes the continuous identity of the subject of which it is a history. We might better understand the role of *Schutz und Schirm* in media history with the help of a term coined by Friedrich Kittler: *implementation*. Implementation, in Kittler's sense of the term, means that some cultural or social function is

---

37   J.H. Campe, *Wörterbuch der deutschen Sprache* (1746-1808), IV, p. 146.

realized—implemented—by a technical solution.[38] The continuous identity of a history's subject matter can then be expressed through the technical implementation of a given cultural or social function. The cultural or social function in question may even be only defined retroactively through a certain technical implementation. The history of the screen in these terms is the account of either the function implemented by the optical device called the 'screen' or of the optical apparatus developed in order to make such implementation possible.

Technical implementation defines retroactively what the problem was that it is to solve, or what the social function is for which it provides the solution. In both cases, implementation characterizes a teleological history, a history of the invention of its own subject matter. There is no doubt, however, that implementation can also mean—and does mean, according to Kittler—the primary act of implementing something in a world that has still to be prepared for the implementation or that still has to search for propitious places to bring it about. This primordial meaning of implementation is where the practices of screening come into play in the background of the media history of the screen. Something exists in the world that can be used (even in the violent sense of 'using') in order to function as a technical device. Or something exists in the world that invites or even seduces people (in often latent and indirect manners) to use it in unforeseen ways. This primordial act of implementation is ahistorical. There is no continuity either in terms of agent or action. There is no continuous narrative of it and hence no narrative at all. One may rather speak of a scene than a history of implementation in this primordial context.

This scene is, however, not without parameters in which the implementation process is structured. The primordial scene of the *Schirm*'s implementation discloses two such parameters. While they are highly specific to the screen, we may surmise that, with some flexibility and abstraction, they can be further developed into a model of how implementation works in general.

First of all, the primal scenes of *Schutz und Schirm* do not share the same subject matter with the media history of the optical device called *Schirm*. Practices, norms, strategies, and legal procedures were developed in the seventeenth and eighteenth centuries that focused on protection and safeguarding as well as screening and filtering, but these either had nothing to do with the visual at all (the rights of *Schutz und Schirm*) or they involved visuality in an utterly different, even opposing sense (the *Jagd-Schirm*). In particular, these practices made no significant use of

38   On implementation in Kittler, see R. Campe, *Kittler's Humanities*.

optical screens while, at the same time, the optical screens used for windows and doors hardly had the elaborate functions of *Schutz und Schirm*. Only in retrospect, from our experience of the cinema, radar, and other screen-based media, can we bring the optical device and the functions of *Schutz und Schirm* together.

When and under what conditions can we bridge the discontinuity between the early modern practices of *Schutz und Schirm* and the media history of the optical screen? There is an unavoidable metaphoricity at play when we take the *Jagd-Schirm* to define the function of optical projection ('seeing something in such a way that one's own gaze is not seen') or when we think of the legal right of protection as characterizing the development of optical media ('a zone of surveillance erected between protector and protected without sovereignty and citizenship'). Under what circumstances is this metaphoric transition vague and rushed, and when does it stand on solid ground? There is probably no completely satisfactory answer to this question. However, a second parameter may help in addressing the issue. This parameter considers the integration of screens in the set-up of a technological optical apparatus for which they serve as 'flat surfaces' for image display. These flat surfaces were perhaps even more prevalent in the early modern household than today, whether in the form of transparent surfaces ('through-screens') or support surfaces for painting ('on-screens'). But the early modern technical assemblage that exhibited the most sophisticated use of optical projection—the magic lantern—shied away from identifying the support surface as a distinct technical component. When the screen was made an explicit part of the technical set-up, it was marginally mentioned as the *paries*, the wall, as in Huygens's construction draft. However, only this one element of the dispositive, which stubbornly remained pre-technological for a long time, finally turned the dispositive into a closed technological system. Only when the screen closed the technological system of screening did it become a technical object in its own right. The magic lantern never reached this point unequivocally. The phantasmagoria of the early nineteenth century probably took an initial step toward this stage, while in certain Western cultures, this transformation was only secured with the assembled apparatus of the cinema. It can, however, also be argued that only Braun's cathode ray tube—the electron canon with the monitor—fully integrated the visual display into the technical being-there of the optical apparatus. Certainly, with the development of radar and similar systems, *Jagd-Schirm* and *Schutz und Schirm* no longer have merely metaphorical status in describing what the screening technology of the optical system accomplishes. The metonymic question of whether the support device is an integral part of the technological system or a coincidental phenomenon in its surrounding world thus appears decisive.

It remains challenging to pinpoint the threshold at which the meta-phorical understanding of the function of the screen becomes cogent as a technological phenomenon or where the metonymic relation of the two being mere co-phenomena is transformed into an integrated technological system. However, the interplay between these two parameters can serve as a model for implementation; it can also provide a new starting point for the study of the screen and other technical media as well.

Works Cited

Agamben, Giorgio. 'The Messiah and the Sovereign. The Problem of Law in Walter Benjamin.' In Agamben, *Potentialities*, translated by Daniel Heller-Roazen, pp. 160-174. Palo Alto: Stanford University Press, 1999.

——. *The State of Exception*. Translated by Kevin Attell. Chicago: Chicago University Press, 2005.

——, *What is an Apparatus? and Other Essays*. Translated by David Kishik and Stefan Pedatella. Palo Alto: Stanford University Press, 2009.

Ahl, Diane Cole. 'The Misericordia *Polytych*.' In *The Cambridge Companion to Piero della Francesca*, edited by Jeraldyne M. Wood, pp. 14-29. Cambridge: Cambridge University Press, 2002.

van Asperen, Hanneke. 'The Sheltering Cloak. Images of Charity and Mercy in Fourteenth-Century Italy.' *Textile* 11 (2013): 262-281.

Benjamin, Walter. *Origin of the German Mourning Play*. Translated by Howard Eiland, Cambridge: Harvard University Press 2019.

Campe, Joachim Heinrich. *Wörterbuch der deutschen Sprache*. Braunschweig: Schulbuchverlag, 1818.

Campe, Rüdiger. 'An Outline for a Critical History of *Fürsprache: Synegoria* and Advocacy.' *Deutsche Vierteljahreschrift für Literaturgeschichte und Geistesge-schichte* 82 (2008): 355-381.

——. 'Kittler's Humanities: On Implementation.' In *The Technological Introject: Friedrich Kittler Between Implementation and the Incalculable*, edited by Jeffrey Champlin and Antje Pfannkuchen, pp. 9-26. New York: Fordham University Press, 2018.

Casetti, Francesco. 'What is a Screen Nowadays?' In *The Screen Media Reader: Culture, Theory, Practice*, edited by Stephen Monteiro, pp. 29-38. New York: Bloomsbury Academic, 2017.

Corvol, André. *Histoire de chasse: L'homme et la bête*. Paris: Perrin, 2010.

Cröker, Johann Melchior. *Der wohl anführende Mahler, welcher curiöse Liebhaber lehret, wie man sich zur Malerei zubereiten … solle*. Edition Jena 1736, edited by Ulrich Schiessl. Mittenwald: Mäander, 1982.

Deleuze, Gilles and Felix Guattari. *Kafka: Toward a Minor Literature*. Translated by Dana Polan. Minneapolis: Minneapolis University Press, 1986.

Diderot, Denis. *Preliminary Discourse to the Encyclopedia of Diderot. Jean Le Rond d'Alembert*. Translated by Richard N. Schwab. Chicago: Chicago University Press, 1995.

Fontin, François. *Amusemens de la chasse et de la peche*. Amsterdam, Leipzig: Arkstée & Merkus, 1743; originally published in Paris, 1660. Translated into German as *Adelicher Zeit-Vertreiber / Oder Neu-Erfundene Jagdergötzungen*. Augsburg: Wagner, 1696.

Foucault, Michel. 'The Confession of the Flesh.' In *Power/Knowledge: Selected Interviews and Other Writings, 1972-1977*, edited and translated by Colin Gordon et al., pp. 194-228. New York: Pantheon Books, 1980.

Geoghegan, Bernard. 'An Ecology of Operations: Fire-Control, Vigilance, and the Birth of the Digital Screen', Manuscript, forthcoming in *Representations* 145 (2019).

Gravesande, Willem Jacob s'. *Mathematical Elements of Natural Science*. Translated by John Theophilus Desaguliers. London: Innys, Longman, Shewell 1726. Originally published in Latin in 1720-1721.

Grimm, Dieter. 'Das staatliche Gewaltmonopol.' In *Internationales Handbuch der Gewaltforschung*, edited by Wilhelm Heitmeyer and John Hagan, col. 1297-1313. Wiesbaden: Westdeutscher Verlag, 2002.

von Grimmelshausen, Jakob Christoffel. *Der abentheuerliche Simplicissimus Teutsch*. In Grimmelshausen, *Werke*, edited by Dieter Breuer. Frankfurt: Deutscher Klassiker Verlag, 1989-1997. For an English translation, see *Adventures of Simplicius Simplicissimus*. Translated by J.A. Underwood. London: Penguin Books, 2018.

Grosser, H. Marc. 'Kircher and the Laterna Magica—A Reexamination.' *SMPTE Journal* 90 (1981): 972-978.

The Holy Bible, Containing the Old and New Testaments. King James Version, 1611. New York: American Bible Society, 1980.

Huhtamo, Erkki. 'Elements of Screenology: Toward an Archaeology of the Screen.' *ICONICS (International Studies of the Modern Image)*, 7 (2004): 31-82.

Huygens, Christiaan. *Œuvres complètes*, edited by the Société hollandaise des sciences. The Hague: M. Nijhoff, 1888-1950.

Kircher, Athanasius. *Ars magna lucis et umbrae*. 2 vols. Rome: Hermann Scheus, 1646.

Krahmann, Elke. *States, Citizens and the Privatization of Security*. Cambridge, UK, and New York: Cambridge University Press, 2010.

Latour, Bruno. 'Visualization and Cognition: Thinking with Eyes and Hands.' *Knowledge and Society* 6 (1986): 1-40.

Luther, Martin. *Werke. Kritische Gesamtausgabe.* Weimar: Böhlau, 1883-2009.

Mager von Schönberg, Martin. *De advocatia armata, sive Clientelari patronorum iure et potestate clientumque officio, vulgo Schutz- und Schirm-Gerechtigkeit, in & extra-Romano Germanicum Imperium.* Basel: König, 1625. First edition Frankfurt, 1619.

Mannoni, Laurent. *The Great Art of Light and Shadow: Archaeology of the Cinema.* Exeter: Exeter University Press, 2000.

Mitchell, W.J.T. 'Screening Nature (and the Nature of the Screen).' *New Review of Film and Television Studies* 13 (2015): 231-246.

Sartre, Jean-Paul. *Being and Nothingness.* Translated by Hazel E. Barnes. London, New York: Routledge, 2003.

Schmitt, Carl. *Concept of the Political.* Translated by George Schwab. Chicago: Chicago University Press, 2007.

Siegert, Bernhard. *Cultural Techniques.* Translated by Geoffrey Winthrop-Young. New York: Fordham, 2015.

Smith, A. Mark. *From Sight to Light. The Passage from Ancient to Modern Optics.* Chicago: Chicago University Press, 2015.

Tänzer, Johann. *Der Dianen Hohe und Niedere Jagd-Geheimnüß.* Copenhagen: Schmedtgen, 1686.

Weber, Samuel. *Theatricality as Medium.* New York: Fordham University Press, 2004.

Zedler, Johann Heinrich. *Grosses vollständiges Real-Lexikon aller Wissenschaften und Künste.* Halle, Leipzig: Johann Heinrich Zedler, 1732-1754. http://daten.digitale-sammlungen.de/~db/0000/bsb00000396/images/. Accessed 11 November 2018.

About the Author

Rüdiger Campe is the Alfred C. and Martha F. Mohr Professor of Germanic Languages & Literatures and Professor of Comparative Literature at Yale University. Before joining the Yale faculty, he taught at Johns Hopkins and Essen University, and has held visiting professorships at NYU, Konstanz, Siegen, European University at Frankfurt/Oder, and other institutions. He is author of *Game of Probability. Literature and Calculation from Pascal to Kleist* (2012; German, 2002) and co-editor with Julia Weber of *Rethinking Emotion. Interiority and Exteriority in Pre-Modern, Modern, and Contemporary Thought* (2014). Further book publications include *Baumgarten-Studien* (with Anselm Haverkamp and Christoph Menke, 2014), *Affekt und Ausdruck* (1990), and *Penthesileas Versprechen* (2008). He has published on science and literature, literature and law, rhetoric, media theory and history, and the theory of communication.

3. Face and Screen: Toward a Genealogy of the Media Façade

Craig Buckley

Abstract

Craig Buckley questions the tendency to see the multi-media façade as paradigmatic of recent developments in illumination and display technologies by reconsidering a longer history of the conflicting urban roles in which façades, as media have been cast. Over the course of the nineteenth century, façades underwent an optical redefinition parallel to that which defined the transformation of the screen. Buildings that sought to do away with a classical conception of the façade also emerged as key sites of experimentation with illuminated screening technologies. Long before the advent of the technical systems animating contemporary media envelopes, the façades of storefronts, cinemas, newspaper offices, union headquarters, and information centres were conceived as media surfaces whose ability to operate on and intervene in their surroundings became more important than the duty to express the building's interior.

Keywords: Urban Screens, Architecture, Space, Physiognomy, Glass, Projection, Billboard

Introduction

One no longer need travel very far to encounter façades that pulse and move like electronic screens. Media façades have spread far beyond the dense commercial nodes with which they were once synonymous—New York's Times Square, London's Piccadilly Circus, Berlin's Alexanderplatz, or Tokyo's Shibuya. Some of the most ambitious media façades are today realized in places such as Birmingham, Graz, Tallinn, and Jeddah; Abu Dhabi, Tripoli, Montreal, and San Jose; Lima, Melbourne, Seoul, and Ningbo. Within the darkness of

Buckley, C., R. Campe, F. Casetti (eds.), *Screen Genealogies. From Optical Device to Environmental Medium*. Amsterdam: Amsterdam University Press, 2019

DOI 10.5117/9789463729000_CH03

a global night this emerging network of cities registers itself through a call and response of ever-changing luminous façades designed not only to mark a place in the city but also to circulate across television, laptop, and smartphone screens. The animated colours, images, and patterns on such façades are massive, hybrid, hardware/software interfaces that modulate and liquefy the apparent stability of the buildings they enclose. Media façades arguably exemplify architecture's loss of material gravity, a victory of ephemeral images over solid stuff that coincides with, and reflects, the competition between world cities to attract tourism and investment. And yet the temptation to see media façades in terms of dematerialized illusions and fleeting animations overlooks the fact that screens inevitably possess their own materiality. As the substance and technique of façade construction increasingly assume performance requirements once limited to optical screens, a building's ability to display and control moving images, graphics, patterns, and text has become a requirement as important as its material, shape, weatherproofing, or security. Broadly speaking, accounts of the media façade remain divided between those that analyze materials, techniques, and aesthetic possibilities as part of an operative project and those that decry their spectacular effect as a species of 'architainment'. The former often claim to renew the meaning and performance of the façade by linking it more intrinsically with digital media and interactivity, whereas the latter, in Luis Fernàndez-Galliano's memorable phrase, see the media façade as a symptom of how architecture's symbolic universe has been 'devoured by media'.[1] To grasp the transformation underway, neither an operative history of the media façade nor a dismissal of its spectacular effects seem sufficient. Rather than insist on an opposition between a symbolic domain proper to architecture and another belonging to 'the media', a historico-critical reflection might begin by recognizing and reconsidering the façade's deep and unstable historical role *as* a medium. Façades involved mediation long before building envelopes assimilated qualities formerly associated with optical screens. In keeping with the argument of this book, the media façade will not be understood primarily as an optical screen whose origins lie in recent technical developments. Rather, these surfaces represent a more fundamental opportunity to embark on a media genealogy of the façade. To do so calls for a deeper history of the tensions and conflicts manifested in debates over these entities. Screens assumed architectural and environmental meanings and functions long before they were autonomous planes for the optical display, and these screening functions intersect in complex ways with the roles that façades have been expected to play.

1   Fernàndez-Galliano, 2.

Amid the considerable and growing literature on screens, accounts of the media façade's history remain nascent. One dominant narrative has emphasized technology; seeing media façades as the result of efforts to integrate new illumination technologies—from neon and fluorescent tubes to high-power projections and LED screens—with the material surfaces of buildings. Yet how have such processes accommodated themselves to the history of the façade while also changing in turn its meaning and purpose? If we are to understand the media façade as a screen, what kind of screen is it? M. Hank Heausler's *Media Façades: History, Technology, Content* (2009), the first book that sought to compile this entity's global proliferation, adopts a technical definition: a media façade is any external building surface with an integrated capacity to display dynamic graphics, images, texts, and spatial movement.[2] The emphasis placed on the façade as a means for controlling images, patterns, graphics, and text distinguishes the media façade from light architecture, in the sense of illumination applied to buildings. In stressing the integration of a dynamic display with a building envelope, the media façade is a more restricted category than the urban screen. The latter, a term developed in media studies over the last decade, seeks to account for screens that are neither television nor movie screens, ranging from mobile screens associated with smartphones, tablets, and laptops to large-scale electronic advertising billboards, public displays, scoreboards, and information kiosks.[3] While the definition of the media façade is narrower than that of the urban screen, both bodies of literature tend to agree that the phenomena are recent. *The Urban Screens Reader,* edited by Scott McQuire, Meredith Martin, and Sabine Niederer, points to the Spectacolor Board in Times Square (1976) as the point of origin for their inquiry.[4] Heausler cites Renzo Piano and Richard Rogers's unrealized design for a large-scale media screen in their winning 1971 entry for the Centre Beaubourg competition as the historical origin for the current proliferation of contemporary media façades.[5] In contrast to these technical accounts of origin, Erkki Huhtamo has advanced a media archaeology of public display screens that goes back to the middle of the nineteenth century. The video billboards populating early twenty-first-century cityscapes emerge, Huhtamo argues, from an earlier

---

2   Heausler further distinguishes between mechanical façades and three general electronic techniques: the use of projection, illuminant control, and digital display surfaces. See, Heausler, pp. 13-14.

3   Among the growing literature on urban screens, see McQuire, Martin, and Niederer, 2009; Verhoeff, 2012; Berry, Harbord, and Moore, 2013; Papastergiadis, Barikin, McQuire, and Yue, 2017.

4   McQuire, Martin, and Niederer, p. 9.

5   Heausler, p. 21.

formative stage defined by urban banners and bill-posting practices on the one hand, and public magic lantern displays on the other.[6] Uta Caspary, by contrast, offers a different perspective. Analyzing the patterns assumed by digital media incorporated in façades, she argues that these surfaces should be understood and interpreted as part of a continuous history of architectural ornament.[7]

This essay builds on, but also differs from, these accounts. Seeking to critically reframe the question of the media façade's historicity, it retraces shifting articulations of the relationship between façade and face in architectural theory. More than the historical continuities of ornament or the intersection of bill-posting and projection, media façades can be understood within the intensified competition between building fronts and commercial messages—a cultural, technical, and political conflict that entailed a transformation in the face/façade relationship. As vertical surfaces in the metropolis came to be established as a form of private property distinct from the buildings to which they were physically attached, a struggle over visibility played out between proponents of the free and unfettered development of advertising and cultural efforts to preserve the city's architectural façades from what was seen as commercial defacement. In this sense, a technology like the magic lantern is less consequential for the emergence of the media façade than the spread of electrification around the turn of the twentieth century. Indeed, it was by seeking to reconceptualize the façade in electrical terms that architects sought to resolve the conflict between billboard and building face, making this cultural-technical transformation into something of crucial consequence for a genealogy of the media façade.[8]

It is also important to remember that the things we today call media façades were conceptualized and envisioned long before it was technically and economically feasible to integrate large scale audio-visual displays into building envelopes. Architects produced remarkably detailed visions for incorporating changing texts, images, and moving images into façades already in the 1920s and 1930s, and science fiction authors had ventured such ideas as far back at the 1880s. Given that the concept of the media façade precedes its realization, how might one understand the social emergence of this desire and its technological configuration(s)? The understanding of

6   Huhtamo, pp. 15-16.
7   Caspary, 2017.
8   There is substantial and growing literature on the consequences of electrification for architecture. Cf. Schivelbusch, 1988; Nye, 2018; Neumann, 2002; Isenstadt, Petty, and Neumann, 2015.

what is called a media façade might change when considered in light of a series of historical events in which the concept and practice of the façade was radically transformed as the result of cultural and technological conflicts. The aim is to grasp not the origins of the media façade but its emergence within a much longer line of descent, in which the mediating functions of the façade were inscribed into a new and conflicted system of purposes. In such an account, Piano and Rogers's competition entry for the Centre Beaubourg can be understood not as a beginning but as a recent descendant of a longer and more complex story. The following proposes a working outline of some of the key events within such a genealogy.

Façades and faces

Among the ancestors proposed for contemporary media façades, one of the most distant are the large expanses of stained glass characteristic of medieval cathedrals. Heralded as precursors to twentieth-century avant-garde light experiments since the 1920s at least, the stained-glass window has also been taken up by more contemporary critics seeking to historicize the integration of media screens into buildings.[9] Writing at the beginning of the 1990s, Martin Pawley saw both stained-glass windows and movie screens as illuminated surfaces designed to 'convey visual information to large numbers of people'.[10] Yet such a comparison, however thought-provoking, neglects the vastly different historical functions and meanings of such illuminated surfaces. To frame the problem of the media façade, the genealogy outlined here asks how the functions and operations of screening have intersected with the functions and operations of façades. Consequently, it begins at a later moment, when the façade came to be defined as an architectural concept.

The term *facciata* emerges in fourteenth century Florence and was etymologically rooted in the Latin *facies*—face, countenance, or visage.[11]

9   Moholy-Nagy points to the medieval stain glass windows as a partial beginning for the light experiments of the 1920s, though one which was 'not consistently carried through.' Moholy-Nagy, 1925, p. 17. For a reflection on stained glass windows in relation to vertical screens, see Elcott's contribution to this volume. For a historical analysis of the Gothic choir screen as medium, see Jung, 2012.

10   Pawley, p. 119. The text was reprinted in a special issue on façades by the Berlin magazine Arch+ in 1990, which was the source in turn for Caspary's account, which argues for the stained-glass window as a key precursor of the media façade.

11   See Rossi, p. 308. On the regularization of façades in Florence as part of the efforts to open up the urban plaza around the Baptistery, see Trachtenberg, pp. 32-41.

The emergence of *facciata* likened a building's front to its *faccia*, or face, and belongs among those analogies to the human body central to Renaissance architectural theory. To conceive of a building's front as a face was to endow it with at least two functions. According to physiognomic discourses that go back to antiquity, the face was the part of the body that most vividly and unmistakably manifested the affections of the soul. Despite the variety of its elements, a face displayed an exemplary unity and was for this reason the most individual and unique part of the body. That which was internal and otherwise unseeable acquired visibility on the face. Such a surface was defined by a complex, expressive relation of inside to outside. Surveying key moments in architectural theory and practice, we might identify three different ideas of the face that inform changing conceptions of the façade. In the Renaissance, one encounters a model of the face as public image. In the eighteenth-century context of the French Royal Academy of Architecture, a revival of physiognomic ideas contributed to a more systematic theory of the face/façade as a 'mirror of the soul'. In the nineteenth century, a rationalist investigation of structure turned against such an idea of the face, drawing instead on analogies rooted in comparative anatomy. Attending to these very different ideas of the face, and the divergent understandings of the relation of interior to exterior characteristic of each, highlights the various kinds of screening expected of the façade.

Façade was a term notably absent from Vitruvius's *De Architectura*, the only surviving antique treatise on architecture. The text of Vitruvius had served as a central authority for Renaissance architects since its rediscovery in 1414, yet as Werner Oechslin has noted, while architects were readily able to codify its precepts concerning the order of building fronts, they long struggled to articulate anything like a clear concept of the façade.[12] The Renaissance palace façade was worked out in practice more than it was in theory; its paradigmatic form was rectilinear in outline, symmetrical in appearance, and hierarchical in organization. As a self-contained representation composed of classical motifs, such façades were also spatially and stylistically separated from their urban surroundings. Analyzing one of the earliest and most canonical Renaissance façades—the Palazzo Rucellai (1442-1451), attributed to Leon Battista Alberti—highlights how such early façades were not the outward face of newly designed buildings but often

---

12   Oechslin, p. 33. While there are a number of excellent studies of the theory of the façade in relation to periods or buildings, there is as yet no comprehensive genealogy of theories of the façade. See Burroughs, 2002; Schumacher, 1987; Szambien, 1996; Vidler, 1992.

exteriors that consolidated formerly separate buildings into an appearant unity. (Figure 3.1) More than a simple addition, the façade of the Palazzo Rucellai, like many other Renaissance palaces, necessitated the elimination of late-medieval elements such as porticos and loggias that had formerly served to mediate between street and building.[13] The façade's unity was thus not rooted in anything like an underlying, inner wholeness. It was, rather, a superficial unity that sought to reorganize the building from outside in. It is for these reasons that Renaissance scholar Charles Burroughs had argued for the Rucellai façade to be understood as an 'opaque screen'.[14] Such a façade enacted the qualities of a screen in presenting an outward image of classical unity that masked and integrated the heterogeneity of the pre-existing medieval urban fabric. The façade of the Palazzo Rucellai created a system of pilasters, windows, entablatures, and rustication as a public image, one that was at once a new, idealized representation of principles of classical unity and the primary face of the patron's cultural and civic ambitions.[15] The alignment of screen and façade was forged in the tenuous physical relation between outward appearance and underlying building substance. The screen-face relationship signified unity yet marked a lack of organic connection between face and body, between surface and soul. In this, such early façades troubled the basic premises of the physiognomic analogy through which they were coming to be theorized.

Such a Renaissance example can be productively compared with the shifts taking place in eighteenth-century France. In the context of the Académie Royale d'Architecture, the authority of the Vitruvian canon became more contentious, and with it came an intensified debate over the normative proportions of the orders and of their relative character.[16] In such a context, academic theory sought to articulate principles that would bring the façade into a more regular and substantial relation to the interior. The architect, professor, and theorist Jean-Francois Blondel made the analogy of façade and face explicit, drawing on a renewed interest in

13   For a detailed account of façade and the relation to the underlying urban parcels, see Mack, 1974.

14   Burroughs, pp. 16-18.

15   The patron, Giovanni di Paolo Rucellai (1403-1481), was a wealthy Florentine merchant navigating a role between Florence's most powerful families, the Strozzi and the Medici.

16   The introduction of the concept of character in architectural discourse is credited to the architect Germain Boffrand and was subsequently elaborated by Jean-Francois Blondel, Le Camus de Mézières, Jean-Jacques Ledoux, and John Soane, among others. For an account of the changed attitude to Vitruvius under the Academie Royale d'Architecture, see Kruft, 1994. For an overview of theories of character, see Forty, 2000.

(Ed.ni Alinari) P.ª I.ª N.º 5013. FIRENZE – Via della Vigne Nuova. Palazzo Ruceliai. (L. B. Alberti.)

3.1:   Palazzo Ruccellai, (1442–1451), Florence, Italy. Attributed to Leon Battista Alberti (1404–1472). © Alinari / Art Resource.

ancient physiognomic ideas. In the entry devoted to the term 'Façade' in Denis Diderot and Jean le Rond D'Alembert's *Encyclopédie*, he wrote, 'The façade of a building is to the edifice what physiognomy is to the human body; the latter reflects the qualities of the soul, the former permits a judicious judgment of the inside of a building'.[17] Academic neo-classicism sought to overcome the separation between outside and inside that was characteristic of the Palazzo Rucellai. Only if the façade communicated a character appropriate to the building type could the architect ensure an integral and 'true' relation between a building and its purpose.[18] As Anthony Vidler has shown, for Blondel's students, most prominently Claude-Nicholas Ledoux, the face/façade analogy was crucial and served to advance an idea of character understood in terms of universal sensations legible to a broad public rather than strictly an elite.[19] Ledoux's enthusiasm for physiognomy as a 'natural language' echoed the writings of his infamous contemporary, Johann Kaspar Lavater. Such a physiognomic conception of the face was neither that of an opaque public image that screened off and separated the domestic from the civic, nor was it a literal correspondence between interior and exterior. Lavater's physiognomy posited an interior that was crucially about the soul, a metaphysical entity that, while itself invisible, could be revealed through visual interpretation. In this sense, the physiognomic façade was less an opaque barrier and more like the paper screens used to produce the period's physiognomic silhouettes. Such silhouettes were the result of a media apparatus that carefully assembled and regulated the proper relations between light source, subject, draftsperson, and drawing instrument around a vertical sheet of paper. Unlike the myth of Butades recounted by Pliny, analyzed in this volume by Francesco Casetti, Lavater's paper silhouettes were not singular traces but inherently multiple, endowed with the rigorous graphic consistency required for comparing numerous likenesses. (Figure 3.2) Similarly, for an architect like Ledoux, deducing the interior from the exterior was not about seeing what was literally inside a building. Rather, it entailed interpreting an individual profile by reference to an understanding of different character types.[20] If the façades of Ledoux aspired to communicate character, this was not the emanation of something

---

17 Blondel, p. 355.

18 Blondel enumerated a range of different characters—from the sublime, noble, and free to the elegant, pastoral, and mysterious—to be used to determine the form and decoration of various building types. On 'caractère vrai', see Blondel, pp. 385-391.

19 See Vidler, 1987.

20 Lavater's *Physiognomische Fragmente* (1775-1778) aimed to provide a more scientific basis for the ancient discourse of physiognomy—distinguishing it from pathognomy, which analyzed the changing manifestations of facial expression. Physiognomy concerned permanent qualities of character deduced from the permanent features of the face and head. As Graham Tytler has observed, what set Lavater apart from other contemporary physiognomists was his insistence that it was not moral character and habits that affected physical appearance but rather that the physical substance of the skull and face embodied aspects of the soul. See Tytler, pp. 51-55.

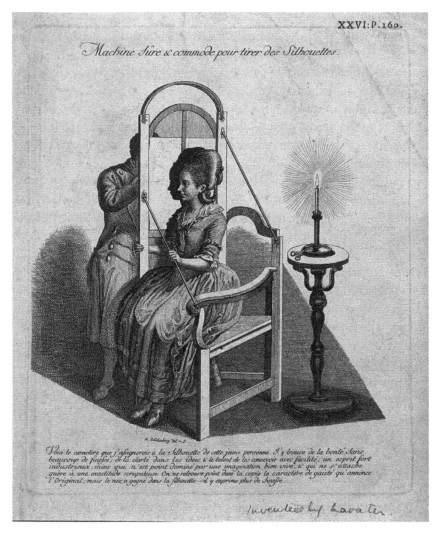

3.2:   Johann Kaspar Lavater (1741–1801), "Machine sûre et commode pour tirer les Silhouettes," from *Essai sur la physiognomie*, 1783.

unique. Rather, it aimed to express the typical purposes and moods of the emerging institutions of a mass society, such as prisons, hospitals, factories, and toll gates. (Figure 3.3)

By the middle of the nineteenth century, however, a distinct hostility to the importance placed on façade design was articulated in ways that would be consequential for the later course of modern architecture. The architect Eugène-Emmanuel Viollet-Le-Duc's monumental *Dictionnaire*

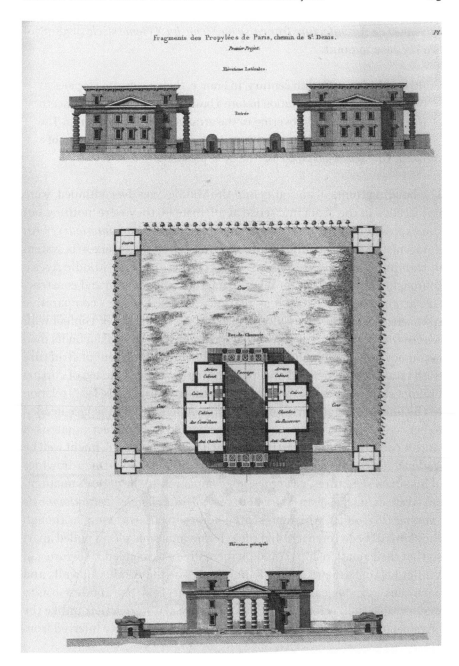

3.3:   Nicolas Claude Ledoux (1736–1806), "Propylées de Paris Chemin St. Denis,"
L'Architecture considérée sous le rapport de l'art, des mœurs et de la législation. Edition
ramée, 1847.

raisonnée de l'architecture francaise du XIeme au XVIeme siècle (1858-1870)
is a key case in point:

> [It] is only since the 16th century, in France, that one erected façades as
> one might put up a decoration before a building, without much concern
> for the relation of this covering to the arrangement of the interior. The
> ancients, like the architects of the middle ages, had no conception of a
> façade dressed solely to please the eyes of passersby.[21]

The building fronts of antiquity and the Middle Ages, he continued, were
not façades in the academic sense at all; instead, they were 'nothing but
the expression of the internal arrangement *(disposition intérieur)'.*[22] An
antagonist of the academic tradition ensconced in the Beaux-Arts system
of training, Viollet-le-Duc saw in the architecture of the Middle Ages a
thoroughly rational basis for relating internal organization and constructive arrangement to exterior appearance. Unlike Lavater's comparative
silhouettes, the rationalist mode of visualization could not be content with
external comparison; the outward appearance of a face taken on its own
could not yield true knowledge. Viollet-le-Duc's alignment of structure
with rationality depended on a penetrating gaze, one capable of cutting
buildings and faces open. To visually grasp the integrity of the face's relation
to the interior, the specific and inviolable appearance of the face needed
to be sacrificed. The drawings that accompanied the architect's analysis of
Gothic construction, as Martin Bressani has aptly observed, might well be
understood as 'clinical' in a Foucauldian sense.[23] Viollet-le-Duc's drawings
of historical structures, he argues, are comparable to the period's anatomical treatises such as Jean-Marc Bourgery's *Traité complet de l'anatomie de
l'homme* (1831-1854), which presented bodies in cutaway view, as though
the skin had been removed, and the relevant anatomic pieces pulled apart
so that their relationships could be mentally re-assembled.[24] (Figure 3.4)
Viollet-Le-Duc's views similarly penetrate the materiality of walls and
partitions, paradoxically pulling elements apart from one another so as to
make visible their internal relations. (Figure 3.5) Construction, unlike the
physiognomic idea of character, was not an inward quality inferred from

21 Viollet-Le-Duc, 1858-1870.
22 Ibid. '[...] *ce que nous entendons aujourd'hui par façade n'existe pas dans l'architecture du
moyen âge.'*
23 Bressani, pp. 126-128.
24 The illustrations were painted by Nicholas-Henri Jacob, a pupil of Jacques-Louis David.

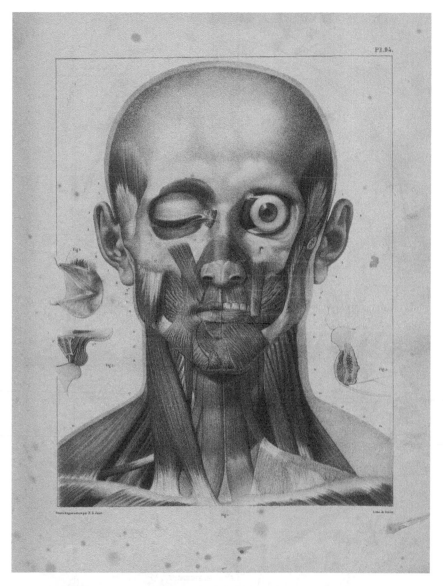

3.4:   Jean-Marc Bourgery (1797–1849), Plate 94 from *Traité complet de l'anatomie de l'homme comprenant la médecine opératoire*, 1849. Illustration by Nicholas-Henri Jacob. © Universitäts Bibliothek Heidelberg.

secondary signs; it was a logical and functional relation between parts that was to be pursued in depth, an aesthetic continuity between structure and surface rooted in a constructive rationale. For the tradition of structural rationalism that Viollet-Le-Duc influentially codified, the ideal façade was to possess a conceptual transparency, guiding the reasoning mind to

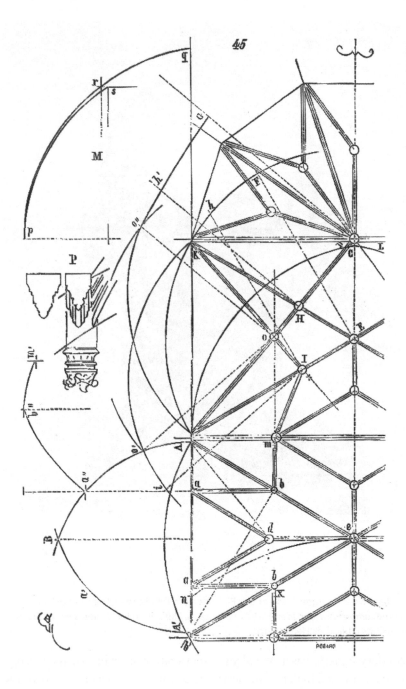

3.5:   Eugène-Emmanuel Viollet-le-Duc (1814–1879), Plan and cutaway perspective illustration of Gothic vaulting, from the article "Construction," in *Dictionnaire raisonné de l'architecture française du XIe au XVIe siècle*, (1858–1870).

penetrate the opacity of experience layer by layer. This anatomical disposition, premised on a direct correspondence between interior arrangement and exterior appearance, aimed to discipline the dangerous independence of the face and to keep façades from becoming superfluous masks.

As the use of iron and reinforced concrete grew in the late nineteenth and early twentieth centuries, frame construction became increasingly dominant, throwing the architectural status of the non-load-bearing wall, and thus the façade, into question. The rationalist suspicion of the façade expressed in Viollet-le-Duc's writings would be amplified by the historians and critics who theorized the modern movement during the first decades of the twentieth century. From critics such as Adolf Behne and Sigfried Giedion to architects and artists like Le Corbusier, Frank Lloyd Wright, and László Moholy-Nagy, it was not only a question of disciplining the building's façade but of declaring its obsolescence, of breaking it open, or of making it disappear.[25] Yet, in an unexpected twist, it was among those currents most committed to attacking the façade, notably interwar constructivism, that efforts to integrate the independence of the face would paradoxically provide the conditions for the emergence of what we currently call a media façade.

Billboards and façades

To follow such a twist, it is important to consider two events whose emergence and unfolding during the second half of the nineteenth century complicated the inside-outside relationship established by these three different ideas of the face/façade. Neither event had any precedent within architectural theory concerning the façade and could not be readily assumed into them. Both remain crucial for comprehending the changes in the façade's role as screen. The first concerns the creation, legitimization, and normalization of systems that allowed for the proprietary control of large vertical surfaces for

25   While the contextual motivations of these arguments differed in each case, in this context it will suffice to note a shared hostility to the façade as a concept. Adolf Behne's *Modern Functional Building* (1926), a pioneering effort to collect and theorize Germany's 'Neues Bauen' (New Building), opposed the concern for building with a concern for the façade in an opening chapter titled: 'Nicht mehr Fassade, sondern Haus.' Sigfried Giedion's 1928 history of reinforced iron and concrete described Le Corbusier and Pierre Jeanneret's Villa Stein de Monzie as having 'attacked the façade of the building with enormous boldness and left it so penetrated with air that one can almost speak of crushing the actual house volume'. Giedion, 180. Moholy-Nagy's *Von Material zu Architektur* (translated into English as *The New Vision*) reproduced an image of showgirls stretching on the marquee of the Scala theatre next to a declaration that the 'concept of the façade is already eliminated from architecture.' Moholy-Nagy, p. 179.

the dissemination of commercial messages in urban contexts. The second concerns the impact of electricity upon the design of façades.

In the middle decades of the nineteenth century, poster advertising in the major cities of Europe and America grew exponentially as billposters, who were paid directly by advertisers, competed to place as many signs as possible on façades, walls, fences, and lampposts. (Figure 3.6) Initially this practice was conducted without permission or by means of ad hoc exchanges with individual building owners.[26] The increasingly fierce and chaotic competition among billposters resulted in the creation of special hoardings for the posting of bills as early as the 1860s in London and Paris and by the 1870s in New York. In the later 1880s and early 1890s, trade organizations that had been formed by consolidating groups of billposters began to regulate the practice and proposed standardized display structures for urban advertisements.[27] By the first decade of the twentieth century, the Billposters' Association of the Americas required that members only post in spaces owned or rented by the association, specifying which posters could be assigned to what locations and for how long. Such self-regulation, Catherine Gudis has argued, was crucial to establishing billposting as a legitimate enterprise, with a rightful basis for the ownership and use of vertical property in urban contexts.[28] Billboards were thus distinct from hoardings, to the extent that they were governed by exclusive ownership rights that could be traded and transferred. From the late nineteenth century, as the volume of urban advertising grew, billboards began to compete with façades for visibility in the metropolitan centres.

The billboard, like the façade, was a vertical urban surface whose value derived from its visibility. Yet unlike the façade, the billboard's value lay in the ability to organize (and profit from) a continually changing set of words, forms, and colours. This type of visibility was incompatible with architectural notions of character, which had sought the typical, unchanging, and metaphysical qualities of the face, not its temporary expressions. The visibility of the billboard was even more unlike the ideal façade of the structural rationalist tradition, which disavowed any purely superficial and arbitrary relation between inside and outside. It was precisely the competition between billboards and façades that led reformers, particularly the Beaux-Arts-inspired City Beautiful movement in the United States, to oppose billboards. Two very different notions about the legitimacy of vertical urban

26 See Gudis, pp. 14-15.
27 Gudis pp. 20-23, and Baker, 2007.
28 Gudis, p. 23.

3.6:   Gilbert Abbott à Beckett (1811–1856), The Billstickers' Exhibition, Punch, 29 May 1847, p. 226.

surfaces struggled for dominance: on the one hand, the idea of a free and unfettered pursuit of attention and profit in the marketplace, and on the other, the argument that an ideal of civic beauty, exemplified by the façades of Beaux-Arts buildings, ought to be protected from the untrammelled excess of commercial persuasion.[29] For detractors, the billboard was screen-like to the extent that it concealed and disfigured building façades, exposing passers-by to unsolicited messages sometimes of an unwelcome or inappropriate kind.

It was the billboard's capacity to obscure façades that led architects to search for methods by which to control and direct its effects—leading them, eventually, to incorporate aspects of billboards into the design of façades. The means for doing so depended less on traditions of projection derived from the magic lantern than on the electrification of major metropolitan centres from the 1880s onwards. As David E. Nye has observed regarding turn-of-the-century America, the conflict between the elite City Beautiful movement and populist proponents of unfettered commercial lighting pitted advocates of a harmonious and unified approach that sought to integrate electric light into the massing and ornamentation of buildings against the push for brighter and bigger 'spectaculars' (as electrified billboards were called) designed to dazzle the eye rather than integrate into façades.[30] The former were modelled on techniques of outline lighting developed at world fairs, where strings of incandescent bulbs were used to trace architectural features, together with a judicious illumination of niches and porticos.[31] The goal was to clearly demarcate the façade's silhouette and enhance its main

29   Baker, p. 1188.
30   Nye, p. 133.
31   See Nye, 2016; Champa, 2002.

elements. (Figure 3.7) Urban advertising spectaculars and fairgrounds such as Coney Island's Luna Park linked electric light to large-scale pictures, words, and movement effects. In such signs, slogans, brand names, and advertising copy came together with images of pickles, fishermen, and chariots to form an urban image-text that was alien to the historical vocabulary of façade design and aimed to compete with these cultural forms. In the American context, elite cultural opinion would fight to restrict and remove the proliferation of such commercial lighting well into the 1930s.[32] During the same years in Europe, the situation was different. Particularly in Weimar-era Berlin, the architectural avant-garde began to embrace rather than reject the illuminated advertisement, or *Lichtreklame*, as it was known in German.

As Berlin recovered from WWI, it aimed to position itself as a world city, and it was within this discourse on the metropolis that ideas about illuminated advertising began to shift. Commercial signage came to be seen as a uniquely powerful element of the façade rather than its antithesis. Photographs of New York's Broadway circulated intensively in the books and journals of Weimar Berlin—one of the best known being Fritz Lang's double exposure of Times Square's illuminated signs in Erich Mendelsohn's *Amerika: Bilderbuch eines Architekten* (1926).[33] (Figure 3.8) Writing in the German Werkbund's journal *Die Form,* the architect Alfred Gellhorn exemplified a broad shift in attitude to the façade. Rather than reject illuminated commercial billboards, he raised the question of reforming and reshaping them:

> As long as our cities are ugly stone deserts, we will want to make over the walls of the streets and squares with colour and light.... Rather than billboards in front of the windows as in America, where you buy entire façades and work behind them in artificial light, seize the façade itself and form it in such a way that it yields the spatial possibilities missed when they were erected.[34]

Rather than presenting incompatible alternatives, an opportunity lay in forming the façade and the illuminated billboard so that they might incorporate each other. For leading architects and critics in the German avant-garde in the 1920s, illuminated billboards shifted status; the thing that threatened the façade was seized as the very material for reshaping a building's face, producing new 'spatial possibilities' and effects in

32   See Wood, pp. 25-26; Gray, 2001.
33   Mendelsohn, 1926. For an overview see Neumann, 2002.
34   Gellhorn, pp. 134-135.

3.7: An example of outline lighting. Panoramic view of Festival Hall, Louisiana Purchase Exhibition, St. Louis, 1904. From *The Universal Exposition Beautifully Illustrated*, St. Louis, MO.: Official Photographic Company, 1904). Courtesy Beinecke Rare Book and Manuscript Library, Yale University.

time that earlier generations of architects were not originally able to comprehend.[35]

Nor was it only in Berlin that the interest in light and illuminated advertisement propelled a rethinking of the façade. A crucial project in this regard was Alexander and Victor Vesnin's 1924 competition entry for the Moscow headquarters of the Leningradskaya Pravda newspaper. (Figure 3.9) Designed for a tiny 6 x 6 metre site, the building was conceived not as a printing facility but as a site for editorial work, sales, urban communication, and advertisement. The Vesnin brothers' combination of steel frame and sheer glass exposed everything to the exterior including a kiosk, reading room, editorial offices, and even the elevators. If the building's reductive use of steel and glass exemplified a rationalist ideal of constructive transparency, it was this very clarity that began to incorporate multiple media systems. Presenting the project in the journal *Sovremennaia Arkitektura* in 1926, they noted: 'The façade fronting Strastnaia square includes: a vitrine for moving messages (*tekushchikh soobshchenii*), an apparatus for illuminated advertising, clocks, a loudspeaker, and a projector.'[36] On the sloped portion of the glass façade, the Vesnin brothers' drawing indicated news from Paris and Berlin to suggest that this surface was

---

35 Here one might include the architect Hugo Häring's claim that 'commercial buildings don't have a façade anymore, their skin is merely scaffolding for advertising signs, lettering, and luminous panels' together with his belief that the 'nocturnal face' of architecture would become its most important attribute. See Haring, 'Lichtreklame und Architektur', cited in Neumann, p. 39.

36 Vesnin, p. 1. Special thanks to Richard Anderson for assistance with the translation and for sharing his knowledge of the project.

3.8:   Fritz Lang (1890–1976), Photograph of Broadway at Night, reprinted in Erich Mendelsohn *Amerika: Bilderbuch eines Architekten*, 1926. Courtesy, Haas Arts Library Special Collections | Yale University Library.

conceived as a projection screen for changing editorial content.[37] Neither an opaque billboard in front of the façade nor an extension added to it, here a mixture of public messaging and news became integrated, visually and tectonically, with rationalist transparency. The expectation that the façade express the building's interior continued, yet it belonged to a very different system of purposes. It was neither strictly a notion of character nor a constructive system that was expressed; it was, rather, a building devoted to intellectual production that projected its own activities onto the surface of its façade. Such activity was not of the same order as the skeleton but was an index of the accelerated temporal rhythms of metropolitan communication. The project's reference was not primarily to the billboards of the capitalist metropolises but to the graphic mechanisms found in the period's revolutionary propaganda. The Vesnin's project was indebted to Vladimir Tatlin's proposal for a *Monument*

37 Jean-Louis Cohen notes that the searchlight on the building's roof was to be used to project messages in light upon the clouds. See Cohen, p. 165. On the importance of wireless image transmission for Ivan Leonidov's 1928 Project for a Worker's Club of a New Social Type in *Sovremennaia Arkitektura*, see Anderson, 2013.

to the Third International (1919-1920), whose rotating cylindrical volume was to house a communication office incorporating newspaper and manifesto production, a telegraph station, and projectors for a large screen. Yet by 1924 it could also have been inspired by numerous projects for kiosks, loudspeaker stands, rostrums, street decorations, and stage designs that flourished in the years following the Bolshevik revolution.[38] Here the conceptual transparency demanded by structural rationalism merged with a desire to integrate the mechanisms of news production with media oriented to consumption, a condition in which the absence of a typical façade was conceptualized as a new kind of broadcast screen.

The vision of integrating news production, public projection, and telecommunication into a single building was, however, already in circulation well before Soviet Constructivism, notably in nineteenth-century science fiction. Albert Robida's novel *Le vingtième siècle* (1882) described the headquarters of the twentieth-century newspaper *L'Époque* as a 'truncated pyramid' constructed from iron and agglomerated paper, flanked by two electrically illuminated screen disks. The first was devoted to projected advertisements, the other was a 'telephonoscope' screen allowing the newspaper's reporters to send moving images of live events back to Paris from any point on the globe.[39] In Robida's illustration, the separation of the screens from the building remains a crucial detail. (Figure 3.10) While all the elements of the early twentieth-century media façade—electrification, ferrous metallic structure, large glass surfaces, projected images, dynamic control mechanisms, news, and advertising—are present in Robida's headquarters, they are still not yet conceived as a single, integrated façade in the manner that emerges in the 1920s.

Other buildings of the interwar years sought to link the integration of artificial light in the façade with the control over changing combinations of words and images. Jan Buijs and Joan Lürsen's headquarters of the Dutch Socialist Cooperative *Vollharding* (1928) in The Hague alternated plate glass windows with translucent illuminated opal glass panels. The gridlines within these panels were designed to accommodate letters and various forms, which made these portions on the building's façade into a dynamic messaging system.[40] Here too, notably in a socialist cooperative, the conversion from billboard to illuminated media façade was pursued. A similar shift appears in the media window included in Alvar Aalto's 1931 design

38   S.O. Khan-Magomedov has stressed Alexandr Vesnin's designs for the staging of *The Man Who Was Thursday* as an influence in this regard. Khan-Magomedov, pp. 134-135.

39   Albert Robida, p. 177.

40   Neumann, p. 132.

СОВРЕМЕННАЯ АРХИТЕКТУРА

Редакция: Москва, Новинский бульвар, 32, кв. 63.
Тел. 5-76-95.

НОВЫЕ МЕТОДЫ АРХИТЕКТУРНОГО МЫШЛЕНИЯ

Одно десятилетие отделяет нас от архитектурного „благополучия" довоенного времени, когда в Ленинграде, Москве и других крупных центрах лучшие русские зодчие беззаботно насаждали всевозможные „стили".

Много ли десятилетие?

Маленькая трещинка времени. Но революция, уничтожив косные предрассудки и отжившие каноны, превратила трещинку в пропасть. По ту сторону пропасти остался последний этап увядания одряхлевшей системы европейского мышления, беспринципный эклектизм, имеющий наготове тысячу художественных рецептов, апробованных нашими дедами и прадедами, готовый черпать истину откуда угодно, — но только в прошлом.

По эту сторону открывается новый путь, который еще надо прокладывать, новые просторы, которые нужно еще заселить. В обстановке сегодняшнего дня куется миросозерцание современного зодчего, создаются новые методы архитектурного мышления.

Вместо старой системы архитектурного творчества, где план, конструкция и внешнее оформление задания постоянно находились во взаимной вражде и где архитектор был по мере сил своих примирителем всех этих неразрешимых конфликтов, — новое архитектурное творчество, прежде всего, характеризуется своим единым нераздельным целевым устремлением, в котором органически выковывается задача и к которому сводится созидательный процесс от начала до конца.

Вместо отвлеченного и крайне индивидуалистического вдохновения старого архитектора — современный зодчий твердо убежден в том, что архитектурная задача решается, как и всякая иная, лишь в результате точного выяснения неизвестных и отыскания правильного метода решения.

Зодчий видит вокруг себя смелое творчество изобретателя в разных областях современной техники, гигантскими шагами побеждающей землю, недра и воздух, с каждым часом отвоевывающей все новые и новые позиции. Не трудно понять, что этот изумительный успех человеческого гения объясняется, главным образом, правильным методом творчества. Изобретатель твердо знает, что как бы ни был ярок подъем его творческого энтузиазма — он будет бесцелен без трезвого учета мельчайших обстоятельств, окружающих его деятельность. Он во всеоружии современного знания, он учитывает все условия сегодняшнего дня, он смотрит вперед, завоевывает будущее.

Конечно, наивно было бы подменить сложное искусство архитектуры подражанием тем или иным, хотя бы

1

ПРОЕКТ

здания Московского отделения конторы и редакции газеты „Ленинградская Правда", Москва, Страстная площадь. Архитектора А. А., В. А. Веснины. 1924 год.

Основная задача при проектировании заключалась в том, чтобы при данной минимальной площади основания здания (6×6 mtr) наиболее рационально разместить все необходимые для данного производственного процесса помещения и выразить в фасадах производственный и агитационный характер сооружения.

Здание спроектировано в 5 этажей из железа, стекла и железо-бетона.

I этаж — газетный киоск, помещение для сторожа.
II „ — читальный зал.
III „ — общая контора и контора объявлений.
IV и V этажи — редакция.

Подвал — отопление.

По фасаду на Страстную площадь спроектировано: витрина для текущих сообщений, установка для световой рекламы, часы, громкоговоритель, прожектор.

3.9: Alexander Vesnin (1883–1959) and Viktor Vesnin (1882–1950), Moscow Bureau of the Newspaper "Leningrad Pravda" Competition project, unexecuted. Moscow, 1924. Reproduced in *Sovremennaia arkhitektura* (Contemporary Architecture) 1, 1925. Courtesy Beinecke Rare Book and Manuscript Library, Yale University.

LES BUREAUX DE L' « ÉPOQUE ».

3.10: Albert Robida (1848 –1926), Headquarters of the Newspaper *L'Epoque*, with twin circular urban screens From *Le Vingtième Siècle: La Vie Electrique*, 1883.

for the Turun Sanomat Building—the headquarters and printing works for a newspaper in Turku, Finland. In Aalto's delicate nocturnal drawing, a solitary worker intently reads an enormous illuminated projection of that day's paper which fills the entirety of the building's vast plate glass show window.[41] A similar desire to combine illumination technology with a system for controlling and changing words and images motivated one of the most ambitious proposals for a media façade to emerge from this period. Avant-garde graphic design had begun to influence the design of neon façades in Paris, Amsterdam, London, and Berlin in the early 1930s, notably in projects for newsreel cinemas. Some of the most notable were Jan Duiker's Handelsblad Cinéac in Amsterdam (1933) as well as the numerous Cinéac cinemas designed by Adrienne Gorska and Pierre de Montaut in France, Belgium, and Greece. (Figure 3.11) The business model for such newsreel cinemas was to partner with local newspapers, who purchased the rights to use their names on the cinema façade, which served as a billboard that generated revenue for the cinema.[42] While such compositions of neon lights could produce the impression of motion, they could not convey different images or change their messages from day to day. The French architect

41 See Pelkonen, p. 56. My thanks to Eeva-Liisa Pelkonen for drawing my attention to this drawing.
42 On the Cinéac chain, see Meusy, pp. 93-119.

Oscar Nitzchke developed his contemporaneous project for a Maison de la Publicité (1935) in a manner that sought to resolve this problem. (Figure 3.12) An admirer of Soviet Constructivism, which he had encountered at the 1925 Exhibition of Decorative Arts in Paris, it is unclear if Nitzchke knew of the Vesnin's Leningradskaya Pravda project.[43] Unlike the Pravda building or the Cinéacs, Nitzschke's project was not conceived for news but for an advertising publisher. Whereas the Pravda used a single portion of the façade for illuminated messages, preserving the rest as transparent glass, nearly the entire façade of the Maison de la Publicité was envisioned as a support system for signboards, neon letters, illuminated signage, posters, and projection screens.[44] Like the period's newsreel cinemas, the billboard-like quality of the façade was to generate revenue, yet here it was to change on a regular basis. And like the Vesnin's Leningradskaya Pravda, the project never got further than drawings and photomontages, a number of which Christian Zervos published in his journal *Cahiers d'art*. In a text on the project, Zervos stressed how the building itself had become a new kind of screen:

> [Nitzchke's] very beautiful project for an advertising building realizes a screen on which powerful appeals for attention could move or be fixed. This screen allows them to become easily interchangeable, to play with them as on a keyboard, making it simple to change the forms almost instantly, as if by magic.[45]

The screen in question is a system of optical display, yet Zervos's reference to the manipulation of interchangeable elements by keyboard highlights the façade's role as a means for controlling different technical media—type-based texts, continuous tone images, and linear graphics—through a single mechanism. In this sense, Nitzchke's façade was neither quite a billboard nor a movie screen. It sought to create a form of technical control that would only much later become a property of optical displays with the emergence of discretely addressable pixel grids characteristic of computer graphics.[46] The interchangeability of film, letters, printed images, and illuminated neon was not achieved by projection but by an ingenious architectonic system; the exterior surface of the building was a cross-braced, light metallic framework made up of tightly spaced horizontal tubes that provided electricity and

43   Abram, p. 75.
44   Zervos, p. 206.
45   Ibid., p. 207.
46   On this distinction, see Kittler, 2001.

3.11: Adrienne Gorska (1899–1969) and Pierre de Montaut (1892–1947), *Trois Salles Marseille at Night*, 1935. Digital image © RIBA.

anchorage points. The materials arranged on the façade would be produced on the building's top floor and then lowered into position by workers operating inside a metal armature placed roughly one and a half metres outboard of a sealed interior façade of glass brick.

With such a screen-façade, we see a starker separation of inside and outside than with the Vesnin brothers's Leningradskaya Pravda. As the entire façade becomes a fully controllable optical screen capable of handling advertising, film projection, and news, it also had to become a much more sophisticated environmental conditioning system. The mechanism supporting this interchangeable system of signs, letters, and moving images meant that window openings needed to be suppressed. The offices inside received light from the glass bricks, yet they were 'hermetically' detached from the outside, their interior atmosphere controlled by mechanical heating and air conditioning.[47] Across this thickened optical and atmospheric barrier, the structural rationalist tradition asserts itself faintly as the tripartite division

47 Abram, p. 68, Zervos, p. 207.

3.12:   Oscar Nitzchke (1900–1991). Maison de la Publicité Project, Paris, France, *Elevation*, 1934–36. Ink, color pencil, gouache, and graphite on lithograph on spiral-notebook card stock. Gift of Lily Auchincloss, Barbara Jakobson, and Walter Randel. Digital Image copyright The Museum of Modern Art/Licensed by SCALA / Art Resource, NY.

of the metallic frame mimics the placement of interior columns, and the horizontal metal tubes echo the layers of glass brick. Such a façade was animated by the graphic elements produced or assembled in the interior, which were themselves dependent on an economy of advertising and attention that was not reducible to the building's literal insides. Just as the technical requirements of the media façade dictated the constraints, materials, and environmental systems of the building's interior, the screen envisaged by the Maison de la Publicité reversed the inside-to-outside communicational directionality assumed by theories of the façade since the eighteenth century. Amid such a reversal, this complex and layered display mechanism assumed a more literally human countenance: in all the views of the project Nitzchke created, the most prominent advertising feature is a female face. As familiar architectonic elements disappear, a surrogate physiognomy appears on this surface, a literal face whose condition of possibility was the more complete extension of urban exchange value into the vertical dimension of the building envelope.

Interest in the media façade was anything but a linear progression. Projects such as Vesnin's Leningradskaya Pravda, Buijs and Lürsen's Vollharding, or Nitzchke's Maison de la Publicité were forgotten for decades before they slowly resurfaced in the work of a younger generation in the 1960s. In the intervening decades, the architectural interest in nocturnal illumination proliferated in scope and intensity, yet it was largely detached from the aspiration to make technologically mediated façades for controlling changing arrays of images, words, and symbols. During the Second World War and in the years immediately following, proponents of the 'New Monumentality' such as Sigfried Giedion, Josep Luis Sert, and Fernand Léger advocated for the role of large-scale projections in the design of new civic centres demanded by postwar reconstruction. Distinct both from the pseudo-monumentality of the 1930s and from the commercial façades of the metropolis, they envisioned a 'lyrical' monumentality characterized by buildings whose large blank surfaces were like screens ready to receive abstract projections of moving colours and forms.[48] While such vast complexes did not emerge as envisioned by Giedion, Sert, and Leger, the role of electric light indeed became more integral to the external appearance of corporate office buildings such as Skidmore Owings and Merrill's (SOM) Manufacturer's Trust Bank in New York (1955) or Ludwig Mies van der Rohe's Seagram Building (1958). Yet these extensively glazed buildings were neither projection screens nor surfaces for communicating with changing pictures and letters. Those architects who

48   See, in particular, Sert, Leger, and Giedion's 1943 manifesto 'Nine Points on Monumentality'.

would begin to re-engage the kinetic pictorial and textual qualities of the media façade during the second half of the 1960s were linked by a shared antipathy to such late modernist buildings.[49] Robert Venturi and Denise Scott Brown would stake their position against the modernist privileging of form over ornament and communicative elements through their desire to learn from the billboards, strip hotels, and dazzling, electronically controlled 'electrographic architecture' of Las Vegas.[50] It was not simply a question of recovering interwar designs for media façades but of the different significance these façades acquired in the 1960s. Whereas Vesnin, Nitzchke, and Duiker sought to integrate a vocabulary of abstract forms and rationalist structure with the culture of news and publicity, Venturi and Scott Brown mobilized the iconographic and popular aspects of such media screens against the hegemonic role assumed by late modern architecture. The giant screen was particularly apt, they argued, for suburban postwar America with its dependence on automobility. Such an argument was part of their larger critique of the modern movement's subordination of façade to interior organization, a legacy which, they argued, had given up the architect's freedom to vary different façades in relation to the specific requirements of urban context.[51] Such an interest was particularly evident in their 1967 competition entry for the National Football Hall of Fame, whose façade was an electronic billboard designed to be visible from the highway. (Figure 3.13) Like the era's drive-in movie theatres, the Football Hall of Fame was a building that could be watched from the parking lot. The interior of the museum was spatially subordinated to such a screen-façade; its vaulted hall, running perpendicularly behind its façade, served both as a buttress for the façade and as a linear exhibition space replete with multi-media displays that included film projections, objects, and illuminated graphics. However much Venturi and Scott Brown played with the iconography of the drive-in, the façade was not a movie screen. Rather, it adapted systems first used for advertising signs and news tickers and later employed in stadium scoreboards. To be made up of 200,000 electronically programmable lightbulbs, it was to produce 'moving sequences of naturalistic images, words, phrases, and diagrammatic choreographies of famous football

49 Sybil Moholy-Nagy played an important role in bringing Nitzchke's project back to attention in the later 1960s; see Abram. In this context, it was interpreted as a precursor of rubric of Pop, rather than for its innovative media systems. The project was also invoked in the debates over the politics of Pop between Kenneth Frampton and Denise Scott Brown. See Frampton, 1971 and Scott Brown, 1971.

50 See Venturi, Scott Brown, and Izenour, 1972.

51 Venturi, 1966, p. 118.

3.13:   Venturi, Scott Brown and Associates, National Football Hall of Fame Competition, 1967. Photograph of model. © Venturi, Scott Brown and Associates.

plays'.[52] The desire was for a programmable face, one capable of consolidating control over formerly distinct elements of letter, picture, and diagram.

The London-based Archigram group also took a major interest in developing an architecture of the media screen during these years. Rather than seek to re-engage the façade with a more popular repertoire of signs explored by Venturi and Scott Brown, they gravitated to the technological affordances of contemporary screen technologies. In not less than a dozen projects between 1963 and 1972, the group envisioned screens in a dizzying variety of roles: as interior partitions, frameworks for ephemeral audio-visual events, pneumatic membranes for living capsules, public feedback mechanisms, subterranean entertainment centres, or mobile, networked, audio-visual educational systems.[53] In the group's Instant City project (1968-1972), provincial towns, villages, and suburbs were to be 'bombarded' with an expanding catalogue of 'environ-poles', pneumatic enclosures, and hybrid screen robots delivering a dose of metropolitan intensity by truck or hovering airship before being packed up and moved on. Rather than fixed in place like billboards, the screens of Instant City were multi-part assemblages, coming together to form freestanding audio-visual 'arenas' or affixing themselves temporarily to extant façades. (Figure 3.14) Indeed, in such projects, any concern with the façade-as-barrier seems to have disappeared; the various screens and

52   Venturi, Scott Brown, and Izenour, p. 117.
53   For an account of Archigram's screen architecture, see Buckley, 2019.

media elements create relations of attraction and attention rather than divisions between interior and exterior. Multi-part, ephemeral, and temporary, Archigram's screens articulated a diffuse landscape in which mobile spectators 'tuned into' the array of screens the way one might tune into a television channel.[54] Such screen systems were conceived to be portable. Even more so, they aimed to catalyze emerging forms of virtual mobility; the multi-directional movement of audio-visual information and messages across a network of towns was to transform a given location by accelerating the adoption of tele-communication links to other places.[55] The screens that serve as the face for such projects emerged amid particular struggles over the function of emerging audio-visual technologies, the qualities of vernacular landscapes, and the legacy of the modern movement, yet they also share something of the autonomy of the face from the interior which had characterized the opaque screens of early modern palace fronts. Even as these post-modern screen-faces take on the guise of a human countenance, they loosen any integral relationship with a body or soul. Yet the opaque screens of the 1960s are less a historical return than they are a reconfiguration, in which the face paradoxically came to mark a non-identity between inside and outside. In so doing, façades acquired a different set of purposes.

Convergence, information, place

It is worth turning now to the project that Heausler and others have pointed to as an 'origin' for the contemporary media façade, in order to emphasize how far along it appears within a genealogy of the screen. One of the historical ironies of Renzo Piano and Richard Rogers's winning entry for the Centre Beaubourg competition is that while the media façade played an important role in their winning the competition, the proposed large-format screen was eliminated during the design development process and was never constructed. Rather than a unified origin, we are looking at the conflicted relationship between design intentions and real technical and political constraints as these were negotiated in the translation of a public competition into a building.[56] (Figure 3.15) Two key shifts can be highlighted

54 Archigram, 1972, p. 96.
55 When first presenting the project in *Architectural Design,* the group explained that the arrival of *Instant City* was to be 'the first stage of a national hook-up. A network of information-education-entertainment-"play and know yourself" facilities'. See, Archigram, 1969, p. 277.
56 Heausler, 2009; see also Foth, Brynskov, and Ojala, pp. 41-42.

3.14:   Archigram (drawing by Peter Cook), Instant City Program, 1970. © Archigram.

relative to the media façades encountered thus far. The first concerns screen's relationship to information and the second its relationship to place.

When French President Georges Pompidou announced the competition in December of 1969 for the largest cultural centre to be realized in Paris since the 1930s, it was under an explicitly interdisciplinary banner. The goal was integration; a single complex was to house a large public library, a museum of contemporary art, a centre for experimental music, and a centre for industrial design. Piano and Rogers's entry responded to the competition brief by proposing not an updated museum but 'a "Live Centre of Information" covering Paris and beyond'.[57] Screen façades were crucial to envisioning the concept. Piano and Rogers described their visualization of the screen façade as a site for the convergence of multiple, formerly distinct entities into a single surface of appearance, relaying 'constantly changing information, news, what's on in Paris, art works, robots, television, temporary structures, electronic two-way games and information, etc.'.[58] Much like Nitzchke's drawing of the Maison de la Publicité, of which the team was

57   Ibid. The building has since been the subject of several monographs. See Piano and Rogers, 1987; Silver, and Dal Co, 2016.
58   Piano and Rogers, 'Competition Statement', cited in Crompton, 1977.

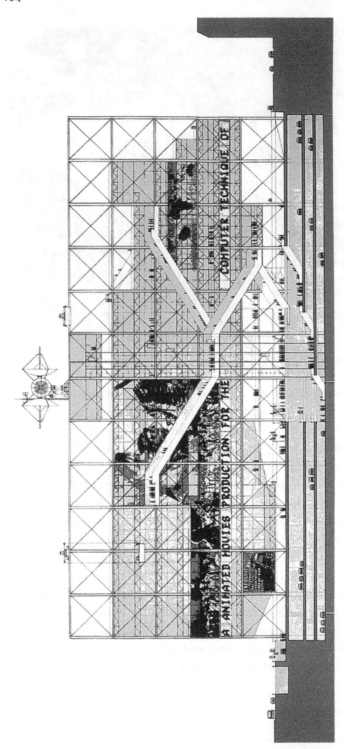

3.15: Renzo Piano and Richard Rogers, with Arup Engineers, Competition Entry for the Centre Pompidou (West Elevation), 1971. © Piano + Rogers, courtesy of Rogers Stirk Harbour + Partners; Fondazione Renzo Piano and Centre Pompidou.

aware, the Pompidou screen looked to assimilate heterogeneous technical media—words, projections, neon, and banners—into a single surface encompassing the entire façade. The photomontage submitted to the competition indicates how technically and formally this role has changed. The solvent transfer technique used by the architects endowed drawing, letters, and photographic media with a consistent quality, their material differences dissolving into the substance of paper just as distinct media channels were to merge into an electronic mosaic.[59] Literal human faces again dominate the façade, yet these are no longer advertisements. The largest profiles, of two female guerrilla soldiers, evoking the ongoing war in Vietnam, were an indication of the televisual images to be displayed on the building. These surmount a separate, panoramic view of a crowd scattered in a field. Such a field appears, in turn, above a horizontal news ticker telegraphing brief phrases and to the left of a large-scale visualization of the world as map. The convergence of various different technical media was visualized in terms of an emerging logic of the pixel grid, yet this convergence was also an effort to highlight the coming together of different information sources, from local information and projections to coded signals received from around the globe by virtue of the massive satellite dish crowning the elevation.[60] Where Nitzchke's façade brought together distinct technical media under the rubric of *publicité*, Piano and Rogers promised greater access to, and control over, 'information'. Here, the term 'information' was deployed in a sense descended from the mathematics of information theory, an approach that treated any number of messages from the vantage point of signal transmission, discarding their cultural and semantic differences. Piano and Roger's information screen aspired to a degree of neutrality; unlike 'publicity', 'information' was ostensibly separate from persuasion and was instead something to be scanned and interpreted with distance and detachment. Both the flexible, wide-span steel framework within and the information screen without sought to resolve a key tension of the competition brief: to support an effort to break down cultural hierarchies while at the same time allowing for an open-ended reintegration and programming of 'productive' relations between

59   I would like to thank Mike Davies in the office of Rogers Stirk Harbour + Partners for archival information concerning the drawing.
60   Scarcely legible toward the bottom of the drawing, one can make out the phrase: 'Caroline, go to canvas city immediately—your friend Linda has been busted', suggesting that portions of the screen were to function as a public-address system for individual messages. The text fragment was clipped from the headline of a critical article in *Architectural Design*, penned by Martin Pawley in 1970, on the chaos surrounding that year's Isle of Wight Pop Festival. See Pawley, 1970.

these formerly separate elements.[61] As a number of critics, including Jean Baudrillard, Alan Colquhoun, and Annette Michelson, noted at the time, the rhetoric of information and its placement as the key element of a new cultural centre was anything but politically neutral; rather, it aimed to replace a modernist commitment to aesthetic autonomy with a managerial model of creative programming and a consumerist model of choice.[62]

The proposals for media façades seen so far in the twentieth century were envisioned for newspaper headquarters, worker's cooperatives, and advertising firms—that is, small-scale private enterprises or civil society organizations. However much the cultural model of the Pompidou mirrored aspects of the liberal consumer economy, it was, at the time, the largest state-sponsored cultural commission in post-World War II France. Here, the screen must be understood not as a loss of materiality but as an integral part of the larger urban demolition and redevelopment project essential to restructuring a key urban node within a plan for the overall metropolitan territory. The unprecedented size of the screen was a factor of the enormous site, which was available only due to the state's highly controversial decision to demolish and redevelop the nearby Les Halles market. It is for this reason that the project's media façade risked being seen from the beginning as a surface that dissimulated state messaging, no matter how open, informational, and indeterminate its programming.

The media faces envisioned on the western elevation of the Centre Pompidou did not simply seek to capitalize on the latent value of attention existing in urban circulation; it aimed to use this enormous screen to produce a new kind of public space.[63] Piano and Rogers's competition project stipulated a plaza that would face the screen and be roughly equal in size to the building's footprint. Screen and plaza were assembled into a perpendicular co-dependence. The sloped public square was designed to emulate the raked floor of an auditorium, yet the relation of public to screen is something other than that found in the

61   The competition brief stated: 'The meeting, in one place, of books, the fine arts, architecture, music, cinema and industrial design [...] is an idea of great originality. This confrontation should enable a far greater public to realize that although creativity affects an appearance of liberty, artistic expression is not inherently autonomous, its hierarchy is merely fictitious, and that there is a fundamental link between today's art forms and the productive relations within society.' 'Centre Beaubourg Competition Brief,' 1977.
62   'The organs of culture,' Alan Colquhoun remarked, 'were now to be reduced to a single entity, the prototype of which was the self-service store—the emblem of the liberal consumer economy'. Colquhoun, 1977, n.p. See also, Baudrillard, 1982 and Michelson, 1975.
63   Such a turn anticipates what more recent discourse on urban screens has come to call 'digital place-making'. See for instance the texts gathered in Foth, Brynskov, and Ojala, 2015; and in Hespanhol et al., 2017.

cinema. The relationship was constituted by and across Piano and Rogers's exposed metallic frame, a device technically reminiscent of Nitzchke's layered media façade. Here, the structurally integral external grid was populated not by advertising workers but by promenading visitors, locating the audience both before and within the physical space of the screen façade. Given the controversy surrounding the commission, it is not surprising that the architects took pains to suggest that such screens were not 'façades, properly speaking', adding that the 'transparency and sense of scale result mainly from the activities within the metallic skeleton' (ossature metallique).[64] Drawing on anatomic metaphors descended from Viollet-le-Duc, the architects insisted that the screen was transparent not only in a literal sense but also in its appeal to a reasoning and reasonable public, as it rationally exposed the principles of indeterminate and open programming taking place behind it. Yet such claims glossed over the complex historical transformation taking place. The distinct separation of the visual content of the façade—channelled by the principles of an emergent computer interface and composed from a changing array of images, texts, and graphics and the disposition of the interior spaces was characteristic of a type of public image akin to the opaque screens of an earlier modernity. From this longer historical perspective, the paradoxical status of the Pompidou screen becomes clearer; its claims for literal, informational, and institutional transparency rested on a more subtly opaque and arbitrary detachment between inside and outside.

The very real technical difficulties that Piano and Rogers, together with the engineering firm Arup, encountered in seeking to the realize the imagined screen façade remain important. After 1971, the technical requirements of the massive display systems proved more difficult than the logistical, fabrication, engineering, and political complexities of the building's remarkable steel structure. The design team turned first to the sort of programmable bulb-based systems used for Olympic scoreboards, yet the costs for producing and maintaining these for even a small portion of the proposed surface proved prohibitive.[65] Large-scale Eidophor projectors, of the kinds used in control rooms, as well as more recent laser systems developed by Hitachi for Osaka '70 were explored, yet none could achieve satisfactory results in daylight. Billy Klüver, the former Bell Labs engineer and co-founder of Experiments in Art and Technology, was invited to assist and proposed a lenticular screen, a surface made up of thousands of individual reflective disks that was capable

64   Piano and Rogers, 1977.
65   Nathan Silver provides an overview of the demise of the audio-visual systems. See Silver, pp. 162-164.

of operating in daylight.[66] Yet even the largest of such screens would only be visible from very specific viewing angles and could not exceed twenty by thirty feet. By the mid-1970s, the screen was quietly dropped from the project, even as the team held out hope for future realization. In addition to technical limitations, some members of the team believed that, ironically enough, it was a political reticence—particularly the uncertainty about who would control the information coursing across the face of the French state's most visible cultural institution—that helped bring about the screen project's demise.[67]

In the years following the completion of the Pompidou in 1977, the questions of interaction and control associated with the large audio-visual façades became more technically feasible. By the mid-1980s, large-scale Cathode Ray Tube screens such as Sony's Jumbotron were realized, and by the early 1990s, innovations in LCD and LED technology for lighting and displays laid the foundation for the current technologies used in billboards and media façades. The greater accessibility of these technologies, together with the steady decrease in LED prices since 2000, has contributed to the expansion of media façades around the globe. Yet technology and economics are not sufficient to explain this phenomenon.

As the techniques for realizing media façades became increasingly viable in the 1980s, their cultural connotations were refracted through a darker lens. One of the enduring popular images of such a shift can be found in Ridley Scott's film *Blade Runner* (1981), in which massive media façades again carry faces that speak and move in the permanent gloom of a dystopian future. (Figure 3.16) Architectural critics also expressed distinct wariness about the effects of such a transformation.[68] For someone like Paul Virilio, who was one of the first to theorize the incorporation of electronic displays into architecture in the 1980s, the key problem was neither spectacular deceit nor authoritarian control. The integration of such optical screens with telecommunication was about a fundamental loss of face, a breakdown of the terms through which a stable spatial difference could be marked. 'The screen interface (computers, television, teleconferencing)', he argued, produced a form of 'visibility without direct confrontation, without a *face-à-face*, in which the old vis-à-vis of streets and avenues is effaced and disappears'.[69] In an interview with Jean Nouvel, he addressed the problem

66   Midant, p. 135.
67   See Banda, pp. 140-141.
68   For an index of this debate, see the articles by Martin Pawley, Paul Virilo, and Vilem Flusser in the special issue of *Arch+* devoted to façades.
69   Virilio, 1988, pp. 17-18.

3.16:   Ridley Scott (director, b. 1937), Frame enlargement from *Blade Runner*, Warner Brothers, 1982.

of the media façade directly. With the potential to incorporate electronic display technologies into building surfaces, he argued, 'everything can be contained in the façade. The boundary was what separated one world from another. Today the world can be completely contained in that boundary'.[70]

Virilio theorized the urban screen interface as part of a technological lineage running from the magic lantern to cinema, television, and computer screens. His analysis, as Anne Friedberg acutely observed, remained in a metaphoric register, disinterested in the technical and historical specificity of different kinds of screens.[71] For Virilio, it was most urgent to think of the screen as a site of loss, whether it be the collapse of presence, of dimension, or of the ability to distinguish inside from outside. Virilio reminded us of the profound difference between the logic of the interface and that of the façade at the very moment when these were being aligned. The former creates relations between things that can no longer be judged according to inherited categories of space and time; the latter serves as a boundary that continues to reference the distinction between interior and exterior, surface and depth. Such a critique remains important amid the current proliferation of screens, particularly as media façades are readily promoted as the bright 'new face' of a 'massively digital urban design'.[72] Yet Virilio's critique relies on

70   Nouvel, p. 105.
71   Friedberg, p. 182.
72   Barker, p. 6.

an overly teleological schema, in which the outcome of optical technologies and their accelerating links with telecommunications carry predictably deleterious results. Just as pertinently, in presenting the mediated screen interface as the antithesis of the directness of face-to-face encounters, Virilio presumes a directness and integrity of the face that downplays its role as media. As Nikos Papastergiadis, Amelia Barikin, Scott McQuire, and Audrey Yue have helpfully argued, in order to consider the public role of urban screens, the traditional emphasis on face-to-face relationships as constitutive of the bourgeois public sphere might be rethought in light of increasingly prevalent face-screen-face relationships.[73]

The media façade combines the seemingly incompatible functions of face and interface; it is at once a technology whose actions relate humans and machines, connecting things disparate and distant, while also operating as a physical surface that constructs and controls the spatial relationships between inside and out. Rethinking the media-architectural genealogy of the face-façade relationship provides an opportunity to hold onto the strangeness of the media façade in the era of its banalization. Yet it might also help to critically retrace the historically changing functions and roles for the human face: an entity that, increasingly, does not simply look at an environment of screens but is being produced by them.

Works Cited

Abram, Joseph. 'Oscar Nitzchke: Projet pour la Maison de la Publicité.' *AMC* 6 (December 1984): 66-79.

Anderson, Richard. 'A Screen that Receives Images by Radio.' *AA Files* no. 67 (2013): 3-15.

Arch+ 108. Special issue: Fassaden, August 1991.

Archigram. *Archigram*. London: Studio Vista, 1972.

——. 'Instant City Primer.' *Architectural Design* (May 1969): 277-278.

Baker, Laura E. 'Public Sites Versus Public Sights: The Progressive Response to Outdoor Advertising and the Commercialization of Public Space.' *American Quarterly* 59, no. 4 (December 2007): 1187-1208.

Banda, Ewen. *The Architecture of Information at Plateau Beaubourg*. Phd Diss., UCLA, 2012.

Barker, Tom. 'Foreword.' In *Media Façades: History, Technology, Content*, edited by M. Hank Heausler, pp. 6-11. Ludwigsburg: Avedition, 2009.

---

73   Papastergiadis, Barikin, and McQuire, pp. 4-5.

Baudrillard, Jean. *L'effet Beaubourg: Implosion et dissuasion*. Paris: Editions Gallilée, 1977. Translated as 'The Beaubourg Effect: Implosion and Deterrence.' *October* 20 (Spring, 1982): 3-13.

Berry, Chris, Janet Harbord, and Rachel Moore, eds. *Public Space, Media Space*. London: Palgrave MacMillan, 2013.

Blondel, Jacques-Francois. *Cours d'architecture, ou Traité de la décoration, distribution & construction des bâtiments*. Paris: Desaint, 1771-1777.

———. 'Façade.' In *Encyclopédie, ou dictionnaire raisonné des sciences, des arts et des métiers, etc.*, edited by Denis Diderot and Jean le Rond d'Alembert, p. 355. University of Chicago: ARTFL Encyclopédie Project, edited by Robert Morrissey and Glenn Roe (Autumn 2017), http://encyclopedie.uchicago.edu/. Accessed 21 October 2018.

Bressani, Martin. 'Viollet le Duc's Optic.' In *Architecture and the Sciences: Exchanging Metaphors*, edited by Antoine Picon and Alessandra Ponte, pp. 118-139. New York: Princeton Architectural Press, 2003.

Buckley, Craig. *Graphic Assembly: Montage, Media and Experimental Architecture in the 1960s*. Minneapolis: University of Minnesota Press, 2019.

Burroughs, Charles. *The Italian Renaissance Palace Façade: Structures of Authority, Surfaces of Sense*. Cambridge, UK: Cambridge University Press, 2002.

Caspary, Uta. 'Digital Media as Ornament in Contemporary Architecture Façades: Its Historical Dimension.' In *The Screen Media Reader: Culture, Theory, Practice*, edited by Stephen Monteiro, pp. 43-152. London: Bloomsbury, 2017.

Champa, Kermit Swiler. 'A Little Night Music: The Play of Color and Light.' In *Architecture of the Night: The Illuminated Building*, edited by Dietrich Neumann, pp. 16-27. Munich: Prestel, 2002.

Cohen, Jean-Louis. *The Future of Architecture Since 1889*. New York: Phaidon, 2012.

Colquhoun, Alan. 'Critique.' *Architectural Design Profiles*, 2 (1977), unpaginated.

Couldry, Nick and Anna McCarthy, eds. *MediaSpace: Place, Scale and Culture in a Media Age*. London: Routledge, 2003.

Crompton, Dennis. 'Centre Pompidou: A Live Center of Information.' *Architectural Design Profiles* 2 (1977), unpaginated.

Dal Co, Francesco. *Centre Pompidou: Renzo Piano, Richard Rogers, and the Making of a Modern Monument*. New Haven: Yale University Press, 2016.

Fernandez-Galliano, Luis. 'Spectacle and Its Discontents; or, The Elusive Joys of Architainment.' In *Commodification and Spectacle in Architecture*, edited by William Saunders, pp. 1-7. Minneapolis: University of Minnesota Press, 2005.

Forty, Adrian. 'Character.' In *Words and Buildings: A Vocabulary of Modern Architecture*, pp. 120-131. London: Thames & Hudson, 2000.

Foth, Marcus, Martin Brynskov, and Timo Ojala, eds. *Citizen's Right to the Digital City: Urban Interfaces, Activism, and Placemaking*. Singapore: Springer Singapore, 2015.

Frampton, Kenneth. 'America 1960-1970: Notes on Urban Images and Theory.'
    Casabella 359-360 (December 1971): 24-38.
Friedberg, Anne. 'Virilio's Screen.' In *The Virtual Window: From Alberti to Microsoft*,
    pp. 182-190. Cambridge, MA: MIT Press, 2005.
Gellhorn, Alfred. 'Reklame und Stadtbild.' *Die Form: Zeitschrift für gestaltende
    Arbeit*, no. 7 (1926): 134-35.
Giedion, Sigfried. *Building in France, Building in Iron, Building in Ferro-Concrete*.
    (Translation of *Bauen in Frankreich, Bauen in Eisen, Bauen in Eisenbeton*, [1928]).
    Translated by J. Duncan Berry. Santa Monica, CA: Getty Center for the History
    of Art and the Humanities, 1995.
Gray, Christopher. 'Streetscapes/Billboards: The Battle over Outdoor Ads Go Back
    a Century.' *The New York Times*, 17 June 2001.
Gudis, Catherine. *Buyways: Billboards, Automobiles, and the American Landscape*.
    London: Routledge, 2004.
Heausler, M. Hank. *Media Façades: History, Technology, Content*. Ludwigsburg:
    Avedition, 2009.
Hespanhol, Luke M., Hank Haeusler, Martin Tomitsch, and Gernot Tscherteu.
    Media Architecture Compendium: Digital Placemaking. Stuttgart: Avedition, 2017.
Huhtamo, Erkki. 'An Archaeology of Public Visual Displays.' In *The Urban Screens
    Reader*, edited by Scott McQuire, Meredith Martin, and Sabine Niederer, pp. 31-48.
    Amsterdam: Institute of Network Cultures, 2009.
Isenstadt, Sandy, Margaret Maile Petty, and Dietrich Neumann, eds. *Cities of Light:
    Two Centuries of Urban Illumination*. New York: Routledge, 2015.
Jung, Jacqueline. *The Gothic Screen: Space, Sculpture, and Community in the
    Cathedrals of France and Germany, ca. 1200-1400*. Cambridge, UK: Cambridge
    University Press, 2012.
Khan-Magomedov, S.O. *Alexandr Vesnin and Russian Constructivism*. New York:
    Rizzoli, 1986.
Kruft, Hanno Walter. 'The Foundation of the French Academy of Architecture
    and the Subsequent Challenge to It.' In *A History of Architectural Theory from
    Vitruvius to the Present*, pp. 128-141. New York: Princeton Architectural Press, 1994.
Mack, Charles Randall. 'The Rucellai Palace: Some New Proposals.' *The Art Bulletin*
    56, no. 4 (December, 1974): 517-529.
McQuire, Scott, Meredith Martin, and Sabine Niederer, eds. *The Urban Screens
    Reader*. Amsterdam: Institute of Network Cultures, 2009.
Mendelsohn, Erich. *Amerika: Bilderbuch eines Architekten*. Berlin: R. Mosse, 1926.
Meusy, J.J. 'Cinéac: un concept, une architecture.' *Cahiers de la cinematheque* no.
    66 (July 1997): 97-119.
Michelson, Annette. 'Beaubourg: The Museum in the Era of Late Capitalism.'
    Artforum (April 1975): 62-67.

Midant, Jean-Paul. 'Le Projet de Façade Audio-Visuelle.' In *Centre Pompidou: Trente Ans D'histoire*, pp. 135-138. Paris: Editions du Centre Pompidou, 2007.

Moholy-Nagy, Laszlo. *Malerei Fotografie Film*. Munich: Albert Langen, 1925.

———. *The New Vision*. New York: Norton, 1938.

Neumann, Dietrich. 'Lichtarchitekur and the Avant-Garde.' In *Architecture of the Night: The Illuminated Building*, edited by Dietrich Neumann, pp. 36-53. Munich: Prestel, 2002.

Nouvel, Jean. 'Interview with Paul Virilio and Patrice Goulet.' *Jean Nouvel*, edited by Patrice Goulet, pp. 105-114. Paris: Electa Moniteur, 1987.

Nye, David E. *American Illuminations: Urban Lighting 1800-1920*. Cambridge, MA: MIT Press, 2018.

Oechslin, Werner. 'Fassade—ein später Begriff.' *Daidalos* 6 (1982): 33-36.

Papastergiadis, Nikos, Amelia Barikin, Scott McQuire, and Audrey Yue. 'Introduction: Screen Cultures and Public Spaces.' In *Ambient Screens and Transnational Public Spaces*, edited by Papastergias, Barikin, McQuire, and Yue, pp. 3-28. Hong Kong: Hong Kong University Press, 2016.

Pawley, Martin. 'Information, the "Gothic Solution."' *Theory and Design in the Second Machine Age*, pp. 114-139. Oxford: Basil Blackwell, 1990.

Pelkonen, Eeva-Liisa. *Alvar Aalto: Architecture, Modernity, Geopolitics*. New Haven: Yale University Press, 2009.

Piano, Renzo and Richard Rogers. *Du plateau Beaubourg au Centre Georges Pompidou*. Paris: Le Centre, 1987.

Robida, Albert. *Le Vingtième siècle: La vie électrique* (1882). Paris: 1893. Translated as *The Twentieth Century* by Philippe Willems; edited by Arthur B. Evans. Middletown, CT: Wesleyan University Press, 2004.

Rossi, G.M. 'Facciata.' *Dizionario enciclopedico di architettura e urbanistica*. Vol. 2, 308. Rome: Istituto Editoriale Romano, 1969.

Trachtenberg, Marvin. *Dominion of the Eye: Urbanism, Art, and Power in Early Modern Florence*. Cambridge, UK: Cambridge University Press, 1997.

Tytler, Graham. *Physiognomy in the European Novel: Faces and Fortunes*. Princeton: Princeton University Press, 2014.

Schivelbusch, Wolfgang. *The Disenchanted Night: The Industrialization of Light in the Nineteenth Century*. Berkeley: University of California Press, 1988.

Schumacher, Thomas. 'The Skull and the Mask.' *The Cornell Journal of Architecture*, 3 (1987): 4-12.

Scott Brown, Denise. 'Learning from Pop.' *Casabella* 359-360 (December 1971): 14-23.

Sert, Josep Luis, Fernand Léger, and Sigfried Giedion, 'Nine Points on Monumentality.' In *Architecture Culture 1943-1968*, edited by Joan Ockman, pp. 27-30. New York: Rizzoli, 1993.

Silver, Nathan. *The Making of Beaubourg: A Building Biography of the Centre Pompidou, Paris.* Cambridge, MA: MIT Press, 1994.

Szambien, Werner. 'La Dialectique du Facadisme.' *Monumental: Revue scientifique et technique de la sous-direction des monuments historiques* 14 (1996): 16-27.

Venturi, Robert. *Complexity and Contradiction in Architecture.* New York: Museum of Modern Art, 1966.

——, Denise Scott Brown, and Steven Izenour. *Learning from Las Vegas* Cambridge, MA: MIT Press, 1972.

Verhoeff, Nanna. *Mobile Screens: The Visual Regime of Navigation.* Amsterdam: Amsterdam University Press, 2012.

Vesnin, Alexander and Viktor Vesnin. 'Leningradskaya Pravda.' *Sovremennaia Arkitektura* 1 (1926): 1.

Vidler, Anthony. 'Losing Face.' In *The Architectural Uncanny: Essays in the Modern Unhomely,* pp. 85-100. Cambridge, MA: MIT Press, 1992.

——. *The Writing of the Walls: Architectural Theory in the Late Enlightenment.* Princeton: Princeton Architectural Press, 1987.

Viollet-Le-Duc, Eugène-Emmanuel. 'Façade.' In *Dictionnaire raisonnée de l'architecture francaise du XIeme au XVIeme siècle.* 10 vol. Paris: B. Bance, 1858-70.

Virilio, Paul. 'The Overexposed City.' *Zone* 1 (1988): 15-31.

Wood, Anthony C. *Preserving New York: Winning the Right to Protect a City's Landmarks.* New York: Routledge, 2008.

Zervos, Christian. 'Architecture et Publicité.' *Les Cahiers d'art* 6-7 (1936): 206-207.

About the Author

Craig Buckley is an assistant professor of modern and contemporary architecture in the Department of the History of Art at Yale University. His research interests include the intersections of modern architecture with avant-garde movements; the entanglement of architectural design with the poetics, technics, and politics of media; and the historiography of modern architecture in the nineteenth and twentieth centuries. His essays and criticism have appeared in *Grey Room, Log, October,* and *Texte zur Kunst.* He is the author of *Graphic Assembly: Montage, Media and Experimental Architecture in the 1960s,* published by University of Minnesota Press (2019) as well as a number of edited collections including *After the Manifesto: Writing, Architecture, and Media in a New Century* (2015), *Utopie: Texts and Projects 1967-1978* (with Jean-Louis Violeau, 2011), and *Clip/Stamp/Fold: The Radical Architecture of Little Magazines* (with Beatriz Colomina, 2010).

4.   Sensing Screens: From Surface to Situation

Nanna Verhoeff

Abstract
Nanna Verhoeff considers recent screen-based public art installations that extend from their architectural site into surrounding urban space in order to engage techniques of 'remote sensing', interactivity, and public display. In these installations, Verhoeff identifies a genre of artwork that aims to raise awareness of urban social issues by visualizing and making 'present' otherwise invisible crises relating to the meeting of the social and the environmental. These installations compel one to look past the *surface* of the screen to its surrounding *situation*. Verhoeff thus reorients cinematic concepts of the *dispositif* towards a broader spectatorial territory, which she identifies by its building-scaled interfaces that reach beyond their location to remake, create, and influence the physical context by sensibly linking it to other, more distant spaces.

Keywords: *Dispositif,* Locative Media, Space, Urban Screen, Spectatorship, Aesthetics

In the Air Tonight

The recent public art installation *In the Air Tonight* uses light and architectural surface for data visualization. (Figures 4.1 and 4.2) The project, by Toronto-based artists Patricio Davilla and Dave Colangelo of Public Visualization Studios, makes use of a LED façade of the Ryerson Image Center in Toronto. It is a temporary but recurring installation for a pre-existing and fixed architecture. It was on display for one month in 2014, and again in 2015 and 2016, with the aim of raising awareness of homelessness in the city. Throughout the cold winter evenings, a blue wave on the façade

Buckley, C., R. Campe, F. Casetti (eds.), Screen Genealogies. From Optical Device to Environmental Medium. Amsterdam: Amsterdam University Press, 2019
DOI 10.5117/9789463729000_CH04

4.1:   Public Visualization Studio, *In the Air Tonight*, Ryerson Image Arts Centre, Toronto, Canada 2014–2016. LED Media Façade, Website, Smartphones, Weather Sensors, Video, Twitter, Facebook. © Public Visualization Studio.

4.2:   Public Visualization Studio, *In the Air Tonight*, Ryerson Image Arts Centre, Toronto, Canada 2014–2016. LED Media Façade, Website, Smartphones, Weather Sensors, Video, Twitter, Facebook. © Public Visualization Studio.

displayed fluctuating information about changing temperatures and wind speed. With the colour blue, it visualizes the feeling of being outside and exposed to the elements. This presents a translation from one sense (touch) to the other (sight). The data in between—from qualitative to quantitative and back—came from a weather station located on the roof of the building. Tweets that used the hashtag *#homelessness* generated a red pulse on the building's surface. In response to financial donations, the façade intermittently turned white. A webcam enabled remote participants in the project to witness the building as it changed colours in real time.[1]

This work made use of the material architecture in which it was embedded to combine forms of *remote* sensing, *individual* interactivity, and *public* display. As such, the work aimed to raise public awareness for social concerns by visualizing and making present what is otherwise invisible—at the intersection of social and environmental problems specific to contemporary urban space. As an 'object to think with', this installation compels us to zoom out from the *surface* of screens to their *situation*.

In the Air Tonight embodies many of our contemporary fascinations: public spectacle, digital experimentation, and the affordances of new display technologies. And, like many other screen-based urban interfaces—from artistic screen installations and media façades to more mundane displays of information, advertisements, and commercial entertainment on the streets of our cities today—it also activates and updates characteristics of preceding screen paradigms. While addressing the present, such new assemblages invoke environmental aspects of panoramas, dioramas, and other visual spectacles from the past, especially from the eighteenth and nineteenth centuries. These historical spectacles created a mobile, pedestrian form of spectatorship that contributed to the rise of urban *flânerie*, which contemporary urban installations reference alongside optical illusions like the camera obscura, magic lanterns, and phantasmagorias.[2]

Recent public screen installations thus integrate visual technologies that recall early forms of urban lighting and display but infuse these with more activating, interactive possibilities. As environmental attractions, they bring back to the present a rich history of public performances and happenings at fairgrounds and other festivals and exhibitions. Moreover,

1   Drucker, p. 1. For more information about *In the Air Tonight*, see http://intheairtonight.org (accessed June 2017).
2   Although there is no end to the number of examples, the commitment to address social issues in their artistic form in other screen works is usefully discussed in the following studies. See Pop et al., 2017; McQuire, 2008.

by working with light, colour, and movement for various optical effects, they examine and extend the city's material surfaces in line with a long tradition of ornaments and *trompe l'oeil* in architectural monuments such as cathedrals. As Joanna Drucker succinctly phrases it, 'Meaning is use, as Ludwig Wittgenstein famously said, to which we can add, such use is always circumstantial and situational'. And use is not a thing but an event that happens in the present.[3]

In this essay, I discuss *In the Air Tonight* and some other comparable installations, treating these works as vehicles that can guide us toward a more in-depth understanding of urban screens in general. Specifically, through a somewhat detailed consideration of a few such installations, I will focus on some of the ways in which these works use technologically enabled 'remote sensing' to address spectators as responsible subjects by putting them into new sensory relationships with their broader urban environment. These artworks stand for a wider variety of screen installations that infuse material architectural surfaces in our urban public spaces with *matter*—both in the sense of materiality and of social concern—by means of light and reflection, the latter in its double meaning of image and thought. These installations compel *sensations*: the activation of the senses that allow humans' bodies and minds to perceive and communicate with one another and with their material environment. Sensations are the events such artworks activate.

In the Western tradition, we distinguish five senses, some of which we assume require direct bodily contact (touch, taste) while others need only bodily tools (such as ears for hearing, noses for smelling, and eyes for vision) for experiencing at a distance. Vision is usually considered the most 'remote' of the senses, the one most capable of connecting over distances—even if there, too, sensing is based on the material contact of light. Today, we use the term 'remote sensing' to describe technology-driven productions of visual sensations at great distances. Yet this term in fact describes nothing more than an extension of what (human) vision has always been capable of

---

3   In *The Lumière Galaxy*, Francesco Casetti provides a perspective on the history of the cinema as one of changing assemblages. The cinematic assemblage is an 'alterable complex of components' and this concept allows us to recognize a dynamic field of technological changes and emerging practices. For a rich archaeology of the panoramic paradigm, see Huhtamo, 2013. About mobile spectatorship and immersion, see also Griffiths, 2002 and 2008. For an archaeology of urban screens as part of a longer history of what he calls 'public media displays', see Huhtamo, 2009. On the connection between contemporary urban screens and the historical, architectural ornament, see Caspary, 2009. About revisiting early travelling cinema, see Loipedinger, 2011. For a study of early cinema and the trope of travel and mobility, see Verhoeff, 2006.

doing. Only the particular sensations produced, the experiences compelled, and the effects created by these two forms of 'remote sensing' differ from one another. Hence my claim that it is the situation, aided by technological affordances, that can make for a different kind of sensation that, being only 'remote' in appearance, is capable of encouraging engagement with our environment. With their display and interactive visualizations of remote sensing, the installations I discuss in this chapter align with Lev Manovich's statement that 'architects along with artists can take the next logical step to consider the "invisible" space of electronic data flows as *substance* rather than just as void—something that needs a structure, a politics, and a poetics'. That is, these artworks produce effects that the viewer can process as sensible material, according to my understanding of the relation between the senses and the sensations they produce. An important element of the specific works that I will discuss is that these sensations function in, and thus have an impact on, public space.[4]

To explore this paradoxical fusion of remote sensing and substance, I will consider how remote sensing shifts the screen's operations from surface to situation. In particular, I focus on works that visualize data generated from elsewhere. The screen projects under scrutiny here experiment with both optical and environmental qualities, as they provide visual interfaces to digital data that is either extracted from their direct environment—the spaces within which they are situated—or from more distant locations with which they are connected, by means of various sensing and display technologies.[5] I will thus conceive of the screen's work as *situated, architectural,* and *eventful.*

In addition to *In the Air Tonight,* I will consider two other examples of the contemporary urban installation, both by Los Angeles-based artist Refik Anadol. Many of Anadol's installations interrogate the conventions of architectural screen-spaces. His *Infinity Room* and *Virtual Depictions: San Francisco* will be central to this essay. Anadol calls these works 'data sculptures', but in light of my own argument I propose the term 'screen-architectures' to describe them. I choose this term in order to situate them alongside other examples of media architecture that work with screens or screen-like displays as well as more temporary and mobile screen-based installations that are—as screens always necessarily are—architectural.[6]

4   Manovich, 2006, p. 237.
5   On screen-based installations, see Mondloch.
6   Anne Friedberg makes the most convincing claim for this architectural perspective on the screen, in her landmark work, *The Virtual Window* (2006).

These specific cases serve as my theoretical objects. That is, I look to specific artworks in order to explain the wider 'genre' of contemporary screen-architectures, a genre that I consider to be fundamentally site specific, or rather, *site responsive*.[7] Screen-architectures enable and propose various forms of interface between an individual and his or her surroundings, whether those surroundings are immediate or more remote. These screen-architectures not only display spectacular optical sights but also produce emergent environmental situations. This perspective on installations as screen-architectures expands on the concept of the *dispositif* to include the spatio-temporal assemblage of screening situations, an assemblage that includes the respective arrangement of spectator, screen, and image.[8]

Once we understand the *dispositif* as a fundamentally material and spatial arrangement, we can further analyze this arrangement as a *spectatorial territory*: it produces not only a spectator but also the territory within which spectatorship can occur. The particular screening situation of each spectatorial territory is layered and porous: each territory is permeable and opens up to other spaces. As we will see below, approaching the screen as part of a spectatorial territory can help us understand contemporary screen installation as historically connected to other mobile screening practices from the past, which entailed their own comparable and yet different spectatorial territories: the camera obscura, the magic lantern, and various forms of urban lighting being a few examples. These screening practices likewise shaped fields of vision for spectators who were positioned behind or in front of screens, or amidst the architectural façades that surrounded them. Within the spatial arrangements of these projection-based *dispositifs*, the image emerges as either transported from another realm, beyond the screen, or in continuity with the surrounding spectatorial space. However, the territorial aspects of spectatorship may not have been sufficiently analyzed to grasp the role of interactive digital urban interfaces in our contemporary moment. As I have argued elsewhere, mobile screens and

7   See Morra, 2017.

8   Hubert Damisch introduced the notion of theoretical objects, saying that such an object '[...] obliges you to do theory but also furnishes you with the means of doing it. Thus, if you agree to accept it on theoretical terms, it will produce effects around itself ... [and] forces us to ask ourselves what theory is. It is posed in theoretical terms; it produces theory; and it necessitates a reflection on theory'. (Bois et al., 1998, p. 8). As Mieke Bal has pointed out, his concept 'sometimes seems to suggest these are objects around which theories have been produced. At other times, [...] he attributes to the artwork the capacity to motivate, entice, and even compel thought'. (Bal, p. 8). In line with this latter capacity, I attribute to the works a theorization of their own status as elaboration of this genre of 'sensing screens'.

location-based technologies have reorganized the *dispositif* in a variety of ways.[9] Not only have they given screens a sense of physical mobility—of vehicular, portable, or wearable transportation—but they have also shifted the terms of interactivity and spectatorial agency. They make the spectator mobile in multiple senses of the word. But there is also a mobility implied in the variability of screens' operations, given that digital interfaces afford many different uses. Hence, mobile screen technologies reveal the *dispositif* to be fundamentally *performative*. Our processes of interfacing with screens within a *dispositif* and the ways we actively engage with those screens produce complex, changing, and interactive spaces. This process is a making of place that renders that place emergent; the place that hosts a site-specific screen is not pre-existing. Hence, the interfacing of viewer, screen, and *dispositif* is not only situated in the sense of *taking* place in a particular location. It also *makes* place as it creates or influences surrounding (urban) spaces. In this sense, it is also situating.[10]

Site-responsivity: From translation to transformation

In view of my brief description of this work at the beginning of the essay, let me now first address an interactive urban installation that, like many other works of screen-architecture, aims to raise awareness and solicit civic participation in urban social issues.

In the Air Tonight is an example of responsive architecture used for (real-time) data visualization that raises social awareness about urban issues (here: homelessness) by deploying—and reflecting on—sensing technologies. Under the surface, it is more complex than meets the eye, due to the way in which the interface translates a social issue (homelessness) into physical and experiential categories (feeling cold). It transfers something we can *measure* (temperature) and subsequently *evaluate* and *display*. Here, this display has a metaphorical visual form: a blue wave signifies 'coldness'. Yet it combines one data source (temperature) with other information (such as the number of tweets using the hashtag *#homelessness*), thus drawing different registers of information from different locations and material contexts and symbolizing different indexical relationships between image and world. The installation makes a connection between very different

---

9   See Verhoeff, 2012.
10   Ibid. Erkki Huhtamo discerns vehicular, portable, and wearable mobile (screen) practices. See Huhtamo, 2015.

spaces, making digital communication visual and hence *sense-able*. This particular form of interface makes perceptible the urban challenges we often take for granted, a transformation that attempts to change our attitude. As such, the installation aims to produce attentiveness and reflexivity and to compel viewers to action. The spectator is positioned as an insightful and conscientious citizen, aware of the presence and situation of others. This may stimulate donations, which might improve and transform the environment surrounding the installation itself.[11]

Responding to its immediate environment—that is, its site of installation—this work demonstrates how data visualization not only communicates data from and about 'here' and 'there' but also allows an interface between these disparate spaces. It also represents the 'now' of the viewing subject in relation to this data as it extracts, translates, connects, and makes 'present'—both temporally and spatially—data about elsewhere in the 'now,' thus producing relations and, perhaps most pertinently, performing the act of *sensing*. The thrust of urban projects like *In the Air Tonight* is to activate local publics by stimulating reflection on their situation and transforming this reflection into social action. Sensing thus implies a distillation of information from the environment to which the perceiving subject becomes attuned—and is thus able to respond to the particulars of that environment. Sensing is not only subjective but also social; it can thus put the self and the senses in an ethical relation to others.[12]

Joanne Morra has proposed that we consider as 'site-responsive' any artwork that responds to its site of installation. An installation can act site-responsively when a work engages a space that is not primarily a site for exhibition. Morra writes that site-responsive interventions aim 'to render historical space contemporary, to critically engage with the museum, its collection, display strategies, narratives, and history, or to open the space up to a broader cultural context that includes artistic practice.' They can activate potential narratives, experiences, and meanings not otherwise obviously primary in the experience of a space. As a result of this activation, the work responds to the site and enables us to understand it differently from how we routinely perceive it. Because the viewer and the work interact, there is a clear reciprocity at play. 'Site-responsivity', Morra writes, 'acknowledges

11   See Verhoeff and Van Es, 2018. For a comparable installation that neatly resonates with the title of the present article, see *Sensing Water* by Seattle-based artist Dan Corson. For more about this work, see http://dancorson.com/sensing-water (accessed June 2017).
12   Urban screens and installations and their possible use for social awareness and civic participation are usefully discussed in Pop et al., 2017. About sensing technologies, smart technologies, and urban experiences, see Shepard, 2011.

the way in which the artworks and space dynamically relate to, and respond to, one another'.[13]

This work in Toronto produces a new situation that moves very literally from the environmental to the optical, and which feeds back into the environment: environmental data about the climate affects a visual display, which in turn transforms its environment. I wish to underscore how this relation between the environmental and the optical is not a one-directional causal process but is complexly intertwined. Accordingly, I propose we understand these site-specific architectural and situated screens as *site-responsive urban interfaces*. This change in terminology emphasizes how the screening situation not only takes place within a space that produces subjectivity but also produces a spectatorial territory that allows possibilities for action and transformation to emerge. While we perhaps tend to understand screen-based spectatorship first and foremost as based on attraction or immersion, we see here how site-responsivity combined with interactivity may yield situations that are performative: fundamentally emergent, dynamic, and transformative of the subject.

Drowning in dimensions

The following case may seem a bit exceptional—let's say, literally out of place—considering my focus on public screening situations. Contrary to exterior displays that cover the city's building façades, Refik Anadol's *Infinity Rooms* are closed interiors that fully immerse the spectator in an abstract spectacle of light and sound (figure 4.3). It is difficult to describe in words what we see in the rooms. Changing black-and-white light patterns (projected by lasers) surround the spectator. Mirrors cover the walls of the small space, visually effacing its boundaries. Engulfing sounds accompany the flow of light patterns. In this audio-visual spectacle, the visitor loses the visual boundaries and surfaces that typically serve as points of sensory reference. The projections of kaleidoscopic light patterns visually encompass the spectator and fill his or her entire field of vision, without the borders of a frame and without discernible walls, floor, and ceiling. As a consequence, the illusion of being both detached and then immersed is very powerful.

The work has appeared in various settings—for example, at the Istanbul Biennial (2015) and the SXSW festival in Austin, Texas (2017). Thus, the rooms

13   See the introduction in Morra, 2017.

travel and are (hence) *site-adaptive*—a form of site-specificity characteristic of many travelling installations that appear in different locations and for different publics, in each instance framed differently by the various occasions of their 'happening'. Another example would be the project *Portals* by Shared Studios, which in various locations places shipping containers that contain screen-based connections by means of live video links to other locations. Or, as the exhibition text by Shared Studios announced: 'Portals are gold spaces equipped with immersive audiovisual technology. When you enter a Portal, you come face-to-face with someone in a distant Portal, live and full-body, as if in the same room'.[14]

We can locate the historical roots of the *Infinity Rooms*—and by extension the *Portals* and other similar installations—in the intersecting optical and environmental aspects of these works. In particular, the early history of virtual reality would be an antecedent. As an immersive environment that travels to and is installed in various public spaces, it recalls early cinema exhibition, which often took place in fairgrounds, markets, circuses, and other travelling shows. It also recalls the mirrored rooms created by artists such as Lucas Samaras and Yayoi Kusama since the 1960s—rooms that used multiple facing mirrors to produce an effect of *mise-en-abyme*. These works are, in a sense, in line with the early nineteenth and twentieth-century practice of travelling exhibitions, which provided local spectators with a sort of virtual travel by showing both local and more exotic sights. *Infinity Rooms*, on the other hand, presents abstract visual forms based on programmed algorithms. Rather than visualize data from outside or elsewhere, the visual spaces are created in the 'here and now' by means of these algorithms that generate new, emergent environments. Compared to earlier practices, this shift from the transmission and representation of data to the construction of data space radically changes the spectator's optical and sensory experience. Anadol's immersive and box-like installations are perhaps more similar to early Virtual Reality, or the CAVES (Cave Automatic Virtual Environments) developed in the 1990s. The difference here, however, lies in the position of the subject. Rather than simply immersive—rather than entice people to drown in dimensions—Anadol's installation is interactive in the *active* sense. The spectator's awareness of his or her own body is not effaced but is instead foregrounded.[15]

14 See Shared Studios website, https://www.sharedstudios.com/ (accessed July 2018).
15 We can recognize a parallel with the Hales' Tours exhibition, even in the way the visual field is radically cut off from the outside, effacing the perspectival cues of horizon and scale, maximizing the optical effect of light and movement. For the connection between Hale's tours

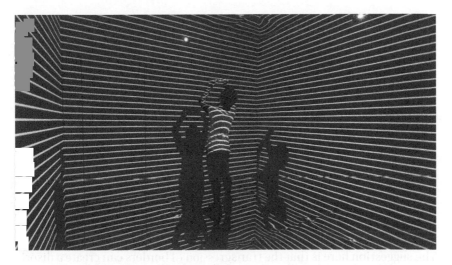

4.3:   Refik Anadol (b.1985), *Infinity Rooms*, Instambul. 2015. Four channel Audio/Visual Installation running on custom software. © Refik Anadol.

The work seems to be inspired by two trends that, put together, create a paradox. On the one hand, the artist suggests that the range and variety of screen technologies have caused us to become increasingly detached from our direct environment. This produces a sense of displacement. On the other hand, his artworks install a media architecture that makes explosive and innovative use of light and screen technology. Anadol thus proposes a temporary synthesis of the two poles of this paradox: between the displacing effects of media on the one hand, and their production of new, albeit temporary, spatialities on the other. His *Infinity Rooms* are part of an ongoing project that he calls 'Temporary Immersive Environment Experiments', intimating his attitude towards this paradox. Anadol understands the immersion produced by his *Infinity Rooms* as a 'state of consciousness where an immersant's awareness of physical self is transformed by being surrounded in an engrossing environment; often artificial, creating a perception of presence in a non-physical world'.[16] What Anadol calls immersion needs

and modern ride films, see Rabinowitz, 1998. This historical connection also segues to a different track, connecting to the immersive environments of virtual reality; see Cruz-Neira et al., 1992. Interestingly, Anadol also experimented with VR versions of his Infinity Rooms but preferred the material, architectural version. In his words: 'We have so many opportunities in the physical world that we have never explored. [...] If you know this much better, then the leap to VR experiences will be much more meaningful, much more impactful.' See also Souppouris, 2017.
16   See Anadol's website at http://www.refikanadol.com/aboutrefikanadol (accessed June 2017) and http://www.refikanadol.com/works/infinity-room (accessed June 2017). On media

a bit of elaboration. The artist creates the impression of boundlessness by taking away borders and surfaces. Immersion, here, is the result of the strategic production of a limitless visual space. The visitor's disembodied visual experience breaks with the dimensions of our common perception and experience of space. However, with these installations, Anadol aims at more than just disorientation:

> In this project, 'infinity' is chosen as a concept, a radical effort to decon-struct the framework of this illusory space and transgress the normal boundaries of the viewing experience to set out to transform the conven-tional flat cinema projection screen into a three-dimensional kinetic and architectonic space of visualisation by using contemporary algorithms.[17]

The suggestion here is that the transgression of borders can create a disori-entation that produces transformation. And that, of course, is the point. One might describe this as producing a different kind of spectatorial territory, an alternate scenography in which the screen becomes coterminous with every interior surface rather than serving as a singular focal point of attention, as in classical theories of the *dispositif*.[18]

The work's elimination of boundaries troubles the certainty of perspecti-val viewing inherent in the model of a single screen facing an audience. As Maaike Bleeker has written, perspectival projection 'creates a "scenographic space" in which all that is seen is in a sense staged for a viewer. At the same time, this staging aims at an effect that is quite the opposite of being theatrical: the promise presented by perspective is one of directness, im-mediacy, it is the promise of Alberti's *finestra aperta*'.[19] Or, as Anadol puts it, 'the experiment intends to question the relativity of perception and how it informs the apprehension of our surroundings'.[20] Anadol's installations thus raise a question: can a different scenography for the screen be mobilized (that is, made mobile and also, literally, transformed) in more fundamental ways than its effacement?[21]

architecture, see Wiethoff and Hussmann, 2017.

17   See http://www.refikanadol.com/works/infinity-room (accessed June 2017).

18   It would be relevant, but take too much space, to involve dramaturgy as a critical concept, as it is discussed in Turners and Behrndt. For more about dramaturgy in relation to digital media, see Eckersall, Grehan, and Scheer. On scenography, see McKinney and Palmer, 2017.

19   Bleeker, 99.

20   See http://refikanadol.com/works/infinity-room/ (accessed June 2017).

21   Surface is a cultural issue in many different fields. For an interdisciplinary take on surfaces, see Bruno, 2014.

Moving surfaces: Situating spectacle

Another project by Anadol addresses this question: *Virtual Depictions: San Francisco*, a video wall created for the 350 Mission building. (Figures 4.4 and 4.5) Visible from the street but displayed on a surface lying behind a large glass façade, the work is literally situated both inside and outside of public space. It is a media wall: a screen surface that wraps around corners and which has the visual effect of a thick mass. Called a 'parametric data sculpture' by the artist, it is a work of *screen-architecture*; between screen surface and material, it is an architectural component.

Virtual Depictions fluidly displays changing abstract vistas—sometimes colourful, sometimes black-and-white—that, with special optical effects, visualize and animate otherwise static numeric, digital data from various sources. Though made visible and animated, this data is not 'legible' as such; there is no way to interpret or distil information from these spectacular and also enigmatic visuals. The images are abstract and are not accompanied by a legend, scale table, or other tools for interpretation. For example, the media wall might display information about the geographic origins of a series of tweets—but not in a map-like, readable image. Instead, the data sets are translated into a gripping visual spectacle. A *trompe l'oeil* effect enhances the kinetic and haptic appearance of the screen and its images, whose movement makes it seem as though the visual material protrudes from, and almost spills out of, its frame. This makes the screen, indeed, look more like a moving sculpture than a flat surface, even if it is actually the latter.

In his reflection on this work, Anadol invokes the installation's historical roots in the phantasmagoria and the cinematic screen. His media wall, in his words, 'turns into a spectacular public event making direct and phantasmagorical connections to its surroundings through simultaneous juxtapositions'.[22] With this invocation of the phantasmagoria, the connection to pre-cinematic kinetic art and other forms of experimentation with visual movement brings a retrospective—or, as Mieke Bal would have it, a 'pre-posterous'—connection to historical moments and their meanings, yet to be disclosed. The work establishes an architectural hybridity. Its mobile surface expands and transforms its surroundings. It not only makes dynamic the appearance of the material structures but also suggests permeability

22   See http://www.refikanadol.com/works/virtual-depictions-san-francisco (accessed June 2017). Anadol's phrasing suggests he is purposefully alluding to the phantasmagorial tradition. About the legacy of the phantasmagoria and magic lantern in digital interfaces and media art, see Grau, 2010.

4.4:   Refik Anadol (b.1985), *Virtual Depictions*, San Francisco. 2015. 6mm LED Media Wall.
© Refik Anadol.

of its terrain. A crucial part of the work's situation is its positioning behind
a glass façade; it thus displays a flowing spectacle of digital data layered
under the reflected image of pedestrians passing by. As *screen-architecture*,
this work expands and infuses its environment with optically vibrant
visuals. Its visual suggestion of material fluidity brings life into the static
surface of the façade. It speaks to our senses as we behold its movement. It
is spectacularly beautiful, yet it firmly situates its spectacle in the everyday
space that surrounds it. But does the spectacle also situate us? Or do we
just look at it?[23]

Mobilizing the senses

The sensing and sensuous site-specificity of these works raises questions
about their specific aesthetics. The three works discussed here are theoretical objects, illustrating the conceptual frameworks of *remote-sensing*, the
spectatorial territory, and *site-responsivity*. All explore the relationship
between the optical and the environmental—how the one infuses and
intervenes in the other, and vice versa. The remote sensing technologies

23   On phantasmagoria as a tool for 'cultural optics', see Gunning. On the retrospective look
at past art or 'pre-posterous' history, what has later been called 'anachronism' as a productive
take on historical relations going in two directions, see Bal, 2010.

4.5: 350 Mission Street, San Francisco, a commissioned digital artwork animates a 70-by-38-foot LED screen that is visible from the street. © Skidmore, Owings & Merrill LLP | Cesar Rubio.

that enable these data visualizations reference, but do not require, the direct contact of bodily senses such as touch. How, then, ought we to understand the subject's own position and agency within this spatial screening situation?

I want to suggest that by screening, filtering, and territorializing, these works have a relationship of what we can call the 'curating' of the subject, in three different senses. First, the works design the space in which the subject is situated and construct or curate this space as emergent. Second, these works also curate data by filtering: selecting, processing, showing, and activating it. Third, as interfaces to this data, these works also curate a field of relations. Enclosing the subject with screens establishes a territory that is paradoxical: physically closed, yet apparently infinite. Screens in these works establish multiple pathways between a viewing subject and the data they display, so as to produce a *dispositif* through which subjects can constitute and transform themselves. This, then, is the emergent and relational situation that they produce: the territory of spectatorship's emergence. Hence my earlier claim that screen-architectures generate situations that can instigate specific kinds of sensations and that stimulate relational connections so as to infuse our environment with active, and actively curated, subjectivities. The kind of spectatorship at stake varies, however, depending on the specific screen-architecture at hand. *In the Air Tonight* aims to create a social consciousness in the spectator by linking specific stimuli to specific data, but *Virtual Depictions: San Francisco* does not. Instead, the latter work creates lush patterns and relief effects that do not allow viewers to recognize in familiar forms the data they depict.

What is at stake, then, when we consider the screen as a situation? This question, too, has a historical antecedent, which has recently resurfaced as an object of concern in media studies as well: the question of aesthetics. The mid-eighteenth-century philosopher Alexander Gottlieb Baumgarten is considered the founder of aesthetic theory. He described aesthetic experience as a mode of connecting, or binding, through the senses. And, since binding exceeds individual subjectivity, we can add: *binding through the senses, in public space. Binding* can connote sociality; the *senses* can be activated by encounters with artworks; and *public space* can be found in the urban environment. The works I have described in this essay offer exemplary intersections of these three aspects of aesthetic experience. All mobilize the senses. *In the Air Tonight* deploys colour to convey temperature. Anadol's *Infinity Rooms* amplify tactility and hearing in tandem while also enhancing but 'problematizing' vision through their disorientating effects. As such, the rooms simultaneously isolate and augment the visitor's senses. And *Visual Depictions: San Francisco* limits senses to vision, even when the work's haptic texture invokes the idea of touch. The work's animated materiality turns vision into more than itself. It makes vision tactile and hence binds viewers by mobilizing the desire to touch what they see and thus to come closer.[24]

24   As far as I know, and to my astonishment, Baumgarten's *Äesthetik I* has not been translated into English. Even the recently republished *Encyclopedia of Aesthetics* devotes a scant two pages to this work. For a relevant, politically oriented discussion of Baumgarten's aesthetics, see Gaygill, pp. 148-186. About the bond between aesthetics and practical life, as she calls it, Jill Bennett writes: '[Aesthetics] inclines not only toward the judgment of art [...] but also toward a more general theory of sensory-emotional experience, potentially crossing from the arts into psychology and social science.' Bennett, 2012, pp. 1-2. Earlier, Bennett recalled Baumgarten's

Binding and public space, taking up the consequences of Baumgarten's view, operate in relation to each other. This is necessarily the case because binding not only happens through the senses but also between entities: between subjects and the objects they bind themselves to—such as, in this case, the installations. Binding is more than just enjoying. It is the transformation of the self under the influence and impact of an art object or sensory experience. In the cases I outline in this essay, the impact lies in how the works organize space, in the sensory appeal of screens and projections, and in the transformational appeal emanating from the experience of the work. This is where public space comes in: all three works use data visualization to truly impact the environment and thus augment the binding effect of the art object. More than just positioning the subject, binding invites the subject—or perhaps provokes the subject—to position him or herself in a bond with the environment. *Situation*, as I have used the concept here, implies that relations are not detached from the subjects; on the contrary, these works solicit subjects to participate in them, they persuade spectators to *want* to engage with them.

These installations, with their 'high-tech' look and feel, strongly evoke the idea of the contemporary: they project a sense of being in the now, and (with consideration of the spatial aspect) in the here-and-now. As such, they bring to fruition a latent aspect of older location-based cinematic screens: the capacity to bring the subject into direct relation with her environment. This type of screening is fundamentally and explicitly situational. However, more so than before, urban screen interfaces compel social engagements with the environments that surround them—including the city's problems, such as homelessness and social disconnection. Thus, the situation surrounding the screen becomes as 'animate' as the moving images projected upon it. Indifference in the face of these works is hard to sustain. Immanuel Kant— strongly influenced by, and yet polemical against, Baumgarten—proposed 'disinterestedness' as a condition for aesthetic experience. This has been much misunderstood as a form of indifference. But the detachment from self-interest, from the selfishness so rampant in contemporary capitalist culture, is also a necessary condition enabling individuals to reach out and engage—and to engage in the binding through the senses that Baumgarten proposed. We can say that these installations are exemplary acts of sense-making: they bring a space, a subject, and data into sensitive connection.

conception of sensitive or sensuous knowledge: 'As a primary encounter, unconstrained by the categories, methods, and demarcations of other disciplines and practices, aesthetic perception is a unique nonscientific basis for inquiry.' Bennett, 2011, p. 119.

Works Cited

Anadol, Refik. http://www.refikanadol.com/works (accessed June 2017).

Bal, Mieke. *Of What One Cannot Speak: Doris Salcedo's Political Art*. Chicago: University of Chicago Press, 2010.

——. *Quoting Caravaggio: Contemporary Art, Preposterous History*. Chicago: University of Chicago Press, 1999.

Baumgarten, Alexander Gottlieb. *Äesthetik I* (1750). Hamburg: Meiner Felix Verlag, 2007.

Bennett, Jill. *Practical Aesthetics: Events, Affects and Art after 9/11*. London: I.B. Tauris, 2012.

Bleeker, Maaike. *Visuality in the Theater: The Locus of Looking*. London: Palgrave, 2008.

——. 'Migratory Aesthetics: Art and Politics beyond Identity.' In *Art and Visibility in Migratory Culture: Conflict, Resistance, and Agency*, edited by Mieke Bal and Miguel Á. Hernández-Navarro, pp. 109-126. Amsterdam: Rodopi, 2011.

Bruno, Giuliana. *Surface: Matters of Aesthetics, Materiality, and Media*. Chicago: University of Chicago Press, 2014.

Casetti, Francesco. *The Lumière Galaxy: Seven Key Words for the Cinema to Come*. New York: Columbia University Press, 2015.

Caspary, Uta. 'Digital Media as Ornament in Contemporary Architecture Façades: Its Historical Dimension.' In *Urban Screens Reader*, edited by Scott McQuire, Meredith Martin, and Sabine Niederer, pp. 65-74. Amsterdam: Institute of Network Cultures, 2009.

Chateau, Dominique and José Moure, eds. *Screens: From Materiality to Spectatorship—A Historical and Theoretical Reassessment*. Amsterdam: Amsterdam University Press, 2016.

Corson, Dan. Sensing Water. See http://dancorson.com/sensing-water (accessed June 2017).

Cruz-Neira, Carolina, Daniel J. Sandin, Thomas A. DeFanti, Robert V. Kenyon, and John C. Hart. 'The CAVE: Audio Visual Experience Automatic Virtual Environment.' *Communications of the ACM* 35, no. 6 (June 1, 1992): 64-72.

Drucker, Johanna. 'Performative Materiality and Theoretical Approaches to Interface.' *DHQ: Digital Humanities Quarterly* 7, no. 1 (2013). Published at http://www.digitalhumanities.org/dhq/vol/7/1/000143/000143.html.

Eckersall, Peter, Helena Grehan, and Edward Scheer, eds. *New Media Dramaturgy: Performance, Media and New-Materialism*. Basinstoke, UK: Palgrave, 2017.

Gaygill, Howard. *Art of Judgment,* Oxford: Blackwell, 1989.

Grau, Oliver. 'Remember the Phantasmagoria! Illusion Politics of the Eighteenth Century and its Multimedial Afterlife.' In *Media Art Histories*, edited by Oliver Grau, pp. 137-161. Cambridge, MA: MIT Press, 2010.

Griffiths, Alison. *Shivers Down Your Spine: Cinema, Museums, and the Immersive View*. New York: Columbia University Press, 2008.

——. *Wondrous Difference: Cinema, Anthropology and Turn-of-the-Century Visual Culture*. New York: Columbia University Press, 2002.

Gunning, Tom. 'Phantasmagoria and the Manufacturing of Illusions and Wonder: Towards a Cultural Optics of the Cinematic Apparatus.' In *The Cinema: A New Technology for the Twentieth Century*, edited by André Gaudreault, Catherine Russell, and Pierre Véronneau, pp. 31-44. Lausanne: Edition Payot, 2004.

Huhtamo, Erkki. *Illusions in Motion: Media Archaeology of the Moving Panorama and Related Spectacles*. Cambridge, MA: MIT Press, 2013.

——. 'The Four Practices? Challenges for an Archaeology of the Screen.' In *Screens: From Materiality to Spectatorship—A Historical and Theoretical Reassessment*, edited by Domonique Chateau and José Mourre, pp. 116-124. Amsterdam: Amsterdam University Press, 2016.

——. 'Messages on the Wall: An Archaeology of Public Media Displays.' In *Urban Screens Reader*, edited by Scott McQuire, Meredith Martin, and Sabine Niederer, pp. 15-28.

In the Air Tonight. http://intheairtonight.org (accessed June 2017).

Loipedinger, Martin, ed. *Early Cinema Today: The Art of Programming and Live Performance*. KINtop Studies in Early Cinema. Frankfurt am Main and Basel: Stroemfeld Verlag, 2011.

Manovich, Lev. 'The Poetics of Augmented Space.' *Visual Communication* 5, no. 2 (June 2006): 219-240.

McKinney, Joslin and Scott Palmer, eds. *Scenography Expanded: An Introduction to Contemporary Performance Design*. London: Bloomsbury, 2017.

McQuire, Scott. *The Media City: Media, Architecture and Urban Space*. London: Sage, 2008.

McQuire, Scott, Meredith Martin, and Sabine Niederer, eds. *Urban Screens Reader*, INC Reader #5. Amsterdam: Institute of Network Cultures, 2009.

Mondloch, Kate. *Screens: Viewing Media Installation Art*. Minneapolis: University of Minnesota Press, 2009.

Morra, Joanne. *Inside the Freud Museums: History, Memory and Site-Responsive Art*. London: I.B. Tauris, 2017.

Pop, Susa, Tanya Toft, Nerea Calvillo, and Mark Wright, eds. *What Urban Media Art Can Do: Why, When, Where & How*. Stuttgart: avedition GmbH, 2017.

Rabinovitz, Lauren. 'From Hale's Tours to Star Tours: Virtual Voyages and the Delirium of the Hyper- Real.' *Iris* 25 (1998): 133-152.

Shared Studios website, https://www.sharedstudios.com/ (accessed July 2018).

Shepard, Mark, ed. *Sentient City: Ubiquitous Computing, Architecture, and the Future of Urban Space*. Cambridge, MA: MIT Press, 2011.

Souppouris, Aaron. 'Inside "Infinity Room", A Dazzling SXSW Art Installation.' *Endgadget* 13 (March 2017), https://www.engadget.com/2017/03/13/refik-anadol-infinity-room-video.

Turners, Cathy and Synne Behrndt, eds. *Dramaturgy and Performance*. Basinstoke, UK: Palgrave, 2016.

Verhoeff, Nanna. *Mobile Screens: The Visual Regime of Navigation*. MediaMatters. Amsterdam: Amsterdam University Press, 2012.

———. *The West in Early Cinema: After the Beginning*. Film Culture in Transition. Amsterdam: Amsterdam University Press, 2006.

Verhoeff, Nanna and Karin van Es. 'Situated Installations for Urban Data Visualization: Interfacing the Archive-City.' In *Visualizing the Street: New Practices of Documenting, Navigating and Imagining the City*. Cities and Cultures, edited by Padram Dibazar and Judith Naeff, pp. 117-136. Amsterdam: Amsterdam University Press, 2018.

Wiethoff, Alexander and Heinrich Hussmann, eds. *Media Architecture: Using Information and Media as Construction Material* (*Age of Access? Grundfragen der Informationsgesellschaft*). Berlin: De Gruyter Mouton, 2017.

About the Author

Nanna Verhoeff is associate professor in the Department of Media and Culture at Utrecht University. Interested in comparative approaches to changing media forms, she investigates emerging and transforming media cultures from early cinema to contemporary mobile and location-based interactive screens and installations. Besides her work on 3D cinema and immersive screen media, she has published on mobile media, augmented reality, screen-based installations, and media architecture. Her books include *The West in Early Cinema: After the Beginning* (2006) and *Mobile Screens: The Visual Regime of Navigation* (2012). She is co-editor of a special issue on Urban Cartographies in *Television and New Media* (Spring 2017). In 2014, she initiated the interdisciplinary research group [urban interfaces] at Utrecht University—a platform for research on location-based and mobile media, art, and performance in urban public spaces.

5.   'Taking the Plunge': The New Immersive Screens[1]

Ariel Rogers

Abstract

Ariel Rogers addresses the contemporary experience of virtual reality technology and its long and volatile relationship to ideas of immersion. The multiplication and pervasion of screens has often been viewed as a break from previously dominant forms of screen engagement. Whereas viewers' encounters with the twentieth-century cinema screen (conceived as singular and static) has typically been framed as an experience of centred space marked by fixity and transfixion, the experience of enclosure in multiple-screen environments has often been conceptualized via concepts of spatial fragmentation and information flow. Contemporary VR sets confound this distinction: not only are they 'immersive' and centring, they are also unanchored, breaking the tight identification of frame and screen that has dominated much of cinema's history.

Keywords: Virtual Reality, Framing, Spectatorship, Video Games, Media Space

Introduction

A cover story in *Variety* on 22 March 2016 marked a perceived turning point in the emergence of virtual reality (VR), just as the Oculus Rift and HTC Vive headsets were about to be made available to the public. Titled

1   This research was assisted by an ACLS Fellowship from the American Council of Learned Societies. The author would also like to thank Rüdiger Campe, Francesco Casetti, and Craig Buckley for their feedback as this essay developed. Thanks as well to Ozge Samanci for encouraging me to explore virtual reality and to the staff at the Northwestern University Knight Lab for helping me to do so.

Buckley, C., R. Campe, F. Casetti (eds.), *Screen Genealogies. From Optical Device to Environmental Medium*. Amsterdam: Amsterdam University Press, 2019

DOI 10.5117/9789463729000_CH05

'Taking the Plunge', the article featured an illustration depicting three virtual reality users, each wearing opaque goggles and walking blindly toward the edge of a high dive, about to fall into a pixelated abyss (Figure 5.1). The would-be cybernauts, improbably dressed in vintage business attire, are equipped with only old-fashioned inflatable lifesavers to buoy them, and one of these has been lost over the precipice. The playful suggestion was that prospective users of virtual reality were ill-prepared (and improperly suited) for the dangerous waters into which the new screens were about to plunge them. Computer-aided head-mounted displays had, as the article acknowledged, been in existence for almost fifty years, and virtual reality—as both a concept and a technology employed across commercial, military, scientific, and artistic contexts—enjoyed an earlier heyday in the 1980s and 1990s.[2] But the release of the Oculus Rift and HTC Vive, together with the anticipated launch of Sony's Playstation VR headset later in the year, represented, as the article put it, 'the first time that these kinds of devices, capable of delivering immersive VR experiences, are going to make it to consumers' living rooms'.[3] Virtual reality has indeed experienced something of a renaissance since Oculus began shipping prototypes to developers in 2013, as these headsets, alongside more inexpensive devices powered by smartphones, have promised to integrate themselves into a media landscape already characterized by proliferating and pervasive screens.[4] As the *Variety* illustration neatly conveys, this new situation both resuscitates long-standing notions of mediated immersion and suggests that they, like so many of our devices, may require updating.

Taking the recent boom of experimentation with virtual reality as a case study, this essay explores the ways in which contemporary screens are associated with the concept of immersion. These screens often seem to disappear, whether by virtue of their proximity to the eyes (as with virtual-reality headsets) or through their sheer ubiquity and integration with the built environment.[5] Screens, however, continue to contribute materially to the experience of immersion, even (indeed, especially) when they recede from the user's consciousness. Within the immersive *dispositifs* in which the new screens participate, both immersion and screens play particular,

2   Roettgers, p. 31. For histories of virtual reality, see Hillis, 1999 and Grau, 2003. For a detailed nonacademic narrative, see Rheingold, 1991.
3   Roettgers, p. 30.
4   On the reemergence of virtual reality, see Rose, SR5; and Suellentrop, C1.
5   On the idea and history of disappearing technological objects, see Spigel, 2012.

5.1:   Depiction of virtual reality accompanied an article titled "Taking the Plunge"
Variety, March 22, 2016. Illustration by Daniel Downey. Courtesy of the artist.

historically contingent roles. Specifically, I will argue that these *dispositifs* bind immersive experience to physical space and frame screens themselves as a means of penetrating that space. The notion of plunging—which simultaneously implies falling, penetration, and submersion—will help us map the contours of these formations.

Immersive screens

The concept of immersion, deriving from the Latin *immergĕre* (to dip or plunge), refers to the action of dipping or plunging into a liquid, or of being buried or embedded within another material or space. Figuratively, it extends to the experience of absorption into an action or condition.[6] This concept was widely applied to new digital media in the 1990s—and into the early 2000s—when a range of developments including the rise of computer-aided image creation, interactivity, and multimedial forms were perceived to have transformed images into spaces users could enter,

6   *Oxford English Dictionary Online*, s.vv. 'immersion, n.', 'immerse, v.' Accessed June 4, 2017. http://www.oed.com

experience multisensorily, and intervene upon.[7] Within scholarly discourses
at that time, the notion of immersion was bound up with other concepts
attributed to new digital media, especially simulation, virtuality, and
interactivity.[8] Experimentation with interactive virtual-reality systems,
together with a perceived pervasiveness of screens (here gracing devices
such as televisions and personal computers), contributed to the notion that
people were increasingly plunging into the dematerialized, fabricated realm
of 'cyberspace'. In this context, immersion was thus conceptualized in terms
of various and contested ideas about how new media were transforming
representation, presence, materiality, embodiment, and agency.

Since the early 2000s, as screens have continued to multiply, scholars have
challenged the sense of rupture the concept of virtuality had once suggested.
In particular, they have historicized 'virtuality' as a concept, emphasized the
role the user's body plays in the experience of digital media, and highlighted
the materiality of screens themselves.[9] Bound up with those projects, there has
also been a significant effort to construct historical genealogies of immersive
media. These histories encompass a range of forms, from spaces of illusion
(associated with frescoes, panoramas, and certain film and video formats
such as Cinerama, Sensorama, and IMAX) to multiscreen and multimedia
installations (in the context of fairs and exhibitions, expanded cinema,
and experimental work at the juncture of art, performance, and film/video
installation).[10] Taken as a whole, this body of work reveals within conceptualizations of immersion faultlines that had been papered over in the 1990s
discourses that aligned the term 'immersion' with virtuality, simulation,
interactivity, and 'cyberspace'. Although the concepts of presence, illusion, and
transparency are routinely employed to define particular forms of immersion,
attending to the diverse practices encompassed by these histories makes
it clear that such concepts, together with differing ideas about agency and
embodiment, come together—or don't—in a variety of ways.[11]

In the remainder of this essay, I will therefore largely bracket the notions
of presence, illusion, and transparency that are frequently, if ambiguously,

7   See Murray, 1997; Manovich, 2001; Packer and Jordan, 2001.
8   See Friedberg, 1993; Morse, 1998; Rosen, pp. 338-349.
9   For the effort to historicize virtuality, see Grau, 2003; Friedberg, 2006. On embodiment, see
Hansen, 2004. On the materiality of screens, see Straw, 2000; Doane, 2003; Wasson, 2007.
10   See Huhtamo, 1995; Colomina, 2001; Grau, 2003; Marchessault, 2007; Griffiths, 2008; Turner,
2013.
11   I am guided here by Jonathan Sterne's point that concepts such as immersion, high definition,
aesthetic pleasure, contemplation, and attention 'have no necessary relationship to one another'
and 'can exist in many different possible configurations'. Sterne, p. 5.

associated with immersion and hew closely to the concept's most literal use to indicate a specific kind of spatial relationship between a body and an environment or enveloping substance. This approach, as I hope to show, offers the benefit of revealing connections among practices whose relationships to other concepts often accompanying the notion of immersion, such as illusion, diverge. The spatial relationship between an object and environment implied by the concept of immersion entails (at least) three specific qualities. This relationship is marked, first, by a relative scale. In order to accommodate plunging or embedding, the environment must be construed as larger than the object it is to encompass. Indeed, the capacity to surround, envelop, or enclose—to act, in other words, as a container—is one of the qualities that Susan Stewart attributes to the figure of the gigantic.[12] Second, the notion of immersion implies proximity. Bodies cannot become immersed in a substance or environment from a distance; there must be contact, or the prospect of contact, between a body and its environment. Although we may apprehend a landscape in the distance, for instance, we are only immersed in that landscape if we conceive our bodily space as continuous with it. Thus, the experience of immersion proffered by contemporary virtual reality has been attributed to the sensation that 'there is no distance between you and the environment'.[13] Finally, the concept of immersion suggests a multidimensional relationship. To be immersed, a body must not only come into contact with a larger environment but be surrounded by it.

This formulation of immersion as a particular kind of spatial relationship is especially useful for assessing screen practices, since screens themselves also construct spatial relationships. As an object, a screen supplies means of sheltering, concealing, filtering, partitioning, or revealing spaces (whether actual or virtual); as an action, to screen is, similarly, to protect, conceal, filter, divide, or display.[14] The history of film theory enumerates the varied and often contradictory ways that audiovisual screens mediate virtual and actual spaces; screens function alternately—and sometimes simultaneously—as apertures, thresholds, barriers, masks, frames, mirrors, and skins.[15] Screens' material qualities contribute to these functions in a variety of ways. The screen's borders work to enclose, obscure, reveal, or demarcate the spaces within and surrounding its edges, enabling the screen to function as a

12 Stewart, p. 71.
13 Lelyveld, p. 78.
14 *Oxford English Dictionary Online*, s.vv. 'screen, n.', 'screen, v'. See also Huhtamo, 2004; Friedberg, 2006; Acland, 2012; Verhoeff, 2012; Bruno, 2014; Casetti, pp. 155-178.
15 Sobchack, pp. 14-17; Friedberg, 2006, pp. 15-18; Casetti, pp. 157-169.

frame, mask, aperture, or connector. Factors contributing to those functions include the scale and shape of the screen, the rigidity or flexibility of its boundaries, and its proximity to the beholder. The screen's surface enables it to function as a threshold, barrier, reflector, membrane, interface, or vehicle for light and sound, thus joining, separating, or reconfiguring the spaces in front of and behind it. Factors contributing to those functions include the screen's transparency, texture, and material composition. Additionally, the mobility of screens, achieved through their capacity to both move and display movement, renders these spatial mediations fluid and dynamic.

   There are many ways in which these material qualities can be harnessed, together with particular types of representation, to form the relationships of scale, proximity, and multidimensionality facilitating immersion. Indeed, we can chart the flexibility and historical contingency of the notion and experience of immersive screens by mapping the diachronic and synchronic permutations of such *dispositifs*. Delineating these formations provides insight into conceptualizations of mediated environments—and bodies' relationships to them—in particular historical contexts. At the same time, it highlights screens' diverse and protean roles in structuring those environments and relationships. In what follows, I will explore one such formation, looking closely at contemporary uses of virtual-reality headsets.

Plunging into virtual reality

The term 'virtual reality' was reportedly coined by the computer scientist and entrepreneur Jaron Lanier in 1989, but this concept drew on, and drew together, an array of more long-standing ideas and achievements.[16] By the late 1980s, key components of the technological assemblage that would come to be associated most strongly with virtual reality—a head-mounted display (HMD) paired with computers and input devices such as data gloves or controllers—had been in existence for decades.[17] Despite virtual reality's eventual association with forms of commercial entertainment such as video games, much of the development of this technology took place in academic and military research laboratories as well as in commercial laboratories focused on industrial applications, with projects ranging from flight and weapons simulators to scientific visualization, surgical training, and architectural walkthroughs.

16 Krueger, p. xiii.
17 See Biocca, 1992.

For instance, Ivan Sutherland, working at MIT and then the University of Utah with funding from the Advanced Research Projects Agency (ARPA) and the Office of Naval Research, developed and refined a computer-aided HMD in the late 1960s and early 1970s. Nicknamed the 'Sword of Damocles', the device employed two small cathode ray tubes (CRTs) and a series of lenses and half-silvered mirrors to project 3D computer graphics (depicting objects such as cubes and molecular models) 14 inches in front of the user, hovering within the actual environment and thus functioning more as augmented than virtual reality. The system tracked the position of the user's head and updated the visual display to correspond with its changing perspective.[18] Claiming to have been stimulated by Sutherland's writing—specifically his 1965 essay, 'The Ultimate Display', which concep-tualizes a multisensory encounter of virtual worlds—researchers at the University of North Carolina, led by Frederick Brooks, Jr., were by the late 1960s experimenting with the use of haptic feedback in conjunction with visual displays, particularly as a tool for scientific visualization.[19] Research at the U.S. Air Force, led by Tom Furness, had focused on visual displays for cockpits since 1966; in 1982, Furness and his colleagues introduced the Visually Coupled Airborne Systems Simulator (VCASS), which featured a helmet that employed miniature CRTs and mirrors to display computer-generated maps of the landscape synchronized with radar information. Later iterations, eventually under the aegis of the Super Cockpit program, included eye tracking, voice command, 3D sound, tactile gloves, and new helmets which used half-silvered mirrors to overlay graphics on the actual cockpit.[20] In the mid- to late 1980s, researchers at NASA's Ames Research Center—including Scott Fisher, who had been involved with interactive displays at MIT in the late 1970s and worked at Atari in the early 1980s—developed the Virtual Environment Display (VIVED) and then the Virtual Interface Environment Workstation (VIEW) systems. Both systems employed HMDs with stereoscopic displays and allowed for input not only through position tracking but also through gesture, thanks to the incorporation of the data glove developed by Fisher's former Atari colleague Thomas Zimmerman (who had since teamed up with Lanier, another Atari alumnus, to form the commercial firm VPL Research). The VIEW system also provided 3D sound and speech recognition.[21]

18   Rheingold, pp. 104-109.
19   Ibid., pp. 20-21, 37-43. See also Brooks, Jr. et al., 1990; Sutherland, 2001.
20   Rheingold, pp. 205-208.
21   Ibid., pp. 128, 131-154. See also Fisher, 2001.

In uniting various academic, military, and commercial projects undertaken in the preceding decades, the notion of virtual reality identified
what was taken to be an emerging form of mediated experience. Although
the term has long conjured the HMD-centred technological assemblages
described above, by the early to mid-1990s it was conceptualized more
broadly in terms of the experience of presence in mediated spaces. In
particular, it was taken to denote simulated environments that functioned
as if authentic by proffering the experience of presence. In some formula-
tions, the notion of virtual reality could also encompass the mediated
perception of temporally or spatially distant actual environments via the
concept of 'telepresence'.[22] As Jonathan Steuer argued at the time, virtual-
reality systems sought to evoke the sensation of presence in artificial or
distant spaces through a combination of sensory breadth (a multisensory
address), sensory depth (resolution), and interactivity (understood as the
user's capacity to modify the mediated environment).[23] The concept of
virtual reality thus encompassed technological configurations beyond the
'goggles and gloves' arrangement, including physical installations such as
the 'responsive environments' that Myron Krueger developed in the 1970s
and the Cave Automatic Virtual Environment (CAVE) that Daniel Sandin,
Thomas DeFanti, and Carolina Cruz-Neira created in 1991.[24] The interest in
interactive simulated environments and mediated presence was, to be sure,
bound up with developments in computing as well as cultural responses to
them, especially William Gibson's 1984 science-fiction novel *Neuromancer*,
which popularized the term 'cyberspace'. But it also drew on other recent
trends—including immersive film and video formats such as Cinerama and
Sensorama as well as practices in art and performance—which harnessed
various configurations of multisensory address, high resolution, and spectator engagement.[25]

In bringing together this range of practices through the alignment of immersion with presence, the notion of virtual reality as it was conceptualized
in the 1990s thus downplayed the significant material differences among
various technological arrangements, including the use of screens with
dramatically divergent sizes and levels of mobility. In doing so, it upheld
the emphasis on dematerialization associated with virtuality generally. In
line with my effort to parse particular immersive *dispositifs*, the analysis

22   See Steuer, 1992.
23   Ibid., pp. 81-86.
24   Krueger, pp. 12-64. See also Sandin, DeFanti, and Cruz-Neira, 2001.
25   See, for instance, Fisher, 260-261; and Krueger, 6-8.

I undertake here, by contrast, focuses on the conjunction of a particular technological arrangement and form of representation. Specifically, I examine how the visual logic associated with spectacles of airborne action—a mainstay of immersive cinema formats—operates in conjunction with contemporary virtual-reality headsets. Attending to the persistence of such spectacles across media makes it possible to chart how the small, mobile screens gracing the new headsets transform the relationship between users' bodies and their environments. Doing so thereby reveals how practices associated with the new virtual-reality screens reframe the experience of immersion.

In adopting certain imagery, contemporary commercial applications of virtual reality seem to reiterate the means by which other media have exploited and flaunted their immersive nature. Consider, for instance, the virtual-reality video game *The Climb* (Crytek, 2016), which positions the player in a series of exotic mountainous landscapes (Figure 5.2). The game has the player attempt to scale the steep edifices only to plummet upon misplacing her grip. As with a film such as *Avatar* (James Cameron, 2009), whose visual style the game recalls, *The Climb* thus harnesses a supposedly (but not actually) new immersive technology, together with digital imaging, both to plunge users into a spectacular space and to provide the visceral experience of plunging through that space.[26] In employing virtual reality to engulf players in awe-inspiring realms, *The Climb* falls in line with a range of older immersive forms, from cathedrals to panoramas.[27] In its focus on provoking the sensation of movement through such realms, it aligns itself especially closely with immersive cinema formats such as Cinéorama, Vitarama, Cinerama, 3D, and IMAX, as well as flight simulators, which have long harnessed the spectacle of aerial motion in particular to display the technologies' capacity not only seemingly to position viewers high above the earth but also to provide a visceral experience of kinesis.[28] In virtual reality, as in these cinema formats, immersive screens contribute to the experience of kinesis by provoking the visual sensation of motion despite the user's or viewer's simultaneous felt experience of bodily stasis.

Such aerial spectacles have also become a prominent component of contemporary blockbuster movies employing digital visual effects, often in conjunction with immersive exhibition formats such as 3D and IMAX. As Kristen Whissel argues, such spectacles shift emphasis away from the

26 See Ross (Miriam), 2012; Rogers, 2013, pp. 210-222.
27 See Grau, pp. 56-139; Griffiths, pp. 15-78.
28 See Belton, 1992; Huhtamo, 1995; Griffiths, pp. 79-113; Ross (Sara), 2012; Taylor, 2013.

5.2:   The virtual-reality video game *The Climb* has players ascend to vertiginous heights. *The Climb* 2016 Crytek GmbH. All rights reserved.

screen's x axis and toward its y and z axes, producing what she identifies as a 'new verticality', which exploits the capacity of visual effects to create spectacles that defy the laws of physics. In emphasizing descent and ascent within the frame—and foregrounding the pull of gravity and its defiance within the diegesis—such spectacles dramatize a range of polar oppositions relevant to global audiences and mark moments of temporal rupture and historical transition within and surrounding the films.[29] Especially insofar as many films and games being produced for virtual reality also make use of digital imaging, they are particularly closely aligned with recent films such as *Avatar* and *Gravity* (Alfonso Cuarón, 2013), which employ both immersive exhibition formats and computer-generated imagery to supply the sensation that viewers are defying gravity by flying or hovering in aerial environments alongside the characters.[30] Such works thus exemplify how the visual logic of verticality (if not necessarily its narrative function as what Whissel calls an 'effects emblem') traverses a range of forms, as she argues, aligning virtual reality with cinema, gaming, and comics.[31]

Virtual-reality headsets, however, transform the way screens collaborate with such spectacles to elicit immersion. Film formats have historically achieved their claim to immersivity by virtue of the scale—and sometimes

29   Whissel, 2014, pp. 21-58.
30   See Richmond, pp. 121-143; Whissel, 2016.
31   Whissel, 2014, p. 21.

also the curvature—of the screen, often together with the employment of high-resolution and/or three-dimensional images and surround sound systems. Not only does a large scale enable screens to function as environments but it also collaborates with other components of exhibition and representation to facilitate the perception of continuity between actual and depicted space, suggesting the extensiveness of the represented realm as well as the viewer's proximity to it.[32] Virtual-reality headsets, by contrast, push the boundaries of the screen frame beyond the viewer's field of vision not by virtue of the screen's scale but rather through its proximity to the eyes. By virtue of this arrangement, virtual-reality headsets emulate other 'peeping' devices such as stereoscopes, kinetoscopes, or—anticipating the connection to x-rays I will make later—certain early fluoroscopes.[33] Contemporary virtual-reality headsets, we might note, can incorporate either dual screens (one screen for each eye) or a single screen divided into two images (one image for each eye). As with 3D cinema, the use of stereoscopy facilitates a sense of continuity between the bodily space of the viewer and the represented imagery. Although the screens themselves do not possess the immense scale necessary to engulf viewers, virtual-reality headsets can proffer a sense of vastness and depth through the representation of environments. They do so not only by depicting the environments' extension into the distance but also by rendering their extensiveness multidirectional so that the viewer understands their reach only over time through exploration.[34]

This arrangement transforms the construction of verticality, including the portrayal of aerial spectacles, and alters the forms of experience it elicits. With cinema, verticality is conveyed representationally (with relation to the depicted world) and graphically (with relation to the frame of the screen). These two forms of verticality often coincide, as when a figure leaping from a tall building in the diegesis also moves down along the y axis in the frame. But they can also diverge, as in the shot of L.B. Jeffries (James Stewart) falling out of the eponymous aperture in *Rear Window* (Alfred Hitchcock, 1954), where the high-angle view of the falling figure exploits z axis movement. Moving-camera shots depicting the action of falling or diving can also exploit the z axis, as when the camera is mounted at the front of a plunging roller coaster in *This Is Cinerama* (Merian C. Cooper, 1952). Significantly,

32   See Rogers, 2016.
33   See Huhtamo, 2012.
34   See Susan Stewart's discussion of the gigantic as something we know 'only partially'. Stewart, p. 71.

however, in a traditional cinematic arrangement the vertical orientation of the screen itself remains steadfast in all of these cases, matching the upright orientation of the heads and bodies of seated viewers. Even when the onscreen depiction of vertical movement diverges from the vertical orientation of the screen, as with the depiction of a descent that moves along the z axis, the screen's position persists in grounding that depiction, providing it a particular situation in actual space. Such instances of disjuncture in orientation provoke the form of pleasure that Scott Richmond attributes to conflict between the viewer's visual and vestibular senses—for example, by making it look as though one is horizontal to the earth when one also feels oneself sitting upright—especially when portrayed on large screens, which allow the spectacle to fill the viewer's field of vision.[35]

Contemporary employments of virtual reality also emphasize verticality representationally, as *The Climb* exemplifies. The animated virtual-reality film *Allumette* (Eugene Chung, 2016) also takes place in an aerial environment and articulates danger and redemption in terms of descent and ascent within that space. In this case, the viewer hovers alongside the characters, capable of looking up into the sky and down into the atmospheric depths. The prospect of catastrophe emerges when a burning ship threatens to fall onto a crowd gathered below (Figure 5.3). The protagonist's mother averts that disaster, sacrificing herself in the process, by boarding the ship and steering it high into the sky, where it finally explodes, raining embers. The virtual-reality film *Take Flight* (Daniel Askill, 2015), like *The Climb*, proffers the experience of vertical motion, here through the portrayal of an ascent. In this case, the viewer's perspective begins on a city street, only to rise quickly through the skyscrapers to a space above the clouds where that perspective hovers alongside several floating celebrities.

Despite these connections, such spectacles, as they are presented through contemporary virtual-reality headsets, diverge from cinema by divorcing vertical articulation from the frame of the screen and establishing it instead in relation to the user's body as it is oriented and positioned in space. Since the screen is now affixed to the user's face and mounted on the axis of her neck, screen space can appear not only to ring her body panoramically but also to exist above and below her head. Indeed, the capacity to present mediated space above and below the user's head represents a prevalent preoccupation of the films and games produced for the new systems. While the experience is similar to having a screen on the ceiling of a small exhibition space, it is different from having a screen on the floor (as in the CAVE

35   Richmond, pp. 134-135.

5.3:   In the virtual-reality film *Allumette* (Penrose Studios, 2016), the prospect of catastrophe emerges when a burning ship threatens to fall onto a crowd gathered below.

system) since mediated space now rises to the level of the user's face, even in the place where she feels her body to be. Many virtual-reality applications portray the space below the user's head as empty, so that in looking down toward one's own body one instead sees vacant diegetic space. However, some examples, such as the virtual-reality film *Invasion!* (Eric Darnell, 2016), present animated bodies in the space below the user's neck. Others can make it seem as though the user is up to her neck in components of the setting: for example, the virtual-reality film *Dear Angelica* (Saschka

Unseld, 2017) allows the viewer's visual perspective to hover just above the surface of a represented bed so that her felt body seems buried inside the mattress, and the virtual-reality application *The Night Café* (Mac Cauley, 2015) makes it possible for the user to embed herself up to the neck in a represented bar counter.

The availability of mediated space above and below the head not only further enables represented space to surround the user but imbricates that gesture with the articulation of verticality. With *Allumette*, for instance, the looming catastrophe is only visible if the viewer looks down to below the place where she feels her body to be. *Take Flight* enables the viewer to watch the city recede in that space. And *The Climb* conveys how far the player has ascended—and how far she has to fall—by depicting the depth below her. Other virtual-reality applications emphasize verticality through the depiction of objects descending from above. Both *Invasion!* and the virtual-reality game *Trials of Tatooine* (Lucasfilm, 2016), for instance, feature spaceships that seem poised to land on top of the user. The virtual-reality film *Colosse* (Fire Panda, 2015) depicts a looming creature. Both *Invasion!* and *Colosse* alert the user to these overhead threats by having small characters run around and hide behind her, looking up in fear. Taking a cue from these characters, the user also cranes her neck and looks up in order to see the ship or creature approaching from above. In such cases, verticality is not relative to the screen nor to the user's head but rather to the remainder of her body and her experience of gravity. In other words, although the depicted ship and creature appear to move forward on the z axis relative to the user's face, their motion is perceived as a descent because it travels along the y axis relative to her torso and felt position on earth.

Underlying this shift in the articulation of verticality is a transformation in the relationship between the user's body, the screen, and represented space. With cinema, the space that appears onscreen—whether diegetic or graphic, representational or abstract, static or moving—bears a stable relationship to the screen itself. Neither movement of the screen nor the position of the viewer affects that relationship. The screen may incorporate multiple images as with split screen, and its dimensions may change as with the Magnascope system of the 1920s.[36] But even in such cases the screen continues, if dynamically, to operate as what Stephen Heath describes as both receiver and provider of the frame. As Heath puts it, the screen's alignment with the frame is 'the basis of the spatial articulations a film

36   On split screen, see Friedberg, 2006, pp. 199-206. On Magnascope, see Belton, pp. 36-38.

will make, the start of its composition'.[37] With virtual-reality headsets, screens continue to give support to images, but they no longer anchor spatial articulation. Instead, space is articulated through the mapping of orientation, position, and movement across actual and virtual realms.[38] It is this mapping itself that remains stable (if the system is functioning according to design), enabling the screen's relationship to represented space to become volatile. Hence movement of the screen, propelled by the user's movement, results in onscreen transformation. While no movement of the film screen or viewer will alter James Stewart's position in the frame in *Rear Window*, the positions of onscreen elements in *The Climb* shift as the player does—if she moves her head to look down, the screen image shifts accordingly to provide a vertiginous, high-angle view.

In permitting and emphasizing the correspondence of such movements, films and games produced for virtual reality alter the relationship between represented and actual space. The works I have discussed map the orientation, position, and movement of the user's head onto the orientation, position, and movement of the visual perspective supplied by a virtual camera. As with the earlier use of HMDs such as Sutherland's 'Sword of Damocles', the new systems achieve this mapping through a process that involves tracking the user within actual space and updating the image display accordingly. Oculus Rift headsets, for instance, contain motion and position sensors (gyroscopes, accelerometers, and magnetometers) that work together to track the orientation of the user's head. The headsets also contain infrared LEDs that function in connection with external infrared cameras to track the user's position in space. Dynamic information on the orientation and position of the headset in actual space is, in turn, employed to orient, position, and move the field of view within a virtual environment.[39] Despite the fact that represented space has been untethered from the screen, it has not become unmoored. The employment of tracking systems—which measure movement not only in relation to the user's previous orientation and position but also in relation to external forces (e.g., gravity) and reference points (e.g., the infrared camera)—ties representation even more firmly to actual space.[40]

37   Heath, p. 393.

38   On the significance of such mapping for the development and operation of virtual-reality technologies, see Biocca, p. 27, pp. 49-56; Steuer, pp. 86-87.

39   See the discussion of Oculus's tracking system in its outline of best practices for developers, online at https://developer.oculus.com/design/latest/concepts/bp_app_tracking (accessed June 5, 2017).

40   Stanković, pp. 92-97.

In response to the notion that virtual reality enables users to escape their bodies, scholars have long emphasized how it activates and indeed relies upon users' bodies.[41] Although my observations about the exploitation of verticality support that argument, they also make a further point. Far from tools for dematerialization, these applications of virtual reality rematerialize representation by anchoring it not only to users' bodies as they interact with virtual environments but also to the users' physical environment.[42] Through the use of tracking systems, onscreen representation is made to index the orientation and position of the user's body in actual space. The user's experience of represented space is also tied to actual space, especially in the exploitation of verticality, since it relies on her capacity to gauge up and down proprioceptively, a capacity that is anchored to the earth in part through the way gravity acts on the musculature and inner ear.[43] When an upright viewer sees James Stewart fall in *Rear Window*, his movement along the z axis conflicts with her own bodily experience of space, but with *Allumette* the act of looking down to see the threatened townspeople is grounded in the user's bodily position and experience.

As applied to illusionistic media such as virtual reality, immersion is often described as the experience of being 'in the picture'.[44] This experience is frequently conceptualized as a movement into another space. For instance, Mel Slater and Sylvia Wilbur contend that the 'grand aim of immersive virtual environments research is to be able to realize that same "stepping through the glass" or "rolling down the window" with respect to computer-generated environments as can be experienced when stepping through a barrier that in normal circumstances screens some aspect of reality from us.[45] Other conceptualizations of immersion—especially those addressing the multiple-screen displays associated with expanded cinema, video art, and the historical avant-garde—describe screens as components of an architecture that surrounds the viewer, allowing screen space to shape actual space.[46] The contemporary applications of virtual reality that I have discussed, however, neither evoke the experience of movement into differ-ent spaces nor operate as architectures forming new spaces. Rather, they

41   Huhtamo, 1995, pp. 176-177; Hansen, 2004, pp. 161-196. For a more recent discussion, see Popat, 2016.
42   For an argument about the imbrications of body and environment in virtual reality, focusing on the body's relation to virtual environments, see Hansen, 2001.
43   Richmond, pp. 6-9, 134-135.
44   Grau, p. 141. Also see, for instance, Belton, p. 98; Lelyveld, p. 78.
45   Slater and Wilbur, p. 604.
46   See, for instance, Marchessault, p. 39.

immerse users in a familiar, worldly space imbricated with representation. This formulation may recall descriptions of 'cyberspace' as an immaterial realm that substitutes for the material world, but I am suggesting something different. These applications of virtual reality spectacularize the forms of connection and tracking that enable the user's felt experience of the world to drive representation. In doing so, they are exposing phenomena (forms of connection and tracking) that constantly surround us but often remain invisible. Far from displacing the material world, these uses of virtual reality, in short, penetrate its surface.

Penetrating screens

Against the tendency to contrast illusionistic and non-illusionistic screen practices, this formulation of immersion aligns the experiences provided by contemporary applications of virtual reality with those associated with the proliferation of screens more broadly. As Francesco Casetti has argued, contemporary proliferating screens function as 'junctions of a complex circuit, characterized both by a continuous flow and by localized processes of configuration or reconfiguration of circulating images'.[47] As a result, we find ourselves immersed, as he contends, within the circulation of information.[48] As our interfaces to technological, social, political, and economic networks, screens operate as interlinked nodes in constantly changing formations. Although the screens themselves may be small, these formations are so boundless and complex that they bear comparison to the sublime.[49] In this context, our proximity to a range of screens (especially those we wear or hold in our hands), in conjunction with the sheer scale of the networks to which they connect us, provokes experiences of immersion. Like other spaces of immersion—such as the panoramas of the nineteenth century and the multiscreen displays of the twentieth—the networks of the twenty-first century, as many have argued, are not only sites of apparent agency but also, increasingly and pervasively, means of control and capture.[50]

At roughly the same time as the resurgence of virtual reality, there has also been a swell of interest in practices that exploit the proliferation of screens by encouraging simultaneous engagement with multiple screens. Some of these

47   Casetti, p. 156.
48   Ibid., p. 170.
49   For a discussion of this comparison, see Jagoda, pp. 20-21.
50   For a gloss on these ideas, see Galloway, 2010.

map the screens' relationships to actual space and to one another, as with *KL Dartboard* and *Darts* for iPad and iPhone (2010), which enabled players to launch virtual projectiles from phone to tablet.[51] With others, screens' relationship to one another is more informational than explicitly spatial, as with 'second-screen' applications tied to television broadcasts.[52] Such multi-screen practices, like the virtual-reality practices I have discussed, manifest the screen's relation to other devices (e.g., through network connections) and to physical space (e.g., through the use of sensors and location tracking). In doing so, they also make visible the often hidden but nevertheless constant connections among our devices as well as the often hidden but materially and geographically situated infrastructures supporting them.[53] Multiscreen practices reveal such connections and infrastructures by materializing particular, though fleeting, configurations, thus providing users a (small) point of access to the vast and dynamic networks that pervade our environment yet, as Patrick Jagoda puts it, remain 'accessible only at the edge of our sensibilities'.[54]

In making such hidden connections and structures visible, these screens do not function as apertures, thresholds, or components of architecture but rather as a means of penetration. In this regard, they are aligned less closely with objects such as windows, doors, or walls than with devices such as probes, x-rays, and scanners.[55] Upon their discovery at the end of the nineteenth century, x-rays presented the possibility of rendering the invisible visible by penetrating the body and revealing the skeleton, offering a form of 'penetrating vision' that was considered both macabre and erotic.[56] In the second decade of the twenty-first century, a different kind of penetrating vision is revealing a different kind of skeleton. In this case, however, our bodies do not contain that framework; rather, it contains us. Whereas x-rays provided a means of plunging into the body, the new screens uncover structures underpinning a space in which we already find ourselves immersed.

This conceptualization of contemporary screen practices suggests a genealogy of immersive screens, supplementing those that trace concepts such as illusion and presence, tied instead to the notion of penetration. The idea of penetration highlights the way in which immersion arises in

51   See Levin, 2014.

52   See Holt and Sanson, 2014.

53   See Chun and Friedland, 2015; Starosielski, 2015.

54   Jagoda, p. 3.

55   Thomas Elsaesser has similarly argued that attention to imaging practices (especially 3D) in realms such as the military frames contemporary imaging technologies as 'technologies of probing and penetration'. Elsaesser, p. 242.

56   Cartwright, p. 111; Tsivian, p. 82.

and through the act of plunging, an act that entails not only entry into an environment but also the formation of an environment as such. An attunement to the idea of penetration, for one thing, re-centres the close historical proximity between the film screen and the x-ray screen at the time of their mutual emergence, highlighting their shared application to the transgression and reconfiguration of spaces. (Although the term 'x-ray' often conjures photographically fixed images, Wilhelm Conrad Röntgen's initial x-ray apparatus of 1895 employed a screen, as did the fluoroscopes that Thomas Edison and others had developed by 1896.)[57] Indeed, cinema was what Tom Gunning has described as a 'sister technology' of the x-ray, presented in its earliest years as a similar kind of technological wonder.[58] And, as scholars such as Lisa Cartwright and Yuri Tsivian have shown, the forms of visuality proffered by x-rays and cinema were intertwined, especially via what Tsivian identifies as a shared investment in the principle of penetrating vision.[59] In proffering entry into the bodily interior, x-rays crossed the boundary marked by the skin and, concomitantly, reconfigured the relationship between the interior and exterior. Insofar as this form of penetrating vision offered access to invisible realities and conjured spatial reorganizations via transparency, it was, like the new mode of vision offered by cinema, as several scholars have argued, bound up with the spatial reconfigurations associated with modernism and modernity more broadly.[60]

The concept of penetration, moreover, reveals how the spatial transgressions that screens achieve have themselves taken up and reconfigured other practices. Perhaps most notably, an investment in penetrating vision also characterized the form of medical perception that, as Michel Foucault contends, emerged around the turn of the nineteenth century in conjunction with the embrace of practices such as dissection.[61] In this context, the use of the scalpel contributed to what Foucault describes as the emergence of a modern conception of the bodily interior as a perceptible space: as a means of penetrating into the depth of the body, the scalpel, as he puts it, rediscovered 'organic space'.[62] Insofar as x-rays also permitted penetration of the body and inspection of the interior, they thus took over medical functions that were previously associated primarily with cutting

57   Glasser, pp. 3-5, 233-243; Curtis, p. 239.
58   Gunning, 1994, p. 196; Gunning, 1990, p. 58.
59   Tsivian, p. 82. Also see Cartwright, pp. 107-142.
60   See Henderson, 1988; Gunning, 1997.
61   See Foucault, 1994.
62   Foucault, p. 141.

it open.[63] Walter Benjamin famously described cinema's achievement of spatial reconfiguration with reference to a similar form of penetration through incision. Likening the camera operator to a surgeon, he argued that the 'cinematographer penetrates deeply into [the] tissue' of reality in order to assemble its parts anew.[64] Mapping these connections allows us to recognize the ways in which the screen itself has also operated as a tool not only for visualization but also for cutting, akin not only to medical imaging technologies but also to more long-standing means of bodily penetration, especially the scalpel. Indeed, like the scalpel, as well as the editor's splicer, both the surface and the frame of the screen at once sever spatial entities and create new spatial junctions.[65]

In connection with virtual reality's medical applications, HMDs were, early on, conceived—perhaps only half-jokingly—as 'x-ray glasses'.[66] This association frames certain HMD screens not only as technologies of vision but also as a means of peeling back the surface of the body and entering its interior. As I have argued, many contemporary screen practices, from the new virtual-reality systems to smartphones more generally, conduct a similar operation on the space of everyday experience. While the scalpel and the x-ray simultaneously plumbed and constructed bodily space as a penetrable depth, these new screen practices both expose and actualize the expansiveness of the mediated space surrounding us.

Works Cited

Acland, Charles R. 'The Crack in the Electric Window.' *Cinema Journal* 51, no. 2 (Winter 2012): 167-171.

Belton, John. *Widescreen Cinema*. Cambridge, MA: Harvard University Press, 1992.

Benjamin, Walter. 'The Work of Art in the Age of Its Technological Reproducibility,' Second Version. In *Selected Writings*, edited by Michael W. Jennings et al., translated by Rodney Livingstone, Edmund Jephcott, Howard Eiland, et al., 4 vols., 3:19-55. Cambridge, MA: Harvard University Press, 1996-2003.

63   Van Dijck, p. 4. Also see Cartwright's discussion of medical transillumination practices employing endoscopic devices. Cartwright, p. 113.

64   Benjamin, III, p. 35.

65   Also see Friedberg's contention that the screen frame marks an 'ontological cut' between 'the material surface of the wall and the view contained within the frame's aperture'. Friedberg, 2006, p. 157.

66   Rheingold, pp. 22, 33.

Biocca, Frank. 'Virtual Reality: A Tutorial.' *Journal of Communication* 42, no. 4 (Fall 1992): 23-72.

Brooks, Jr., Frederick P. et al. 'Project GROPE—Haptic Displays for Scientific Visualization.' *Computer Graphics* 24, no. 4 (August 1990): 177-185.

Bruno, Giuliana. *Surface: Matters of Aesthetics, Materiality, and Media*. Chicago: University of Chicago Press, 2014.

Cartwright, Lisa. *Screening the Body: Tracing Medicine's Visual Culture*. Minneapolis: University of Minnesota Press, 1995.

Casetti, Francesco. *The Lumière Galaxy: Seven Key Words for the Cinema to Come*. New York: Columbia University Press, 2015.

Chun, Wendy Hui Kyong and Sarah Friedland. 'Habits of Leaking: Of Sluts and Network Cards.' *differences* 26, no. 2 (2015): 1-28.

Colomina, Beatriz. 'Enclosed by Images: The Eameses' Multimedia Architecture.' *Grey Room* 02 (Winter 2001): 6-29.

Curtis, Scott. 'Still/Moving: Digital Imaging and Medical Hermeneutics.' In *Memory Bytes: History, Technology, and Digital Culture*, edited by Lauren Rabinovitz and Abraham Geil, pp. 218-254. Durham, NC: Duke University Press, 2004.

Doane, Mary Ann. 'The Close-Up: Scale and Detail in the Cinema.' *differences* 14, no. 3 (2003): 89-111.

Elsaesser, Thomas. 'The "Return" of 3-D: On Some of the Logics and Genealogies of the Image in the Twenty-First Century.' *Critical Inquiry* 39, no. 2 (Winter 2013): 217-246.

Fisher, Scott. 'Virtual Interface Environments.' In *Multimedia: From Wagner to Virtual Reality*, edited by Packer and Jordan, pp. 257-266. New York: Norton, 2001.

Foucault, Michel. *The Birth of the Clinic: An Archaeology of Medical Perception*. Translated by A.M. Sheridan Smith. New York: Vintage Books, 1994.

Friedberg, Anne. *Window Shopping: Cinema and the Postmodern*. Berkeley: University of California Press, 1993.

———. *The Virtual Window: From Alberti to Microsoft*. Cambridge, MA: MIT Press, 2006.

Galloway, Alexander R. 'Networks.' In *Critical Terms for Media Studies*, edited by W.J.T. Mitchell and Mark B.N. Hansen, pp. 280-296. Chicago: University of Chicago Press, 2010.

Glasser, Otto. *Wilhelm Conrad Röntgen and The Early History of the Roentgen Rays*. Springfield, IL: Charles C. Thomas, 1934.

Grau, Oliver. *Virtual Art: From Illusion to Immersion*. Cambridge, MA: MIT Press, 2003.

Griffiths, Alison. *Shivers Down Your Spine: Cinema, Museums, & the Immersive View*. New York: Columbia University Press, 2008.

Gunning, Tom. 'The Cinema of Attractions: Early Film, Its Spectator and the Avant-Garde.' In *Early Cinema: Space Frame Narrative*, edited by Thomas Elsaesser with Adam Barker, pp. 56-62. London: BFI, 1990.

——. 'The Whole Town's Gawking: Early Cinema and the Visual Experience of Modernity.' *Yale Journal of Criticism* 7, no. 2 (1994): 189-201.

——. 'From the Kaleidoscope to the X-Ray: Urban Spectatorship, Poe, Benjamin, and *Traffic in Souls* (1913).' *Wide Angle* 19, no. 4 (Oct. 1997): 25-61.

Hansen, Mark B.N. 'Embodying Virtual Reality: Touch and Self-Movement in the Work of Char Davies.' *Critical Matrix* 12, no. 1-2 (2001): 112-147.

——. *New Philosophy for New Media*. Cambridge, MA: MIT Press, 2004.

Heath, Stephen. 'Narrative Space.' In *Narrative, Apparatus, Ideology: A Film Theory Reader,* edited by Philip Rosen, pp. 379-420. New York: Columbia University Press, 1986.

Henderson, Linda Dalrymple. 'X Rays and the Quest for Invisible Reality in the Art of Kupka, Duchamp, and the Cubists.' *Art Journal* 47 (Winter 1988): 323-340.

Hillis, Ken. *Digital Sensations: Space, Identity, and Embodiment in Virtual Reality*. Minneapolis: University of Minnesota Press, 1999.

Holt, Jennifer and Kevin Sanson, eds. *Connected Viewing: Selling, Streaming, & Sharing Media in the Digital Era*. New York: Routledge, 2014.

Huhtamo, Erkki. 'Encapsulated Bodies in Motion: Simulators and the Quest for Total Immersion.' In *Critical Issues in Electronic Media*, edited by Simon Penny, pp. 159-186. Albany: State University of New York Press, 1995.

——. 'Elements of Screenology: Toward an Archaeology of the Screen.' *Iconics* 7 (2004): 31-82.

——. 'Toward a History of Peep Practice.' In *A Companion to Early Cinema,* edited by André Gaudreault, Nicolas Dulac, and Santiago Hidalgo, pp. 32-51. Malden, MA: John Wiley & Sons, 2012.

Jagoda, Patrick. *Network Aesthetics*. Chicago: University of Chicago Press, 2016.

Krueger, Myron W. *Artificial Reality*. Second edition. Reading, MA: Addison-Wesley, 1991.

Lelyveld, Philip. 'Virtual Reality Primer with an Emphasis on Camera-Captured VR.' *SMPTE Motion Imagining Journal* 124, no. 6 (Sept. 2015): 78-85.

Levin, Michal. *Designing Multi-Device Experiences: An Ecosystem Approach to User Experiences Across Devices*. Sebastopol, CA: O'Reilly Media, 2014.

Manovich, Lev. *The Language of New Media*. Cambridge, MA: MIT Press, 2001.

Marchessault, Janine. 'Multi-Screens and Future Cinema: The Labyrinth Project at Expo 67.' In *Fluid Screens, Expanded Cinema*, edited by Janine Marchessault and Susan Lord, pp. 29-51. Toronto: University of Toronto Press, 2007.

—— and Susan Lord, eds. *Fluid Screens, Expanded Cinema*. Toronto: University of Toronto Press, 2007.

Morse, Margaret. *Virtualities: Television, Media Art, and Cyberculture*. Bloomington, IN: Indiana University Press, 1998.

Murray, Janet H. *Hamlet on the Holodeck: The Future of Narrative in Cyberspace.* Cambridge, MA: MIT Press, 1997.

Oxford English Dictionary Online. 'immersion, n.', 'immerse, v.' http://www.oed.com. Accessed 4 June 2017.

——. 'screen, n.', 'screen, v'. http://www.oed.com. Accessed 4 June 2017.

Packer, Randall and Ken Jordan, eds. *Multimedia: From Wagner to Virtual Reality.* New York: W.W. Norton & Company, 2001.

Popat, Sita. 'Missing in Action: Embodied Experience and Virtual Reality.' *Theatre Journal* 68, no. 3 (September 2016): 357-378.

Rheingold, Howard. *Virtual Reality.* New York: Simon & Schuster, 1991.

Richmond, Scott C. *Cinema's Bodily Illusions: Flying, Floating, and Hallucinating.* Minneapolis: University of Minnesota Press, 2016.

Roettgers, Janko. 'Taking the Plunge.' *Variety*, 22 March 2016.

Rogers, Ariel. *Cinematic Appeals: The Experience of New Movie Technologies.* New York: Columbia University Press, 2013.

——. 'Scaling Down: Cinerama on Blu-ray.' In *Screens*, edited by Dominique Chateau and José Moure, pp. 82-96. Amsterdam: Amsterdam University Press, 2016.

Rose, Frank. 'Movies of the Future.' *The New York Times*, 13 June 2013, SR5.

Rosen, Philip. *Change Mummified: Cinema, Historicity, Theory.* Minneapolis: University of Minnesota Press, 2001.

Ross, Miriam. 'The 3-D Aesthetic: *Avatar* and Hyperhaptic Visuality.' *Screen* 53, no. 4 (Winter 2012): 381-397.

Ross, Sara. 'Invitation to the Voyage: The Flight Sequence in Contemporary 3D Cinema.' *Film History* 24 (2012): 210-220.

Sandin, Daniel, Thomas DeFanti, and Carolina Cruz-Neira. 'A Room with a View.' In *Multimedia: From Wagner to Virtual Reality*, edited by Packer and Jordan, pp. 286-292. New York: Norton, 2001.

Slater, Mel and Sylvia Wilbur. 'A Framework for Immersive Virtual Environments (FIVE): Speculations on the Role of Presence in Virtual Environments.' *Presence* 6, no. 6 (December 1997): 603-616.

Sobchack, Vivian. *The Address of the Eye: A Phenomenology of Film Experience.* Princeton: Princeton University Press, 1992.

Spigel, Lynn. 'Object Lessons for the Media Home: From Storagewall to Invisible Design.' *Public Culture* 24, no. 3 (2012): 535-576.

Stanković, Stanislav. *Virtual Reality and Virtual Environments in 10 Lectures.* Williston, VT: Morgan & Claypool, 2016.

Starosielski, Nicole. *The Undersea Network.* Durham, NC: Duke University Press, 2015.

Sterne, Jonathan. *MP3: The Meaning of a Format.* Durham, NC: Duke University Press, 2012.

Steuer, Jonathan. 'Defining Virtual Reality: Dimensions Determining Telepresence.' *Journal of Communication* 42, no. 4 (Fall 1992): 73-93.

Stewart, Susan. *On Longing: Narratives of the Miniature, the Gigantic, the Souvenir, the Collection.* Durham, NC: Duke University Press, 1993.

Straw, Will. 'Proliferating Screens.' *Screen* 41, no. 1 (Spring 2000): 115-119.

Suellentrop, Chris. 'Virtual Reality Is Here. Can We Play With It?' *The New York Times*, 24 March 2014, C1.

Sutherland, Ivan. 'The Ultimate Display.' In *Multimedia: From Wagner to Virtual Reality*, edited by Packer and Jordan, pp. 252-256. New York: Norton, 2001.

Taylor, Giles. 'A Military Use for Widescreen Cinema: Training the Body through Immersive Media.' *The Velvet Light Trap* 72 (Fall 2013): 17-32.

Tsivian, Yuri. 'Media Fantasies and Penetrating Vision: Some Links Between X-Rays, the Microscope, and Film.' In *Laboratory of Dreams: The Russian Avant-Garde and Cultural Experiment*, edited by John E. Bowlt and Olga Matich, pp. 81-99. Palo Alto: Stanford University Press, 1996.

Turner, Fred. *The Democratic Surround: Multimedia & American Liberalism from World War II to the Psychedelic Sixties.* Chicago: University of Chicago Press, 2013.

Van Dijck, José. *The Transparent Body: A Cultural Analysis of Medical Imaging.* Seattle: University of Washington Press, 2005.

Verhoeff, Nanna. *Mobile Screens: The Visual Regime of Navigation.* Amsterdam: Amsterdam University Press, 2012.

Wasson, Haidee. 'The Networked Screen: Moving Images, Materiality, and the Aesthetics of Size.' In *Fluid Screens, Expanded Cinema*, edited by Janine Marchessault and Susan Lord, pp. 74-95. Toronto: University of Toronto Press, 2007.

Whissel, Kristen. *Spectacular Digital Effects: CGI and Contemporary Cinema.* Durham, NC: Duke University Press, 2014.

———. 'Parallax Effects: Epistemology, Affect and Digital 3D Cinema.' *Journal of Visual Culture* 15, no. 2 (2016): 233-249.

About the Author

Ariel Rogers is assistant professor in the Department of Radio/Television/Film at Northwestern University. She is the author of *Cinematic Appeals: The Experience of New Movie Technologies* (2013) as well as articles on widescreen cinema, digital cinema, and special effects in classical Hollywood. Her research interests also include spectatorship, new media, melodrama, and women in film. She has taught media and film studies at the University of Southern Maine and The New School and was a Mellon Postdoctoral Fellow in Cinema Studies at Colby College.

6.   The Atmospheric Screen: Turner, Hazlitt, Ruskin

Antonio Somaini

Abstract

Antonio Somaini questions the veils, mists, and fogs that appear in the late works of J.M.W Turner, suggesting that here the canvas gains the status of an 'atmospheric screen'. Drawing on the etymology of the term 'medium', Somaini probes the re-emergence in the nineteenth century of an environmental media concept in relation to the rediscovery of the environmental nature of the screen. Their parallel genealogies, he suggests, intersect in Romantic landscape painting as well as in German *Naturphilosophie* and Romantic Literature, each of which might be situated within a line of descent running from Aristotle's notions of *metaxy* to mediaeval theories of *media diaphana*. The controversies over Turner's canvases, exemplified by the debate between Ruskin and Hazlitt, are a potent reminder of the unsettled status of the atmosphere at a moment when the optical conception of the screen was not yet dominant.

Keywords: Romanticism, Painting, Medium, Atmosphere, Landscape

In his 'Notes on a Genealogy of the Excessive Screen'—the text that introduced Yale's Mellon Sawyer Seminar, *Genealogies of the Excessive Screen*, from which the essays in this volume originate—Francesco Casetti presents the history of screens and of the very term 'screen' as the intertwining of two different traditions. On the one hand there is a tradition, beginning in the early nineteenth century, that considers the screen to be first and foremost an *optical* device: a material surface onto which an image is projected or from which an image emanates. On the other hand, there is an older tradition within which the term 'screen' suggests a number of *spatial* entities producing some kind of division in the physical environment. Casetti writes:

Buckley, C., R. Campe, F. Casetti (eds.), *Screen Genealogies. From Optical Device to Environmental Medium.* Amsterdam: Amsterdam University Press, 2019
DOI 10.5117/9789463729000_CH06

Screens are not only optical devices. Since the 15th century the English word *screen*, as well as the French *écran*, the Italian *schermo*, the German *Schirm*, have denoted objects that perform functions other than supporting a projected representation. A screen was a contrivance for warding off the heat of a fire or a draft of air, a partition of wood or stone dividing a room or a building into parts, a wall thrown out in front of a building to mask the façade, a tactical deployment of soldiers to conceal the movement of an army, an apparatus used in the sifting of grain and coal. It was a filter, a divide, a shelter, a camouflage. These functions underscored not so much the optical qualities of a screen but rather its environmental character—its nature as a prop to be used within and towards a space.[1]

If analyzed from an archaeological perspective—one that studies the present from the vantage point of the past and the past from the vantage point of the present, recognizing the fact that our historical reconstructions are often the result of some kind of 'retroactive causality'—then the transformations that screens are currently undergoing may be interpreted in relation to the intertwining of the two different traditions highlighted by Casetti.[2] The fact that the ubiquitous screens of our computers, tablets, and smartphones are at the same time both *optical* displays and highly networked digital devices (which perform crucial *spatial* and *environmental* operations in terms of mapping, orientation, geolocalization, and even concealment) invites us to rediscover the older spatial and environmental meanings of the term 'screen'. As Casetti writes: 'Screens have become again filters, shelters, divides, and camouflage. They remain surfaces that display images and data, and yet their opticality is deeply rooted in their spatial and environmental conditions.'[3]

A similar dynamic, I would like to argue, may be detected if we turn from the history of the term 'screen' to that of another term that is firmly connected to it: the term 'medium'. An archaeological approach to the history of the medium as a concept—a *medium archaeology* that tries to understand what media are becoming today by exploring the multiple

1   Casetti, 2017. In a footnote of his text published in this volume (Casetti's footnote n.23), Casetti suggests that the first occurrence of the optical meaning of the English term 'screen' can probably be found in two notices referring to the patent granted on 26 January 1802 to Paul De Philipsthal, which is probably the English name used by Paul Philidor, a magician and pioneer of the Phantasmagoria shows.
2   On media archaeology and the idea of 'retroactive causality', see Elsaesser, pp. 71-100, in particular pp. 80-86.
3   Ibid.

meanings that have been associated with the term 'medium' in the past—comes to conclusions similar to Casetti's. If the spatial and environmental functions performed by contemporary, digitally networked screens invite us to rediscover a past in which screens were considered to be 'filters, shelters, divides, and camouflage', then the current interest in the *environmental* and *ecological* dimensions of media—in the ever-deeper intertwinings of nature and communication technologies and in how contemporary media serve as infrastructural environments that reorganize the human sensorium—invites us to re-explore the *longue durée* of a tradition in which the term 'medium' did not indicate, yet, a series of technical means of (mass) communication but rather the environment, the *milieu*, or the *Umwelt* in which sensory experience takes place. This tradition was recently highlighted by John Durham Peters in *The Marvellous Clouds: Towards a Philosophy of Elemental Media*. As he writes, 'the concept of media [...] was connected to nature long before it was connected to technology [...]. Medium has always meant an element, an environment, a vehicle in the middle of things'.[4] If we want to understand the spatial, environmental dimension of contemporary media, Peters writes, we need to revisit 'the older, environmental meaning of medium' and the 'elemental legacy of the media concept'.[5]

If we accept both Casetti and Peters's suggestions—that both screens and media are currently undergoing a series of transformations that can be better understood if we rediscover their older spatial and environmental dimensions—we may ask ourselves when and how the history of the 'screen' and that of the 'medium' intersected one another, and what was the result of such intersections. Several historical periods and several constellations of discourses and practices could be studied in this perspective. For example, in the 1920s and 1930s, László Moholy-Nagy used the term 'medium' to refer to the environmentally diffused element of light, imagining a future in which an art conceived as a form of 'light configuration' (*Lichtgestaltung*) could completely transform the cinematic *dispositif* by projecting 'light plays' (*Lichtspiele*) onto clouds and other 'gaseous formations' rather than onto the traditional flat, bidimensional screen.[6] Or, in the 1960s and 1970s,

4　Peters, p. 46.
5　Ibid., pp. 3-4.
6　See Moholy-Nagy, 1923; Moholy-Nagy, 1936, p. 40. See also the way in which Moholy-Nagy, in his *von material zu architektur* (German edition 1929, published in 1938 in English in a revised version as *The New Vision*), presents his camera-less *Fotogrammen* as a technique in which 'the surface becomes a part of the atmosphere [*atmosfäre*], of the atmospheric background, in that it sucks up the light phenomena produced outside itself'. Moholy-Nagy, 2001, p. 90; Moholy-Nagy, 1975, p. 86.

Marshall McLuhan insisted that media be understood as 'environments', while a number of artistic practices within the field of so-called 'expanded cinema' explored the screen in its spatial, environmental, and atmospheric dimension.[7] Among the many examples one might refer to is Joan Brigham and Stan VanDerBeek's *Steam Screens* (1979), a performance in which film images were projected onto clouds of steam in the sculpture garden of the Whitney Museum of American Art in New York.

Rather than focusing on two foundational periods in the history of media theory, such as the 1920s-1930s and the 1960s-1970s, this essay will take a step back in time and consider the case of an earlier intersection between screen and medium. This earlier intersection can be found during the first decades of the nineteenth century within the context of British Romanticism, when critics and essayists such as William Hazlitt and John Ruskin reflected on the representation of atmospheric elements in the work of Joseph Mallord William Turner, while Turner himself revolutionized the tradition of landscape painting. It is in this period that we find some of the most interesting occurrences of the idea of the medium as a sensible, atmospheric environment, one that is characterized by the presence of natural screening and veiling entities such as clouds, fog, and mist. And it is in this same period, in the late paintings of Turner, that the canvas—rather than being treated as a flat, opaque surface or as an open, transparent window—becomes something different: an *atmospheric screen* capable of capturing and visualizing the turbulent fusion of the atmospheric elements and of leading the spectator right in the midst of it, abolishing any clear-cut separation between seer and seen and becoming itself, one might say, a part of the atmosphere.

'The medium through which they are seen'

In order to investigate the intersection between the ideas of screen and medium taking place during the early nineteenth century in England, we may take as a starting point a passage from an essay by William Hazlitt entitled 'On Imitation': a text published in 1817 in the second volume of *The Round Table: A Collection of Essays on Literature, Men, and Manners*.[8] In it, Hazlitt tries to respond to the old question of why 'objects in themselves disagreeable or indifferent, often please in the imitation'.[9] 'One chief reason

---

7   See McLuhan, 1997; Youngblood, 1970.
8   Hazlitt, 1817.
9   Ibid., p. 11.

[...] why imitation pleases', writes Hazlitt, 'is because, by exciting curiosity, and inviting a comparison between the object and the representation, it opens a new field of inquiry, and leads the attention to a variety of details and distinctions not perceived before'.[10] Drawing a parallel between *scientific* and *artistic* visual representations, Hazlitt sees in imitation a form of *knowledge* based on the capacity of capturing a series of 'details' and 'distinctions in nature' that are not accessible to any kind of unmediated perception.[11] This is true also of objects that are at first displeasing: 'Imitation renders an object displeasing in itself a source of pleasure, not by repetition of the same idea, but by suggesting new ideas, by detecting new properties, and endless shades of difference.'[12]

In the second half of his essay, Hazlitt highlights the excesses to which this idea of imitation may lead. Too much attention to the reproduction of details, distinctions, and 'shades of difference' may produce a form of 'picturesque' in which the pictorial representation becomes an end in itself.[13] Instead of promoting 'a more intense perception of truth' based on 'the powers of observation and comparison', artistic imitation may turn into 'pedantry and affectation', into an excessive attention to academic skills and technical execution that only artists can appreciate.[14] It is this kind of 'excess' that Hazlitt finds in the paintings of Turner.[15] In a passage often quoted in the literature on the painter:

> We here allude particularly to Turner, the ablest landscape painter now living, whose pictures are, however, too much abstractions of aerial perspective, and representations not so properly of the objects of nature as of the medium through which they are seen. They are the triumph of the knowledge of the artist, and of the power of the pencil over the barrenness of the subject. They are pictures of the elements of air, earth, and water. The artist delights to go back to the first chaos of the world, or to that state of things when the waters were separated from the dry land, and light from darkness, but as yet no living thing nor tree bearing fruit was seen upon the face of the earth. All is 'without form and void'. Some one said of his landscapes that they were *pictures of nothing, and very like*.[16]

10   Ibid., pp. 11-12.
11   Ibid., pp. 12-13.
12   Ibid., p. 13.
13   Ibid., p. 15.
14   Ibid., pp. 16, 18.
15   Ibid., p. 19.
16   Ibid., pp. 19-20.

'Pictures of nothing.' This is the title that—according to Pierre Wat in his book *Turner, menteur magnifique*—the art historian Lawrence Gowing wanted to give to the exhibition of Turner's paintings that he organized in 1966 at the Museum of Modern Art in New York.[17] The title that was finally chosen was *Turner: Imagination and Reality*, but the initial idea of a *painter of nothingness* was preserved.[18] Focusing on the (often unfinished) paintings and watercolours produced during the last two decades of his life, Gowing's exhibition promoted the vision of a Turner who, with his unique 'absorption in the intrinsic character of paint', could be considered to be a precursor of modernist abstraction. According to Gowing, in Turner's paintings 'no single touch of paint corresponded to any specific object', producing as a result the impression of an 'endless continuum' and of a 'return to a primal flux which denies the separate identity of things'.[19]

In 1961, just a few years before Gowing's exhibition, the art historian Robert Rosenblum formulated the idea of Turner as the precursor of modern abstract painting in an article published in *Art News* with the title 'The Abstract Sublime' and later developed into the 1975 book *Modern Painting and the Northern Romantic Tradition: Friedrich to Rothko*.[20] According to Rosenblum, one could trace a direct genealogical line leading from the Romantic land-scapes of Caspar David Friedrich and Joseph Mallord William Turner to the abstract expressionism of Clyfford Still, Mark Rothko, Jackson Pollock, and Barnett Newman. Linking these artists together was, according to Rosenblum, a common search for the sublime, running from the 'Romantic Sublime' of Friedrich and Turner to the 'Abstract Sublime' that could be found in paintings such as Rothko's *Light Earth over Blue* (1954), with its 'infinite, glowing voids'.[21] The reference to the Book of Genesis that we find in Hazlitt's passage—'The artist delights to go back to the first chaos of the world, or to that state of things when the waters were separated from the dry land, and light from darkness, but as yet no living thing nor tree bearing fruit was seen upon the face of the earth. All is *without form and void*'—returns in Rosenblum's text. He sees in the work of Newman, Still, Rothko, and Pollock 'a post-World-War-II myth of Genesis' animated not so much by Romantic 'pantheism' but rather by a new, modernist '*paint-theism*': a belief in the possibility of conveying 'supernatural experiences [...] through the medium of paint alone'.[22]

17   Wat, p. 109.
18   Gowing, 1966. For a reference to the title Gowing had initially chosen, see Wat, p. 109.
19   Goring, pp. 43, 13, 38, 16.
20   Rosenblum, 1961; Rosenblum, 1977.
21   Rosenblum, 1961.
22   Ibid.

In recent years, another phrase extracted from Hazlitt's passage has become a focus of the literature on Turner: 'pictures of the elements of air, earth, and water'. The exhibition *Turner and the Elements*, curated in 2011-2012 by Inés Richter-Musso and Ostrud Westheider, focused precisely on the way in which Turner represents the four classical elements of air, water, earth and fire.[23] As Richter-Musso reminds us in her essay in the catalogue, Hazlitt's claim that Turner's paintings are 'pictures of the elements of air, earth, and water' probably referred to two oil paintings previously exhibited at the Royal Academy: *Fall of an Avalanche in the Grisons* (exhibited in 1810) and *Snow Storm: Hannibal and his Army Crossing the Alps* (exhibited in 1812). (Figure 6.1) Both depict scenes in which nature suddenly manifests its overwhelming, destructive force. As Richter-Musso writes, 'critics widely reproached Turner for allowing the elements of air, earth, and water to entirely subsume the historical subject matter'. In the middle of a historical phase in which modern chemistry was introducing new elements, thus putting into question the classical quaternary—around 1800, thirty chemical elements had been identified, forming the basis of the modern table of the elements—Turner chooses to focus on those natural, meteorological, and atmospheric phenomena that highlight the *fusion* of the four classical elements rather than their distinction. Following his programme of a renewal of landscape painting through its merging with history painting, Turner presents nature as a 'cosmic force-field', the site of a tragic struggle among elements and forces that manifests itself in a variety of phenomena characterized by a constant 'dissolution and creation of forms'.[24] With their mutability and fleetingness, waves, rain, smoke, mist, and clouds are signs of the powers of an 'eternally changing matter', and the 'formative processes' of evaporation and condensation, accumulation and flow reveal 'the transitory nature of the natural world'.[25]

From the perspective we are exploring in this essay—the intersection of screen and medium—there is yet another phrase in Hazlitt's passage from 'On Imitation' that needs to be highlighted: the phrase in which Hazlitt writes that Turner's paintings are 'too much abstractions of aerial perspective, and representations *not so properly of the objects of nature as of the medium through which they are seen*'. What is of particular interest in this phrase is precisely the meaning Hazlitt assigns to the term 'medium' and the implications this meaning has in relation to both the status of the canvas and the visual experience of the spectator.

23 Richter-Musso and Westheider, 2011.
24 Richter-Musso, 2011, pp. 45, 48.
25 Ibid., pp. 46, 49.

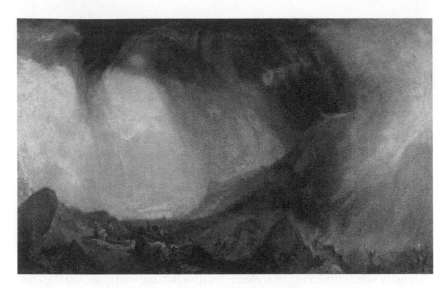

6.1:   J.M.W. Turner (1775–1851), *Snow Storm: Hannibal and his Army Crossing the Alps*, Exhibited 1812. Oil paint on canvas, 146 × 237, 5 cm. © Tate, London 2018.

As I have tried to show elsewhere—in an essay dedicated to the meanings of the German term *Medium* and on the idea of a 'medium of perception' [*Medium der Wahrnehmung*] in the writings of Walter Benjamin—the way in which the term 'medium' is used by Hazlitt in this passage can be located within one of the multiple genealogical lines that characterize the history of the very concept of 'medium'.[26] Along this line, the medium is conceived neither as an intermediary between the world of the living and the world of the dead (as in the occult, spirit tradition) nor as a set of supports and techniques defining the specificity of some kind of artistic representation, such as painting and sculpture; neither as an 'extension of man', as in Marshall McLuhan's famous definition in *Understanding Media* (1964), nor as a series of techniques and operations capable of storing, processing, and transmitting signals and information, as in Friedrich Kittler's notion of *Medien*. Even though these different meanings are often historically intertwined with one another, the way the term 'medium' is used in Hazlitt's passage is firmly rooted in a tradition that interprets as 'medium' those atmospheric substances (such as air, ether, clouds, vapour, smoke) that, taken together, constitute the environment, *milieu*, or *Umwelt* in which sensory experience unfolds. Authors such as Stefan Hoffmann and Dieter Mersch have rightly qualified such understanding of the concept

26 Somaini, pp. 6-41.

of medium as 'aisthetic' [*aisthetisch*], since it is primarily correlated to a theory of perception (*aisthesis*) and of its spatial and material conditions of possibility.[27]

Considered in this perspective, Hazlitt's reference to 'aerial perspective' just before stating that Turner's paintings are 'representations not so properly of the objects of nature as of the medium through which they are seen' is directly related not only to Leonardo da Vinci's famous statements in *A Treatise on Painting* on the way in which the vision of objects at a distance is conditioned by the air that 'interposes between' them and the eye but also to the *longue durée* of a tradition that interprets the idea of medium in environmental and atmospheric terms.[28] The 'medium through which' objects of nature are seen is not, here, the 'medium of *paint*', as in the modernist readings of Turner suggested by Gowing and Rosenblum. It is rather an *atmospheric medium* whose representation turns the canvas itself into an *atmospheric screen*. A brief detour into this idea of an atmospheric medium will help us further substantiate this idea.

Clouds, ether, and the 'medium of perception'

In his 1942 essay 'Milieu and Ambiance: An Essay in Historical Semantics', the literature historian, philologist, and critic Leo Spitzer gives a fundamental contribution to the reconstruction of what Hoffmann and Mersch present as an 'aisthetic' understanding of the medium.[29] He underlines the fact that 'the history of the word [*ambiance*] cannot be separated from that of *medium* and *milieu*', which is itself linked 'to the German *Umwelt*, the Spanish *medio*, the Italian *ambiente* and the English *environment*'.[30] His essay begins with the Greek notion of *periechon* (τὸ περιέχον, from the verb περι-έχειν), meaning 'that which surrounds, encompasses': a term 'used to refer to the all-embracing air, space, sky, atmosphere, climate'.[31]

A further, crucial step in this tradition can be found in the notions of *diaphanes* and *metaxy* in Aristotle's treatise *De Anima*, which was later to

---

27   On the history of the concept of medium up to the beginning of the 20th century, with a special focus on the idea of an 'aistetic concept of medium' [*aisthetischer Medienbegriff*], see Hoffmann, 2002 and Hoffmann, 2006.

28   Leonardo da Vinci, p. 180.

29   Spitzer, 1942.

30   Ibid., p. 2.

31   Ibid.

be translated in Latin with the terms *diaphanum* and *medium*.[32] According to Aristotle, every form of sensory perception requires the presence of an intermediary element, the *metaxy*, between the perceiving body and the perceived objects. Vision, in particular, is made possible by a specific kind of *metaxy* called *diaphanes*. Although itself colourless and not visible, the *diaphanes* may be activated by colour, thus passing from a state of *potency* to a state of *act*, which allows it to transmit the action of colour from the object to the human sensorium, the *aistheterion*.[33]

The way the term *medium* is used in medieval and modern optics, especially in the expression *media diaphana*, is likewise related to a theory of perception invested in the material, environmental conditions influencing the transmission of light and colour. For instance, Isaac Newton's *Opticks: or a Treatise of the Reflexions, Refractions, Inflections and Colours of Light* (1704, translated in Latin in 1706) analyzes the transmission of light through transparent ('pellucid') and diaphanous mediums that are both man-made and natural. Some are artificially produced and, in many ways, reminiscent of screens: prisms, lenses, crystals, and sheets of glass. Others are spatially diffused in the environment: water, oil, air, and the ether flowing between all bodies, a substance that Newton calls the 'Æthereal medium', always with a capital Æ.[34]

According to Spitzer, in Newton's idea of an 'Æthereal medium' we find again 'the ancient idea of a *medium of perception*'.[35] Just as artificial entities such as lenses, prisms, and sheets of glass—all with their different degrees of transparency and opacity—are capable of influencing the transmission of light and the conditions of sensory perception, so is the ether, with its 'fluid' and 'vibrating' nature. As an 'ambient medium', the ether, according to Newton, can be 'denser', 'rarer', 'subtler', 'fluid', 'elastick', even 'quiescent', but it is never a static, passive entity.[36] Rather, it is an intermediary agent, a transmitter of attractive forces, and a conveyor of light.[37] The ether, in other words, is an active substance endowed with functional properties. As Spitzer writes,

32   The term *metaxy* was translated in Latin as *medium* by Michael Scotus, in his translation, around 1225, of Averroes's *Commentarium Magnum in Aristotelis De Anima*: a treatise in which the *medium* becomes the condition of possibility not only of sensation but also of thought.

33   Aristotle, *De anima*, B VII, 418 b, 5-6, and 419 a, 15.

34   On the notion of 'Æthereal medium', see Newton, pp. 324, 327, 328, 343.

35   Spitzer, p. 5.

36   Newton, pp. 195, 205, 229. The terms 'denser', 'rarer', 'subtler', 'fluid', 'elastick', and 'quiescent' appear throughout Newton's *Opticks*. See Newton, pp. 5, 183, 326, and 329.

37   See Spitzer, p. 35. On the ether as a medium, see Milutis, 2006; Kümmel-Schnur and Schröter, 2008. See also Henderson, 2002.

a functional connotation (of varying intensity) is ever present [in the way in which Newton uses] the term *medium*; the very choice of this word in reference to the various elements reflects the point of view of a scientist conscious of the potentialities, the properties of all elements with which he has to deal; who in his experiments, in the formulation of his theories, sees any given element as a 'factor': as, in some way, an active entity, a means to an end—in the largest sense, as a means through which the efficacy of physical laws manifests itself. Thus, regardless of the multiplicity of references of which *medium* is capable, there is perhaps one 'meaning' throughout: an element envisaged as a factor.[38]

During the first decades of the nineteenth century, we find in England a whole series of examples of uses of the term 'medium' in the same material, environmental, atmospheric sense we find in Hazlitt—often by scientists with whom Turner was in direct contact. Among them, the physicist and astronomer Mary Somerville presents, in *The Connexion of the Physical Sciences* (1834), air, ether, and atmosphere as the 'surrounding medium' through which light and sound propagate, often using the same expression 'ethereal medium' that we find in Newton's *Opticks*.[39] Three years before, in a letter to C.R. Leslie dated 26 September 1831, it was the painter John Constable—author of a series of *Cloud Studies* painted between 1821 and 1822, and accompanied by detailed meteorological 'inscriptions'—who wrote that nature is never 'divested of her chiaroscuro [...], for we never see her but through a medium'.[40]

References to an ambient medium that pervades the atmosphere and conditions our visual perception of the surrounding environment through its different degrees of transparency and its reflecting and refracting properties can be widely found throughout the first decades of the nineteenth century: not only within the domain of British science, literature, and painting but also within the tradition of German Romantic literature and *Natur-philosophie*. Before returning to Turner, a few examples from this second tradition may give us an idea of the various perceptual, epistemological, and environmental meanings that were assigned to the term *Medium*, directly derived from Latin, and to its German translation, *Mittel*.

In his *Vom Erkennen und Empfinden der menschlichen Seelen* (1778), Herder refers to the ether as a *Medium* in the sense of a fluid that pervades body

---

38 Spitzer, pp. 39-40.
39 Sommerville, p. 208. On Turner and Somerville, see Wagner, pp. 103-104.
40 Leslie, p. 50. Quoted in Wagner, p. 50.

and soul and makes all forms of sensory and cognitive experience possible.[41]
In the later *Ideen zur Philosophie der Geschichte der Menschheit* (1784-1791),
it is the 'air' (*Luft*) that is presented as a *Medium* and a 'general vehicle
(*allgemeines Vehikel*) of things' pervaded by 'effective, spiritual forces'.[42]
A few years later, Schelling, in *Ideen zu einer Philosophie der Natur* (1797),
presents heat and light as pervasive 'fluids' (*Fluida*) that keep natural bodies
together. Together with the air, they are 'the general medium (*das allgemeine
Medium*) through which the higher forces of nature act onto dead matter':
'the medium', adds Schelling, 'in which we live, that surrounds everything,
penetrates everything, and is present in everything'.[43]

A metaphorical use of the term *Medium* can be found in Johann Wilhelm
Ritter's *Fragmenten aus dem Nachlasse eines jungen Physikers. Ein Taschenbuch für Freunde der Natur* (1810), in which every individual entity existing
in nature is presented as a prismatic, screen-like, 'light-refracting medium'
(*Brechungsmedium*) that breaks the unity of the universal force and of the
universal, divine light that pervades the created world. Life, continues Ritter,
is the play of colours that is produced by such prismatic medium.[44] A few
years earlier, in his novel *Godwi, oder das steinerne Bild der Mutter* (1801),
Clemens Brentano directly associates the concept of *Medium* with the idea
of the 'romantic' (*das Romantische*), which in the eighth chapter is the object
of a conversation among the protagonists: Godwi, Haber, and Maria, the
narrator. The romantic artwork is here presented as a form of representation
that does not limit itself to an imitation of the object but rather presents
it through a specific, emotionally charged mediation. Maria states that
'everything that lies as an intermediary (*als Mittler*) between our eye and
a distant object to be seen, everything that brings the distant object closer
to us, and at the same time confers to it something of itself, is romantic'.
Godwi adds to this the idea that the 'romantic' may be better understood if
we compare it with the experience of seeing through a coloured, telescopic
lens: 'the romantic is like a telescope (*ein Perspectiv*) or, more precisely, the
colour of the glass and the determination of the object through the shape
of the glass.[45]

A material, environmental idea of medium—formulated through the
concepts of *Trübe* (the 'opaque', 'cloudy', or 'turbid') and *Mittel*, often

---

41 Herder, 1892. Quoted in Mersch, pp. 37-38.
42 Herder, 1989, p. 35. Quoted in Hoffmann, 2002, pp. 74-75.
43 Schelling, pp. 116, 177.
44 Ritter, p. 139. Quoted in Hoffmann, 2002, p. 61.
45 Brentano, p. 314

associated in the expression *'das trübe Mittel'* ('the opaque medium')—
plays a very important role in Goethe's *Theory of Colours* (*Farbenlehre*,
1810) and in his later writings on clouds and other atmospheric phenomena. In the 'Didactic Part' of his radically anti-Newtonian treatise,
Goethe presents 'physical colours' (distinguished from 'physiological'
and 'chemical' ones) as phenomena that appear within and thanks
to some kind of material, colourless, and opaque medium.[46] Colours,
writes Goethe, are 'actions and passions of the light' (*Taten und Leiden
des Lichts*); they are constantly transforming 'half lights' or 'half shadows' (*Halblichter* or *Halbschatten*) that manifest themselves across an
intermediary region spanning between the polar opposites of light and
darkness, or 'light and non-light' (*Licht und Nichtlicht*).[47] In a short text
entitled 'Das Trübe', this intermediary realm is presented as having a
crucial epistemological and ontological significance, since it is in it,
according to Goethe, that one finds the first manifestation of some
kind of space-filling materiality, the 'first layer of corporeality' (*die erste
Lamelle der Körperlichkeit*)[48].

In his 1840 English translation of Goethe's treatise, Charles Lock Eastlake
translates the expression *'trübes Mittel'* with the English 'semi-transparent
medium': a medium that can change in density, becoming thicker or thinner
and 'more transparent'.[49] As is well known, Turner, who owned a copy of
Eastlake's translation and made several annotations in it, mentions Goethe
explicitly in a painting entitled *Light and Colour (Goethe's Theory) – the
Morning after the Deluge – Moses Writing the Book of Genesis* (exhibited
1843). (Figure 6.2) The painting is part of a sort of diptych with *Shade and
Darkness – the Evening of the Deluge* (exhibited 1843).[50]

Although the extent of the actual influence of Goethe's *Farbenlehre* on
Turner has been and continues to be the object of contrasting views among
art historians, we may still notice how, in the painting *Light and Colour
(Goethe's Theory)*, the turbulent, circular vortex of atmospheric elements
that we find often in Turner's paintings here takes on a series of yellow-red
hues.[51] This particular colour palate may bear a reference to the § 150 in
Goethe's *Farbenlehre*, in Eastlake's translation:

---

46   Goethe, 2003 (1810), pp. 104-107.
47   Ibid., pp. 45, 58.
48   Goethe, 1962, pp. 227-29. On the concepts of '*Trübe*' and '*trübes Mittel*' in Goethe's writings
on colours and clouds, see Vogl, 2005.
49   Goethe, 1840, § 151, p.62.
50   See Gage, 1984.
51   On these two paintings and their contrasting interpretations, see Finley, 1997.

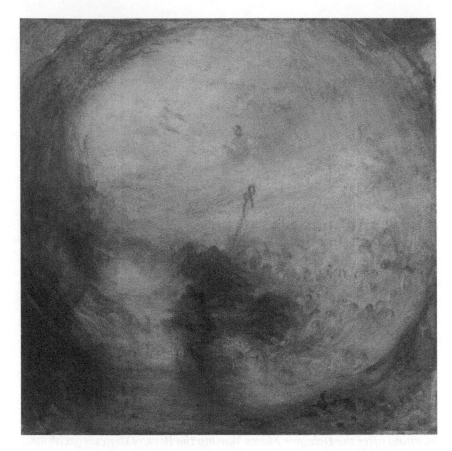

6.2:   J.M.W. Turner (1775–1851), *Light and Colour (Goethe's Theory) – the Morning after the Deluge – Moses Writing the Book of Genesis*, Exhibited 1843. Oil paint on canvas, 78.7 x 78.7 cm. © Tate, London 2018.

The Highest degree of light, such as that of the sun, of phosphorous burning in oxygen, is dazzling and colourless: so the light of the fixed stars is for the most part colourless. This light, however, seen through a medium but very slightly thickened (*durch ein auch nur wenig trübes Mittel gesehen*), appears to us yellow. If the density of such a medium be increased (*Nimmt die Trübe eines solchen Mittels zu*), or if its volume become greater, we shall see the light gradually assume a yellow-red hue, which at last deepens to a ruby-colour.[52]

52   Goethe, 1840, § 150, p.61.

In the years following the publication of *Farbenlehre*, Goethe's interest in the *'trübes Mittel'* developed into a wider interest for clouds and other atmospheric, meteorological phenomena.[53] After discovering Luke Howard's *Essay on Modifications of Clouds* (first published in 1803, translated into German in 1815)—a text in which we find an occurrence of the term *medium* in the material, environmental sense we are analyzing here—Goethe dedicated a number of studies and poems to the figure of Howard and to the study of clouds:[54] for example, the poems *'Atmosphäre'* and *'Howards Ehrengedächtnis'*, this last one divided in four parts entitled *'Stratus'*, *'Cumulus'*, *'Zirrus'*, and *'Nimbus'*, following Howard's cloud classification.[55] Howard was for Goethe the one who, for the first time, had been capable of 'distinguishing between clouds', establishing divisions into what seemed to be indivisible, fixating and defining what seemed to be utterly ephemeral and indefinable.[56] As we read in a letter to Carl Friedrich Zelter dated 24 July 1823, Goethe's interest in atmospheric phenomena and their metamorphic fleetingness—clouds were for him the quintessential realm of 'the transitory' (*das Übergangliche*)[57]—had a strong epistemological dimension, which linked it to the other areas of Goethe's natural studies, beginning with geology, that realm of stones and solid grounds that seemed to lie at the opposite of the vaporous instability of clouds:

> Just as I have engaged in the study of the earth (*Erdkunde*) perhaps longer than I should have, I begin now to interest myself in the atmospheric realm (*den atmosphärischen Reichen*); and were it just to experience how one thinks and can think (*wie man denkt und denken kann*), that would already be an advancement (*ein Vorgewinn*).[58]

The idea that the study of clouds has a quintessential epistemological value lies at the centre, as we will now see, of John Ruskin's writings on Turner, which appear across the different volumes of his *Modern Painters* (1843). And it is here that the idea of a painting explicitly conceived to be 'in the service of clouds' is strictly connected to an understanding of the spectator's experience as a form of *seeing through*, a capacity of penetrating through

---

53 On Goethe's writings on clouds and other atmospheric and meteorological phenomena, see Badt, 1960; Vogl, 2005; Beyer, 2004.
54 Howard, 1865, p. 28.
55 Both poems are quoted in Badt, pp. 19-20.
56 Ibid.
57 Goethe, 1989, p. 244. Quoted in Vogl, p. 72.
58 Quoted in Badt, p. 19.

the canvas as atmospheric screen, that 'veil (...) of 'intermediate being' that constitutes the sensible environment.[59]

'Something which has no surface and through which we can plunge farther and farther'

Ruskin's vision of Turner is almost diametrically opposed to that of Hazlitt in the essay 'On Imitation'. If Hazlitt condemns the way in which Turner insists on the mingling and the fusion of the elements within the 'medium', leading the spectator 'back to the first chaos of the world', Ruskin finds in Turner's paintings a forceful depiction of the atmosphere, allowing the spectator to experience a heightened, perceptual, and emotional immersion in the infinity of the natural environment. In watercolours such as *Long Ship's Lighthouse, Land's End* (1834-35) (Figure 6.3), Ruskin sees a kind of pictorial representation that is 'not formless, but full of indications of character, wild, irregular, shattered, and indefinite, full of the energy of storm', adding that 'it is this untraceable, unconnected, yet perpetual form—this fullness of character absorbed in the universal energy—which distinguish nature and Turner from all their imitators'.[60]

Contrary to Hazlitt, Ruskin believed that Turner's paintings, through their very insistence on the properties of the environmental 'medium', could provide a powerful epistemological tool, establishing the foundations of 'a science of the aspects of things', a science capable of studying the 'vibrations of matter' and the various forms of diaphanous, atmospheric, and ultimately *screen-like* mediation that could be found in nature:

> there is a science of the aspects of things, as well as of their nature; and it is as much a fact to be noted in their constitution, that they produce such and such an effect upon the eye or heart [...] as they are made up of certain atoms or vibrations of matter. Turner [...] is the master of the science of aspects.[61]

After formulating in his 'Remarks on the Present State of Meteorological Science' (1839) the dream of 'a vast machine [...] omnipotent over the globe, so

---

59   Ruskin, 1903, III, p. 318; Ibid, IV, p. 101. See also Part VII ('Of Cloud Beauty'), Chapter 1 ('The Cloud-Balancings'), ibid.
60   Ibid., p. 404.
61   Ibid., p. 387.

6.3:   J.M.W. Turner (1775–1851), *Long Ship's Lighthouse, Land's End*, c.1834–1835. Watercolor and gouache, scraped by the artist 28.6 × 44 cm. Digital image courtesy of the Getty's Open Content Program.

that it may be able to know, at any given instant, the state of the atmosphere at every point of its surface',[62] in the various chapters of the first volume of *Modern Painters* dedicated to the 'truths' of 'tone', 'colour', 'chiaroscuro', 'space', 'skies', 'clouds', 'earth', 'water', and 'vegetation', Ruskin describes the constant transformations, the infinite *nuances* of the ever-changing nature that is captured by Turner's paintings: 'This is nature! The exhaustless living energy with which the universe is filled (...) how various, how transparent, how infinite in its organization!'[63]

Clouds play, from this perspective, a crucial role. With their division into different 'regions' (the upper region of the 'cirrus', the central region of the 'stratus', and the lower region of the 'rain-cloud'), their endless transformations ('they have no sharp edges, they are all fleecy and mingling with each other'), and their various effects of screening, filtering, and layering, they are for Ruskin a primary example of that 'infinity' that characterizes natural, atmospheric phenomena.[64] It is an infinity that could only be

---

62 Ruskin, 1839, pp. 56-59.
63 Ruskin, 1903, I, pp. 383-84.
64 Ibid., p. 359. See also ibid., p. 387: 'If we wish, without reference to beauty of composition, or any other interfering circumstances, to form a judgement of the truth of painting, perhaps

visualized by a form of painting explicitly conceived to be 'in the service of clouds'.[65]

Being 'in the service of clouds' meant for Ruskin being capable of seizing those 'wreaths', 'halos', and 'films' on which he insists in *Modern Painters*: those layers and folds of a natural landscape characterized by 'an infinity of gradation [...] from the highest film that glorifies the ether to the wildest vapour that darkens the dust'.[66] Situated between these various layers, human existence unfolds within an *intermediate realm* characterized by the presence of a number of screen-like, *veiling* entities, of which the cloud and the leaf are the most emblematic manifestations. As we read in the fifth volume of *Modern Painters*, published in 1860:

> We have seen that when the earth had to be prepared for the habitation of man, a veil, as it were, of *intermediate being* was spread between him and its darkness, in which were joined, in a subdued measure, the stability and insensibility of the earth, and the passion and perishing of mankind.
> But the heavens, also, had to be prepared for this habitation.
> Between their burning light—their deep vacuity, and man, as between the earth's gloom of iron substance, and man, *a veil had to be spread of intermediate being*;—which should appease the endurable glory to the level of human feebleness, and sign the changeless motion of the heavens with a semblance of human vicissitude.
> Between the earth and man arose the leaf. Between the heaven and man came the cloud. His life being partly as the falling leaf, and partly as the flying vapour.[67]

In Turner's paintings, Ruskin found a form of representation capable of visualizing and penetrating these various intermediate layers, exploring 'all those passages of confusion between earth and air, when the mountain is melting into the cloud, or the horizon into the twilight'.[68] As opposed to

the very first thing we should look for, whether in one thing or another—foliage, or clouds, or waves—should be the expression of *infinity* always and everywhere, in all parts and divisions of parts. For we may be quite sure that what is not infinite cannot be true'.

65   Ibid., p. 318. (On the question of the representation of clouds in the history of painting, and in particular on Ruskin's idea of a painting 'in the service of clouds', see Damisch, pp. 253-276.)

66   Ibid., pp. 414-415.

67   Ibid., p. 101.

68   Ibid., p. 410

what happened in the paintings of the 'old masters', in which 'the blue sky [is] totally distinct in its nature, and far separated from the vapours which float in it', giving the impression that 'cloud is cloud, and blue is blue, and no kind of connection between them is ever hinted at', Ruskin believes that the way in which Turner represents clouds gives the spectator the impression of looking 'through' the skies rather than 'at' them.[69] Turner, we read in the first volume of *Modern Painters*, represents the sky as 'a deep, quivering, transparent body of penetrable air', producing a kind of 'painting of the air, something in which you can see, through the parts which are near you, into those which are far off; something which has no surface and through which we can plunge farther and farther, and without stay or end, into the profundity of space'.[70]

Turner—who, around 1810, for his lectures in perspective, produced multiple drawings and diagrams in different techniques studying the transmission of light and colour through diaphanous media (see, for example, the *Lecture Diagrams: Reflections in Two Transparent Globes*, 1810) (Figure 6.4)—promoted himself this idea of a painterly style stemming from a direct, penetrating, immersive, sensorially exposed experience of nature. In a title that refers to what is very likely a fictional anecdote, he suggests that the painting *Snow Storm – Steam Boat off a Harbour's Mouth making Signals in Shallow Water, and going by the Lead. The Author was in this Storm on the Night the Ariel left Harwich* (exhibited in 1842) (Figure 6.5) was conceived while being tied to the mast of a ship during a violent storm at sea, in direct contact with the natural elements. In this case the natural elements are mingled with the artificial smoke produced by the steam boat: a theme—that of the fusion of natural cloud-like vapour and man-made steam produced by boats and trains—which was to be at the centre of several of Turner's paintings during the 1830s and 1840s, such as *Rain, Steam and Speed. The Great Western Railway* (exhibited in 1844).[71] (Figure 6.6)

As Lawrence Gowing writes in *Turner: Imagination and Reality*, 'Snow Storm is a picture of *being in it*': a picture in which the canvas allows the spectator to experience the environmental, atmospheric medium in which

69   Ibid., p. 347.

70   Ibid., pp. 347-348.

71   For an analysis of the implications of the mingling of nature and technique in Turner's paintings (in particular in *Snow Storm – Steam Boat off a Harbour's Mouth* and *Rain, Steam, and Speed*), see Wagner, pp. 101-105. Wagner—who refers to the connection between Turner and thermodynamics discussed by Michel Serres in his 'Turner Translates Carnot' (1982, pp. 54-62)—underlines the fact that Ruskin, who was generally hostile to the process of industrialization, does not emphasize this aspect in his analysis of Turner's paintings.

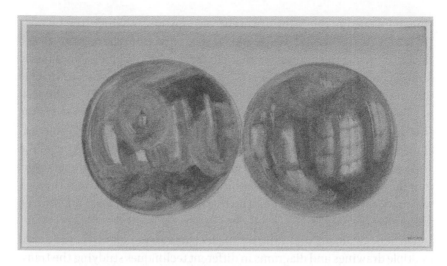

6.4:   J.M.W. Turner (1775–1851), *Lecture Diagrams: Reflections in Two Transparent Globes*, c.1810. Pencil and oil paint on white wove paper, 21.7 x 40.4 cm. © Tate, London 2018.

6.5:   J.M.W. Turner (1775–1851), *Snow Storm – Steam Boat off a Harbour's Mouth making Signals in Shallow Water, and going by the Lead*. The Author was in this Storm on the Night the Aerial lift Harwich, Exhibited 1842. Oil paint on canvas, 91.4 x 121.9 cm. © Tate, London 2018.

6.6:   J.M.W. Turner (1775–1851), *Rain, Steam and Speed. The Great Western Railway*, 1844. Oil paint on canvas, 91 x 121.8 cm. © National Gallery, London/Art Resource, NY.

the elements and the forces of nature intersect and transform one another.[72] And this idea of *being in it*, of using painting in order to stage a state of *immersion* and even a *dissolution* into the atmospheric medium through the erasing of any kind of clear-cut separation between the perceiving body and the surrounding environment, is what we find in another famous painting by Turner, *Regulus* (1828, reworked in 1837). (Figure 6.7) The title refers to the story of a consul of the Roman Republic who served in the First Punic War (256 BC), defeating the Carthaginians in a naval battle at Cape Ecnomus near Sicily. After having invaded North Africa, Regulus was himself defeated and captured at Tunis in 255 BC. Having been sent to Rome to negotiate peace, he urged the Roman Senate to refuse the offer of the Carthaginians, who took revenge on him by torturing him to death: his eyelids were removed, and he was forced to stare into the sun until he became blind.[73]

---

72   Gowing, p. 48.

73   In his *Turner, menteur magnifique*, Pierre Wat draws a comparison between the historical anecdote behind the title of Turner's *Regulus* and a text by Heinrich von Kleist on Caspar David Friedrich's *Mönch am Meer* (1808-1810), in which we find another reference to a vision without eyelids: see Kleist, 1810. See also Wat, pp. 57-68.

6.7:   J.M.W. Turner (1775–1851), *Regulus*, 1828, reworked 1837. Oil paint on canvas, 89.5 x 123.8 cm. © Tate, London 2018.

In his *Techniques of the Observer*, Jonathan Crary sees in this painting—and in later paintings such as the already mentioned *Light and Colour (Goethe's Theory)*—a major sign of 'the breakdown of the perceptual model of the camera obscura', with its strict separation between seer and seen. 'Seemingly out of nowhere, [Turner's] paintings of the late 1830s and 1840s signal the irrevocable loss of a fixed source of light, the dissolution of a cone of light rays, and the collapse of the distance separating an observer from the site of optical experience.'[74] This 'collapse', adds Crary, is most evident in paintings such as *Regulus* and *The Angel Standing in the Sun* (exhibited in 1846) (Figure 6.8), in which Turner stages a condition of full exposure to the first source of light and heat: 'in Turner all of the mediations that previously had distanced and protected an observer from the dangerous brilliance of the sun are cast off', and what we are left with is a real 'fusion of eye and sun'[75] that, during the early decades of the nineteenth century, can also be

74   Crary, 1990, p. 138.
75   Ibid., p. 139.

6.8:   J.M.W. Turner (1775–1851), *The Angel Standing in the Sun*, Exhibited 1846. Oil paint on canvas, 78.5 × 78.5 cm. © Tate, London 2018.

found in Goethe's understanding of the eye as 'sun-like' (*sonnenhaft*)[76] and in Gustav Fechner's view of the eye 'as a creature of the sun on earth, a creature dwelling in and nourished by the sun's rays'.[77] In a text written over ten years later in an exhibition catalogue that revisits and reformulates the idea of a Turner precursor of abstraction—*Aux origines de l'abstraction. 1810-1914* (2003-2004)[78]—Crary adds that through the exposure to the '*aveuglante lumière*' of *Regulus*, the spectator is presented with an experience '*effroyable*

76   I am referring here to the famous verses mentioned by Goethe in the 'Einleitung' of the *Farbenlehre*: 'Wär' nicht das Auge sonnenhaft, / Wie könnten wir das Licht erblicken? / Lebt' nicht in uns des Gottes eigne Kraft, / Wie könnt' uns Göttliches entzücken?' Goethe, 2003 (1810), p. 57.
77   Fechner, pp. 39-58. Quoted in Crary, 1990, p. 142.
78   Lemoine and Rousseau, 2003. For another recent exhibition on the idea of Turner precursor of abstraction, see Rosenberg and Hollein, 2007.

et hallucinatoire' at the same time, in which *'la distance entre le sujet et l'objet, soit entre un spectateur et le monde, s'abolit au profit d'une inscription physique du soleil dans le corps'*, up to the point that *'le corps du spectateur et le monde extérieur des phénomènes physiques ne forment qu'un tout indivisible'*.[79]

Interpreted from the perspective of a study of the intersections between the environmental meanings of the terms 'screen' and 'medium', the 'fusion of eye and sun' highlighted by Crary in his reading of Turner's *Regulus* cannot be interpreted as a 'casting off' of all of the 'mediations' that had previously framed the observer's vision. On the contrary, what we find not only in *Regulus* but also in *Snow Storm* and in many of Turner's later paintings is an emphasis on 'mediation' that takes the form of an immersion within an atmospheric environment conceived itself as a 'medium'—an immersion within 'something which has no surface and through which we can plunge farther and farther', made possible by a canvas that has turned into an atmospheric screen.

Works Cited

Aristotle. *De anima* [On the Soul]. Translated by Hugh Lawson-Tancred. New York and London: Penguin Classics, 1987.

Badt, Kurt. *Wolkenbilder und Wolkengedichte der Romantik*. Berlin: De Gruyter, 1960.

Beyer, Andreas. 'Die "Physiognomie der Atmosphäre": Zu Goethes Versuch, den Wolken Sinn zu verleihen.' In *Wolkenbilder: Die Entdeckung des Himmels*, exhibition catalogue edited by Bärbel Hedinger, Inés Richter-Musso, and Ortrud Westheider, pp. 172-78. Munich: Hirmer, 2004.

Brentano, Clemens. *Godwi, oder das steinerne Bild der Mutter*. In *Sämtliche Werke und Briefe*, vol. 16. Stuttgart, Berlin, Köln, Mainz: Kohlhammer, 1978.

Casetti, Francesco. 'Notes on a Genealogy of the Excessive Screen.' In *SCREENS: Genealogies of the Excessive Screen, A Mellon Sawyer Seminar at Yale*. New Haven: Department of Film and Media Studies, 2017. http://dev.screens.yale.edu/sites/default/files/files/Screens_Booklet.pdf. Accessed 12 December 2018.

Crary, Jonathan. *Techniques of the Observer: On Vision and Modernity in the Nineteenth Century*. Cambridge, MA: The MIT Press, 1990.

——. 'Aveuglante lumière.' In *Aux origines de l'abstraction, 1800-1914*. Exhibition catalogue, pp. 104-109. Paris: Édition de la Réunion des musées nationaux, 2003.

Damisch, Hubert. *Théorie du nuage. Pour une histoire de la peinture*. Paris: Seuil, 1972.

---

79 Crary, 2003, pp. 106-107.

Elsaesser, Thomas. *Film History as Media Archaeology*. Amsterdam: Amsterdam University Press, 2016.

Fechner, Gustav. 'On the Comparative Anatomy of Angels.' (1825) *Journal of the History of the Behavioral Sciences* 5, no 1 (1969): 39-58.

Finley, Gerald. 'The Deluge Pictures: Reflections on Goethe, J.M.W. Turner and Early Nineteenth-Century Science.' *Zeitschrift für Kunstgeschichte* 60. no. 4 (1997): 530-548.

Gage, John. 'Turner's Annotated Books: Goethe's Theory of Colours.' *Turner Studies* 4, no. 2 (1984): 34-52.

———. *Farbenlehre*, 1810. Stuttgart: Verlag Freies Geistesleben, 2003.

Goethe, Johann Wolfgang. *Theory of Colours*. Translated by Charles L. Eastlake. London: Murray, 1840.

———. 'Das Trübe.' In *Naturwissenschaftliche Hefte*, edited by D. Kuhn, pp. 227-229. Book 1, Volume 7 of *Die Schriften zur Naturwissenschaft (Leopoldina Ausgabe)*, edited by D. Kuhn, R. Matthei, W. Troll and K.L. Wolf. Weimar: Verlag Hermann Böhlaus Nachfolger, 1962.

———. 'Wohl zu merken.' In *Schriften zur allgemeinen Naturlehre, Geologie und Mineralogie*, edited by W. van Engelhardt and M. Wenzel, pp. ??. Book 1, volume 25 of n *Sämtliche Werke, Briefe, Tagebücher und Gespräche (Frankfurter Ausgabe)*, various editors. Frankfurt am Main: Deutscher Klassiker Verlag, 1989.

Gowing, Lawrence. *Turner: Imagination and Reality*. New York: Museum of Modern Art, 1966.

Herder, Johann Gottfried. *Vom Erkennen und Empfinden der menschlichen Seelen* (1778). In *Sämmtliche Werke*, edited by Bernhard Suphan. Berlin: Weidmann 1892.

———. *Ideen zu einer Philosophie der Geschichte der Menschheit* (1784-1791). In *Werke in zehn Bänden*, edited by Martin Bollacher and Günther Arnold, pp. ??. Frankfurt am Main: Deutscher Klassiker Verlag, 1989.

Hazlitt, William. *The Round Table: A Collection of Essays on Literature, Men, and Manners*. Edinburgh: Archibald Constable and Co., 1817.

Henderson, Linda. 'Vibratory Modernism: Boccioni, Kupka, and the Ether or Space.' In *From Energy to Information: Representation in Science and Technology, Art, and Literature*, edited by Bruce Clarke and Linda Dalrymple Henderson, pp. 126-149. Redwood City, CA: Stanford University Press, 2002.

Hoffmann, Stefan. *Geschichte des Medienbegriffs*. Hamburg: Meiner, 2002.

———. 'Medienbegriff.' In *Handbuch Medienwissenschaft*, edited by Jens Schröter, pp. 13-20. Stuttgart, Weimar: Metzler, 2014.

Howard, Luke. *Essay on the Modification of Clouds* (1803). Third Edition. London: John Churchill & Sons, 1865.

Kleist, Heinrich von. 'Empfindungen vor Friedrichs Seelandschaft.' *Berliner Abendblätter*, 1810.

Kümmel-Schnur, Albert and Jens Schröter, eds. *Äther. Ein Medium der Moderne.* Bielefeld: Transcript, 2008.

Lemoine, Serge and Pascal Rousseau. *Aux origines de l'abstraction. 1800-1914.* Exhibition catalogue. Paris: Édition de la Réunion des musées nationaux, 2003.

Leonardo da Vinci. *A Treatise on Painting.* Translated by J.F. Rigaud. London: Nichols and Son, 1835.

Leslie, Charles Robert. *Life and Letters of John Constable.* London: Chapman and Hall, 1896.

McLuhan, Marshall. 'Environment and Anti-Environment.' (1966) In *Media Research: Technology, Art, Communication,* edited by M.A. Moos, pp. 110-120. New York: G+B Arts International, 1997.

Mersch, Dieter. *Medientheorie. Zur Einführung.* Hamburg: Junius, 2006.

Milutis, Joe. *Ether: The Nothing that Connects Everything.* Minneapolis and London: University of Minnesota Press, 2006.

Moholy-Nagy, László. 'Light: A Medium of Plastic Expression.' *Broom* 4, no. 4 (March 1923): 283-284.

———. *Von material zu architektur* (1929). Edited by by Hans M. Wingler. Berlin: Gebr. Mann, 2001.

———. 'Problems of the modern film.' *Telehor* (1936): 37-40.

———. *The New Vision.* Mineola, NY: Dover, 1975.

Newton, Isaac. *Opticks, or a Treatise of the Reflections, Refractions, Inflections and Colours of Light.* Fourth corrected edition. London: William Innys, 1730.

Peters, John Durham. *The Marvelous Clouds. Toward a Philosophy of Elemental Media.* Chicago: University of Chicago Press, 2015.

Richter-Musso, Inés. 'Fire, Water, Air and Earth: Turner as a Painter of the Elements.' In Richter-Musso and Ostrud Westheider, *Turner and the Elements,* 41-51.

——— and Ostrud Westheider. *Turner and the Elements.* Exhibition catalogue. Munich: Hirmer, 2011.

Ritter, Johann Wilhelm. *Fragmente aus dem Nachlasse eines jungen Physikers. Ein Taschenbuch für Freunde der Natur* (1810). Leipzig and Weimar: Müller and Kiepenheuer, 1984.

Rosenberg, Raphael and Max Hollein, eds. *Turner Hugo Moreau: Entdeckung der Abstraktion.* Exhibition catalogue. Munich: Hirmer, 2007.

Rosenblum, Robert. 'The Abstract Sublime.' *Art News* 59, no.10 (February 1961), 350-359. Available online at ArtNews.com. http://www.artnews.com/2015/03/27/beyond-the-infinite-robert-rosenblum-on-sublime-contemporary-art-in-1961/. Accessed July 2018.

———. *Modern Painting and the Northern Romantic Tradition.* Boulder, CO: Westview Press, 1977.

Ruskin, John. 'Remarks on the Present State of Meteorological Science.' In *Transactions of the Meteorological Society* 1 (1839): 56-59.

——. *Modern Painters. The Works of John Ruskin: Library Edition*. Edited by E.T. Cook and A. Wedderburn. London: George Allen, 1903.

Schelling, Friedrich Wilhelm Joseph. *Ideen zu einer Philosophie der Natur* (1797). Vol. 5 of *Werke. Historisch-Kritische Ausgabe*, edited by Hans Michael Baumgartner. Stuttgart: Frommann Holzboog, 1994.

Serres, Michel. 'Turner Translates Carnot.' (1974) *Hermes: Literature, Science, Philosophy*, edited by Josué Harari and David F. Bell, pp. 54-62. Baltimore & London: The Johns Hopkins University Press, 1982.

Somaini, Antonio. 'Walter Benjamin's Media Theory: The *Medium* and the *Apparat*.' *Grey Room* 62 (Winter 2016): 6-41.

Sommerville, Mary. *The Connexion of the Physical Sciences* (1834). New York: Harper and Brothers, 1871.

Spitzer, Leo. 'Milieu and Ambiance: An Essay in Historical Semantics.' Part 1. *Philosophy and Phenomenological Research* 3, no.1 (September 1942): 1-42.

——. 'Milieu and Ambiance: An Essay in Historical Semantics.' Part 2. *Philosophy and Phenomenological Research* 3, no. 2 (December 1942): 169-218.

Vogl, Joseph. 'Wolkenbotschaft.' In *Wolken*, edited by Lorenz Engell, Bernhard Siegert, and Joseph Vogl, pp. 69-78. Weimar: Bauhaus Universität Weimar, 2005.

Wagner, Monika. *William Turner*. Munich: C.H. Beck, 2011.

Wat, Pierre. *Turner: Menteur magnifique*. Paris: Hazan, 2010.

Youngblood, Gene. *Expanded Cinema*. Introduction by R. Buckminster Fuller. New York: E.P. Dutton, 1970.

About the Author

Antonio Somaini is full professor in film, media, and visual culture theory at the Université Sorbonne Nouvelle – Paris 3. He co-directs the *Laboratoire International de Recherches en Arts* and is on the steering committee of the European Network for Cinema and Media Studies. He has been fellow at the *Zentrum für Literatur- und Kulturforschung* in Berlin (2013) and senior fellow at the International Research Institute for Cultural Technologies and Media Philosophy in Weimar (2014-15). Major publications include *Cultura visuale. Immagini, sguardi, media, dispositivi* [*Visual Culture. Images, Gazes, Media, Dispositives*] (with Andrea Pinotti, 2016) and *Ejzenštejn. Il cinema, le arti, il montaggio* [*Eisenstein. Cinema, Art History, Montage*] (2011; 2017 in English).

7. The Fog Medium: Visualizing and Engineering the Atmosphere[1]

Yuriko Furuhata

Abstract

Yuriko Furuhata explores the fog sculptures of artist Nakaya Fujiko. Nakaya's deployment of fog and smoke recalls other expanded cinema practitioners and environmental artists in the postwar period, yet her experiments take on a different significance when seen not as a descendant of the phantasmagoria but as part of an assemblage linked to the development of smoke screens for aerial warfare. Paying particular attention to the dual function of fog screens—which obfuscate visibility yet also make visible such qualities as temperature, humidity, and wind—Furuhata historicizes the epistemological and political conditions behind the turn to fog and smoke within expanded cinema and the environmental arts during the Cold War. In so doing, Furuhata provides a geopolitically nuanced twist to the recent interest in 'atmospheric media' and 'elemental media'.

Keywords: Cold War, Pepsi Pavilion, Atmosphere, Peter Sloterdijk, Expanded Cinema

Introduction

Fogs, as Japanese artist Nakaya Fujiko once noted, are clouds that descend on earth.[2] Recently, clouds have become a much-debated and researched topic in film and media studies. Terms such as 'atmospheric media' and

---

1   I want to thank Nakaya Fujiko, the Nakaya Ukichirō Foundation, and Julie Klüver Martin for their kind permission to reproduce images related to Nakaya Ukichirō's scientific research and the Pepsi Pavilion in this article. All the Japanese names follow the customary order of the family name first. All translations from Japanese sources are mine.
2   Nakaya, 1970, p. 106.

Buckley, C., R. Campe, F. Casetti (eds.), *Screen Genealogies. From Optical Device to Environmental Medium*. Amsterdam: Amsterdam University Press, 2019
DOI 10.5117/9789463729000_CH07

'elemental media' have gained popularity, alongside the metaphor of the cloud in cloud computing. Scholars as diverse as Weihong Bao, Mark Hansen, Tung-Hui Hu, John Durham Peters, Nicole Starosielski, and Antonio Somaini have prompted us to look at the affinity between media and atmospheric environment in a new light.[3] To put it schematically, the old framework of media ecology represented by the Toronto School of communication studies *à la* Marshall McLuhan that regarded media *as environments* has given way to a more materialist, infrastructural, and genealogical study of technical media that *become environmental*. Conversely, scholars are now paying renewed attention to the mediating function of environmental elements such as air, water, and light as communicative and expressive media.

This chapter joins this growing field of atmospheric and elemental media studies by providing a genealogy of artificial fog as medium. More specifically, I turn to the dual functions of fog as both a screening device (which visualizes or obfuscates the environment) and as an atmospheric phenomenon in its own right. A focal point of this genealogical investigation is Nakaya Fujiko's 'fog sculptures'. First presented as an integral component of the Pepsi Pavilion at Expo '70, an event designed by the artist and engineer collective Experiments in Art and Technology (E.A.T.) to which Nakaya belonged, this exquisite artwork stands out as both a pioneering work of Japanese environmental art (*kankyō geijutsu*) and a salient example of what might be called an atmospheric screen. Consisting of water-based artificial fog, softly concealing the outer shell of the dome-shaped pavilion, this delicate work pushes our understanding of the screen beyond the assumed planarity of the projection surface. Unlike the common understanding of screen as a passive surface onto which images are projected, the atmospheric screen of the fog sculpture foregrounds its paradoxical capacity to conceal. And by concealing, it makes explicit the atmospheric phenomena that may otherwise go unnoticed. In other words, the making-visible of the atmosphere by the fog both parallels and goes beyond the making-visible of the image by the screen.

In what follows, I argue that an environmental artwork like Nakaya's fog sculpture not only participates in what Peter Sloterdijk has called the process of 'atmospheric-explication'—a process that transforms the taken-for-granted givenness of the environment into an explicit object of manipulation—but also links the history of art to the history of science and technology.[4] Read through this framework of atmospheric-explication, the fog sculpture appears as more than a mere device for visual obfuscation

---

3   See Bao, 2015; Hansen, 2015; Hu, 2015; Peters, 2015; Starosielski, 2015; Somaini, 2016.
4   See Sloterdijk, 2009.

and serves as a means of calling attention to larger historical processes of studying and controlling atmospheric phenomena. An exploration of this work also allows me to trace the genealogical background of artificial fog and its entanglement with warfare, cloud-seeding, and geoengineering.[5]

My argument is that the work of fog sculpture serves as a unique point of convergence between two heterogeneous lines of descent: on the one hand, the practice of *visualizing* atmospheric phenomena such as air currents, in which fog serves as projection and camouflage screen; and on the other, the practice of *engineering* the atmosphere, including weather control that artificially produces fog, rain, and snow. To trace a genealogy of the fog medium is to investigate how and why these lines of descent intersected at a specific moment through an interdisciplinary group of artists, scientists, and engineers coming from Japan and the United States, whose political alliance cemented during the Cold War. Seen from this geopolitical perspective, the historical timing of the fog sculpture matters a great deal. That is, the emergence of artificial fog as an artistic medium is inseparable from the larger geopolitical conditions of modernity in which the atmosphere was articulated with and as technical media.

Visualizing the atmosphere

Before turning to the fog sculpture at the Pepsi Pavilion, I want to briefly summarize the ways in which fog (and cloud-like substances in general) has long functioned as a screening and visualizing device. With the invention of electric light, clouds in the night sky became a medium of telecommunication. The nineteenth century witnessed an increased desire to reach the sky and turn clouds into a surface for projection. The clouds became a medium of 'celestial projection', a surface for projections that ranged from flashing Morse code for military communication to illuminated letters and pictures for commercial advertisements. In one such experiment with 'cloud telegraphy', a large mirror was used to bounce electric light as projected signals onto clouds. Some inventors such as Amos Dolbear even imagined that weather forecasts could one day be 'given by a series of flashes' reflected onto clouds.[6] The idea of using clouds as a screen was also behind the 1893

5   An affinity between the fog sculpture and media is present in Peters's passing comment; artworks like fog and mist installations befittingly belong to 'an age of poison gas, cloud seeding, and geoengineering'. Peters, p. 255.

6   Quoted in Marvin, p. 184.

Chicago World's Fair's 'electric cloud projector' used to 'project the daily number of visitors in the daytime, and to beam texts and pictures in the clouds after dark'.[7]

The idea of projecting images onto clouds, however, was not limited to marketing and military strategists. Magicians, artists, and scientists also saw the potential in combining electric light projections and gaseous screens. In the early nineteenth century, Belgian physicist and magician Étienne-Gaspard Robertson made use of smoke to enhance ghostly spectacles of his phantasmagoria.[8] A similar desire to use the visual effect of smoke, fog, and cloud pervaded visual artists in the twentieth century. One salient example is László Moholy-Nagy's whimsical proposal to use 'clouds or artificial fog banks' for light projection work.[9] His dream came true with the artistic use of dry ice and fog machines in theatrical performance, projection-based light art, and expanded cinema that flourished from the 1960s onward. The most well-known work in this context is Anthony McCall's 'solid light film', *Line Describing a Cone* (1973), a work that combines the sculpting force of the light beam emitted by a film projector with the ambient effect produced by a smoke machine (or, in its early exhibition, cigarette smoke).[10]

A number of other artists and filmmakers have made similar attempts to incorporate cigarette smoke, dry ice fumes, and other gaseous substances as projection surfaces in their filmic and installation works. Japanese experimental filmmaker Matsumoto Toshio, for instance, initially planned to use smoke grenades and dry ice to create a three-dimensional ambient screen for his expanded cinema piece, *Projection for Icon,* at the international event *Cross Talk/Intermedia* in Tokyo in February 1969. Matsumoto ended up using helium-filled giant balloons as the projection surface, but his proposal speaks to the contemporaneous interest by experimental filmmakers who saw cloud-like substances as a potential technical support for expanded cinema.[11] At *Cross Talk/Intermedia*, these same buoyant balloons were also used by the experimental filmmaker Iimura Takahiko and composer David Rosenbaum.

Cross Talk/Intermedia was conceptualized in the wake of *9 Evenings: Theater and Engineering* (1966), a landmark intermedia event in New York.

7   Huhtamo, p. 335.
8   Williamson, p. 107.
9   Casetti, p. 93.
10   MacDonald, p. 164.
11   Matsumoto Toshio writes: 'I had a desire to project onto something that was not [regular] screen [...] First, I imagined this work as a projection onto a gaseous body.' Matsumoto, n.p.

Initiated by artist Robert Rauschenberg and Bell Laboratories engineer Billy Klüver, the occasion emblematized the art-and-technology movement of the era. Similarly, *Cross Talk/Intermedia*—the largest event in a series sharing its name—was intended to bring artists and engineers together, but this time with an explicit emphasis on facilitating collaborations among Japanese and American composers, musicians, and filmmakers. Experimental composers and musicians Roger Reynolds, Karen Reynolds, Akiyama Kuniharu, and Yuasa Jōji were the main organizers, and they invited filmmakers such as Matsumoto, Iimura, and Stan VanDerBeek as well as musicians such as Gordon Mumma, Robert Ashley, and Salvatore Martirano on board. Incidentally, Pepsi was one of the official sponsors, along with the United States Information Agency, which saw an opportunity to fold the event into its Cold War cultural diplomacy efforts that increasingly targeted left-leaning youths who vehemently opposed the Cold War military-industrial alliance between Japan and the United States.[12]

The artistic use of helium gas and inflatable, pneumatic objects also became popular during the 1950s and 1960s. From Gutai group artist Kanayama Akira's *Balloon* (1956) to Robert Whitman's *The American Moon* (1960) and Andy Warhol's *Silver Clouds* (1966), artists frequently made use of plastic, a synthetic material whose availability increased in the postwar years, and helium-filled objects for their installation and film projection works.[13] Similarly, visual artist Azuchi Shūzō Gulliver used a gigantic cylinder-shaped inflatable for his expanded cinema piece, *Flying Focus* (1969). Reminiscent of the early practice of celestial projection, images emitted from a slide projector were projected onto an upright cylinder floating against the night sky.[14] This turn towards ephemeral screens made of vaporous particles in the air was also evident in a more commercially oriented attraction at Expo '70. The Japanese Tobacco Company's Rainbow Pavilion featured a 'smoke show' that combined spectacular light and film projections with a gigantic smoke screen generated by dry ice. This smoke screen belongs to the same lineage as Robertson, Moholy-Nagy, and Matsumoto's proposals to use vaporous particles hanging in the air as projection surfaces.

Yet light and film projections are only one part of the lineage of visualizing the atmosphere. Fog and smoke have also served as scientific instruments inside the laboratory. Given that the industrial pollution

---

12   Reynolds, pp. 9-10. See also Sas.
13   Ross, pp. 139-146.
14   Gulliver, 2017. For more on Gulliver's work, see Ross, 2014.

known as 'smog'—a combination of smoke and fog—is associated with
aerial invisibility, the use of fog and smoke for visualizing atmospheric
phenomena may seem counterintuitive. However, observing and analyzing
natural atmospheric phenomena, including the formations of clouds and
fog, often required their mimetic replication inside the enclosed space of
the laboratory.

At the beginning of the twentieth century, French physicist Étienne-Jules
Marey made use of chronophotography and smoke as instruments for visualizing and observing otherwise invisible atmospheric phenomenon of air
currents, turning the malleable and opaque substance of smoke into a means
of visualization. He built glass wind tunnels attached to a 'smoke machine'
that spouted smoke streaks from a row of parallel nozzles. He would then
place tiny objects in these wind tunnels to disturb the flow of air—and thus
to alter the visible path of the smoke streaks. Marey documented the patterns
created by these smoke trails in a series of stunning chronophotographs.
Smoke here functioned as a sculptural medium for visualizing airflow, and
photography worked as a graphic medium for recording this movement.[15]

Marey was by no means the first scientist to notice smoke's potential as
a tool for the visualization and observation of airflow. French aeronautical
engineer Alphonse Pénaud also observed how 'dust particles lit up by the
sun would give a graphic picture of the disturbance of the air around birds'.
In order to replicate this natural optical condition, Pénaud used jets of
smoke to further study air turbulence, an experiment that anticipated the
use of dust, smoke, and chemical fog by expanded cinema and light art
practitioners in the mid-twentieth century.[16]

Such scientific deployment of cloud-like substances is an essential part
of the history of the laboratory. Take, for instance, the invention of the
cloud chamber by Scottish physicist and meteorologist Charles Thomson
Rees Wilson. The cloud chamber is a scientific instrument used by atomic,
nuclear, and particle physicists to visualize otherwise invisible atmospheric
phenomena such as the passages of charged particles. Wilson's original

15   Hinterwaldner, p. 9. While Marey's proto-cinematic invention of chronophotography and his
attention to the indexical trace of time occupies an important place in film and media studies,
what draws my attention to his experiments is not the photographic record per se but his use
of the smoke machine to visualize airflow. On Marey's experiments with the indexical trace of
time, see Doane, 2002.

16   Braun, p. 217. Some critics have compared Nakaya Fujiko's fog sculpture to Marey's smoke
photographs. Anne-Marie Duguet, for instance, notes that although Nakaya's primary objective
is aesthetic, her creative process relies on rigorous scientific protocols of observation and
experimentation. Duguet, p. 35

impetus for building a sealed container with super saturated water vapour was to reproduce the cloud formations he observed as a meteorologist. The cloud chamber, in other words, was first designed to create artificial clouds in a controlled environment. To use Peter Galison's term, the cloud chamber was an instrument of 'mimetic experimentation', a term he uses to describe a series of scientific 'attempt[s] to reproduce natural physical phenomena, with all their complexity, in the laboratory'.[17]

It was these mimetic experiments—the reproduction and analysis of atmospheric phenomena such as rain, clouds, fog, lightning, and snow inside the simulated environment of the laboratory—that informed the later invention of the water-based artificial fog used by Nakaya Fujiko and her collaborators for the Pepsi Pavilion. To fully understand the genealogical significance of this fog sculpture therefore requires that we pay attention to the technological and scientific conditions that enabled the artist to turn artificial fog into an artistic medium. Just as the material history of microphysics cannot be narrated without the understanding of technical and epistemological impacts of instruments and machines that assisted scientists in their attempts to visualize, document, measure, and compute their experiments, unpacking the invention of the fog medium in a genealogical fashion demands that we understand the technological apparatus that supported this artwork: the fog-making machine. Furthermore, just as the construction of scientific instruments for experiments is bound up with their institutional as well as theoretical contexts, the fog-making machine used for the Pepsi Pavilion has its own historicity.

In order to understand the historicity of this apparatus, however, we must not simply look at the instrument itself but also broaden our scope to trace another genealogical connection: a familial connection between the artist and her father, Nakaya Ukichirō, a famed physicist who invented artificial snowflakes in the mid-1930s. (Figure 7.1) While critical and historical writings on Nakaya Fujiko's fog sculpture have made customary reference to this father-daughter relationship, they hardly go beyond anecdotal interpretations of their shared interests in meteorological phenomena.[18] As we will see below, however, the connection between their work goes beyond their bloodline; it is the practice of engineering the atmosphere that binds the artist and the scientist.

17   Galison, p. 75.
18   Art critic Okazaki Kenjirō suggests that Nakaya Fujiko's keen interest in the observation of the structure and metamorphic process of fog formation comes from her father Ukichirō's devotion to the scientific analysis of the principles of snow crystallization. Okazaki, p. 69.

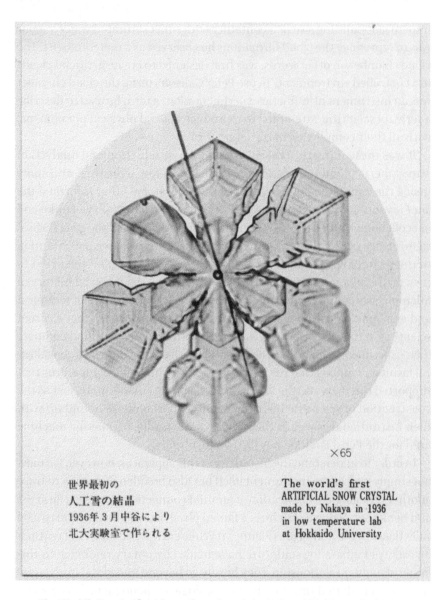

世界最初の
人工雪の結晶
1936年3月中谷により
北大実験室で作られる

×65

The world's first
ARTIFICIAL SNOW CRYSTAL
made by Nakaya in 1936
in low temperature lab
at Hokkaido University

7.1:   The World's First Artificial Snow Crystal made by Nakaya Ukichirō at the low-temperature lab, Hokkaido, Japan, 1936. © Nakaya Ukichiro Foundation.

Engineering the atmosphere

According to Sloterdijk, the invention of poison gas in the early twentieth century weaponized the very act of breathing air—a hitherto latent possibility.[19] The atmosphere thus became a medium for distant killing through the spread of poison gas, and along with this change came the use of smoke screens, fog machines, and fog dispersal techniques in the service of aviation.

As James Fleming notes, 'The dawn of aviation brought new deeds and challenges, with fog dispersal taking centre stage'.[20] Natural fog, in other words, became an explicit object of systematic technological manipulation through its deployment in aerial warfare. The rise of fog along with clouds, snow, and rain as objects of military research is intimately tied to this strategic understanding of the atmosphere as a prime battlefield in the twentieth century. Pilots especially needed a clear view of the runway, requiring fog dispersal; battleships also benefited from the fog-dispersal technology. Henry G. Houghton, a physical meteorologist from the Massachusetts Institute of Technology, invented an experimental fog clearing machine in the mid-1930s. Houghton created 'artificial fogs in his laboratory and tested means of dispersing them' using pressure nozzles. And his research had direct implications for the technical component of the fog sculpture.[21]

The first successful case of large-scale fog dissipation was the British Royal Air Force's Fog Investigation and Dispersal Operation (FIDO) system deployed in 1944. The chemical engineers working on this project came up with a device to heat up the airfield so that Allied pilots could safely take off and land during foggy conditions.[22] On the other side of the globe, a team of Japanese scientists led by Nakaya Ukichirō embarked in June 1944 on a similar project to observe and disperse summer sea fog. Having worked on several wartime research projects related to frost heaving, aircraft icing, and lightning at the Institute of Low Temperature Science in the 1930s and early 1940s, Nakaya was a scientist whom the Japanese military entrusted with the strategic task of developing a fog dispersal system.

With the assistance of researchers at the central meteorological observatory, military engineers, and his students from Hokkaido University, Nakaya directed a project studying summer sea fog. In order to collect comprehensive data on density, humidity, scale, and fog droplet size, they rode balloons provided by the Japanese Army and photographed fog droplets day after day. These photographic records provided the visual means of gauging the size

---

19   Sloterdijk, p. 57.
20   Fleming, p. 6.
21   *Popular Science*, p. 39. Houghton's research on pressure nozzles is also mentioned by Nakaya Fujiko. See Nakaya, 1972, p. 220.
22   Fleming, p. 6.

and density of droplets in the atmosphere. The researchers also deployed time-lapse cinematography to document the appearance and disappearance of sea fog from the top of a nearby coastal mountain.[23] Along with the prevention of icing on aircraft propellers and frost heaving on the railroad, the clearing of the visual field for aviators became particularly urgent as Japan consolidated its territorial control over northern climate regions such as Manchuria and the Kuril Islands. The scientific study of fog was implicated in the expansion of the Japanese empire—and its eventual demise.

From 1944 to 1945, Nakaya's team tirelessly gathered atmospheric data using balloons, cameras, desiccators, and daily weather maps. They finally devised a 'fog dispersal truck' using makeshift materials one month before Japan's surrender in August 1945.[24] The end of the war did not bring an end to Nakaya's atmospheric science research, however. And his collaboration with experts from other fields continued. After the war was over, Nakaya worked on the agricultural impact of snow, ice, and frost in the hope of improving the productivity of his war-torn nation after the loss of its oversea colonies. Later he also worked on resource development projects.[25] In order to continue his research on artificial snow and artificial rain, he sought financial assistance from governmental agencies, including the Allied occupation forces and the U.S. Air Force. Not surprisingly, his involvement in both Japanese and American military research was quite controversial to some.[26] Others were more forgiving, since Nakaya regarded his involvement in military research as a necessary evil and upheld his ideal of engaging in 'useful' basic research that served the common good.[27]

Between 1952 and 1954, Nakaya joined and worked for the U.S. Army Corp's Snow, Ice, and Permafrost Research Establishment (SIPRE), an organization that he helped establish by serving as an international consultant. It is this type of participation that places Nakaya in the transnational orbit of the military-industrial-academic complex that bridged wartime Japan and Cold War America. To put it differently, by following Nakaya's career we can trace Japan's geopolitical reorientation from World War II to the Cold War period.

One of the American meteorologists Nakaya knew was Vincent Schaefer at the General Electric Research Laboratory. During the Occupation, Schaefer had personally helped Nakaya by procuring American film stock to reshoot his film

23   Higashi, pp. 70-96.
24   Sugiyama, p. 84.
25   Machimura, p. 45.
26   Kobayashi, pp. 21-22.
27   See Nakaya Ukichirō, p. 28.

Snow Crystals (1939), which documented his experiments with artificial snow.[28] Schaefer procured the necessary funds from the classified cloud-seeding project called Project Cirrus (1947-1952), for which he served as a coordinator.[29]

During World War II, Schaefer—like Nakaya—worked on military research related to de-icing techniques. Together with Irving Langmuir, a Nobel Prize-winning chemist who also worked for the GE Research Laboratory, Schaefer developed a method of cloud seeding to artificially induce precipitation. They were the literal 'rainmakers' who contributed to the dual-use technology of weather modification during the Cold War.[30]

Researchers involved in Project Cirrus 'conducted about 250 experiments involving modification of cold cirrus and stratus clouds, warm and cold cumulous clouds, periodic seeding, forest fire suppression, and a notable attempt to modify a hurricane'.[31] The promise of freely engineering meteorological phenomena seemed like a near-future reality. (Figure 7.2) A 1954 *Collier's Magazine* article, tantalizingly titled 'Weather Made to Order', describes such futuristic scenarios as 'milking rain or snow from reluctant clouds at the proper time and place'.[32] The practice of weather control, in short, is described as a domestication of nature. The gendered analogy of milking rain or snow also betrays a masculine fantasy of extraction, extended to the atmosphere.

The author of the article, Howard T. Orville, chairman of the Advisory Committee on Weather Control under the Eisenhower administration, further speculated on the future:

> How will you have your weather—wetter, drier, warmer in winter, cooler in summer? Or would it appeal to you to have every weekend a fair one, and rain only on Wednesdays? (Even that's conceivable, by stimulating an apparent natural weather 'cycle' of about a week.) Whatever your choice, the time may not be far away when the weather-makers can deliver it.[33]

Orville, a retired Navy officer, also discussed the possible military uses of weather modification, such as intercepting clouds in order to dry up crops and thus to 'strike at an enemy's food supply'.[34]

28   Sugiyama, p. 155.
29   Ibid., p. 174.
30   Harper and Doel, p. 118.
31   Fleming, p. 150.
32   Orville, p. 26.
33   Ibid.
34   Ibid., p. 29.

7.2: "Weather made to order? Man's Progress in Weather Control." *Collier's Magazine*, May 28, 1954.

By the mid-1960s, such speculation became a harrowing reality. The political destabilization of Southeast Asia during the Vietnam War and the military potential of 'weather warfare' seemingly convinced the Pentagon to launch weather control as part of its experimental warfare. In preparation, the U.S. government under President Lyndon Johnson tested its secret weather modification techniques for the purportedly humanitarian project of alleviating droughts in India. Once it proved effective, large-scale cloud-seeding techniques were employed to steer hurricanes above Laos and Vietnam with the intention of prolonging the monsoon season and thus disrupting 'North Vietnam's supply lines that snaked through the Laotian panhandle and into South Vietnam'.[35] In short, the military use of weather control up in the air became a potential means of disrupting enemy logistics on the ground.

Such tactical use of weather control further integrated meteorological phenomena into warfare. In so doing, it propelled the ongoing process of atmospheric-explication that began with the invention of poison gas and continued with fog dispersal and its counterpart, smoke screen technology.[36] While the commercial use of cloud-seeding promised a rosy future for weather on demand—turning arid deserts into fertile croplands by modulating rainfall, preventing flooding, and feeding hydroelectric power plants—the development of weather control is inseparable from its military applications. Of course, this does not mean that the military use of weather control overshadowed its civilian counterpart. In 1950s and 1960s Japan, for instance, research projects on experimental weather control, especially on artificial precipitation, were carried out mainly by meteorologists affiliated with hydroelectric power companies supported by the state, which hoped to multiply the production of electricity needed for the nation's rapid economic recovery and further industrial growth.[37]

Regardless of its applications, however, there is one common element to these diverse forms of weather control: their inseparability from the question of security. From its military application to warfare to its civilian application to ensure food and water security, controlling weather became tied to the geopolitics and biopolitics of the twentieth century. That is to say, the military application of weather control became inseparable from the geopolitical influences of nation-states over their given or disputed territories, as well as the biopolitical management of populations and their access to crops or water. Weather control in this sense was a dual-use technology;

---

35   Harper and Doel, p. 130.
36   Citing the 1996 study by the U.S. Air Force titled 'Weather as a Force Multiplier: Owning the Weather in 2025', Sloterdijk lists possible means of weather control: 'Based on current projections, the range of weather weapons will include: the maintaining or hindering of vision in air space; the increasing or decreasing the troops' comfort levels (i.e. their morale); thunderstorm enhancement and modification; rainfall prevention over enemy territories and the inducing of artificial drought; the intercepting and blocking of enemy communication; and preventing the enemy from performing analogous weather activities.' Sloterdijk, p. 64.
37   See, for instance, Yoshimoto, pp. 12-21.

at the most basic level, it was an instrument for managing the environment in both peacetime and wartime, an instrument that both sustained the biological life and ensured the survival of the modern nation-state.

In this regard, it is worth remembering Sloterdijk's point that explicating the atmosphere reveals the existential insecurity of living in a technologically mediated environment. With the militarization of poison gas and weather control, technological modernity intensified the sense of insecurity associated with the environment, as the air we breathe potentially contains poison, and the clouds above us are possible meteorological weapons. In the compensatory manner, this intensified sense of atmospheric insecurity further propels technological inventions to create countermeasures, such as the inventions of the gas mask, air-purification, and so on. The eventual establishment of the regulatory Weather Control Commission in the United States (directly modelled after the Atomic Energy Commission) fits this framework.[38] The weaponization of weather control could—like nuclear weapons—become lethal if it got out of control. Even uncontrolled air pollution can be lethal, as indicated by deaths caused by heavy smog. Such incidents of industrial air pollution are considered 'inadvertent weather modification'.[39]

The sense of insecurity posed by weather modification is, however, not an exception but a rule of technological modernity. It is a salient example of the paradoxical process of atmospheric-explication in general. According to Sloterdijk, 'modernity conceived as the explication of the background givens thereby remains trapped in a phobic circle, striving to overcome anxiety through technology, which itself generates more anxiety'.[40] That is to say, the explication of the atmosphere creates a vicious cycle: the more we learn about the vulnerability of the atmosphere, the more we turn to technology to compensate for and control this vulnerability.[41] The military investment in the weaponization of the weather, in this regard, is part of the ongoing process of atmospheric-explication that also reveals the human desire to dwell inside a 'climate-controlled' environment.[42] The revelatory capacity of technology to explicate the atmosphere is inseparable from the artifice of human dwelling

38   Harper and Doel, p. 119.
39   Tsuchiya, p. 213.
40   Sloterdijk, p. 79.
41   Ibid.
42   As Eduardo Mendieta puts it, all technology for Sloterdijk is primordially 'space-originating technology'. Mendieta, 73. In his essay 'The Age of the World Picture,' Heidegger criticized this way of conceiving technology as an instrument as a hallmark of modernity when the objectification of the world vis-à-vis the relational centre of the subject becomes the basis of knowledge production.

as a constant effort to engineer the environment. Needless to say, the effort to secure and expand habitable environments through engineering the land, ocean, and sky is a continuous thread that runs through the history of industrialization and colonialism and that characterizes modernity.

Fog sculpture

It is against this broad context of the ongoing process of atmospheric-explication that I want to situate the invention of artificial fog as an artistic medium by Nakaya Ukichirō's daughter, Nakaya Fujiko. Her innovative use of water-based artificial fog, which generated a microclimate around the Pepsi Pavilion, cannot be separated from the concurrent epistemological and technological process of atmospheric-explication. It is not coincidental that the artistic use of fog became both conceptually salient and technologically feasible at the precise moment when the adverse effects of weather modification (including the inadvertent kind, in the form of air pollution) were slowly becoming clear.

To put it schematically, then, the microclimate control at the Pepsi Pavilion is a scaled-down version of commercial, military, and industrial geoengineering that controlled and modified weather. This is not to disregard the aesthetic intention of the artist who is known for her commitment to environmental activism and her critique of mercury pollution. Rather, I am highlighting the ambivalent duality of the technologically mediated process of atmospheric-explication that binds otherwise heterogeneous experiments undertaken by artists, scientists, and engineers.

Although the ultimate inventor of the pressurized nozzle-based fog-making machine for the Pepsi Pavilion was American cloud physicist Thomas Mee, Nakaya Fujiko settled on this apparatus after a long process of experimentation. To better understand how the fog sculpture sits at the point of convergence between these two lines of descent (of visualizing and engineering the atmosphere), let us look closely at the technological and scientific assistance that Nakaya received to make this artwork. The idea to shroud the exterior of the geodesic dome with artificial fog emerged at the early planning stage of the Pepsi Pavilion by E.A.T., a group to which she belonged since her participation in the *9 Evenings* event in 1966.[43] (She

---

43 Strictly speaking, E.A.T. as a group was formally established after the success of *9 Evenings*. For more on the history of E.A.T., see the 2003 exhibition catalog *E.A.T. – The Story of Experiments in Art and Technology*.

7.3:   Experiments in Art & Technology, The Pepsi Pavilion at Osaka Expo '70, (photo: Shunk-Kender). © Roy Lichtenstein Foundation, courtesy Experiments in Art & Technology.

also served as the coordinator for E.A.T.'s Tokyo headquarters.) Throughout the second half of the 1960s, Nakaya and other Japanese artists including Ichiyanagi Toshi, Takahashi Yūji, Takemitsu Tōru, Isobe Yukihisa, Usami Kenji, Morioka Yūji, and Kobayashi Hakudō participated in E.A.T. projects that included *9 Evenings* (1966), *Some More Beginnings* (1968), the Pepsi Pavilion at Expo '70 (1970), and *Utopia: Q&A 1981* (1971).[44] Among these, the commissioned project of designing the Pepsi Pavilion was by far the largest project that E.A.T. undertook. The project involved 75 artists, scientists, and engineers, nurturing interdisciplinary collaborations among them.

Enveloping the dome with artificial fog was central to the group's overall objective of turning the pavilion into a 'living responsive environment'.[45] They wanted this artificial environment to register and respond to ambient factors such as wind, temperature, humidity, and the movement of visitors in

44   Packer, p. 146.
45   Klüver, 1972, n.p. See also Klüver, 1970.

real time.[46] (Figure 7.3) However, the technical feasibility posed a challenge. According to Nilo Lindgren, a journalist who followed its planning stage, 'No one knew whether or not it was actually possible to make a fog, but the idea persisted and survived'.[47] Nakaya, who had an avid interest in the ephemeral form of clouds, became a key person in charge of executing this ambitious idea.

There are many different ways of artificially creating fog. As Nakaya notes in her essay 'The Making of "Fog" or Low-Hanging Stratus Clouds', one can use water (as she ultimately did for the Pepsi Pavilion), chemicals, oil, or smoke. She opted for using pure water in order to accommodate the aesthetic requirements of the project. Water, rather than other substances, was more suitable for the following reasons:

My choice was based on what I felt were the three most important requirements of the fog for our purpose:

1. Visibility: it should scatter enough light to reduce considerably the visibility of the objects behind, and, at the same time, make visible the otherwise invisible dynamics of atmosphere;
2. Tangibility: it should feel soft and cool to the skin;
3. Vulnerability: it should be subject to atmospheric conditions; it should disappear, not persist.[48]

Among these three conditions, the first (visibility) and the third (vulnerability) are particularly interesting in light of the scientific investment in fog discussed earlier and the weaponization of fog. Fog—or low-hanging stratus clouds, as Nakaya calls them—is marked by its versatility. When used to conceal objects behind it, it works like a smokescreen. But it can also refract and diffuse light. Some of her later projects thus make clever use of laser beams, as in the case of her collaborative work with Bill Viola (*Fog Sculpture*, 1980), which took advantage of fog's optical effects of refraction and diffusion and served as an ambient screen.[49]

Moreover, fog's constant metamorphosis can draw viewers' attention to ambient environmental factors such as wind, temperature, humidity, and even the movement of visitors (which makes it an ideal 'interactive' or 'responsive' medium for environmental art). Put another way, a fog

46 Nakaya Fujiko writes: 'Constantly changing atmosphere acted as a mold; the Fog sculpture was given its form instantaneously by the physical condition of its environment.' Nakaya, 1972, p. 207.
47 Lindgren, p. 23.
48 Nakaya, 1972, p. 209.
49 Viola, p. 150.

sculpture engages in the process of atmosphere-explication; it renders explicit latent conditions of the atmosphere that otherwise remain imperceptible as an environmental given.[50] Generated by atomizing nozzles attached to the roof of the geodesic dome, this site-specific fog sculpture cascaded, drifted, and gathered outside the dome, responding to the ever-changing patterns and density of air currents, temperature, humidity, and light. (Figure 7.4)

What is unique about the technical support of this work is its use of water-based, rather than chemical, fog. In using water, the work *simulated* natural fog and provided the pavilion with its own microclimate. Yet this microclimate was completely artificial. Nakaya notes: 'The only request I made to my partner-scientist was that I wanted dense, bubbling-out fog, as close a simulation as possible to natural fog in its physical nature, to cover the entire Pavilion, with perhaps drop-size control added to make rain once in a while'.[51]

At the preparatory stage for designing the fog-making system, Nakaya spent six months gathering statistical data on the local weather patterns in Senri, where the world's fair was to take place. She carefully studied the layout of the fairground and the topography of the surrounding area to understand its potential physical impact on the aesthetic process of fog-making. She also consulted a number of Japanese physicists and meteor-ologists in order to explore the technical feasibility of producing pure water fog.[52] Two of the scientists she sought advice from were Magono Chōji and Higashi Akira at Hokkaidō University. They were both students of her father, Nakaya Ukichirō, and had participated in his wartime research project on fog dispersal in the first half of the 1940s. Nakaya Fujiko's path thus directly crossed with that of her father in her quest for the scientific and technical support she needed to create this exquisite environmental artwork. By generating simulated fog and rain, this site-specific work also participated in the experimental practice of weather control, which developed in the 1950s and 1960s. As I discussed in previous sections of this chapter, the attempt to visualize otherwise invisible atmospheric phenomena has generated scientific and artistic experiments since the nineteenth century. The attempt to control weather and to engineer man-made fog, rain, and

---

50   Sloterdijk, p. 47.
51   Nakaya, 1972, p. 220.
52   Nakaya Fujiko writes: 'The area around the Pavilion was open except for the southwest side where it was backed up by a small hill; there were no other obstacles nearby, such as tall buildings or trees, to serve as windbreaks.' Nakaya, 1972, p. 208.

7.4:   Billy Klüver, Fujiko Nakaya and Thomas Lee inspecting the pumps for the cloud sculpture at Pepsi Pavilion, Osaka, '70. © Roy Lichtenstein Foundation, courtesy Experiments in Art & Technology.

snow belongs to a different lineage, even though both traditions share a desire to explicate the atmosphere. The genealogical nexus between the two Nakayas point to the intersection of these two lineages.

Site-specific weather

Pushing the line of genealogical thinking that binds fog sculpture to weather control further, we may arrive at a new way of conceptualizing screens and the history of media as well as a new conception of site-specificity as a geopolitically located practice. To begin, we may think of the practice of engineering the atmosphere as both site-specific and scalable. One can move from modulating an atmosphere at the miniature scale of a cloud chamber to the median scale of a pavilion and to a much larger scale of an entire region. Moreover, as one moves from the enclosed space of the laboratory to the larger space of open experiments, the geopolitical configuration of the technology changes as well. Various geographical, climatological, meteorological, socio-political, and technical factors are at play when weather modification is performed. At this point, geopolitics (literally, the politics of the earth) provides a necessary perspective for thinking about the specificity of a given site of weather modification. It is in this sense—of the specificity of the given environment within which the work of weather control takes place—that we may use the term *site-specificity*.

Although this term comes out of the discipline of art history and holds a privileged relationship to the field of sculpture, I am more interested in its literal connotation, of the givenness of the site.[53] What happens if we move away from the formal or conceptual constraints of a site-specific art work (though Nakaya Fujiko's fog sculpture surely can be analyzed from that angle) and towards the geopolitical specificity of the notion of *site* itself? Here, I am using the term to deliberately expand this notion to include a site's environmental constraints, wherein the broadly conceived act of engineering the atmosphere may take place. To do so is to decouple an artwork from its disciplinary context and place it in a different framework of analysis. To read the singular work of fog sculpture and the systematic operations of weather control side by side is to pay attention to their common ground. This ground, I argue, is the epistemological and technological conditions of mimetic experimentation, the attempt to artificially replicate meteorological phenomena.

Expanding the conceptual affordance of the term site-specificity outside the history of art in this manner also allows us to attend to multiple senses

---

53   I am thinking in particular of debates around Rosalind Krauss's seminal 1979 essay, 'Sculpture in the Expanded Field'. For its enduring relevance to the fields of sculpture, architecture, and conceptual art, see Papapetros and Rose, 2014.

of the term *medium*. In the context of art history, the term refers to an artistic medium—the material and technical supports and formal conventions of an artwork—while the same term in the context of media studies predominantly signifies technical channels and intermediary agents of communication, transmission, and storage. The recent recuperation of medium in the spatial and environmental sense of milieu—literally the middle—by media scholars offers a heuristic means of rearticulating the material support of environmental artworks, such as Nakaya's fog sculpture, in terms of this etymological affinity between milieu and medium. The idea of elemental media—water, air, and sky as communication media—proposed by Peters, for instance, pushes this line of thinking to incorporate natural physical phenomena, including the weather, back into the history of technical media. '"Media," understood as the means by which meaning is communicated, sit atop layers of even more fundamental media that have meaning but do not speak', writes Peters. For him, 'the old idea that media are environments' must be flipped if we were to understand media in this expanded sense, since 'media are ensembles of natural element and human craft'.[54] To understand the significance of the fog sculpture from this emergent perspective of environmental media means that we expand the use of the term medium in relation to this artwork. As I have argued throughout this chapter, this expanded sense of the medium allows us to incorporate the development of its technical apparatus through the history of science and technology into its genealogical framework.

Conclusion

In conclusion, I want to briefly discuss an afterlife of the fog-making machine used for Nakaya's fog sculpture at the Pepsi Pavilion. Originally invented by Mee and his engineers for weather control, the apparatus had practical applicability beyond the realm of art. As Billy Klüver proudly notes, it 'offered interesting possibilities for environmental irrigation systems, outdoor air conditioning, and protection of crops from frost'.[55] The original application of the fog machine was aesthetic, but its afterlife was not. This fog-making technology (or more precisely, the evaporative cooling process derived from it, which Mee Industries Inc. developed after Expo '70) is used today to cool

54   Peters, p. 3.
55   Klüver, 1972, p. xii.

down data centres.[56] The metaphorical clouds of networked data storage and processing systems are thus directly linked to the physical clouds of fog sculpture by the historical path of a shared apparatus.

Seen from the standpoint of media studies, then, the invention of the fog medium belongs to the wider history of atmospheric media. Noting the ubiquitous presence of networked computational devices and micro-sensors in our environments and their capacity to filter data and condition our sensory experiences of the world at the imperceptible level, Mark Hansen has proposed the term 'atmospheric media'. Marked by anticipatory temporality, these atmosphere media, he argues, have reconfigured the relationship between humans and their environments.[57]

Recently, Nakaya Fujiko and a collaborator placed meteorological sensors at various places around an installation site in order to record ambient data such as temperature, humidity, and wind speed and direction. These data were then run through a special computer program that controlled the nozzles of a fog-making machine so that the shape of the fog directly responded to, and interacted with, the surrounding environment.[58] Here, current debates about atmospheric media come into sharp focus through the technological articulation of artificial fog and computational media.

Commenting on the contemporary resurgence of meteorological meta-phors in discussions of computational media, Peters writes: 'Fantasies of what Mark Hansen calls "atmospheric media" presupposes an electrical grid. Information is not smokeless. Google's servers burn up millions of dollars of electricity every month and produce an enormous amount of heat that requires cooling.'[59] Mee's fog-making apparatus and other air-conditioning systems installed at data centres worldwide are precisely the infrastructure that sustains the electrically powered servers of today's Internet-related service providers. The fog-making machine, in short, is the infrastructure of contemporary atmospheric media that Hansen discusses. In this regard, it is worth mentioning that the MeeFog system is installed at none other than Facebook's data centre in Prineville, Oregon.[60] The low-hanging cloud or fog that enveloped the Pepsi Pavilion at Expo '70 thus resurfaces not only in Nakaya's later and similarly spectacular artworks (such as the fog

56   'Data Center Uses MeeFog System', Mee Industries Incorporated Homepage. http://www.meefog.com/case-studies-post/data-center/data-center-uses-meefog-system-keep-operating-heat-wave/.
57   Hansen, p. 5.
58   See Ozaki, 2017.
59   Peters, p. 332.
60   'Facebook Uses MeeFog System', Mee Industries Incorporated Homepage. http://www.meefog.com/case-studies-post/data-center/facebook/.

sculpture for the Blur Building designed by architects Elizabeth Diller and Ricardo Scofidio for the 2002 Swiss Expo) but also in the much less visible walls and pipes of data centres where digital clouds are stored, accessed, modulated, and cooled. The distance between these two manifestations of artificial fog may seem far and wide, yet, as I have argued in this chapter, they belong to the same genealogy.

Pointing out the frequent recycling of Cold War bunkers into data centres, which inherit what he calls a 'bunker mentality', Tung-Hui Hu argues that data centres sit at 'the border between the dematerialized space of data and the resolutely physical buildings they occupy'.[61] A similar tension exists between the air-conditioning systems that support the operation of data centres and the engineering of the atmosphere by artists, scientists, and engineers that I traced as the genealogy of the fog medium. Arguably, the bunker mentality oriented towards ensuring security is itself an effect of the existential insecurity generated by the process of atmospheric-explication. The repurposing of the fog-making system invented for the Pepsi Pavilion to cool down data centres partakes in this ongoing process of atmospheric-explication. Going back to Hu's discussion of the bunker mentality for a moment, we may surmise that *in*security about the loss of data stored in the digital cloud is part of what Sloterdijk has called the phobic circle of explication. As we explicate the atmosphere through technology, it amplifies our anxiety about its vulnerability, which in turn prompts more technological solutions to manage and control this vulnerability.

The epistemological implications of atmospheric-explication, however, are not limited to the management of anxiety and insecurity generated by technology. What I have called the lineage of visualizing the atmosphere is a mode of explication that also gave rise to a series of aesthetic experiments that took the ephemeral matter of cloud-like substances (e.g. smoke, mist, fog, and helium-filled balloons) as projection and installation media. The duality of fog as a screening device to conceal and to reveal, to undermine and to increase visibility of the environment has thus served different functions in the realm of contemporary art. One may well read these artworks as symptoms of the existential insecurity generated by the technological explication of the atmosphere. We may also situate them as integral components of the genealogy of atmospheric computational media and the infrastructure that sustains it. To do so enables us to directly link the existential insecurity of atmospheric-explication discussed by Sloterdijk to the material infrastructure of data centres. The increasing embeddedness of

61   Hu, p. 81.

computational media in our physical environment and the ever-intensifying traffic of electronic signals in our everyday lives seem to demand that we shift our perspective from the old model of technical media towards atmospheric phenomena as media. To do so without collapsing metaphors and histories is a challenge to which this chapter has attempted to respond.

When we attend to the genealogical dimension of these media rather than the phenomenological experiences they engender in the present, we inevitably come up against another challenge: the geographically, politically, and institutionally specific contexts within which certain technological apparatus were developed, tinkered with, and put to experimental use. The historicity of the fog-making machine used for the fog sculpture at the Pepsi Pavilion in 1970 is a salient reminder of such specificity. And this specificity, as in many other instances of media, is deeply entangled with the geopolitical configuration and reconfiguration of the world. In other words, the work occupies multiple positions depending on the analytical framework: it is at once an exemplary atmospheric screen; an exquisite environmental artwork; an emblem of the art-and-technology movement that facilitated collaborations among artists, scientists, and engineers; and a scaled-down version of military and civilian applications of weather control and geoengineering. There's no doubt that we can find more instances of such varied articulations among the works of other contemporary media artists. But to overemphasize their technological novelty would risk obscuring their historical conditions of possibility. To look through the dust of archives that led to such articulations of artificial and technical media is a way to see fog in its longer history as a medium of scientific inquiry and artistic experiment.

Works Cited

Bao, Weihong. *Fiery Cinema: The Emergence of An Affective Medium in China, 1915-1945*. Minneapolis: University of Minnesota Press, 2015.

Braun, Marta. *Picturing Time: The Work of Etienne-Jules Marey (1830-1904)*. Chicago: University of Chicago Press, 1992.

Casetti, Francesco. *The Lumière Galaxy: Seven Key Words for the Cinema to Come*. New York: Columbia University Press, 2015.

Doane, Mary Ann. *The Emergence of Cinematic Time: Modernity, Contingency, the Archive*. Cambridge, MA: Harvard University Press, 2002.

Duguet, Anne-Marie. 'Naturally Artificial.' In *Fujiko Nakaya: Fog, Kiri, Brouillard*, 30-39. Paris: Editions Anarchive, 2012.

Fleming, James Rodger. *Fixing the Sky: The Checkered History of Weather and Climate Control*. New York: Columbia University Press, 2010.

Galison, Peter. *Image and Logic: A Material Culture of Microphysics*. Chicago: University of Chicago Press, 1997.

Gulliver, Shuzo Azuchi. 'Flying Focus.' In *Ekusupandeddo shinema saikō / Japanese Expanded Cinema Reconsidered*, exhibition catalogue, 71. Tokyo: Tokyo Shashin Bijutsukan, 2017.

Hansen, Mark B.N. *Feed-Forward: On the Future of Twenty-First Century Media*. Chicago: University of Chicago Press, 2015.

Harper, Kristine C. and Ronald E. Doel. 'Environmental Diplomacy in the Cold War: Weather Control, the United States, and India, 1966-1967.' In *Environmental Histories of the Cold War,* edited by J.R. McNeill and Corinna R. Unger, 115-138. Cambridge: Cambridge University Press, 2010.

Higashi, Akira. *Yuki to kōri no kagakusha Nakaya Ukichirō*. Tokyo: Hokkaido Daigaku Tosho Kankōkai, 1997.

Hinterwaldner, Inge. 'Parallel Lines as Tools for Making Turbulence Visible.' *Representations* 124.1 (Fall 2013): 1-42.

Hu, Tung-Hui. *A Prehistory of the Cloud*. Cambridge, MA: The MIT Press, 2015.

Huhtamo, Erkki. 'The Sky Is (Not) the Limit: Envisioning the Ultimate Public Media Display.' *Journal of Visual Culture* 8.3 (2009): 329-348.

Klüver, Billy. Atarashii taiken no ba: Pepshi kan no 'ikita kankyō.' Translated by Nakaya Fujiko. *Bijutsu techō* (July 1970): 94-108.

Klüver, Billy. 'The Pavilion.' In *Pavilion: Experiments in Art and Technology*, edited by Billy Klüver, Julie Martin, and Barbara Rose, ix-xvi. New York, E.P. Dutton & Co., Inc, 1972.

—— and Julie Martin, eds. *E.A.T. – The Story of Experiments in Art and Technology*, exhibition catalogue. Tokyo: NTT InterCommunication Center, 2003.

——, Julie Martin, and Barbara Rose, eds. *Pavilion: Experiments in Art and Technology*. New York: E.P. Dutton & Co., Inc, 1972.

Kobayashi Hideo. 'Teion Kekyūjo o meguru gunji kenkyū.' *Kokumin no kagaku* (March 1955): 19-25.

Krauss, Rosalind. 'Sculpture in the Expanded Field.' *October* 8 (Spring 1979): 30-44.

Lindgren, Nilo. 'Into the Collaboration.' In *Pavilion: Experiments in Art and Technology*, edited by Billy Klüver, Julie Martin, and Barbara Rose, 3-59. New York, E.P. Dutton & Co., Inc, 1972.

MacDonald, Scott. *A Critical Cinema 2: Interviews with Independent Filmmakers*. Berkeley and Los Angeles: University of California Press, 1992.

Machimura Takashi. *Kaihatsu shugi no kōzō to shinsei*. Tokyo: Ocha no mizu shobō, 2011.

Marvin, Carolyn. *When Old Technologies Were New: Thinking About Electric Communication in the Late Nineteenth Century.* Oxford: Oxford University Press, 1988.

Mee Industries Incorporated. 'Data Center Uses MeeFog System.' MeeFog.com. http://www.meefog.com/case-studies-post/data-center/data-center-uses-meefog-system-keep-operating-heat-wave/. Accessed 26 May 2017.

———. 'Facebook Uses MeeFog System.' MeeFog.com. http://www.meefog.com/case-studies-post/data-center/facebook/. Accessed 27 May 2017.

Mendieta, Eduardo. 'A Letter on Überhumanismus.' In *Sloterdijk Now,* edited by Stuart Elden, 58-76. Cambridge, UK: Polity, 2012.

Nakaya Fujiko. 'Kūki to mizu.' Special Issue on Expo '70, *Bijutsu techō* (July 1970): 105-108.

———. 'Making of "Fog" or Low-Hanging Stratus Cloud.' In *Pavilion by Experiments in Art and Technology,* edited by Billy Klüver, Julie Martin, and Barbara Rose, 207-223. New York, E.P. Dutton & Co., Inc, 1972.

Nakaya Ukichirō. 'Gunji kenkyū to wa nanika.' *Hokudai kikan* (January 1955): 27-28.

Orville, Howard T. 'Weather Made to Order?' *Collier's Magazine,* 28 May 1954.

Okazaki Kenjirō, "The lucid, unclouded fog – the movement of bright and swinging water particles." In *Fujiko Nakaya: Fog, Kiri, Brouillard,* 60-74. Paris: Editions Anarchive, 2012.

Ozaki Tetsuya. 'Nakaya Fujiko + dNA: MU.' *ART iT.* http://www.art-it.asia/u/admin_exrev/HsLPfgloEvCVG1oBUwXu/. Accessed 18 March 2017.

Packer, Randall. 'The Pepsi Pavilion: Laboratory for Social Experimentation.' In *Future Cinema: The Cinematic Imaginary After Film,* edited by Jeffrey Shaw and Peter Weibel, pp. 144-149. Cambridge, MA: The MIT Press, 2003.

Papapetros, Spyros and Julian Rose, eds. *Retracing the Expanded Field: Encounters between Art and Architecture.* Cambridge, MA: MIT Press, 2014.

Peters, John Durham. *The Marvelous Clouds: Toward a Philosophy of Elemental Media.* Chicago: University of Chicago Press, 2015.

Popular Science. 'Fog Wiped Out by Chemical Spray.' October 1934.

Reynolds, Roger. *Cross Talk Intermedia I.* Newsletter for Institute of Current World Affairs, 10 May 1969. http://www.icwa.org/wp-content/uploads/2015/11/PR-20.pdf. Accessed 18 March 2017.

Ross, Julian. *Beyond the Frame: Intermedia and Expanded Cinema in 1960-1970s Japan.* PhD diss., The University of Leeds, 2014.

Sas, Miryam. 'By Other Hands: Environment and Apparatus in 1960s Intermedia.' In *The Oxford Handbook of Japanese Cinema,* edited by Daisuke Miyao, pp. 383-415. Oxford: Oxford University Press, 2014.

Sloterdijk, Peter. *Terror From the Air.* Translated by Amy Patton and Steve Corcoran. Cambridge, MA: MIT Press, 2009.

Somaini, Antonio. 'Walter Benjamin's Media Theory: The *Medium* and the *Apparat*.' *Grey Room* 62 (January 2016): 6-41.

Starosielski, Nicole. *The Undersea Network*. Durham, NC: Duke University Press, 2015.

Sugiyama Shigeo. *Nakaya Ukichirō: Hito no yaku ni tatsu kenkyū o seyo*. Tokyo: Mineruva shobō, 2015.

Tsuchiya Iwao. 'Kishō seigyo, Kikō kaizō.' *Kishō kenkyū nōto* 104 (June 1970): 143-264.

Viola, Bill. 'Music for Fog Sculpture Event by Fujiko Nakaya, Kawaji Onsen, Japan, 1980.' In *Fujiko Nakaya: Fog, Kiri, Brouillard*, edited by Fujiko Nakaya and Anne-Marie Duguet, 150-155. Paris: Editions Anarchive, 2012.

Williamson, Colin. *Hidden in Plain Sight: An Archaeology of Magic and the Cinema*. New Brunswick, NJ: Rutgers University Press, 2015.

Yoshimoto, Hideyuki. 'Denki jigyō to jinkō kōu.' *Denryoku*, 46.5 (May 1962): 12-21.

About the Author

Yuriko Furuhata is associate professor in the Department of East Asian Studies, an associate member of the Department of Art History and Communication Studies, and a faculty member of the World Cinemas Program at McGill University. She works in the areas of film and media theory, Japanese cinema and media studies, visual culture, and critical theory. She is the author of *Cinema of Actuality: Japanese Avant-Garde Filmmaking in the Season of Image Politics* and has published articles in journals such as *Grey Room*, *Screen*, and *New Cinemas*. She is currently working on a book, tentatively titled *Atmospheric Control: A Transpacific Genealogy of Climatic Media*, exploring the historical connections between Japanese environmental art, weather control, and cybernetic architecture.

8.   The Charge of a Light Barricade: Optics and Ballistics in the Ambiguous Being of Screens

John Durham Peters

Abstract

John Durham Peters invites a rethinking of the optical and environmental duality of the screen by examining media practices that link projection to protection and showing to shielding. The ontological ambiguity of the screen—at once a site for the representation of a world and a real element embedded in the world—enables one to think of media as a key part of what Peters calls 'infrastructures of being'. Outlining the historical convergences between cultural practices of targeting and visualizing in Western history, Peters weaves together a rich and unexpected set of voices from the onset of the 'atomic age'—from James Joyce and Vladimir Nabokov to Harold Edgerton and Norbert Wiener—illuminating the connection of detonation to image-making across photographic, filmic, televisual, and celestial screens.

Keywords: Photography, Atomic Bomb, Television, Infrastructure, Literature

SCREEN (NOUN): 1F. 'Any thin extended surface set up to intercept shot in gunnery trials.' SCREEN (VERB): 1A. 'TRANS. To shelter or protect with or as with a screen, from heat, wind, light, missiles, or the like.'—*Oxford English Dictionary*

The ontological ambiguity of screens

When we see, do we see the world or images of the world? Do our eyes give us direct access to reality, or do they construct pictures by means of which

Buckley, C., R. Campe, F. Casetti (eds.), *Screen Genealogies. From Optical Device to Environmental Medium*. Amsterdam: Amsterdam University Press, 2019

DOI 10.5117/9789463729000_CH08

we navigate it? The long history of disputes about the theory of vision could be boiled down to the question of whether sight is immediate or mediated. Certainly in everyday practice, almost everyone votes for the former view. We trust intuitively that our eyes deliver the world to us. The trees, houses, windows, books, and people I see feel like they are simply there and not like neurologically processed artefacts of a narrow band of the optical spectrum. George Santayana wrote of our 'animal faith' in the senses, and Edmund Husserl called our everyday immunity to scepticism about them 'the natural attitude'. The suspension of disbelief may be a practical prerequisite for living, but it does not take much philosophical exertion to reactivate it. Optical illusions, blind spots, floaters, and after-images intrude on the idyll of immediate vision. You can rub your eyes and behold colourful light shows that come from nowhere but the eyes themselves, and you can get even more spectacular results from hallucinogenic drugs. If you stare directly at a star, you can make it disappear; if you stare directly at the sun, you will see it everywhere you look for a long time thereafter. If you spin yourself around and around, the world will keep spinning when you stop. Many are the ways of detaching sight from the world. Thus eyes become media—as always, with biases and specific channel characteristics. Betting that reality is unproblematically given by the senses is a gamble that usually pays off, but it is also an evolutionarily fruitful inurement to fabrications and an overconfidence in the reliability of our instruments.

I start by rehearsing these well-known and elementary observations to make a point about the deep stakes of the concept of *screen*. Its double heritage as both environmental and visual, as explicated in the introduction to this volume, usefully intervenes in the long history of meditations on how we see. As the editors write, a screen can be 'a filter, a divide, a shelter, or a means of camouflage'. The optical view sets us up to view screens as surfaces for stagecraft and illusion—at times perhaps wonderful but never fully real. This view is barely two centuries old. The much older environmental view takes screens as things in the world in their own right—as defensive ploys, parries, blinds, barriers, or sieves. The genealogy of screens bequeaths us, in other words, both a suspicious and an ontological view of screens, a conflict between a dualistic and monistic metaphysics—a face-off, say, between team Adorno and team Deleuze. This tension also informs the long history of debates about the nature of photography, specifically about whether it is the documentary pencil of nature or a kind of natural magic for stunts and tricks.

There *are* good reasons for dualistic suspicion. The negation of that which is immediately before our eyes is the first principle of cognition. Ever since

Moses's proscription on graven images and Plato's attack on idols, at least, expurgating illusions has been an essential ethical and intellectual task. The civilizational heights of philosophy, religion, and science owe much to the spurning of surfaces.

Modernity also has an all too well-known history of suspicion toward the visual. Johannes Kepler, in founding the retinal theory of vision, understood the eye as a *camera obscura* (a term he probably coined) and helped launch the seventeenth-century scepticism about the data of the senses. (As an astronomer, he needed to sort out the play of light on the eyes at night).[1] Galileo worried that his telescope was deceiving his eyes, and Descartes much more radically asked if everything he saw and heard could be an elaborate simulation by some malign *Matrix*-style demon. Locke thought we had no access to the world except through 'ideas', and soon Berkeley gave up on tying such ideas to any external reality whatsoever. Leibniz's cosmos was composed of monads—little images of the world, which happened to lack windows. Modern epistemology was founded as a thoroughgoing critique of direct sight in favour of an analysis of the elaborate mechanics by which pictures are brought before the mind. In a slightly different key, iconoclasm fuelled political reforms from the Calvinist image-storms of the sixteenth century through Milton to the French Revolution. From Kant through Marx and Freud through Adorno and beyond, much intellectual and political energy has been spent on the dialectical unmasking of illusion's intertwinement with the world. Such worries were baked into the cultural reception of optical media such as the magic lantern, the phantasmagoria, photography, and film, and attacks on images remain the ostinato of modern visual culture—often with ample justification, given the alluvion of ballyhoo that covers the globe.

But in tearing off masks, we should stop short of tearing off faces. Some appearances are real things. With productive ambiguity, the environmental concept of *screen* blurs the real and the fabricated, the natural and the techni-cal, the objective and the retinal. In this way, the environmental concept is a kind of corrective to the corrosiveness of the hermeneutics of suspicion. What if screens were a part of—not apart from—the world? What if we took screens as not merely presenting appearances but as performing genuine operations on and with what we pleadingly call reality? Could the world itself be a screen? How might we think of nature's image-inscription surfaces and light sources? The sun writes on the earth's biosphere, hydrosphere, lithosphere, and atmosphere in various ways. (I leave to the side the question

1   Lindberg, pp. 178-208.

whether a screen is definitionally a fully erasable surface or one that, like Freud's *Wunderblock*, leaves behind traces of its various projections.) Deserts, clouds, seas, and forests index both lightfall and albedo—the reflectivity of the earth's surface, which is a key factor in global warming. Chlorophyll is a kind of slow photographic medium, as indeed some bioartists have shown, and the history of temperature and climate is written into tree rings and stone. The earth and sky are screens for light. The universe, if you like, screens its history in the redshifts of the light emanating from distant celestial objects. Screens, in this ample conception, are ubiquitous not only as technical interfaces but also in the natural world. The retina is a peculiar kind of screen, and, like the sky, it has a special vaulted curvature that is the condition of possibility for all seeing. Is the retina a projection surface for pictures or a participant in the being of what it sees? It is hard to say, and that is precisely the point.

In preparing this essay, I have acutely felt the blessing and curse of too many ancestors. (I sometimes thought that I had confused two letters— scream, not screen—as I've torn my hair out.) The head spins with examples of interesting screens. I thought of architectural screens in Japanese or Arab culture, such as those that figure so beautifully in some of Henri Matisse's paintings. (Figure 8.4) I thought of the cloud of the Pentateuch—which both shows and hides the divine presence, both indicating YHWH's nearness and shielding him from the profane gaze of the people—and of the ancient Greek *skēnē*, which is the ancestor of our word 'scene' but originally meant 'tent'. The *skēnē* was both a stage for theatrical spectacles and a shelter from the elements, thus uniting the twinned faces of the screen concept: projection and protection. I thought of so-called screen-savers, those abstract kinetic images designed to preserve one's computer monitor as a genuine tabula rasa devoid of any traces of its habitual pictures.

This ontological expansion of the screen obviously fits the digital Zeitgeist. Screens show up at the gas pump, in classrooms, airports, doctors' offices, and on our persons. In a historical moment when our quotidian lives and natural habitats alike are governed by networked flows of data, it is both urgent and interesting to consider media as actors in the world and not merely as traffickers in simulacra, phantasms, and second-rate copies (with proper dialectical provisos, of course). The weather, the economy, the sea are all natural-technical hybrids. So is the public sphere, whose nature is sensitive to rapid alteration by tweets, rumours, and filter bubbles. (Seeing media as ontological is, of course, not always a happy thought.) The reclaiming of a natural dimension for the screen concept helps us to liberate images and other mediated forms from the cage of representation in which they

8.1:   At the time this photo was made, smoke billowed 20,000 feet above Hiroshima while smoke from the burst of the first atomic bomb had spread over 10,000 feet on the target at the base of the rising column. (Photo: Bob Caron), Source National Archives and Records Administration.

have been crammed, allowing them to become participants in the world, or even in being itself, for good and ill. The question about media and reality is less one of true and fake than of good and evil. A reality cannot be false; it simply is. But it can be bad. Politics, ethics, and aesthetics rather than know-it-all epistemology should be the leading disciplines for media theory, and I take the ontological ambiguity of the screen concept as one push in the broader intellectual direction of understanding media as infrastructures of being, with all the troubles that follow. Screens are preeminent sites for foregrounding the work that media do in the world.

A telling recent example for joining *screen*'s dual senses of projection or protection is the airport security checkpoint, as brilliantly analyzed by Lisa Parks. She sees such screening as a quasi-cinematic apparatus into which billions of dollars have been poured since 2001. Sites of poorly paid, stressful, and dangerous labour, checkpoints are a 'state-led exercise in hand-eye coordination'.[2] Take off your shoes, says the TSA as if speaking to Moses, for this is holy ground: here passengers undergo a public, state-mandated striptease. The monitoring of bodies combines remote-sensing and close-sensing, imaging and touch, in a kind of two-step flow. If a trigger is set off, then you undergo a pat-down by a member of the same sex (here the state enforces the gender binary, just as it enforces the privilege of whiteness). The monitoring of luggage is done by way of an optical screen, which serves as a 'gothic cousin to the television commercial', 'a spectral slide show of 21st-century consumerism' as goods parade across it in constant infomercial without price tags.[3] Airport security is a kind of weapons system whose putative aim is to detect concealed weapons. Here, screening is both an authoritative inspection of populations (as in a 'cancer screening') and a plethora of visual technologies.

Optics and ballistics

The ancient link of optics and ballistics is yet another way that screens are ontologically ambiguous. The reality of a projectile is obvious in a way that that of a picture is not. Theories of vision starting from Aristotle understood the eye as a ballistic screen, capturing 'species' (essences) radiating off of objects. Indeed, it seems to be Thomas Aquinas's rather sheepish translation of a passage about vision from Aristotle's *De Anima* that gave us the media concept—a third term, a middle place, a *medius locus* (which is the origin of the term *milieu*) that connects eye and object. There was no middle term, no exact equivalent in Greek. For Thomas, a medium was a stop-gap accounting for the action at a distance between target and vision.[4] In the atomist psychology of Epicurus and Lucretius, every material object broadcasts superfine corpuscular emissions that, upon striking the human sense organs, cause sensations. For Lucretius, everything threw off images,

2   Parks, p. 186.
3   Ibid., p. 194.
4   Hagen, pp. 13-29.

traces, films—*simulacra* or *membranae*—in the same way that 'wood throws off smoke and fire heat', cicadas molt their shells, calves shed their caul, or a snake sheds its skin.[5] Here, images are not shadows of real things, an ontologically suspicious doubling; they are bits of reality physically partaken of by the eyes. Unsurprisingly, the term that perhaps best embodies the doubleness of the screen concept is 'film'. In older uses, 'film' as a noun could mean a thin sheet, tissue, or membrane, as in Lucretius; as a verb, 'to film' could mean to cover with a layer. Cinema inherits a much longer history of understanding vision as a physical, even projectile event, and of images as physical entities (cf. the comical 'or the like' in the epigraph to this essay, which makes missiles and light equally into projectiles).

The art of ballistics, ancient and modern, played a central role in scientific instrumentation and measurement as well as technical invention. Humans may be the only species that can throw, and we seem deeply fascinated with throwing: 'The parabolic ballista is ours alone.'[6] Media theorist Friedrich Kittler dwelled with martial delight on the ancient tie between acoustics (the lyre) and archery (the bow) as well as the role that the cannon played in early modern science. He was also fascinated by how Renaissance perspective involved what he called the '*Bewaffnung des Auges*', or weaponization of the eye. His case in point was Albrecht Dürer's 1527 treatise on the construction of fortresses, which gives us 'perspective from a ballistic perspective'. The sight lines for fortresses tied the straight lines of linear perspective to the parabolas of bullets. To see was to shoot.[7] This correlation extends to the French and Spanish verbs meaning to fence, *escrimer* and *esgrimir*, which, like the English 'skirmish', are cognate to the Dutch *scherm*, German *Schirm*, or Swedish *skärm*, all of which mean screen or shield. Here, optical media meet swordplay!

War is a regular theme in media theory, and perhaps one reason is the readiness with which war makes problems ontologically specific; the battlefield may be socially constructed, but its reality is obvious to everyone on it. In warfare, there is no sign without *Sein*. In war (as in love), the sign is the thing itself. To signal is not a neutral act: it is to risk blowing your cover. Every message sent potentially discloses your location to the enemy. (Chechen warlords were killed by Russian intelligence agents tracking their cell phones.) Ancient catapults launched balls inscribed with imprecations; soldiers have long christened bullets after their intended targets; and an

---

5   Lucretius, 4: 54-61. On Balzac's reception of such ideas, see Krauss, 1978.
6   Ridley, C4.
7   Kittler, 2002, p. 65; See also Bousquet, 2018.

image of Rita Hayworth may have adorned (much to her distress) one of the bombs dropped on Japan. Cybernetics, the meta-science developed by Norbert Wiener out of his research on anti-aircraft artillery during World War II, turns on the insight that signals are not simply signs; they are weapons, that is, reality-rearranging vectors. Perhaps the young John Langshaw Austin, later famous as the author of *How to Do Things with Words*, first discovered performativity while overseeing British reconnaissance for Operation Overlord, i.e. the D-Day invasion of Normandy in 1944. The battle command is not just a statement about the world; it is a speech act on which life and death hang. For good or ill, war is a destination for those interested in a return to ontology.

The fireball

The atomic bomb was a screen technology. The cityscapes of Hiroshima and Nagasaki famously served as photographic screens: the bomb's heat and radiation left its mark on walls, buildings, and bodies as an exposed image. The cities were made into perverse photographic laboratories for skiagraphy or shadow-writing. For the vaporized bodies, as Akira Mizuta Lippit remarks, no image was 'left but their negatives'.[8] It is a well-known, gruesome, and perhaps exaggerated fact that images of people and objects—so-called 'nuclear shadows'—were written onto walls by the flash of the bomb. (The bomb did burn clothing patterns onto people's skins.) Thomas Pynchon wrote perhaps too graphically that the victims' bodies became 'a fine-vapor deposit of fat-cracklings wrinkled into the fused rubble'.[9] In 1945, Bazin wrote of the ontology of the photographic image, and there could be no clearer example of an image ambiguously suffused with real presence than a nuclear shadow. (Bazin's essay could have been called 'the oncology of the photographic image'.[10]) Paul Virilio and Kittler both compare the bomb dropped on Hiroshima to a camera with a very fast shutter-speed, i.e. one fifteen millionth of a second or 67 nanoseconds. Kittler sees this ultra-rapid-fire flash photography as the inaugural act of cinema that operates according to computer processing speeds.[11] The bomb is the origin of digital media in this as in many other ways.

---

8   Lippit, pp. 81, 93-95, 109, passim.
9   Quoted in Kittler, 1999, p. 261.
10   A pun I owe to Antonio Somaini.
11   Virilio, p. 81; Kittler, 1999, p. 261.

At first it was only the bomb, and not the camera, that could operate at such speeds. The first aerial pictures of the blast over Hiroshima were taken by George Caron, the tail-gunner of the Enola Gay, with a borrowed camera. (The plane with all the photographic equipment that was supposed to document the attack got off course and missed the rendezvous.) Caron's photo, now canonical, is a grainy black and white image of a column of cloud, leaning slightly off the vertical, topped by a separate crown-shaped puff. (Figure 8.1) No sign of the instant disappearance of 80,000 people is to be found in the abstraction of this extreme long shot. Mushroom cloud pictures like this one, which was published in *Life Magazine* two weeks after the assault, remain the iconic image of the nuclear age.

In a brilliant and also slightly terrifying recent article, Ned O'Gorman and Kevin Hamilton argue that the nuclear fireball is actually the more characteristic image.[12] The mushroom cloud can be seen with the naked eyes, but not the thermonuclear fireball itself, at least not in any detail. The fireball of a hydrogen bomb simply explodes too fast, and though filmable with a traditional 24-frame-per-second camera, the complex physical reactions that are of deep interest to scientists elude traditional photographic techniques.

Enter Harold Edgerton, the MIT professor of electrical engineering already famous for his mid-1930s photographs of a milk-drop splashing on a surface. (Figure 8.2) O'Gorman and Hamilton show that his interest in split-second photography emerged in the late 1920s and 1930s as he studied the engineering problem of synchronization among machines. Stroboscopic techniques allowed him to observe and document rapid events that would otherwise elude vision. With two of his former students, Edgerton formed a company called EG&G (Edgerton, Germeshausen, and Grier) that specialized in high-speed images of nuclear explosions, or 'firing and timing'. EG&G was a major defence contractor for the U.S. military during World War II and the Cold War. The company took an aerial photograph of Normandy on 5 June 1944, which revealed a profound lack of preparation by German troops for what was to come the next day. None of the Germans seem to have noticed an uncanny flash in the sky that night—from a camera mounted in the bay of an airplane where a bomb normally would go.[13] This substitution of camera and bomb also took place in the case of Fat Man, the bomb dropped on Nagasaki. Edgerton's company contributed in developing the bomb's

12   See O'Gorman and Hamilton, 2016.
13   The logistical media history of D-Day is at least threefold: the intelligence reports overseen by Austin; the aerial photography overseen by Edgerton; and the weather forecast, one of the most important in history, overseen by a team of American, British, and Norwegian meteorologists.

8.2:   Harold E. Edgerton (1903–1990), *Milk-Drop Coronet Splash*, 1936. © 2010 MIT.
Courtesy of MIT Museum.

detonation mechanism. The workers at Raytheon who built it were kept in
the dark about its ultimate purpose and were told it was an 'advanced version
of equipment for night aerial photography'.[14] That description was, in a way,
technically correct. As O'Gorman and Hamilton note, 'Over Normandy a
camera occupied the bay of a bomber, [and] over Nagasaki a plutonium core

14   O'Gorman and Hamilton, p. 193.

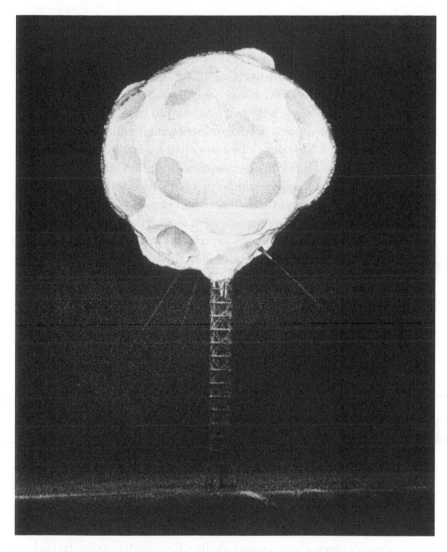

8.3:   Harold E. Edgerton (1903–1990), *Atomic bomb explosion at the Nevada Proving Grounds*, photographed for the Atomic Energy Commission; before 1952. The first microseconds of an atomic explosion captured in a 1/100,000,000-of-a-second exposure, taken from seven miles away with a lens ten feet long. © 2010 MIT. Courtesy of MIT Museum.

occupied the place of a circuit normally reserved for a camera flash'.[15] In the history of photography, the synchronization of light flash and shutter opening was always a challenge. The discovery of EG&G was to use the very same micro-timing mechanisms for both detonation and shutter. EG&G made literal the identity of flash and photograph.

To document hydrogen bombs, EG&G had to find a way to slow the reaction, or rather the camera, down to microseconds (millionths of seconds). In the early 1950s, EG&G developed so-called Rapatronic (*rap*id *action* elec*tronic*) cameras for taking microsecond images of nuclear reactions. Taking pictures of bombs poses unique problems; for one thing, the camera has to be able to withstand the radiation and exposure of a blast over 100 times the intensity of the sun's surface. Here, as with the A-bomb, light is not just an invisible hand tracing images in pixie dust but a grotesquely palpable physical event. ('Screen' is also a term for a shield against radiation.) The details of the camera go beyond our concern here: EG&G's key discovery was that to make images of thermonuclear blasts, the camera must participate in the detonation. Camera and bomb were bound by a single 'firing, timing and exposing' mechanism. It was impossible to tell where the bomb ceased and the picture began.

The resultant microsecond images, like Edgerton's earlier photos of milk drops landing on flat surfaces or later pictures of bullets whooshing through apples, were profoundly unnatural and unlike any that human eyes had ever seen before. Forget Walter Benjamin's tenth of a second or Eadweard Muybridge's horses as a standard for how photography blows apart time—these images isolated millionths of seconds. EG&G's fireball images, captured by slicing time at intervals impossible for the eye, are uncanny and terrifying. Fiery icicles drip from irradiated bone-like balls. The images have the grayscale tones of X-ray films and show toothy baby monsters rearing menacingly on two legs, teratomas, bulbous cauliflowers, mutant navel oranges, aliens, insects, skulls—Rorschach tests for the nuclear age. (Figure 8.3) The work of EG&G provides a radical perspective on the ontology of the photographic image.[16]

15   Ibid., p. 194.
16   We might also consider the film leader countdown as a convergent staging of detonation and pictures, with its radar-like clock-sweep, its NASA-like countdown to blastoff. Bruce Conner exploits this link in *A Movie* (1958).

8.4:   Henri Matisse (1869–1954), *L'Ecran Mauresque (The Moorish Screen)*, 1921. Oil on canvas, 91.9 x 74.3 cm. © 2018 Succession H. Matisse / Artists Rights Society (ARS), New York.

Television as war machine

Television and the bomb were arguably the two main mass media of the postwar era. Both were massive delivery systems, often developed by the same people and institutions, involved similar physical processes and existential worries, similar large-scale capital investment and blankets of fallout.[17] As Kittler flatly declares, 'television is a civilian side-effect of an extensive military electronics'.[18] TV was, hands down, the most important screen of the decades following 1945 and was always deeply connected to radar, radiation, anti-aircraft fire, and weather forecasting, as visionaries as diverse as Paul Virilio, Friedrich Kittler, Joyce Nelson, and Tex Avery have observed in their various ways.[19]

James Joyce portrayed the ballistic dimension of television in *Finnegans Wake* (1939), in a passage beloved by Marshall McLuhan:

> In the heliotropical noughttime following a fade of transformed Tuff and, pending its viseversion, a metenergic reglow of beaming Batt, the bairdboard bombardment screen, if tastefully taught guranium satin, tends to teleframe and step up to the charge of a light barricade. Down the photoslope in syncopanc pulses, with the bitts bugtwug their teffs, the missledhropes, glitteraglatteraglutt, borne by their carnier walve. Spraygun rakes and splits them from a double focus, grenadite, damnyite, alextronite, nichilite: and the scanning firespot of the sgunners traverses the rutilanced illustred sunksundered lines.[20]

I cannot do this passage justice, but I do not think a better account of television's operation as an optical gunnery machine has ever been given. The heliotropic night-time/nought-time tube, with its viseversion (vice versa) of interlacing video, glowing with beams, will teleframe a light barricade—the screen named after TV inventor John Logie Baird, if it is properly tuned. The broadcast sprays bitts between the teffs at the missiled/misled tropes/hopes/anthropes in one of the *Wake*'s 'thunderwords', glitteraglatteraglutt, which could refer to the crackling, statick-y sound or the sparkling snow of the image, the glut of glitter borne by carrier wave

---

17   See Nelson, p. 12.
18   Kittler, 2002, p. 290.
19   Avery's animated short of 1953, 'The T.V. of Tomorrow', brilliantly shows the TV set multifariously as a military and domestic apparatus.
20   Joyce, p. 349.

or carny-valve. The electron spraygun bombards the tube with a scanning firespot traversing the 'sunksundered lines'. Such a treasury of potential media-theoretic vocabulary! Joyce has lent quantum physics terms such as 'quark'; perhaps his 'bitt' should retroactively be awarded the honour of coining the digital 'bit'. If we wanted a good name for screens in their doublings as projection and protection, my nominee would be 'the charge of a light barricade'.

Another brilliant literary treatment comes from 'Pale Fire,' the poem-within-the-book in Vladimir Nabokov's novel *Pale Fire* (1962). The narrator, John Shade, addresses his wife Vanessa at the end of an evening of television, turned nervously on while they wait for their forlorn daughter out on a date:

> Eleven struck. You sighed. "Well, I'm afraid
> There's nothing else of interest." You played
> Network roulette: the dial turned and trk'ed.
> Commercials were beheaded. Faces flicked.
> An open mouth in midsong was struck out.
> An imbecile with sideburns was about
> To use his gun, but you were much too quick.
> A jovial Negro raised his trumpet. Trk.
> Your ruby ring made life and laid the law.
> Oh, switch it off! And as life snapped we saw
> A pinhead light dwindle and die in black
> Infinity. [...][21]

Note the harsh judgment day of the viewer's hand, executioner of images, like a cowboy too quick on the draw to let someone else shoot or a guillotiner mutilating faces. The sovereign dial or ruby ring, making life and law by the sheer caprice of the roulette wheel, is a kind of weapon, beheading commercials, cutting people down in mid-sentence, fencing with the screen.[22] Note the late-night boredom, the 'nought-time', scanning between channels in expectation of something about to take place. (Figure 8.5) When the tube is finally turned off, its light dies cosmically like a vortex in a bathtub drain in black infinity—a vivid image for anyone who

21 Nabokov, pp. 49-50.
22 One of the early TV remote control devices, the Zenith Flash-Matic, was advertised as putting a weapon in housewives' hands that they could shoot at the set to control volume (see Fig. 8.5). As in Shade's poem, the gender polarity of weaponry is reversed when war technology is domesticated.

remembers what happened to the image on the screen when television sets were shut off in the 1950s and 1960s. In the poem, this all happens right before a police car pulls up at midnight, lights flashing, bringing news of their daughter's Ophelia-like death. Nabokov describes the juxtaposition of boredom and disaster, the uneasy but eager scanning of the horizon that Stanley Cavell thinks forms the existential fact of television. TV viewers, like decommissioned radar readers, watch for approaching threats, seeking drama or meaning amid the repetitive tedium. As a system that mobilizes entire populations to monitor and scan air-borne signals sent from afar, television incorporates the Bomb and the Holocaust as unassimilable experiences but does so in an overwhelmingly banal register that can occasionally erupt into something much more urgent. It is this mix of waiting for the coming catastrophe and escaping numbly into fantasy, of on-edge vigilance and opiate boredom, that makes television the true child of the postwar era. It also shows why television is a more cosmic medium than cinema and thus also generally more boring: it has to pull its content from the sky.

Perhaps the least interesting thing about postwar TV was the programs. These were the meat the burglar gives to the guard dog so he can get about his genuine business. The medium's existential profile appeared on its edges when it was turned off, being turned on or off, being listened to but not watched, when the horizontal and the vertical were being tweaked, when the snow between the stations showed up or the antenna didn't pull in the signal. The opening sequence of *The Outer Limits* from 1963 immortalized the creepy effect of messing with the screen:

> There is nothing wrong with your television set. Do not attempt to adjust the picture. We are controlling transmission. If we wish to make it louder, we will bring up the volume. If we wish to make it softer, we will tune it to a whisper. We will control the horizontal. We will control the vertical. We can roll the image, make it flutter. We can change the focus to a soft blur or sharpen it to crystal clarity. For the next hour, sit quietly and we will control all that you see and hear.

(Unfortunately, this uncanny discipline did not apply to the commercials.)[23] The children in *Poltergeist* (1982) discover the 'TV people' in the middle

---

23   Alien possession via broadcast irregularities would later become a topic in Parliament Funkadelic's album *Mothership Connection* (1975), which is also all about The Bomb.

8.5:   Advertisement for Zenith Flash-Matic Tuning, first wireless remote-control device for television sets, c.1955.

of the night after all the regular channels have signed off. Insomnia calls forth the spirits.

Literary examples could be multiplied. Thomas Pynchon's novella *The Crying of Lot 49* (1965) opens with protagonist Oedipa Maas returning home one afternoon to find herself being 'stared at by the greenish dead eye of the TV Tube'.[24] The postwar TV set was a commanding presence, rearranging subjects and objects around it, even when it was turned off. Soon, when Oedipa and a new friend are making love in a hotel, an old war movie plays on TV, offering comic commentary: 'From the other room came a slow, deep crescendo of naval bombardment, machine-gun, howitzer, and small-arms fire, screams and chopped-off prayers of dying infantry'.[25] In Harry Mulisch's *The Discovery of Heaven* (1992), probably the most important postwar novel written in Dutch, a character turns on a TV set without turning on the house lights and 'the reflection of the image flickered through the room as if constant small explosions were going off'.[26] We have all seen this effect: a room lit up by a TV set that we cannot see can look like a flashing war theatre.

24   Pynchon, p. 1.
25   Ibid., p. 25.
26   Mulisch, p. 580.

Perhaps the most famous literary example is the opening line of William Gibson's *Neuromancer* (1984): 'The sky above the port was the colour of television, tuned to a dead channel.' Gibson exploits the environmental-meteorological metaphor of 'snow' for the video noise that possesses a TV channel when there is no signal. The deadpan bit of the line is that such a channel has no colour at all, just a jumpy fuzz of black and white. Video noise, as it is called, is sensitive to cosmic flux and the solar wind. In the United States it is called 'snow', in Sweden 'war of the ants' (*myrornas krig*), and in Hungarian 'ant soccer' (*hangyafoci*). Something must be happening in there—In 'Pale Fire', when the TV is first turned on, 'The screen/In its blank broth evolved a lifelike blur', it is like the primordial ooze bringing forth life for the first time.[27] Viewers still search screens for emerging patterns of life and death.

Whether the *Götterdämmerung* of the ants or the 'technical difficulties' of some atmospheric disturbance, the television screen without a clear picture has rich significance. (Yet again, the medium is the message!) A blank screen can mark the censorship of something not showable, death, an ending, or someone closing their eyes. (For Microsoft-hosted computers, the 'blue screen of death' signified total system failure.) In heist movies, the screens of surveillance or security monitors turn to snow when they are hacked or hijacked. In disaster films, the world will end after a global montage of TV reporters against a backdrop of notable landmarks (the Eiffel Tower, the pyramids at Giza) shows the TV screens, one by one, turning to snow. Snow belongs to a family of 'ominous visual glitches'.[28] Signal degradation is a sure trope of the world being profoundly out of joint. During a bad telephone connection, we say 'you are breaking up', not differentiating the person and their signal. The loss of radio contact in World War II could mean technical difficulties or death ambiguously, as in Randall Jarrell's poem 'A Front' in which a returning bomber, on finding the airbase shrouded with dense fog, disappears from the radio band. There is little that is quite as existentially rich as a TV screen filled with nothing but snow or a radio crackling with the staticky music of the spheres.

No wonder that the central theological, strategic, metaphysical, and epistemological question of the age came down to reading the significance of a fuzzy screen. Was 'jam', as Norbert Wiener called it, the product of a malevolent demon trying to interfere with our equipment or the random flux of cosmic stochastics? Was it an adversary messing with us or just God playing dice with the universe? World War II and Cold War cryptography led

27 Nabokov, p. 47.
28 'Ominous Visual Glitch', *TVTropes.com*, http://tvtropes.org/pmwiki/pmwiki.php/Main/ OminousVisualGlitch (accessed 2018).

Wiener to the deepest questions in the philosophy of science and religion.[29] The fog of war makes the reading of the signal a matter of life and death, and this jumpy hermeneutic burden remained part of the infrastructural unconscious of television screens in the postwar era.

Back to the sky

Snow falls from the sky. TV was an aerial medium, both dependent on the 'air' to carry its signals and the great mouthpiece for the atmosphere's main human manifestation, the weather. TV screens belong to the same family as radar screens, which watch for projectiles such as aircraft and larger formations such as weather fronts. The sky has always been the screen of screens. It is full of clouds, lightning, winds, comets, portents, omens, and *mirabilia*. Epic poets such as Virgil and Milton conjured the sky as a battlefield of the celestial hosts. Chinese emperors ruled by its mandate. In many cultures, new stars mark the birth and death of souls. In Shakespeare's *Hamlet*, the guards atop the castle at Elsinore, still stunned by the apparition of a ghost, while away the night discussing atmospheric omens. Ronald Reagan's 'Strategic Defence Initiative' envisioned a shield or celestial screen against nuclear warheads that was both cinematic and military, as captured in its lasting nickname 'Star Wars'.[30]

Most curiously, the sky is both a protective shield and a space for spectatorship. At night, the sky admits starlight, but by day the celestial canopy blocks out visible light from deep space. Without the enveloping atmosphere, we would wilt at once before the solar wind, and Earth would be a desert like Mars, where any atmosphere has been blown away and all oxygen is tied up in the rusty red lithosphere. Earth's sky is a cosmic shield as well as a cosmic cinema. The sky at day is McLuhan's 'light on' (which he associated with movies) and at night 'light through' (which he associated with television). If we are looking for what Francesco Casetti calls 'a cinema that manifests itself in the broad daylight', no better example could be found than the sky.[31] The sky is our ultimate environment and 'the ultimate art gallery above' (Emerson); it is both ontological and optical, usually indistinguishably so. The celestial vault—like its twin, our retinas—hovers between being and illusion, just like everything else.

---

29   Wiener, pp. 35-6, 93-4, Chapter 11, passim.
30   See Packer, 2013; Huhtamo, 2010.
31   Casetti, p. 207.

Works Cited

Bousquet, Antoine. *The Eye of War: Military Perception from the Telescope to the Drone*. Minneapolis: University of Minnesota Press, 2018.

Casetti, Francesco. *The Lumière Galaxy: Seven Keywords for the Cinema to Come*. New York: Columbia University Press, 2015.

Hagen, Wolfgang. 'Metaxu: Eine historiosemantische Fussnote zum Medienbegriff.' In *Was ist ein Medium?*, edited by Stefan Münker and Alexander Roesler, pp. 13-29. Frankfurt: Suhrkamp, 2008.

Huhtamo, Erkki. 'The Sky Is (Not) the Limit: Envisioning the Ultimate Public Media Display.' *Journal of Visual Culture* 8, no. 3 (2010): 329-348.

Joyce, James. *Finnegan's Wake*. New York: Penguin Books, 1999.

Kittler, Friedrich. *Gramophone, Film, Typewriter*. Translated by Geoffrey Winthrop-Young and Michael Wutz. Palo Alto: Stanford University Press, 1999.

——. *Optische Medien*. Berlin: Merve, 2002.

——. 'Lightning and Series—Event and Thunder.' Translated by Geoffrey Winthrop-Young. *Theory, Culture, and Society* 23, no. 7-8 (2006): 63-74.

Krauss, Rosalind. 'Tracing Nadar.' *October* 5 (1978): 29-47.

Lindberg, David C. *Theories of Vision from Al-Kindi to Kepler*. Chicago: University of Chicago Press, 1976.

Lippit, Akira Mizuta. *Atomic Light (Shadow Optics)*. Minneapolis: University of Minnesota Press, 2005.

Lucretius, *De rerum natura* (On the Nature of Things), translated by W. H. D. Rouse, revised by Martin F. Smith. Cambridge: Harvard University Press, 1992.

Mulisch, Harry. *De ontdekking van de hemel*. Amsterdam: De Bezige Bij, 1992.

Nelson, Joyce. *The Perfect Machine: TV in the Nuclear Age*. Toronto: Between-the-Lines Press, 1987.

Nabokov, Vladimir. *Pale Fire*. New York: Vintage International, 1989.

O'Gorman, Ned and Kevin Hamilton. 'EG&G and the Deep Media of Timing, Firing, and Exposing.' *Journal of War & Cultural Studies* 9, no. 2 (2016): 182-201.

Packer, Jeremy. 'Screens in the sky: SAGE, surveillance, and the automation of perceptual, mnemonic, and epistemological labor.' *Social Semiotics* 23, no. 2 (2013): 173-195.

Parks, Lisa. 'Points of Departure: The Culture of US Airport Screening.' *Journal of Visual Culture* 6, no. 2 (2007): 183-200.

Pynchon, Thomas. *The Crying of Lot 49*. New York: Harper Perennial, 1999.

Ridley, Matt. 'Tracing Those Angry Birds to the Dawn of Man.' *Wall Street Journal*, 15-16 January 2011, C4.

TV Tropes. 'Ominous Visual Glitch.' Last updated June 23, 2018. http://tvtropes.org/pmwiki/pmwiki.php/Main/OminousVisualGlitch

Virilio, Paul. *War and Cinema: The Logistics of Perception*. Translated by Patrick
    Camiller. London: Verso, 1989.
Wiener, Norbert. *The Human Use of Human Beings: Cybernetics and Society*. Boston:
    Houghton Mifflin, 1954.

About the Author

John Durham Peters is the María Rosa Menocal Professor of English and
Professor of Film and Media Studies at Yale University. His first book was
Speaking into the Air: A History of the Idea of Communication (1999). His most
recent publication, *The Marvelous Clouds: Toward a Philosophy of Elemental
Media* (2015) is a re-synthesis of concepts of media and culture, ranging from
planetary motion to bone evolution and calendrical design. His new book,
*Promiscuous Knowledge: Information, Image, and Other Truth Games in
History*, co-authored with the late Kenneth Cmiel, will be published in 2020.

9. Flat Bayreuth: A Genealogy of Opera as Screened[1]

Gundula Kreuzer

Abstract

Gundula Kreuzer challenges common assumptions about the 'screenification' of contemporary opera productions by reconsidering historical screening techniques within staged opera. Beginning with the Baroque picture-frame stage, she highlights how a desire for visual illusion on stage came into conflict with the increasingly complicated array of equipment, scenery, and props required to produce such elaborate scenes. Retracing strategies tested out at Wagner's Festspielhaus at Bayreuth, she argues that the theatre's curtain line came to imply an invisible screen with the capacity to organize the various media on the deep stage into a unified whole, a perception fostered by the visual and acoustic environment of the auditorium. Rather than a part of the telos of modernist painting, she highlights this flattened planar format as the outcome of technical and aesthetic conflict, whose legacy proves highly relevant to contemporary experiments with operatic staging.

Keywords: Auditorium, Stage, Architecture, Set Design, Richard Wagner, Music

Over the last several decades, music scholars have developed a keen interest in opera's relationship to the screen. A substantial number of essays and monographs have addressed such aspects of 'opera on screen' as studio productions of opera, TV relays or videos of live performances, television

1   This essay was developed in successive talks at Yale, Columbia, and Stanford Universities. Among the many stimulating audience responses, I am particularly indebted to Karol Berger, Craig Buckley, Kurt Forster, Brian Kane, and Carol Vernallis. Research has been generously supported by The Whitney and Betty MacMillan Center for International and Area Studies at Yale.

Buckley, C., R. Campe, F. Casetti (eds.), *Screen Genealogies. From Optical Device to Environmental Medium*. Amsterdam: Amsterdam University Press, 2019
DOI 10.5117/9789463729000_CH09

opera, opera films, or the diegetic use of opera in feature films.[2] In this discourse, 'screen' often serves as a shorthand for all manner of cinematic media, which are contrasted to the seemingly independent phenomenon of opera: the screen tends to stand as the 'other' to live operatic performance. This ontological opposition has received ideological fuel since the introduction, in late 2006, of 'Live in HD' simulcasts by the Metropolitan Opera and other major opera houses. For many commentators, the fact that cinematic remediations now claim for themselves the thrill of a live event has heightened the sense of an underlying competition between stage and screen, along with the pervasive anxiety that our ubiquitous digital culture might render live performances obsolete or redundant.[3] As music critic Anthony Tommasini does not tire of arguing, a simulcast of a performance enjoyed in the cinema offers an experience fundamentally different from all prior forms of remediated opera, because the simulcast combines audiovisual immersion with live communal viewing. Thus, Tommasini worries, HD broadcasts might not only lure audiences away from the opera house but also blur our sense of 'what the real thing is'.[4] From this perspective, the silver screen appears as opera's harbinger of death.

Ironically, a number of film scholars have simultaneously raised concerns about the future of the cinema itself, which they see likewise endangered by what we might call the increasing 'screenification' of our world.[5] Indeed, one could consider the very premise of this volume (namely, to rethink the genealogy of the screen) as an attempt to resituate the cinematic screen within an expanded—and ever-growing—panoply of screen practices. Yet with regard to opera, I would like to counter the widespread pessimism (or scepticism) toward its engagement with the screen, which I understand here very broadly as a two-dimensional 'information surface'.[6] Placing opera's relationship to such surfaces in a longer historical context challenges the frequently implied teleology of at least a partial medial succession from opera, via cinema, to digital content.

My essay is not the first, of course, to counter such linear narratives. Some scholars, for instance, have tended to stage competitions between

---

2   Thus the title of Marcia Citron's path-breaking monograph *Opera on Screen*. For select literature on opera on and for television, video, and live cinematic broadcasts, see Senici, 2010; Morris, 2010; Steichen, 2011; and Ward-Griffin, 2014.

3   The concept of remediation is taken from Bolter and Grusin, 1999. For a philosophical challenge to this opposition regarding opera films, see Cachopo, 2015.

4   Tommasini, 2013.

5   See, for instance, Friedberg, 2010; Elsaesser, 2016, p. 388.

6   This definition is from Huhtamo, 2004, p. 4.

opera and cinematic media. A frequent claim is that simulcasts lack the key components defining the live operatic event, namely the co-presence of performers and spectators, and the productive relationships between them.[7] One might also argue that opera—possibly more than film—has always been widely accessible outside the theatre via different media formats (whether as piano transcriptions or collector's cards), or that the cinematic challenge is not new to opera. As early as the 1920s, after all, the rise of film fanned what was widely discussed as an 'opera crisis' and spurred operatic productions to move away from the realism then newly associated with the cinema. Instead of such comparative arguments, however, I will explore features of the cinematic *within* opera, taking a media-archaeological perspective from which the relationship between opera and screening appears more complex than the predominant critical focus on opera's audiovisual remediations implies. First, screens are used not just to remediate opera but to *mediate* it in the first place: a variety of screens are essential to operatic production today. Second, I will propose that nineteenth-century illusionist staging practices themselves involved techniques of screening, which let the cinematic screen emerge less as a rival than as an ally of the proscenium stage. This historically and conceptually extended approach to screening as an operatic technique may, in the end, help reframe some recent developments in opera as well.

Screens onstage

To start with the obvious: video and computer screens have increasingly permeated opera houses since the rise of television. Monitors inside the proscenium and in the wings show a live feed of the conductor that affords onstage singers greater mobility, while additional live projections from the stage help stagehands, technical managers, and backstage singers to coordinate their activities. The continually increasing number of digitally operated props, lights, and stage technologies, meanwhile, require their own fleet of screens to manage. As tools for a performance, however, these screens are supposed to remain as invisible to audiences as the rehearsal process itself. By contrast, the visibility of supertitle screens—themselves initially contested technological additions to operatic performance—is by now deemed so essential as to influence price ranges in many an auditorium, even though supertitles are usually considered external to the 'actual' production.

7   On this conception of live performance, see Fischer-Lichte, 2008, p. 32.

More controversial has been the use of projections in productions proper, whether as part of a set, as a means to simulate scenes that are difficult to mount with conventional stage technologies, or as commentary on the stage action. Although this now-common practice dates back at least to Erwin Piscator's theatre of the 1920s, some pundits have continued to bemoan the inclusion of cinematic projections onto suitable or specially designed surfaces on stage: at best, they hold, this wastes the theatre's own illusionist possibilities; at worst, it destroys them.[8] As theatre scholar Arnold Aronson has argued perhaps most vocally, 'such projections and [moving] images draw upon a fundamentally different vocabulary from that of the stage', to the extent that 'the placement of such [film and video] technology on the stage is tantamount to carrying on a conversation in two languages'.[9] Aronson reasons that the theatre is unique among representational art forms in that it deals 'with real surfaces and volumes. A floor that is treated to look like tile may in fact be made of wood, but it still functions as a floor'.[10] Inserting projected images into this stage representation in most cases interrupts its continuity of space and time and thus dislocates the staged performance; even without a designated screen space, Aronson holds, a projected image infers its own frame within a stage production that is already framed by the proscenium. The presence of a projection and its implied screen thus collapses the basic representational tension between figure and ground into a hotchpotch of different media and materialities, each with 'different systems of reference'; as a result, 'content is overwhelmed by form'.[11] Aronson's key concern, then, is the collapse of the 'space-time continuum' established by living bodies acting in the present moment with, in, and upon the three-dimensional space of a stage.[12]

Yet I would venture that this collapse is less inevitable than Aronson allows. One exception is a type of production that employs screens as part of the staged (twentieth- or twenty-first-century) reality itself. Take, for example, Mariusz Treliński's updated 2016 staging of Richard Wagner's *Tristan und Isolde* (1865), a much-discussed co-production of the Festspielhaus Baden-Baden, the Polish National Opera, the Metropolitan Opera New York, and the National Centre of Performing Arts in Beijing.[13] (Figure 9.1)

8   On Piscator's use of screens and projections, see Fischer-Lichte, 1999, pp. 333-347.
9   Aronson, pp. 86-87.
10   Ibid., p. 87.
11   Ibid., pp. 93, 87.
12   Ibid., p. 88.
13   My discussion is based on my attendance at the Metropolitan Opera performance, conducted by Sir Simon Rattle, on 17 October 2016, as well as the HD broadcast of 8 October 2016,

9.1:   Tristan navigates his warship via radar control while spying on the distraught Isolde below deck with surveillance cameras in Mariusz Treliński's production of Richard Wagner's *Tristan und Isolde*, here at its premiere at the Baden-Baden Festspielhaus in March 2016. Courtesy of Monika Rittershaus.

In Act I, Isolde and Brangäne, the opera's only two female characters, are locked into the lower rooms of Tristan's modern-day warship, rendered as a vertically and horizontally split stage; and surveillance cameras project Isolde's actions live onto a screen on deck. Tristan alternately spies on these images and broods over an outsized digital radar screen. Distracting and crude these screens may be. But they efficiently communicate that Wagner's hero knows to navigate his ship but not his conscience. What is more, they drive home the misogyny at the core of Tristan's ill-fated enterprise—an attitude all too pervasive in our technologically advanced society, as the *#MeToo* movement has since shown. Rather than break the theatrical illusion, Treliński's screens render his staging's contemporary, socio-critical flair in the first place.

Even more radical in its embrace of screen technology is Barrie Kosky's widely travelled production of Wolfgang Amadeus Mozart's *Die Zauberflöte*

video-directed by Gary Halvorson; a recording of the latter is available online via Met Opera on Demand.

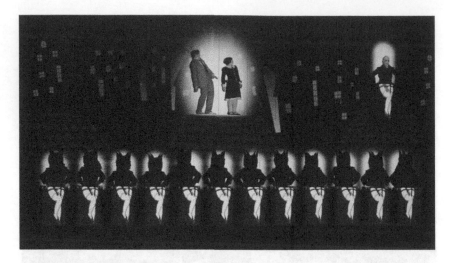

9.2:   Having caught the fleeing Papageno and Pamina, Monostatos and his demonic aids start dancing with digitally animated legs in response to Papageno's magic bells in Barrie Kosky's 2012 production of Wolfgang Amadeus Mozart's *Die Zauberflöte*, here in a 2013 perormance of LA Opera. The soloists are strapped onto semicircular platforms in the upper half of the screen, while the chorus members stand in barrels right in front of the screen. Screen capture from digital video. https://www.youtube.com/watch?v=lS8m-ulLOK8

(1791), premiered at the Komische Oper Berlin in 2012.[14] Counterintuitively for an opera, this staging aspires wholesale to silent film aesthetics. Kosky transplanted Mozart's work to the 1920s, and his only 'set' is a glossy white screen downstage onto which colourful animations are projected. Wearing stylized 1920s garb and mask-like makeup that recalls then-famous film characters, the singers emerge as needed through doors in the screen: they appear as though they were part of the animation, their bodies strapped onto small, rotating semi-circular platforms or stuck into a waist-high barrel downstage. (Figure 9.2) Moreover, the singers are usually whisked away as soon as they are done singing, because Emanuel Schikaneder's often clumsy and offensive spoken dialogues are here replaced by short filmic intertitles—perhaps Kosky's most drastic intervention. In this production, then, projections and screens do not perforate Aronson's 'real-life' stage

14   The staging was co-produced by Suzanne Andrade of 1927 Productions Limited; for more details and the performance history, see http://www.19-27.co.uk/the-magic-flute/ (accessed 30 May 2018). My discussion is based on my attendance at the Opera Philadelphia performance on 15 September 2017.

space; rather, human bodies intrude into an otherwise smooth visual animation.

This inversion raises a host of interesting questions related to audiovisual synchrony, human agency, and techno-determinism in operatic production (and beyond). For instance, the singers are unable to move their legs when fastened onto those platforms, and their limbs are animated by projections instead. (The Queen of the Night suffers the most extensive of such prostheses, with only the singer's head visible atop a monstrous digital spider.) Even during rare moments when—mostly male—characters move about in front of the screen, their gestures and steps are minutely choreographed in order to stay in sync with the ongoing projections: they are but cogs in the machine of filmic fantasy. In a way, each singer appears as the mere image of a character animated audiovisually through pre-conceived music and projections; the singers, that is, seem screened. Perhaps the only more daring—if practically easier—option would have been to disembody them entirely by having them sing in the pit or behind the screen, as was done in some early silent movie theatres.

Remarkably in the context of opera's relation to the screen, though, hardly any critics commented on the complete collapse of the three-dimensional stage space. As soon as the production establishes its aesthetic as a self-conscious imitation of silent film, the frame of reference shifts from the opera house to the cinema. This shift makes the flatness of the stage representation *as screen* an expected (or at least accepted) feature rather than a disturbing intrusion into opera's typically material means of signification and a squandering of its theatrical space. Part of the staging's appeal, of course, is its very defiance of expectation, along with the way in which this new garb for Mozart's beloved warhorse creatively defuses at least some of the libretto's problematic aspects. But the tremendous success of this production and its unusually extended global tour make me wonder whether there is more to its approach than meets the cartoon-watching eye; whether the staging *qua* two-dimensional screening of *Die Zauberflöte* may have enthralled audiences not just because it is so visually alluring and dramatically consequential but also because it has something fundamental to say about the nature of staged opera. In the following sections I will therefore probe what the idea of screening might hold for the 'traditional' production of opera, first by looking into the rise of illusionist stage practices in the nineteenth century and then by zooming in on Wagner's Bayreuth theatre.

Illusionist opera's spatial dilemma

To summarize historical developments rather coarsely: illusionist theatrical practices emerged in the late Renaissance and attached particularly to opera, with its elaborate machineries and audiovisual spectacle. Thus, it was above all opera that popularized across Europe what has tellingly been called the 'picture-frame stage': a designated and elevated stage framed by a proscenium arch and viewed mostly from the front (Figure 9.3), by contrast to thrust stages, theatres in the round, or performances in large halls or open spaces.[15] On these proscenium stages, an opera's diegetic settings were simulated by painted backdrops plus a series of increasingly foreshortened pairs of flats and borders along the sides and the top of the stage, which enclosed the stage picture and hid the necessary machinery. In order to facilitate the stage's spatial illusion, the frontal positioning of at least an important part of the audience (and particularly the patron's central seat) allowed stage designers to translate perspectival painting, with its single vanishing point, from the flat canvas onto the stage.[16] The resulting settings were tailored towards singers who mostly moved along a narrow strip downstage: this ensured both that the footlights would render them visible and that they would not destroy the illusion of the foreshortened sets when moving further upstage (although their integration was somewhat aided by the dimmer light towards the back).[17] In a sense, Baroque opera had singers act in front of a spatial backdrop—or a voluminous surface framed by the proscenium arch.

The successive wings, flats, and drops were thus together intended to create the effect less of a real-world scene than of a well-executed painting thereof—even when, since the mid-eighteenth century, stage floors began to be raked and more complex calculations of spatial perspective liberated the sets from the central vanishing point.[18] This pictorial model for Baroque productions is evinced also by theatrical terminology: the French and Italian terms for painted backdrops are identical with those for the painter's canvas (*toile* or *tela*), while

---

15   See Johnson, 2018.

16   Examples are the ground plans by Joseph Furttenbach of 1640, reproduced in Hewitt, pp. 195, 197. For surveys over the development and mechanics of Baroque operatic scenery, see Glixon and Glixon, 2006; Baker, 2013; and Johnson, 2018. The translation of perspective painting to the stage was not without its problems and worked perfectly only for a single point in the auditorium (typically the aristocratic patron's box); see Damisch, pp. 214-218.

17   See Baker, pp. 45-46.

18   On the latter development, associated above all with Ferdinando Galli-Bibiena's 1711 treatise *L'architettura civile*, see Baker, pp. 49-52.

9.3:   Carl Fredrik Adelcrantz, Drottningholm Slottsteater, near Stockholm, Sweden, 1762–1766. This unusually deep and pristinely preserved Baroque picture-frame stage is shown here with one of its original sets of seven wings and borders and, in the background, a seascape with wave machine. Photograph © Gundula Kreuzer.

the German *Prospekt* specifically indicates a panoramic painting.[19] (Only the British term *backcloth* and its American successor *backdrop* are generic to the theatre.) Vice versa, the painterly aspiration of stage designs manifested in their typical idealizing depictions. William Hogarth's famous painting of the climactic prison scene of John Gay's *The Beggar's Opera* (London, 1728), for example, renders the set as one continuous space rather than breaking it down into its individual drops and wings; only the painted curtain betrays the picture's inspiration in the theatre rather than in real life. (Figure 9.4)[20]

Within the proscenium frame, however, stage practices since the later eighteenth century moved towards less pictorial and ever more realistic means of representation. To name but a few well-known factors in this development, the Romantic fad for historical novels and a shift in operatic

19   See Grimm and Grimm, col. 2173; and *Oxford English Dictionary*. On the painterly model of Baroque stage design, see also Schivelbusch, pp. 192–193.
20   For the 1729 painting, see http://collections.britishart.yale.edu/vufind/Record/1669269 (accessed 31 May 2018).

9.4:   William Hogarth (1697–1764), *The Beggar's Opera* (1729). Oil on canvas, 59.1 x 76.2 cm. Digital image courtesy of Yale Center for British Art.

subject matter from the generically mythological to the concretely historical called for more verisimilitude and characteristic detail in stage sets, while the rise of popular spectacular media such as panoramas, dioramas, and cycloramas further whetted audiences' visual appetite.[21] At the same time, the increased strength of gas lighting (introduced in European opera houses between the 1810s and the 1840s) allowed singers to venture further from the stage front while revealing the flatness and artificiality of the painted sets. This exposure in turn aggravated dissatisfaction with the Baroque system's privileging of a few central seats in the auditorium, which for the majority of the audience left the spaces between wings visible.[22] One result of all this was an increased use of practicable scenery, i.e. 'real' objects that singers could walk upon: wooden ledges, built stairs leading to painted houses, and

21   For more on the developments surveyed here, see e.g. Williams, pp. 58-75.
22   On the introduction of gas lighting on European stages, see Penzel, pp. 53-57; Baumann, 1988, pp. 81-114. On the growing dissatisfaction over the course of the eighteenth century with the undemocratic viewing conditions and unnatural vistas of Baroque stages, see Schivelbusch, pp. 191-199, 204-206.

so on. These furthered a perceived realism not just of the respective settings but also of the acting, since singers now had voluminous scenescapes to engage with. In short, production techniques partially shifted from a series of two-dimensional representations to an assemblage of three-dimensional *presentations* of objects and scenery.

Yet this move had aesthetic and practical drawbacks. For one, the often heavy built scenery obstructed and eventually foiled quick mechanical changes of flats and drops between scenes, traditionally accomplished in full sight of the audience. Elaborate sets were now prepared upstage during an intimate (or so-called 'short') scene that was played in front of a drop hung further downstage; and where that proved impossible, act curtains or drops appeared in the early nineteenth century to cover the transformations, despite misgivings as to their disruption of the scenic illusion.[23] More important in our context was what I might call the chief dilemma of nineteenth-century operatic practitioners: namely, how to reconcile the growing desire for visual illusionism with the proliferation of different media and materialities on stage, some of which were flat depictions of an intended object, others voluminous simulations, and yet others the 'real' thing. To evoke Aronson's terms, how could painted canvases, material structures, mechanical or living animals, real-life objects, coloured light, and costumed bodies be unified in such a way as to suggest a single frame of reference?

Although various architects, designers, directors, and composers individually addressed this issue in theory and practice, the person who has most come to epitomize the envisioned total theatrical illusionism is Richard Wagner (1813-1883). And for my purposes, Wagner offers once more a convenient port of call because his operas, his writings, and the Festspielhaus in Bayreuth all demonstrate an extreme commitment to smoothing over the interstices between his different participating media. One much-discussed way of doing so was to (try and) obscure each medium's technical and material conditioning—an aspiration notoriously critiqued by Theodor Adorno under the label of phantasmagoria.[24] But another way, I argue, was to envision them all as contributing to the effect of a flat surface: that is, an animated and resonant painting.

Wagner's pictorial orientation operated on many levels. To begin with, illusionist painting played a key role in his seminal 1849 treatise 'The Art-Work of the Future'. Visually complementing singers and material objects,

---

23   On the rise of act curtains and drop scenes, see Kreuzer, 2018, pp. 73-77.
24   Adorno, 2005, p. 74. For more on Adorno's concept, see below.

painted scenery was to deck out the rest of the stage with what Wagner called 'artistic truth'—the colours and appearances of nature. In return, the art of painting would be consummated in his *Gesamtkunstwerk*:

> That which the landscape painter [...] has erstwhile forced into the nar-row frames of panel-pictures—what he affixed to the egoist's secluded chamber walls, or offered for the random, incoherent and garbled stacking in a picture-storehouse [i.e. museum]—*with this* he will henceforth fill the ample framework of the tragic stage [...]. The illusion which his brush and finest blend of colours could only hint at and merely distantly approach, he will here bring to perfectly deceptive representation through the artistic use of every known device of optics and artistic lighting.[25]

In the expanded theatrical frame with its real light and living humans, Wagner expected painting to 'effect a livelier impression' and reach larger audiences.[26] Indeed, the stage's enhanced affordances of simulation were the lure with which he hoped to attract the collaboration of visual artists (rather than 'mere' stage designers) in the first place. In a way, these artists did not merely provide the backdrop for the characters' actions; instead, singing bodies and coloured light became animating additions to their pictures. Practicable scenery notwithstanding, Wagner's theatrical vision remained as if painted: designs (or, more often, actual paintings) were translated from flat canvases to spatial models and then onto stage—where they were to achieve a heightened pictorial illusion.

Once again, theatrical jargon reveals that Wagner was not alone with this conception of the three-dimensional stage in terms of two-dimensional, painterly representation. Nineteenth-century German libretti began to subdivide acts not into scenes or *Auftritte* defined by the entrances and exits of characters, but into *Bilder* (pictures or images), defined by settings; while in France, popular shows promoted the equivalent term *tableau*.[27] What is more, these theatrical practices resonated with discourses in the visual arts on how to achieve depth perception in painting and sculpture. In his influential 1893 treatise *The Problem of Form in the Fine Arts*, the sculptor

25 Wagner, 'Das Kunstwerk der Zukunft' (1849), in Wagner, 1911, vol. 3, p. 153. My translation is adapted from Wagner, 1966, vol. 1, pp. 186-187. As is evident from this quotation, Wagner was no fan of the visual arts per se.

26 Wagner, 'Das Kunstwerk der Zukunft', in Wagner, 1911, vol. 3, p. 153; translation in Wagner, 1966, vol. 1, p. 187.

27 Pougin, p. 699. On the eighteenth-century rise of this 'tableau aesthetics', see Frantz, pp. 153-195.

Adolf Hildebrand claimed that 'all spatial relations and all distinctions of form are *read off* from a single vantage point, so to speak, *from front to back.* [...] In artistic representation it is therefore a matter of setting in train this single, unifying movement into depth'.[28] This unification was achieved by tending above all to what would be perceived as the first or frontal plane of the artwork: 'The more coherent and recognizable the surface effect of the object's image is, the more coherent is the idea of depth, for it is then stimulated by the depth relations between these two-dimensional units and not by the spatial values of the individual units that compose the image'.[29] In other words, even sculptors, who worked with homogenous voluminous materials (Hildebrand's chief interest was reliefs), were concerned with ordering their intended objects according to a unifying frame; and that frame was constituted by assuming the effect of a picture plane—by creating the impression as if the beholder were seeing a flat, continuous surface that only perfectly simulated depth.

Wagner's stage directions reveal the same preoccupation with achieving a coherent painterly surface. Already in his early operas he prescribed settings in painstaking detail, and he paid particular attention to audiovisual effects that not only use the full stage space but seek to extend it while keeping in perspective.[30] In the first act of *Lohengrin* (1850), for example, the challenge was to render the protracted mysterious arrival of the Grail knight from the far distance without breaking the perspective. According to an 1854 ground plan for this scene designed at the composer's behest by the Dresden actor Ferdinand Heine (Figure 9.5), as Patrick Carnegy has shown, Wagner had a boy in a miniature swan-boat pulled along a groove upstage before the identically clad Lohengrin singer entered further downstage, drawn by his 'real' swan (complete with movable neck and flapping wings).[31] This substitution was possible—and all the more necessary—because Lohengrin does not sing during his journey, making both the excitedly commenting onstage observers and the offstage spectators focus exclusively on his visual arrival.

Elsewhere, Wagner followed French practices in using music to further the depth effects of explicitly painterly sets.[32] One instance is the opening

28 Hildebrand, p. 243 (emphases in original).
29 Ibid., p. 244.
30 On Wagner's particular penchant for subterranean and deep spaces, see Watkins, pp. 119-120.
31 See Carnegy, pp. 41-42.
32 Since the late eighteenth century, composers of French opera in particular sought to musically evoke their settings at the beginnings of acts; and they increasingly drew on diegetic offstage sound to enhance the emerging scene. A famous example is Fromental Halévy's *La juive* (1835),

LOHENGRIN (I. Act).

Ansicht.

Gerichtsplatz am Ufer der Schelde.

A) Mächtige Eiche, deren Wipfel sich jedoch möglichst nach der Höhe ausbreitet und zugleich die Soufite bildet, um den Zuschauern in den oberen Seitenlogen nicht die Aussicht nach dem Hintergrunde zu benehmen. Der Stamm der Eiche steht quer vor der zweiten Coulisse.
B) Der Schild des Königs, am Stamme aufgehängt.
C) Königsstuhl, auf rohen Steinstufen erhöht.
D) Unregelmässige Terrainerhöhungen, nach der Bühne zu sich abflachend, und in die Coulissen hinein immer höher ansteigend, so dass die darauf Stehenden einander pyramidalisch überragen. Die Schraffirungen auf dem Grundriss deuten die mehr oder minder steile Böschung an. (Für die Sachsen und Thüringer.)
E) Dergleichen Terrainerhöhungen für die Brabanter.
F) Gemaltes Uferversatzstück, rechts ein wenig ansteigend, mit einzelnen niedrigen Buschwerk und G) dem Landungsplatze.
H) Steiler praktikabler Uferhügel, mit einzeln stehenden Eichen, zur Aufstellung von Volksgruppen; das hinten im Bogen vorspringende Stück etwas flacher auslaufend.
J) K) Nur gemalte Uferversatzstücken, mit Buschwerk, und rechts mit einzelnen Bäumen.
L) Jenseitiges Ufer der Schelde, mit der Burg von Antwerpen.
M) Horizontprospekt mit flacher Ferne.

1—7) Waldcoulissen. Die Stufen des Königsstuhles so wie die Terrain-Erhöhungen, als Rasen und Erdreich gemalt.

a) Praktikables Wasserversatzstück.
b) Punktirte Linie, auf welcher ein verkleinerter Schwanennachen, mit einem Kinde als Lohengrin, vorübergezogen wird.
c) Der Raum zwischen J und F mit einer wie Wasser gemalten Leinwand bedeckt, auf welcher, (Linie d) der wirkliche Nachen, worin Lohengrin steht, hinten von rechts kommend, den Bogen bis an den Landungsplatz G beschreibt. Der Schwan mit beweglichem Hals und Flügeln.
e) ✝✝✝ Volksgruppen beiderlei Geschlechts, wovon f) der Perspektive wegen nur Kinder. g) Krieger.

9.5:   Ferdinand Heine (1798–1872), sketch-map of 1854 for Act I of Wagner's *Lohengrin*. Following Wagner's instructions, Lohengrin's arrival from the far distance is effected via a boy actor in a miniature boat moving along the dotted line b (in red in the original) from left to right before the identically clad Lohengrin singer enters along the red line d on his "real" swan boat. Courtesy of Nationalarchiv der Richard-Wagner-Stiftung Bayreuth.

of *Tannhäuser* (1845), where Wagner described the Venusberg grotto as stretching into an unseeable distance.[33] Accordingly, he called for irregular ledges and protruding rocks at various heights and distances that partly obscure the grotto's end and partly enable an increased foreshortening towards the back of the stage, thus facilitating the grotto's spatial simulation. The Venusberg's population was likewise staggered between the protagonists in the foreground and a host of mythical creatures frolicking mid- and upstage. And acoustically, Wagner evoked the grotto's expanse with an exceptionally long stretch of purely orchestral music following the curtain—music whose iridescent shimmering timbre and chromatically

whose curtain opened onto the intricate town square of medieval Constance, with an offstage organ and choral chanting seemingly emanating from its painted church.
33   Stage directions according to Wagner, 2001, p. 67. I have discussed the Venusberg scenes in more detail in Kreuzer, pp. 27–53, especially pp. 31–37.

shifting sound fields evoke static (if sensually charged) space more than kinetic development. It takes about ninety seconds until we finally hear some singing (this is opera, after all); but it is only the gentle sirens' chorus sounding invisibly from afar—an effect that acoustically underscores the optical foreshortening, while making us wait another four minutes until the protagonists raise their voices. In his 1861 and 1875 revisions of the opera, Wagner further amplified the audiovisual stage setting to the point that his optical directions resemble a paint-by-number manual.[34] Not accidentally, this Venusberg scene sparked what is perhaps the most substantial number of stand-alone paintings by non-theatrical artists of any operatic setting.

The conceptualization of operatic scenes as two-dimensional—if moving and sonorous—images also throws new light on Wagner's notorious open transformations. These lengthy transitions are accompanied (or, in fact, rendered) by explicitly illustrative music that sonically depicts the gradual change of locales, so as not to interrupt the theatrical illusion with a curtain or pause. Representing these transformations visually as well was crucial for Wagner's goal of total audiovisual synchrony, but it posed tremendous mechanical challenges. For the paradigmatic transition to Nibelheim's underground smithy in *Das Rheingold* (composed in 1853-1854 and premiered in 1869), a Bayreuth rehearsal score documented Wagner as desiring the following effect: 'not "tableaux vivants"—but a "picture of life" shall unfurl everywhere before us.'[35] His original German formulation ('*nicht "lebende Bilder"—sondern ein "Bild des Lebens" soll sich überall vor uns entrollen*') leaves no doubt about Wagner's technological conception, whereby one single image was to continually unroll before the spectators' eyes. This expression evokes moving canvases (*Wandeldekorationen*), a technology that had been reintroduced from the Baroque era into early nineteenth-century boulevard theatres and popular musical multimedia to emulate the spectacular optical entertainments of the time. In 1882, Wagner himself famously deployed such moving canvases in his premiere production of *Parsifal* for the horizontal Act I transformation from the meadow to the Grail temple, although his machinist Carl Brandt layered three open-worked canvases that moved at different speeds so as to better integrate the singers' simulation of walking through this painted landscape.[36]

34   See Wagner, 2001, pp. 7-10.

35   This comment was probably pencilled by Henriette Glasenapp into the vocal score owned by her husband, Wagner biographer Carl Friedrich Glasenapp, during the 1876 rehearsals; Nationalarchiv der Richard-Wagner-Stiftung Bayreuth, A-M 5153/I: *Das Rheingold*, p. 105.

36   On this transformation and for designs of the moving canvases, see Baumann, 1980, pp. 154-165; and Carnegy, pp. 111-113.

(Again we could speak of a deep surface; as with Kosky's screen, Wagner's protagonists became ornaments within the primarily technical optical animation of this scene.) Yet more significant than Wagner's future literal employment of this technology is that his allusion to it betrays once more a two-dimensional conception of spatial representation. Canvases can unroll horizontally or vertically, but they always move along the chosen plane and in a pre-ordered sequence. The analogy to film is obvious, although it rests on the technology of animating pictures (the unwinding of a canvas or film) more than on its visual affordances: for instance, montage techniques and sudden cuts run counter to Wagner's desired continual transformations. Instead, Wagner's concept of the single evolving *Bild des Lebens* points to a perceptual kinship with cinema: that of the flat surface facilitating life-like moving images—a surface akin to both the painter's canvas and the cinematic screen, whose material identity is rendered obvious in German, where *Leinwand* is the term for both. No wonder that Wagner frequently wrote of stagings as the 'scenic picture'.[37]

Screening in Bayreuth

Wagner's ideal that a staging ought to appear like an animated painting was fortified by some of the celebrated innovations of the Bayreuth Festspielhaus, built on his instructions (and incorporating earlier ideas of Gottfried Semper) by Otto Brückwald in 1872-1876. This two-dimensional approach may seem surprising: after all, the theatre's exposed high stage house widely heralded the spatial abilities of its cutting-edge illusionist technology. (Figure 9.6) Nevertheless, many commentators on the inaugural 1876 production of Wagner's *Der Ring des Nibelungen* admiringly noted its overall smooth picture quality. In comparison to conventional theatres, this effect was enhanced by a plethora of architectural features: the amphitheatrical seating (with its unobstructed sightlines), the row of protruding columns at the side walls narrowing in toward the stage, and the fan-shaped ceiling all directed the gaze to the stage, where two successive proscenia both enhanced the traditional framing function and seemingly further foreshortened the staged image, since the second proscenium was significantly smaller than

37   For instance Wagner, 'Das Bühnenfestspielhaus zu Bayreuth' (1873), in Wagner, 1911, vol. 9, p. 338 ('scenische Bild'); Wagner, 1966, vol. 5, p. 335. The analogy between continuous transformations and moving pictures would be famously enacted with Alban Berg's silent-film interlude for *Lulu*, premiered posthumously in 1937.

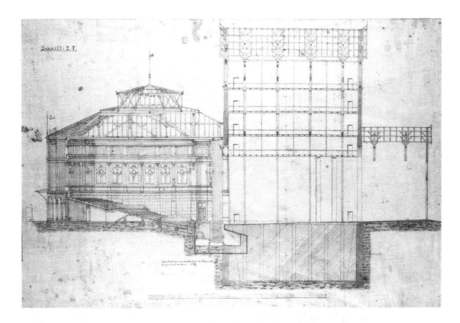

9.6:Longitudinal section of the Bayreuth Festspielhaus, constructed by Otto Brückwald (1841–1917) between 1872 and 1876. The plan shows the building before completion. Already notable are the high stage house and the lowered orchestra pit, although the latter proved too small and had to be significantly expanded in 1875, as indicated in a first revision to the drawing (originally in red) by the construction supervisor Carl Runckwitz. Courtesy of Nationalarchiv der Richard-Wagner-Stiftung Bayreuth.

the first. (Figure 9.7) According to Wagner, Semper had anticipated that this proportion between the two proscenia would create 'the singular illusion of an apparent throwing-back of the scene itself, making the spectator imagine it quite far away, though he still beholds it in all the clearness of its actual proximity'. As with popular optical media such as panoramas, moreover, the actual distance of the stage was veiled by the fact that, in Wagner's words, 'between [the audience] and the picture to be looked at there is nothing plainly visible, merely a floating atmosphere of distance, resulting from the architectural adjustment of the two proscenia; whereby the scene is removed as it were to the unapproachable world of dreams'.[38] The then-unusual (and originally accidental) total darkness of the auditorium further helped to ensure that spectators could look at nothing but this image emerging like

38All quotations Wagner, 'Das Bühnenfestspielhaus zu Bayreuth' (1873), in Wagner, 1911, vol. 9, pp. 337-338. English-language versions in Wagner, 1966, vol. 5, pp. 334-335. For more on the design of the Bayreuth auditorium, see Habel, pp. 399-404.

9.7: View from the side of the auditorium to the stage of the Bayreuth Festspielhaus, showing the 1882 Grail Temple set for Wagner's *Parsifal* and the striped curtain. Courtesy of Nationalarchiv der Richard-Wagner-Stiftung Bayreuth.

a dream out of obscurity—an effect that art historians have long related to the cinematic *dispositif*.[39]

To be sure, Wagner was not the first to ponder architectural changes that might increase the theatre's overall illusionism. Already in the early nineteenth century, to cite but two examples, both the French colonel and inventor Jacques-François-Louis Grobert and the Prussian painter and architect Karl Friedrich Schinkel independently suggested removing the orchestra from sight, dimming auditorium lighting, and abolishing boxes in the proscenium wall and seats for patrons on the sides of the stage, all to enhance the theatre's effect of perspectival illusion.[40] Yet the Bayreuth Festspielhaus was the first opera house to realize such ideas comprehensively. And I want to suggest that its structural means to focus the gaze on the

39   See, for instance, Crary, 2002, p. 19; and Elcott, 2016, p. 51. See also ibid., pp. 54-57, on the enhanced picture quality due to the dual proscenium and darkness.

40   Among other proto-Wagnerian measures, Grobert proposed an amphitheatrical auditorium and advocated moving both prompters and orchestra into the wings on both sides of the stage. Grobert, pp. 227-29, 255-57, 271-72. On Schinkel, who also replaced the Baroque wing-and-fly scenery at Berlin's Nationaltheater with symbolic cycloramic backdrops that allowed for wider viewing angles while depending less on perspectival foreshortening, see Bomberger, 1998, pp. 148-151; and Forster, 2018, pp. 260-277. For earlier theatrical reformers such as the architect Louis Catel, see Biermann, 1928.

performance consciously flattened the transition from auditorium to stage, leaving the impression as if Wagner's 'scenic picture' was not enacted on a deep stage but mounted on an invisible wall right before the audience (see again Figure 9.7). Neither a substantial apron nor a prompter's box protruded from the stage; the footlights were well hidden; and both orchestra and conductor remained invisible, because instead of the customary pit, Wagner's sunken orchestra—what he called his 'mystic abyss'—left but a narrow gap between auditorium and stage, a slightly curved and barely visible line in the ground.[41] Thus, in Bayreuth, the *Spiellinie* or curtain line (the imaginary line downstage beyond which actors would not venture) fell almost in one with both the edge of the stage and the acoustic 'gulf'. Accordingly, some spectators appreciated that Wagner's singers never stepped in front of the curtain line, not even for curtain calls.

The curtain itself also participated in this flattening. Instead of the then-customary red velvet, whose rich folds both evoke depth and attract the eye, Bayreuth's curtain featured stripes; thus it defied the impression of volume without vying for attention with the emerging stage, as did the occasional painted curtains representing allegorical scenes or settings related to the opera. To further deemphasize its presence, the Bayreuth curtain likely used the same brown-and-yellow hues as the interior décor.[42] The curtain was made of a lightweight fabric that could move more speedily, and it utilized a new diagonal pull—the so-called Wagner-curtain mechanism—that opened the curtain gently from the middle and moved it simultaneously to the sides and up, rather than simply parting in the middle or being raised directly upwards. (Figure 9.8) As Yale's music instructor Gustave Stoeckel marvelled, this curtain left 'the impression that some unseen hands have moved it very gracefully out of sight'—which is to say that it eased the technologically mediated transition from auditorium to stage, from sound to vision, from the real to the diegetic world.[43] Even the narrowing series of dual columns at the sides of the auditorium could be seen as a visual remnant of the Baroque paired flats leading towards a foreshortened backdrop; and

41   Wagner, 'Das Bühnenfestspielhaus zu Bayreuth' (1873), in Wagner, 1911, pp. 337-338; translation in Wagner, 1966, vol. 5, p. 334.
42   The exact colours and the direction of the stripes remain unclear, since the curtain of the 1882 *Parsifal* production depicted in Figure 9.7 was likely not the original one. For more on the Bayreuth curtain, see Dombois, 2012; and Kreuzer, pp. 91-97. By 1867, Hermann Helmholtz had established that vertical stripes (as in Bayreuth's 1882 curtain) made a wall or square look taller, while horizontal stripes made it look wider, but neither direction implied a third dimension; see Thomson and Mikellidoju, 2011. On the tradition of painted curtains, see Bachler, 1972.
43   Stoeckel, 1877, p. 266.

9.8:   The curtain mechanism introduced in Bayreuth in 1876 and standardized as "Wagner curtain." Drawing by Walter Huneke, technical director of the Bayreuth Festival from 1966 to 1990. By kind permission of the heirs of Walter Huneke.

they fostered the expectation that the opening of the proscenium contained a painted (if lively) canvas.

   This flattening effect of Bayreuth's technology of image production and perception had an important acoustic equivalent. In the festival theatre's covered pit, the orchestral sound was famously pre-mixed and then projected into the auditorium via what Wagner called an 'acoustic sounding board' (*akustische Schallwand*).[44] (Figure 9.9) For audiences, the resulting sound obscures the exact position of individual instruments in the pit. Incidental noises of tone production were also filtered out (one of Wagner's dreams come true). Thus divested of both its spatial and mechanical origins, which is to say of its concrete sources, orchestral sound appears not only as disembodied but also as flattened—as deprived of the distance at which it is produced. It emanates instead from the same gulf that marks the curtain line. The Bayreuth auditorium complemented this flattened orchestral sound generation with a deepening of sound transmission, or what we might call its proto surround-sound effect: the unusually long reverberation seemed to envelop audiences acoustically, just like those pillars that extended the stage frame into the auditorium incorporated them spatially. According to a cognitive process Michel Chion has discussed for sound film as 'synchresis', the resulting acousmatic music whose source is obscured attaches more easily to the simultaneous visual scenes, boosting the perceived immersive

44 Wagner, 'Vorwort zur Herausgabe der Dichtung des Bühnenfestspieles *Der Ring des Nibelungen*' (1862), in Wagner, 1911, vol. 6, p. 276; translation adapted from Wagner, 1966, vol. 3, p. 277.

realism of the audiovisual representation (particularly in the case of explicitly diegetic or illustrative musical passages, such as those at the opening of *Tannhäuser*).[45] By projecting the sound into the auditorium and back onto the screen-like stage, in short, Bayreuth put into practice Wagner's ideal that the 'ghost-like music' inspire spectators to an 'enthusiastic state of clairvoyance' like the vapours rising from the Delphi oracle.[46]

Ironically, Wagner's emphasis on sound as a medium of immersion became a notorious object of critique. As Friedrich Nietzsche contended in his 1888 pamphlet *The Case of Wagner*, with the latter '[t]he color of the tone [*des Klanges*] is decisive; what it is that resounds is almost a matter of indifference'. Nietzsche took this observation as indicative of the alleged reign of style over thought in Wagner's works—in other words, of surface over depth: through an overwhelmingly sensual exterior, Nietzsche held, Wagner incited the nerves of his spectators and short-circuited their brains. In view of a long aesthetic tradition (particularly in German-language thinking) that valued hidden depth and its alleged meanings over outward façade, this verdict amounted to a profound devaluation of Wagner's artistry.[47] Adorno, too, cited 'the primacy of harmonic and instrumental sound [*Klang*]' as the epitome of Wagner's 'magic delusion' (*Blendwerk*), which the philosopher famously defined as the 'occultation of production by the outward appearance of the product'.[48]

Yet it is telling that Adorno (following Marx) chose as his metaphor for this musical illusionism the optical medium of the phantasmagoria. In this popular entertainment of the late eighteenth and early nineteenth century, the supporting devices (a *laterna magica* and screens) were for the first time masked by total darkness to let projections appear as 'real'.[49] And it was precisely such an immersive deception via smooth surfaces that Wagner pursued visually. Clement Greenberg has famously described the 'ineluctable flatness' of the surface as the defining, unique condition of

---

45 Chion, 1994, especially p. 63.
46 Wagner, 'Das Bühnenfestspielhaus zu Bayreuth' (1873), in Wagner, 1911, vol. 9, p. 339. Translation modified from Wagner, 1966, vol. 5, p. 335. On the acoustic properties of the auditorium, with its reverberation (with audience attendance) of almost 1.6 seconds, see Clarke, p. 155.
47 Nietzsche, p. 624. On the aesthetic value placed on the idea of depth and its related concepts of interiority, inwardness, and meaning in German musical aesthetics, see Watkins, pp. 1-8 and 22-50; on the tensions inherent in this focus on depth by a discipline that traditionally addresses artistic surfaces, see Shusterman, pp. 1-5.
48 Adorno, 1998, p. 82; translation from Adorno, 2005, p. 74.
49 On Adorno's recourse to the phantasmagoria and its implications, see Gunning, 2004. On earlier associations between Wagner and phantasmagoria, see Crary, 1999, p. 254; on the technological conditions of phantasmagoric illusions, see Elcott, 2016, pp. 46-49, 54-57.

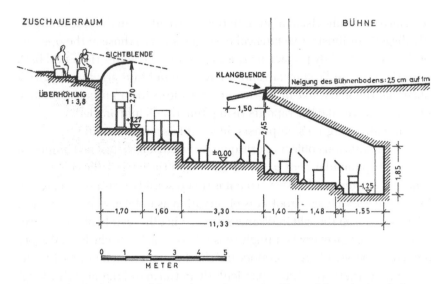

9.9:   Longitudinal section of the sunken orchestra pit—Wagner's "mystic abyss"—in the Bayreuth Festspielhaus. Drawing by W. Rauda, 1953. Visible are the terraced seating for the orchestra (with strings atop and woodwind, brass, and percussion successively further below the stage), Wagner's "sounding board" extending from the front of the stage, and an additional curved screen that conceals the orchestral apparatus and its necessary lights. © Nationalarchiv der Richard-Wagner-Stiftung, Bayreuth.

the art of painting, which otherwise shares with the theatre 'the enclosing shape of the support': until the twentieth century, painters generally worked to evoke three-dimensional spaces through this limit of the flat, framed canvas while simultaneously de-emphasizing its materiality.[50] Vice versa, we could say that the specific, both delimiting and enabling condition of opera was the heterogeneity of its contributing media even on the purely visual level. Three-dimensionality was a given on the proscenium stage; but the challenge, as discussed, was how to meld everything into a unified perspective and thus create an illusionist overall appearance. Thus, if Aronson worried that onstage video projections might disrupt the diegetic space-time continuum, Wagner was concerned about *any* object (including bodies) protruding from his multimedia *Gesamtkunstwerk* and thereby exposing the entire staging as artifice.[51] It is for this reason that his visual ideal remained that of the illusionist surface to which his stagings aspired.

The Bayreuth *Ring* production of 1876 occasionally emphasized this frontal plane literally, as with the partially transparent and painted scrim that

---

50   Greenberg, p. 200.
51   On this key concern of Wagner's, see Kreuzer, pp. 12-21.

covered the stage for the opening underwater scene or the clouds projected onto veils and gauzes.[52] Even the Ride of the Valkyries was feigned at Wagner's request not with actual horses but with lantern slides projected onto the scenery, just as the composer had incorporated dissolving views in his 1861 and 1875 revisions of *Tannhäuser*.[53] Regarding the seamless integration of his different onstage media, we have already witnessed Wagner's efforts to maintain an accurate perspective in the example of the boy actor simulating Lohengrin's faraway entrance. Another case in point was his unprecedented use of water vapours in the *Ring* to mask his stage technologies and amalgamate singers, practicable scenery, and flat canvases into a seemingly natural whole.[54] Wagner's condensation of the space between auditorium and stage into a single thick line, I would propose, served the same purpose. As Sybille Krämer has argued, a line always implies a plane on which it is drawn; it 'is a medium of transmission and transgression. It homogenizes things that are different and thus mediates between heterogeneous worlds'.[55] Bayreuth's visible curtain line-cum-gulf thus implied an invisible scrim or screen at the front of the stage through which the production was viewed and to which its multiple material elements adhered, as it were—just like the individual instruments' sounds gathered at the pit's acoustic baffle before being projected *in toto* to the audience, or like Hildebrand's frontal plane through which an artwork's depth was perceived.

A look at some of the pre-artistic (or pre-proto-cinematic) functions of screens in European culture fortifies this association of the curtain line with an implied vertical plane. Long before the rise in the late eighteenth century of optical media that employed flat surfaces for projections, a screen might serve (according to the editors of this volume) as 'a filter, a divide, a shelter, or a form of camouflage': it was used to partition spaces, to protect the inside from the outside, and to police migration across these demarcations.[56] Among the earliest documented uses were screens against fire and drafts, with the term dating back to the fourteenth century.[57] But the screen's function *as* screen always depended on its situatedness and its application in an individual context. By the same token, the theatre's invisible curtain line traditionally served to contain a performance spatiotemporally and to

52 See Baumann, 1980, pp. 181-183.
53 On the Valkyrie projections (which left much to be desired), see Carnegy, p. 87; on the dissolving views Kreuzer, p. 32.
54 On Wagner's use of steam and its many functions, see Kreuzer, pp. 165-188.
55 Krämer, p. 13.
56 Craig Buckley, Rüdiger Campe, and Francesco Casetti in the introduction to this volume.
57 See Huhtamo, 2004, p. 5.

separate it from the audience. These objectives were reinforced by Wagner materially, architecturally, and acoustically: in Bayreuth, the acoustic gulf doubled as nothing less than a screening technique—or a screen as cultural technique. According to Bernhard Siegert, 'cultural techniques are conceived of as operative chains that precede the media concepts they generate'.[58] In this sense, the Bayreuth theatre's various techniques of flattening the performative surface do point forward towards the cinematic screen and its perceived visual illusionism. At the same time, however, they also reveal that nineteenth-century modes of perception were trained to see a representational surface as deep and a three-dimensional stage as flat—as an animated canvas. Cultivating these modes of perception was Wagner's ultimate means of veiling his stagings' technical origins. He sought to conceal not just the ropes and pulleys of individual stage technologies but the staged-ness of the performance itself, the entire pretence of stage production, to wit: the stage. Wagner's Bayreuth production could thus in fact be viewed like a living and sounding 'image of life' projected onto a wall right in front of the audience.

The notion of the proscenium's opening as an invisible wall would famously be popularized by proponents of naturalist theatre shortly after Wagner's death, with roots reaching back to mid-eighteenth-century discourses by Diderot and other *philosophes*.[59] The implication here was that actors should behave as naturally as if they were enclosed by a solid fourth wall, which would become transparent only to audiences, not performers. Yet the aesthetics inherent in this fourth-wall naturalism and its prototypical setting of the indoor room are different from Wagner's. Rather than observing a seemingly real scene with its heterogeneous materialities (which also, of course, necessitates realistic settings), Wagner aspired to present an *idealized* nature, a higher sense of reality that would immerse and thereby change each spectator; hence also his mythic subjects and grand scenarios. His invisible wall served illusionism, not naturalism. It amounts to a pre-cinematic screen technique no less than those shadow projections, panoramas, and dioramas discussed as such by media scholars Charles Musser and Erkki Huhtamo.[60]

Tellingly, early cinematic practices themselves revealed their partial roots in opera's conflicted negotiation between two- and three-dimensional

58   Siegert, p. 11.

59   On naturalism and late nineteenth-century understandings of realism in theatre, see Fischer-Lichte, 1999, pp. 243-252; and Chothia, 2011; on the history of the concept of the fourth wall, see Lehmann, esp. pp. 57-155.

60   See Musser, 1984; Musser, 1990, pp. 15-54; Huhtamo, 2004; and Huhtamo, 2012.

representations. This was the case not only when films were based on operatic plots, or when they were shown in actual opera houses or in otherwise
darkened auditoria, with a curtain dramatically (un)covering the screen.
As William Paul has demonstrated for American cinemas, the silver screen
was also frequently placed upstage so as not to waste the depth of the stage
and to evoke a Wagnerian sense of distance. It took acoustic arguments to
move the fully flattened image to the front of the stage, eventually doing
away with the stage altogether.[61] Perhaps it was owing to this operatic
genealogy of early cinema that critics so readily embraced Kosky's wholly
screened *Zauberflöte*.

Opera beyond the screen

Against this background, we might re-evaluate recent pushbacks against
the expanding use of screens in operatic (and theatrical) life. To take one
example, in a 2017 advertising campaign for the Yale Repertory Theater,
Meryl Streep addressed common concerns when she proclaimed that 'now,
especially with all the competing screens that you can look at, there's just a
real appetite for the actual as opposed to the virtual. And people are piling
in to see live theater, to see something happen in front of them'.[62] Apart
from the surprising notion that theatrical make-believe might be equated
with 'the actual' (an idea itself conditioned by the digital age), Streep puts
her finger on one possible—and frequently cited—distinguishing factor
between cinematic screening and theatrical performance: that vibration of
embodied presence, along with the possible synergy between spectators and
actors. In doing this, however, Streep takes for granted the picture-frame
stage and its intended frontal spectator. But if productions on such stages
might themselves aspire to an aesthetic of screening (as they did in late
nineteenth-century illusionist opera), their difference from cinema may
not be as categorical as she assumes—at least in comparison to other forms
of theatrical expression.

   It might be precisely because of this illusionist family resemblance that,
over the last decade, opera's increased 'screenification' has been paralleled

---

61   Paul, pp. 223-225, 237-238. Tellingly, the paradoxical relationship between the screen's
flatness and its three-dimensional illusions was an important topic for early film theorists; for
a short summary, see Friedberg, 2006, pp. 153-155.
62   Meryl Streep as quoted in a promotional email from the Yale Repertory Theater, 24 June
2017.

by—or has actually fostered—a less noted opposite trend: an upsurge of
alternative opera companies that break with visually lush yet conceptually
conservative productions and the frontal viewing position associated with
both proscenium theatres and the cinema. Instead, they radically embrace
opera's performative, material, experimental, collaborative, multimedial,
and embodied roots. In New York, that cradle of HD broadcasts, companies
like Loft Opera or On Site Opera proclaim already in their names their
commitment to unusual performance spaces. And even upstart companies
like Heartbeat Opera that perform in traditional studio theatres tend to
liberate the performance from the box set and the orchestra from the pit.

Likely the most radical example of an opera without proscenium was
staged in Fall 2015 by LA's The Industry, an 'independent, artist-driven'
company founded in 2012. For performances of its so-called 'mobile opera'
Hopscotch, it shuttled twenty-four groups of audience members in limousines
simultaneously along three different routes to twenty-four performance
sites across Los Angeles.[63] Each route offered a different selection of eight
ten-minute segments (or chapters), written by six teams of composers
and librettists and performed by different sets of singers representing the
three main characters at different stages of their story, with pre-selected
parts of the cityscape turning into natural settings. All segments were
continuously enacted and broadcast live to twenty-four screens at the
production's 'Central Hub', a temporary tent-like structure located between
the performance sites. Twelve additional chapters fleshed out the story
through multimedia cartoons available only online. Screens and live performance, site-specificity and mobility, diegesis and reality, online content and
embodiment, mediation and presence, nature and culture and technology
all merged geographically, experientially, and conceptually.

Tellingly, the show's director, Yuval Sharon, explicitly declared his resistance to 'an old-fashioned assumption that theater should share classical
painting's focus on a fixed perspective, or the ultra-controlled visual frame of
the film [... which] infantilizes the audience and reduces their perception'.[64]
Along with this illusionist perspective and confined theatrical space, Sharon
shattered the traditional identification of performers and characters, frag-
mented both storyline and audience experience, and abandoned the idea of
a singular composer, while the small and flexible orchestration allowed rare

63   The following discussion is based on press materials and reviews, the programme book
and audio recording, and the online documentation at http://hopscotchopera.com/ (accessed
31 May 2018). Alex Ross described his experience of *Hopscotch* in Ross, 2015.
64   Sharon, p. 132.

spatial suppleness for an opera. Obviously, the coordination and execution of the event crucially depended on digital media, whose influence we might also detect in the idea to serve up a selection of bite-sized fragments. At the same time, without an explicit stage area, *Hopscotch*'s individual scenes depended all the more on the embodied audiovisual establishment of the performative situation in each location, be they abandoned skyscrapers, elevators, beaches, or the limousines themselves. When the MacArthur Foundation recognized Sharon in 2017 for 'expanding how opera is performed and experienced through immersive, multisensory and mobile productions that are infusing a new vitality into the genre', it acknowledged the opportunity he had seized for twenty-first-century opera at large.[65]

Ours, of course, is not the first era in which the rise or proliferation of screened media has challenged the proscenium theatre's illusionist interface and its predominantly passive mode of perception. Walter Benjamin, for one, believed that cinema and radio had rendered the entire operatic apparatus 'obsolete' and had stimulated Brecht's epic theatre reform instead.[66] Aided by digital technologies and a resulting increase of kinesis in both spectators and performers, however, recent explorations of site-specific opera performances have developed new ways to challenge the screen (painted, animated, or implied) as the default model for immersive musical multimedia. Unlike film, in short, opera does not necessarily have to be screened, whether inside or outside the opera house. And, along with the liveness Streep praised, it may be this newfound mobility of performances, audiences, and works as well as the concomitant embrace of opera's mixed media that will support its deliverance from the screen.

Works Cited

Adorno, Theodor. 'Versuch über Wagner.' In *Die musikalischen Monographien*, pp. 7-148. Volume 13 of *Gesammelte Schriften*, edited by Rolf Tiedemann. Darmstadt: Wissenschaftliche Buchgesellschaft, 1998.
———. *In Search of Wagner*. Translated by Rodney Livingstone. London: Verso, 2005.
Aronson, Arnold. 'Can Theater and Media Speak the Same Language?' In *Looking into the Abyss: Essays on Scenography*, pp. 86-96. Ann Arbor: University of Michigan Press, 2005.

65 Tom Huizenga and Robert Siegel on NPR's *All Things Considered*, 2017.
66 Benjamin, pp. 1, 6.

Baker, Evan. *From the Score to the Stage: An Illustrated History of Continental Opera Production and Staging.* Chicago and London: University of Chicago Press, 2013.

Benjamin, Walter. *Understanding Brecht.* Translated by Anna Bostock. Introduction by Stanley Mitchell. London and New York: Verso, 1998.

Baumann, Carl-Friedrich. *Bühnentechnik im Festspielhaus Bayreuth.* Munich: Prestel, 1980.

——. *Licht im Theater: Von der Argand-Lampe bis zum Glühlampen-Scheinwerfer.* Stuttgart: Franz Steiner, 1988.

Biermann, Franz Benedikt. *Die Pläne für Reform des Theaterbaues bei Karl Friedrich Schinkel und Gottfried Semper.* Berlin: Gesellschaft für Theatergeschichte, 1928.

Bolter, J. David and Richard Grusin. *Remediation: Understanding New Media.* Cambridge, MA: MIT Press, 1999.

Bomberger, E. Douglas. 'The Neues Schauspielhaus in Berlin and the Premiere of Carl Maria von Weber's *Der Freischütz.*' In *Opera in Context: Essays on the Historical Staging from the Late Renaissance to the Time of Puccini,* edited by Mark A. Radice, pp. 147-169. Portland, OR: Amadeus Press, 1998.

Cachopo, João Pedro. 'Opera's Screen Metamorphosis: The Survival of a Genre or a Matter of Translation?' *Opera Quarterly* 30, no. 4 (2015): 315-329.

Carnegy, Patrick. *Wagner and the Art of the Theatre.* New Haven, CT: Yale University Press, 2006.

Chion, Michel. *Audio-Vision: Sound on Screen.* Translated by Claudia Gorbman. New York: Columbia University Press, 1994.

Chothia, Jean. '"Zero...Zero...and Zero": Permeable Walls and Off-Stage Spaces.' In *Thinking on Thresholds: The Poetics of Transitive Spaces,* edited by Subha Mukherji, pp. 17-28. New York: Anthem Press, 2011.

Citron, Marcia. *Opera on Screen.* New Haven, CT: Yale University Press, 2000.

Clarke, Joseph. *The Architectural Discourse of Reverberation, 1750-1900.* PhD Dissertation. Yale University, 2014.

Crary, Jonathan. *Suspensions of Perception: Attention, Spectacle, and Modern Culture.* Cambridge, MA: MIT Press, 1999.

——. 'Géricault, the Panorama, and Sites of Reality in the Early Nineteenth Century.' *Grey Room* 9 (2002): 5-25.

Damisch, Hubert. *The Origin of Perspective.* Translated by John Goodman. Cambridge, MA and London: MIT Press, 1994.

Dombois, Johanna. 'Das Auge, das sich wechselnd öffnet und schließt: Zur Szenographie des Wagner-Vorhangs.' In *Richard Wagner und seine Medien: Für eine kritische Praxis des Musiktheaters,* edited by Dombois and Richard Klein, pp. 87-110. Stuttgart: Klett-Cotta, 2012.

Elsaesser, Thomas. *Film History as Media Archaeology: Tracking Digital Cinema.* Amsterdam: Amsterdam University Press, 2016.

Elcott, Noam. *Artificial Darkness: An Obscure History of Modern Art and Media*. Chicago and London: University of Chicago Press, 2016.

———. 'The Phantasmagoric *Dispositif*: An Assembly of Bodies and Images in Real Time and Space.' *Grey Room* 62 (2016): 42-71.

Fischer-Lichte, Erika. *Kurze Geschichte des deutschen Theaters*. Second edition. Tübingen and Basel: Francke, 1999.

———. *The Transformative Power of Performance: A New Aesthetics*. Translated by Saskya Iris Jain. London and New York: Routledge, 2008.

Forster, Kurt W. *Schinkel: A Meander Through His Life and Work*. Basel: Birkhäuser, 2018.

Frantz, Pierre. *L'esthétique du tableaux dans le théâtre du XVIIIe siècle*. Paris: Presses Universitaires de France, 1998.

Friedberg, Anne. *The Virtual Window: From Alberti to Microsoft*. Cambridge, MA: MIT Press, 2006.

———. 'The End of Cinema: Multimedia and Technological Change' (2000). In *The Film Theory Reader: Debates and Arguments*, edited by Marc Furstenau, pp. 272-278. London and New York: Routledge, 2010.

Glixon, Beth and Jonathan Glixon. *Inventing the Business of Opera: The Impresario and His World in Seventeenth-Century Venice*. Oxford and New York: Oxford University Press, 2006.

Greenberg, Clement. 'Modernist Painting' (1960). Revised version in *Esthetics Contemporary*, edited by Richard Kostelanctz, pp. 198-206. Buffalo, NY: Prometheus Books, 1978.

Grimm, Jacob, and Wilhelm Grimm, eds. *Deutsches Wörterbuch*, 13:2173 ('Prospect, prospekt'). Leipzig: Hirzel, 1889.

Grobert, Jacques-François-Louis. *De l'exécution dramatique considérée dans ses rapports avec le matériel de la salle et de la scène*. Paris: F. Schoell, 1809.

Gunning, Tom. 'Illusions Past and Future: The Phantasmagoria and its Specters.' *MediaArtHistoriesArchive* (2004). http://www.mediaarthistory.org/refresh/ Programmatic%20key%20texts/pdfs/Gunning.pdf. Accessed 31 May 2018.

Habel, Heinrich. *Festspielhaus und Wahnfried: Geplante und ausgeführte Bauten Richard Wagners*. Munich: Prestel, 1985.

Hewitt, Barnard, ed. *The Renaissance Stage: Documents of Serlio, Sabbattini and Furttenbach*. Coral Gables, FL: University of Miami Press, 1958.

Hildebrand, Adolf. 'The Problem of Form in the Fine Arts.' In *Empathy, Form, and Space: Problems in German Aesthetics, 1873-1893*, introduction and translation by Harry Francis Mallgrave and Eleftherios Ikonomou, pp. 227-279. Santa Monica, CA: Getty Center for the History of Art and the Humanities, 1994.

Huhtamo, Erkki. 'Elements of Screenology: Toward an Archaeology of the Screen.' *ICONICS: International Studies of the Modern Image* 7 (2004): 31-82.

———. 'Screen Tests: Why Do We Need an Archaeology of the Screen?' *Cinema Journal* 51, no. 2 (Winter 2012): 144-148.

Huizenga, Tom, and Robert Siegel. 'Opera Director Yuval Sharon Awarded MacArthur "Genius" Grant.' *All Things Considered*, WNPR, 11 October 2017. http://www.npr.org/sections/deceptivecadence/2017/10/11/556899374/opera-director-yuval-sharon-awarded-macarthur-genius-grant. Accessed 31 May 2018.

Johnson, Eugene J. *Inventing the Opera House: Theater Architecture in Renaissance and Baroque Italy*. Cambridge, UK: Cambridge University Press, 2018.

Krämer, Sybille. 'Graphism and Flatness: The Line as Mediator between Time and Space, Intuition and Concept.' In *The Power of Line: Linea III*, edited by Marcia Faietti and Gerhard Wolf, pp. 10-17. Munich: Hirner, 2015.

Kreuzer, Gundula. *Curtain, Gong, Steam: Wagnerian Technologies of Nineteenth-Century Opera*. Oakland, CA: University of California Press, 2018.

Lehmann, Johannes Friedrich. *Der Blick durch die Wand: Zur Geschichte des Theaterzuschauers und des Visuellen bei Diderot und Lessing*. Freiburg: Rombach, 2000.

Morris, Christopher. 'Digital Diva: Opera on Video.' *Opera Quarterly* 26, no. 1 (2010): 96-119.

Musser, Charles. 'Toward a History of Screen Practice.' *Quarterly Review of Film Studies* 9, no. 1 (1984): 59-69.

———. *The Emergence of Cinema: The American Screen to 1907*. New York: Scribner, 1990.

Nietzsche, Friedrich. 'The Case of Wagner.' In *Basic Writings of Nietzsche*, edited by Walter Kaufman, pp. 601-654. New York: The Modern Library, 1968.

Oxford English Dictionary. 'Back-cloth *n*. 2' and 'back-drop.' http://www.oed.com. Accessed 21 June 2018.

Paul, William. *When Movies Were Theater: Architecture, Exhibition, and the Evolution of American Film*. New York: Columbia University Press, 2016.

Penzel, Frederick. *Theatre Lighting Before Electricity*. Middletown, CT: Wesleyan University Press, 1978.

Pougin, Arthur. *Dictionnaire historique et pittoresque du théâtre et des arts qui s'y rattachent*. Paris: Firmin-Didot, 1885.

Ross, Alex. 'Opera on Location: A High-Tech Work of Wagnerian Scale is being Staged Across Los Angeles.' *The New Yorker*, 16 November 2015. https://www.newyorker.com/magazine/2015/11/16/opera-on-location. Accessed 31 May 2018.

Schivelbusch, Wolfgang. *Disenchanted Night: The Industrialization of Light in the Nineteenth Century*. Translated by Angela Davies. Berkeley: University of California Press, 1988.

Senici, Emanuele. 'Porn Style? Space and Time in Live Opera Videos.' *Opera Quarterly* 26, no. 1 (2010): 63-80.

Sharon, Yuval. 'A Dialogue [with Josh Raab] in Place of a Director's Note.' *Hopscotch: A Mobile Opera* [program book]. Los Angeles: The Industry, 2015.

Shusterman, Richard. *Surface and Depth: Dialectics of Criticism and Culture*. Ithaca: Cornell University Press, 2002.

Siegert, Bernhard. *Cultural Techniques: Grids, Filters, Doors, and Other Articulations of the Real*. Translated by Geoffrey Winthrop-Young. New York: Fordham University Press, 2015.

Steichen, James. 'HD Opera: A Love/Hate Story.' *Opera Quarterly* 27, no. 4 (2011): 443-459.

Stoeckel, Gustave J. 'The Wagner Festival in Bayreuth,' *New Englander* 36, no. 139 (April 1877): 258-293.

Thompson, Peter, and Kyriaki Mikellidoju. 'Applying the Helmholtz Illusion to Fashion: Horizontal Stripes Won't Make You Look Fatter.' *i-Perception* 2 (2011). https://www.ncbi.nlm.nih.gov/pmc/articles/PMC3485773/. Accessed 31 May 2018.

Tommasini, Anthony. 'A Success in HD, But at What Cost?' *The New York Times*, 14 March 2013. https://www.nytimes.com/2013/03/15/arts/music/mets-hd-broadcasts-success-but-at-what-cost.html. Accessed 31 May 2018.

Wagner, Richard. *Sämtliche Schriften und Dichtungen. Volksausgabe*. 16 vols. Leipzig: Breitkopf & Härtel, 1911.

———. *Prose Works*. Translated by William Ashton Ellis. 8 vols. New York: Broude Brothers, 1966.

———. *Tannhäuser und der Sängerkrieg auf Wartburg: Textbuch der letzten Fassung mit Varianten der Partitur und der vorangehenden Fassungen*, edited by Egon Voss. Stuttgart: Reclam, 2001.

Ward-Griffin, Danielle. 'Virtually There: Site-Specific Performance on Screen.' *Opera Quarterly* 30, no. 4 (2014): 362-368.

Watkins, Holly. *Metaphors of Depth in German Musical Thought: From E.T.A. Hoffmann to Arnold Schoenberg*. Cambridge, UK: Cambridge University Press, 2011.

Williams, Simon. 'The Spectacle of the Past in Grand Opera.' In *The Cambridge Companion to Grand Opera*, edited by David Charlton, pp. 58-75. Cambridge, UK: Cambridge University Press, 2003.

About the Author

Gundula Kreuzer is professor of music at Yale University. Her research interests embrace the history and theory of opera, with a special focus on aspects of performance, staging, technology, mediality, and sound; music and politics; reception studies; and German and European cultural history since the late eighteenth century. Kreuzer is the author of the award-winning *Verdi and the Germans: From Unification to the Third Reich* (Cambridge University Press, 2010) and *Curtain, Gong, Steam: Wagnerian Technologies* *of Nineteenth-Century Opera* (University of California Press, 2018). Her editorial work includes the critical edition of Verdi's chamber music for *The Works of Giuseppe Verdi* (Chicago University Press, 2010) and service as reviews editor for *Opera Quarterly*. In 2019, she received the Dent Medal of the Royal Musical Association and launched the annual symposium Y | Opera | Studies Today (YOST).

10.   Imaginary Screens: The Hypnotic Gesture and Early Film

Ruggero Eugeni

Abstract

Ruggero Eugeni argues that film profited from an insistent reference to hypnosis. If in early depictions, hypnotists were pointing their fingers at the subject in order to hit him or her with a shot of magnetic fluid, by the early twentieth century, subjects were induced into a hypnotic state as the hypnotist's hand waved repeatedly in front of the eyes. This new gestural format, repeatedly staged by the movies of the same period, was instrumental in mirroring and shaping in imaginary terms the film's screening conditions and the viewer's experience. At a moment when a nascent cinema might have been defined in a number of ways, the anachronistic figure of the hypnotist's hand worked to establish the screen rather than the film or the projector as the essential element of an emerging assemblage.

Keywords: Silent Film, *Dispositif*, Vision, Spectatorship

Hypnosis in early cinema: A metaphor of the film-viewing situation

Between the 1910s and 1920s, the iconography of hypnosis in film was changing. The hypnotist no longer pointed his fingers at the subject, hitting him with a shot of magnetic fluid; instead, subjects now fell into hypnosis as a consequence of the hypnotist waving his hand in slow and repeated gestures in front of their eyes. Occasionally, other hypnotic procedures were also shown, such as the gaze of the hypnotist or the movement of shining objects. But the waving gesture of the hypnotist's hand appears to have held primary interest, for even as it remained marginal in the extra-cinematic practice of hypnosis, it was widely staged and represented in the movies of the period.

Buckley, C., R. Campe, F. Casetti (eds.), *Screen Genealogies. From Optical Device to Environmental Medium.* Amsterdam: Amsterdam University Press, 2019
DOI 10.5117/9789463729000_CH10

The predominance of the new hypnotic gesture must be understood in relation to the mutual convergence and progressive overlap between the film-viewing situation experienced by spectators and the hypnotic setup. Such a convergence can be observed from the 1910s, both in film theoretical discourses and in the filmic depictions of hypnosis itself.[1] In this context, the gesture of the hand passing before the eyes of the hypnotized subject introduces—unlike other inductive gestures, and in particular the blow of energy—an explicit reference to the movie screen as both material and imaginary surface; indeed, its predominance over the 'blow' gesture highlights the key role of the silver screen within the imaginary and metaphorical reorganization of the cinematic situation as a hypnotic scene.

I articulate my discussion in two steps. First, I analyze a number of films produced between 1897 and 1923 that feature hypnosis. I emphasize the metaphorical references to the film-viewing situation and outline the role of the hypnotist's hand, in particular, as a reference to the film screen. I then summarize the development of mesmeric and hypnotic scenarios from their origins at the end of the eighteenth century to the first decade of the twentieth. In doing so, I argue that cinema ends up replacing the hypnotic setup within modernity and that the film screen is a key element in this process. In other words, I analyze the role of the hand-as-screen from both sides of the metaphorical equation: first, the cinema as hypnosis, and then, hypnosis as cinema.

It should be clear that my approach occupies a singular position within the current debate on screen theory.[2] Indeed, the discussion is often divided between a technological *archaeology* of the silver screen and its cultural *genealogy*. On the contrary, I insist on the dynamical and reciprocal interactions between material and imaginary aspects of film screens, and I emphasize how such interactions give birth to that particular cultural and theoretical object that we call the film *dispositive*.

Shadows, audiences, hallucinations

In its early period, cinema displayed different representations of hypnosis. At first, when the process of trance induction was staged, the prevailing

---

1   On the relationship between cinema and hypnosis, especially in reference to early cinema, see Alovisio, 2013; Andriopoulos, 2008; Bellour, 2009; Berton, 2015; Eugeni, 2002, 2003; Gordon, 2001; Killen, 2015; Ronetti, 2018; Schweinitz, 2010; and Väliaho, 2010.
2   See Blassnig, Deutsch, and Schimek, 2013; Chateau and Moure, 2016; Huhtamo, 2004, 2009, 2012; Manovich, 2001; Mitchell, 2015; Musser, 1984, 1990; and William, 2005.

mise-en-scène involved the 'classic' gesture of the hands pointed towards the body of the hypnotized subject—see, for instance, *Chez le magnetiste* (Alice Guy Blaché, 1897; Figure 10.1) or *L'antre des ésprits* (George Méliès, 1901; Figure 10.2).[3] In doing so, early filmmakers recovered and remediated within the cinematic domain the most widespread and immediately understandable iconography of hypnotic induction of the time: a gesture rooted in the long-established magnetic tradition, linked to the release of fluid energy, and which had already been adopted by contemporary practitioners of hypnosis (see, for instance, Figure 10.3).

Towards the mid-1910s, however, the iconography of hypnosis began to grow in both variety and complexity. A relevant example is *Trilby* (Maurice Tourneur, 1915), one of the first films to adapt the eponymous best-selling novel by George du Maurier, published in 1894. The plot is centred on a magnetic pair of characters: Svengali, an ambiguous and haunting musician-turned-hypnotist, and Trilby, a humble and compliant girl who, under Svengali's hypnotic spell, turns into a great and famous opera singer.

In the first scene of hypnotic induction, Trilby is posing as a model for her boyfriend, the painter Little Billee, when she is overcome by a sudden headache—though the actress's rendition more closely resembles a hysterical fit. Called upon to help the girl, Svengali hypnotizes her. As Trilby sits in front of him, the man moves his hand, from his eyes to hers, with one or two fingers pointed; then, keeping his palms open, he waves both hands, repeatedly and alternately, in front of the girl's face. At this point she initially composes her body in a *cataleptic* state and then suddenly becomes animated, as if staring at a series of invisible images. (Figure 10.4) The waving gesture is repeated and reversed at the end of the sequence: after a violent backlash by Little Billee and the group of painters living with him, Svengali brings Trilby back to reality and does so by waving his hands in front of her face, twice, as if to dissolve an invisible curtain.

In this example, the gesture of Svengali's hands seems to first compose and then dissolve a sort of invisible screen right in front of Trilby's eyes: some kind of veil or curtain, capable of both isolating the subject from her social environment and of reflecting a series of images, projected directly—or so it appears—by the subject's mind. This last impression is further accentuated in the same sequence by the presence of two other surfaces that are similarly

---

3   In addition, see also *Une scène d'hypnotisme I e II* (Lumière, 1896), *Mesmerist and Country Couple* (Edison, 1899), 1904; *Le Baquet De Mesmer* (Méliès, 1904). For other references to film representing hypnotism in the 1910s, see Andriopoulos, pp. 92-127; and Gordon, p. 128 and pp. 141-166.

10.1:   Alice Guy-Blaché (1873–1968), Frame enlargement from *Chez le Magnétiseur*, 1898.

10.2:   Georges Méliès (1861–1938), Frame enlargement from *L'Antre des Esprits*, 1901.

10.3:   Charles-Émile Carlègle (1877–1937). *Hypnotisme*. 1904. BNF, Collection Jaquet, Dessinateurs et humoristes, Tome 1.

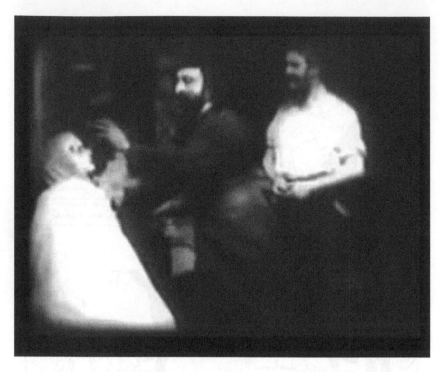

10.4:   Maurice Tourneur (1876–1961), Frame enlargement from *Trilby*, 1915.

capable of supporting images: first, the shower curtain, behind which one of the painters' silhouettes appears just before the sequence of Trilby's hypnosis; second, the canvas on which Trilby's young lover is painting a portrait of her and which appears in the foreground during the first part of the sequence.[4]

A less obvious but equally interesting example can be found in '*Les yeux qui fascinent*' ('Hypnotic Eyes'), episode six of the popular French serial *Les Vampires* (Louis Feuillade, 1916). In this episode, the criminal Moreno hypnotizes his maid and then proceeds to kidnap Irma Vep (a *femme fatale* in the service of the Grand Vampire) in order to replace her with the hypnotized girl. With the purpose of orchestrating the switch, Moreno intoxicates Irma Vep with chloroform before releasing his hypnotized maid from her hiding place in a large trunk. As the girl stands before him, Moreno waves his open

4   Not surprisingly, the gesture of Svengali is also reminiscent of the film projector's shutter, since it alternates light and shadow on the woman's face. For the importance of the visual and pictorial aspects of Tourneur's film, see Askari, 2015. For a more general discussion, see Eugeni, 2014.

10.5:   Louis Feuillade (1873–1925), Frame enlargement from *Les Vampires*, Episode 6: « LesYeux qui Fascinent ». 1916.

hand twice in front of her face, causing her to transition from a *lethargic* to a *catatonic* state: in short, she becomes a puppet, manipulated by Moreno's imperious gestures.[5] (Figure 10.5)

In this case, the gesture of circling one hand in front of the woman's eyes does not induce hypnosis but rather *reactivates* a state in which the (male) hypnotist exerts control over the (female) hypnotized subject. More exactly, the gesture has the effect of animating an inert body, turning it into a moving (albeit controlled) one. Nor should we neglect a series of not-too-implicit meta-cinematographic references embedded within this sequence. Two motifs are at work here: shadows, on the one hand (both the maid and Irma Vep cast masked silhouettes) and doubles, on the other hand (the mirrors, the two interchangeable women, etc.), both alluding in different ways to the nature of cinematic images. Within this network of references, the gesture of Moreno's hands evokes the twofold power of the cinematic situation: the capacity to turn still shadows into moving and living images (with the maid's body acting as a metaphor for the cinematic image), and the power to control, through the display of these images on the screen, the 'automated'

5   The presence of hypnosis in this film has been also analyzed by Weingart, 2014.

viewer's body and its reactions (with the maid also acting as a metaphor of the viewer's body in front of the screen). In sum, the hypnotist appears as a *grand imagier*, able to activate, deactivate, reactivate, and regulate the movements and actions of both images and bodies.

Of *Dr. Mabuse: The Gambler* (Fritz Lang, 1922), Raymond Bellour has written, 'It is with [this double film] that a joint evaluation of the dispositives of cinema and of hypnosis seem to cover the range of their possibilities for the first time'.[6] What is most relevant, from this point of view, is that Lang explicitly overlaps theatrical and hypnotic settings: in fact, in the well-known sequence at the Philharmonic, Mabuse, disguised as the stage hypnotist Sandor Weltmann, causes a collective hallucination in the audience by showing a caravan of Bedouins descending from the stage down the aisles of the hall. Again, I suggest we focus our attention on Mabuse/Weltmann's gestures.[7]

Having delivered a brief introductory speech, Mabuse/Weltmann moves stage left (or, for viewers, to the right end of the frame) and brings his left hand to his face, with his palm turned outwards; then, with a flourish, he slowly lowers the same hand, still open, upon the audience. (Figure 10.6) Two details further amplify the impact of his gesticulation: first, Mabuse, in his disguise, pretends here to be deprived of his right hand; second, because of an 'imperfection' in the editing, his gesture as he lowers his open left hand is shown twice. During the hallucinatory caravan appearance that follows, Mabuse/Weltmann always keeps his hand open, first toward the audience, then toward the images of the moving caravan. (Figure 10.7) Eventually, the man lifts his hand again, slowly, before suddenly closing his palm and yanking back his arm, as if to tear apart an invisible veil: in the hall, the images abruptly disappear.

In this example, *hypnosis works from within a theatrical situation but turns it into a cinematographic one.* If the example from *Les Vampires* discussed above could be seen to signify a shift from photography towards moving images, here we can thus find a similar move from theatre to cinema. In this sense, the role of Mabuse/Weltmann's hand is crucial, since it symbolically replaces the two elements of the cinematic situation that are physically absent from the hall yet that are nonetheless necessary to operate the cinematic machine: the *screen* (his hand stretched out towards the audience) and the *projector* (his hand pointed toward the hallucinatory images of the moving caravan).

6   Bellour, p. 391.
7   According to Tom Gunning, Mabuse appears here as a 'grand enunciator'. Gunning focuses on the *gaze* of Mabuse, while my analysis emphasizes the role of his hand, and in general of his mimicry. Gunning, 2001, pp. 87-116.

10.6:　Fritz Lang (1890–1976), Frame enlargement from *Dr. Mabuse, der Spieler. Zweiter Teil: INFERNO, Ein Spiel von Menschen unserer Zeit*, 1922.

10.7:　Fritz Lang (1890–1976), Frame enlargement from *Dr. Mabuse, der Spieler. Zweiter Teil: INFERNO, Ein Spiel von Menschen unserer Zeit*, 1922.

Dr. Mabuse: The Gambler is not the only film of the Weimar period to combine openly cinematic and hypnotic settings. Another good example is *Schatten. Eine nächtliche Halluzination* (*Warning Shadows*, Arthur Robinson, 1923). In this movie, a mysterious figure infiltrates a mansion where a luxurious party is taking place. After turning the living room into a makeshift screening room, he first proceeds to tell a dramatic story using shadow puppets and then causes a collective hallucination in which both hosts and guests end up witnessing, and even actively participating in, that same story.

Here, two distinct dispositives are deployed in succession: first the shadow play and then the hypnotic hallucinations. Both, however, clearly allude to the cinema. A spatial overlap, in fact, connects the projection screen and the space in which the collective hallucination takes place. In this case, the trance-inducing gesture of waving an open hand is almost absent. It re-appears, however, in a brief moment towards the end of the sequence: as the latest images of the hallucinatory film-inside-the-film fade out, the hypnotist-projectionist appears alongside the shocked viewers, looks into the camera, and passes his hand in front of his eyes, as if to wipe clean his field of vision—a gesture immediately mimicked by the countess who is hosting the party. (Figure 10.8)

In conclusion, considering these meta-cinematic scenes of hypnosis, how, should we regard the transition from the throwing of fluid upon the subjects to the waving of a hand before their faces? In order to answer this question, we must consider this transformation against a wider background. In the same years as the movies we just analyzed were released, much of the emerging film criticism and cinema theory as well as a number of discourses produced by journalists, psychiatrists, and writers emphasized the 'structural affinity' between the film experience and the hypnotic trance.[8] During the 1910s, the metaphorical overlapping of cinema and hypnosis became a widespread *topos*. Some films took part directly in this tendency, and they can be seen, therefore, to use the representation of hypnosis both to mirror and to shape, in imaginary terms, the situation experienced by the film viewer.

Within this context, in fact, the act of launching magnetic energy does not disappear but is deeply transformed into the shining of the hypnotist's eye or into the twinkle of a brilliant object handled by him or her. In this way, a metaphorical relationship between the passage of magnetic power and the beam of the film projector is established: in this respect, we can speak of the (hypnotist's) *hand-as-projector*. At the same time, however, a radically new

8   Andriopoulos, p. 16.

10.8:   Arthur Robison (1883–1935), Frame enlargement from *Schatten. Eine nächtliche Halluzination*. 1923.

metaphor appears: the gesture of the hand passed in front of the hypnotized subject introduces a reference to the other essential component of the film-viewing situation, the *screen*. The hand-as-projector is thus undermined by the new metaphorical gesture of the hypnotist's *hand-as-screen*. Although the two metaphors coexist and compete, *the latter tends to prevail*. Different reasons account for such prevalence, partly linked to the centrality of the screen in the formulation of the filmic-hypnotic situation, which I will discuss below. For the moment, in light of our analysis, we can suggest that the new gesture of the hand-as-screen prevails because it enables a richer and more articulated system of metaphorical references. Indeed, at least three different specific functions of the screen emerge in connection to the gesture.

First, the hand-as-screen refers to the screen as an *environmental* component of the film-viewing situation: it is intended to build a situation of isolation and concentration of the subject's attention. Consequently, as a spatially situated device, it is apparently meant to induce a state of psychic and social separation of subjects from their own environment and their installation in a new, heterotopic scene—an intimate sphere with a private regime of perception and relationships (see, particularly, *Trilby* and *Les Vampires*).

Second, the hand-as-screen represents the actual projection screen as an *operational* component of the film-viewing situation and refers to the hypnotist as the *operator* of the trance induction. It activates (in *Trilby* and *Mabuse*), re-activates (in *Les Vampires*), or de-activates (in *Schatten*) the hypnotic state. Moreover, from this perspective, the gesture expresses a further and deeper meaning of the cinematic situation, since the imaginary screen appears here as a *means for 'handling' both moving images and the bodies of the viewers.*

Finally, the imaginary screen drawn by the hypnotist's hand alludes to the actual screen as a *documental* component of the film-viewing situation: it is intended as a surface allowing the 'resurfacing' of subjective hallucinatory images and by this way their intersubjective observation. It is worth noting an ambiguity in this regard, since the surface evoked by the hand-as-screen gesture can function both as a 'catoptric' and a 'dioptric' surface[9]—that is, as a private and intimate 'image machine' that passively receives and refracts moving images produced elsewhere and projected from a distance (*Trilby, Les Vampires*); and as a public and collective 'visual' or 'sight machine' that actively produces and externalizes moving images (*Mabuse, Schatten*). If in the first case a screen needs a (yet imaginary) projector (for instance, the subject's or the hypnotist's mind), in the second case the screen *is* the projector. At the same time (in *documental* terms), in the first case the film spectator cannot see the hallucinatory image experienced by the hypnotized character, while in the second case characters and spectators share the same visions.

Obsessing images

In this section I intend to further extend my observations and analyze the encounter between cinema and hypnosis from the point of view of an *archaeology of the hypnotic setting*.[10] From this new perspective, cinema no longer appears as the object of a metaphorical transference *from* hypnosis but rather as an essential component of the history *of* 'modern' hypnosis.

9   On this point, I adopt and reinterpret some suggestions from Zielinski, 2013. Note that the screen as a dioptric surface incorporates some of the features attached to the projector's beam-as-blow of magnetic energy within the new and larger metaphorical framework of the hand-as-screen.

10   Here I refer to and expand what I previously argued in my book *La relazione* (Eugeni, 1993). On the history of hypnotism, see Crabtree, 1993; Ellenberger, 1970; Forrest, 2000; Gauld, 1992; Mayer, 2013; Monroe, 2008; Roussillon, 1992.

As it is well known, hypnosis evolved from 'magnetism' or 'mesmerism' with Franz Anton Mesmer's para-healing practices at the end of the eighteenth century. However, the 'classic' magnetic setting took shape when the Marquis de Puysegur transformed the technique in 1784: its purpose was no longer to induce para-epileptic seizures in the patients but rather to immerse them in a state of *artificial sleepwalking*. From this point on, magnetism became, for almost all of the nineteenth century, a show of *public intimacy*: it implied a clearly defined division of roles between the couple immersed in the intense magnetic relationship and an audience carefully observing their movements and poses. Against this backdrop, two different and parallel narrative paths emerged. On the one hand, sleepwalkers could be entirely dependent on the operators for their perceptual ability, emotions, agency, memories, and so on. On the other, they could also reach the status of *seers*: they could guess the thoughts of the attendees, read a book even if blindfolded, penetrate with their sensibility their own bodies and those of others, even access other dimensions, and, afterward, bear testimony to what they had seen.

To sum up, the setting of the classical hypnotic setup is defined and made distinct by three orders of elements: from a *topological* point of view, the delimitation of the magnetic scene through a set of gestures explicitly designed to activate the sleepwalking state; from a *relational* point of view, the distinction between a magnetic pair (doctor/patient) and a collective audience; from an *epistemological* point of view, the sleepwalker's access to the invisible or unknown and the specific modalities of his or her revelations of this 'other scene' to the audience.

Two elements are especially relevant for our purposes. First, classical hypnosis does not entail the use of screens—except, perhaps, opaque surfaces limiting the view of the seer and challenging his or her ability. Indeed, the subject's gaze and body inhabit the invisible rather than just looking at something immaterial on a flat surface. Second, the waving of one's hand before the eyes of the patient is not contemplated as a technique to induce the magnetic state—except, perhaps, in the case of a heretic and anti-fluidic mesmerist such as the Abbé de Faria.[11]

---

11   The abbot José-Custodio de Faria (1756-1819) was an ambiguous figure of a priest coming from Goa, through Rome and Portugal, operating in Paris in the very first years of the nineteenth century. He anticipated the idea of 'suggestion', typical of the end of the century. Indeed, according to him, the state of trance is not due to an exchange of magnetic fluid; instead it depends on a state of suggestion that affects the sleepwalkers (the *époptes*, or seers, in Faria's terms); consequently, the gesture of the hand passed before their eyes is aimed to produce a state of exceptional *concentration*, plunging the *époptes* in their cataleptic state.

The complex and dynamic equilibrium of the classical setting of magnetism is gradually revisited and deconstructed during the 'post-classical' period. At the end of the 1870s, Jean Marie Charcot 'had the idea of artificially reproducing [hysterical] paralyses, and [...] for this purpose he made use of hysterical patients whom he put into a state of somnambulism by hypnotizing them'.[12] With him, hypnosis became a tool to artificially activate, break down, assemble, and replicate the symptoms of hysteria.[13] The hypnotic setup inaugurated by Charcot at the Salpêtrière hospital maintained the relational and topological features of the classical scene, but, crucially, it deconstructed the epistemic ones; more specifically, it *deprived the sleepwalker of the role of seer*. The hypnotized subject became '*la chose de l'expérimentateur*', and his or her speaking body was transformed '*en véritable phonographe d'Edison*'.[14] Towards the end of the century, therefore, the clairvoyance of the seer as a defining trait was eliminated from the hypnosis scene and shifted towards the new experimental and theatrical scene of Spiritualism.[15]

The Nancy School, in its competition with Salpêtrière, was even more radical in deconstructing the classical scene of magnetism. Here, Hippolyte Bernheim (inaugurating his interventions in 1884) focused on the concept of *suggestion*, which he regarded as the influence exerted by a subject on another one by instilling 'ideodynamic' images without the need for specific and ritualized gestures. As a consequence, hypnosis was now merely considered a specific case of suggestion, one that involved the hypnotist as well as the hypnotized—and even the audience. In this way, the *relational* feature of the classical scene is critically undermined. On the other hand, hypnosis as suggestion is no longer limited to a specific setting but can potentially occur, in different forms, in all sorts of social contexts: patients do not need to be hysterical to be suggested, nor does one need to be a hypnotist in order to exert suggestion. In short, the *topological* feature of the classic magnetic scene is also radically deconstructed.

As a consequence of this progressive deconstruction, the setting of post-classical hypnosis became increasingly *de-individuated* and less strictly codified; hypnotic suggestions and resulting hallucinated visions expanded and spread widely across *fin de siècle* society: in the

12   See Sigmund Freud's essay 'Charcot' (1893) in Freud, 1962, III, pp. 7-23.
13   See André, 2011; Carroy, 1991; Didi-Huberman, 2003.
14   Richer and Tourette, pp. 99 and 106. On the 'technologizing' of the sleepwalker within the new 'discourse networks' of the twentieth century, see Kittler, 1997.
15   See Natale, 2016; Peters, 1999.

performances of stage hypnotists, who no longer used trusted sleepwalkers but directly hypnotized members of the audience; in the resulting 'epidemics of hypnotism' that extended beyond performances and worried jurists, moralists, and scientists; in the very mechanics of crowds and societies analyzed by social psychologists; at the root of criminal phenomena investigated by legal and anthropological theorists; and even in the immersive and dreamlike states typical of the aesthetic experience. Once again, it is worth noting that these different and varied types of post-classical hypnosis neither make use of any kind of screens nor specifically use the hand passed before the eyes of the subject as a way of inducing suggestion.

We are therefore led back to the period we started from: the 1910s, the historical background of 'modern' hypnosis. I intend to advance three related hypotheses. First, if classical hypnosis was characterized by the progressive *individuation* of its settings, and if the post-classical period saw a *de-individuation* of them, modern hypnosis entails an opposite process of *re-individuation*. The resulting newly redefined setup, however, no longer requires a magnetic pair acting *in front of* an audience, but rather a hypnotist who acts *on* a group of subjects, thus turning *them* into an audience.

Second, *the film-viewing situation represents the great cultural model for the new hypnotic setting*. From this point of view, the metaphorical overlap of the cinematic situation and the modern hypnotic setup is symptomatic of a deeper phenomenon: *cinema becomes the new hypnotic scene of modernity*. As I said at the beginning of this section, cinema should be considered not simply a metaphor of hypnosis but rather an essential component of its cultural history.

My second hypothesis has an important corollary. Early cinema has often been described as a dispositive able to assemble, revitalize, and give better voice to those visionary practices that could not find a space in its coeval media.[16] From the point of view I propose here, on the contrary, *cinema appears to narrow down and to regulate the forms of artificial production, circulation, and consumption of the visible.* If early cinema reflects a social anxiety related to the uncontrolled spread of images, it does so in order to discipline this circulation and thus reduce such anxieties.

Finally, my third hypothesis is that *cinema can serve as a model for the modern setup of hypnosis thanks to the presence of the screen within the*

16   See Albera and Tortajada, 2015.

film-viewing situation. The screen—which, as we saw, was completely missing in both the classical and post-classical settings—becomes, in turn, the central site of reorganization for the modern setting of hypnosis. This dynamic can therefore explain the key role of the hand-as-screen metaphorical gesture and its predominance over the hand-as-projector metaphor within the meta-filmic representations of hypnosis I analyzed above.

To fully understand this key point, I refer back to the three functions of the hand-as-screen delineated at the end of the previous section and compare them to the three specific features that characterize the hypnotic setting of modernity.

First, the screen as an *environmental* component is a sheltering device that focuses the spectator's attention and retains it within a specific space; it protects the spectator's attention from the break-ins and interruptions of external reality; with its ignition and its extinction, a projection on a screen marks the beginning and the end of the film experience. Thus, the screen appears both as producer and synecdoche of a new *topological* definition of the hypnotic scene.[17]

Second, the screen as an *operational* component marks the presence of the hypnotizer within the setup. The screen takes the role of the hypnotist, while its size and location make him a dominant figure whose influence is aimed at the viewers so that each of them is involved in the suggestion and, at the same time, they are all transformed into a unitary social group. In this way, a new *relational* configuration is built within the hypnotic scene, one based on the model of the hypnotist enchanting a crowd. Even individual hypnosis becomes a different declination of that setting: as Freud argues, *après coup* in 1921, in this new modern magnetic scene, 'the hypnotic relation is [...] a group formation with two members [... so that] hypnosis has a good claim to being described as a group of two'.[18]

Finally, the screen as a *documental* component is the surface on which hypnotic, subjective hallucinations manifest themselves in an objective way and, at the same time, where objective stimuli appear to become subjective hallucinations. Spiritualism and clairvoyance can therefore be reintroduced within the *epistemic* dimension of the new hypnotic scene.

17   On hypnosis and cinema as 'technologies of attention', see Crary, 1999; Rogers, 2014. On the dialectical coexistence of 'protection' / 'concealment' on the one hand, and of 'showing' / 'monstration' on the other, see Avezzù, 2016.

18   Freud, 1949, pp. 78 and 100.

Actual screens, imaginary screens, dispositives

We have, at this point, all the elements to interpret in full the phenomenon from which we started: the changes taking place between the 1910s and the 1920s in the iconography of the hypnotic induction in filmic representations; changes that consist, mainly, of the shift from the motif of the hypnotist's fingers pointed directly at the subject's body to a new gesture, one in which the hypnotizing hand is waved or circled in front of her eyes.

Three closely related events, I believe, explain this situation. The first is the association and merging of cinematic spectatorship and the modern hypnotic setting that takes place during this period. Second, many films further promote this association by the staging of situations of hypnosis in ways that are endowed with rich, articulate, and complex metaphorical references to the film's viewing situation. Finally, the cinematographic screen plays a key role in allowing and encouraging the identification of the hypnotic and the cinematographic: the screen is in fact a *centralized operator of hypnosis* acting on a crowd of viewers, and thus becomes the perfect model of the modern hypnotist. In light of these three elements, the transformation I have described in this essay can be explained as a shift of accent from the metaphor of the hypnotist's hand-as-projector to that of the hypnotist's hand-as-screen.

These conclusions lead me to focus the last section of this essay on the cinematic screen, in order to consider more carefully the radical transformations it underwent during this period. Film historians and media archaeologists have accurately documented a series of material innovations: the 1910s see a new attention to the architectural and technical aspects of the screen, with the transition from the vaudeville curtain and the nickelodeon gilded frame to the larger silver screens of picture palaces.[19] Alongside these, I wish to emphasize another type of transformation, which concerns the symbolic and imaginary values of the film screen. Indeed, at a time when the film's viewing situation ends up coinciding with the hypnotic one, the screen becomes the key element of the induction and maintenance of the state of hypnosis.[20]

19   See Huhtamo, 2004; William, 2005.
20   From this point of view, in addition to what we have observed above on the basis of film analysis, we can consider the journalistic and critical interventions of the same period. These repeatedly describe the film-viewing situation as a hypnotic setting. Not by chance, many writers' focus shifts during those years from the projector's beam to the screen itself as the site and means of inducing a semi- or para-hypnotic trance. In 1918, Emile Vuillermoz can still link the hypnotic nature of film to the action of the projector's beam: '*La foule est attirée par le*

In order to fully grasp the metamorphosis that the screen undergoes at this moment, we must face these transformations jointly. Indeed, the mutual interaction of material and technological aspects on the one hand and symbolic and imaginary ones on the other marks a decisive turning point in the history of the film screen: from a factual component of the film-viewing situation, it becomes a *dispositive*. In fact, we can consider a dispositive as an *assemblage* of different components (topological, technological, operational, symbolic, and imaginary) linked by a network of reciprocal relations of regulation and determination;[21] on this basis, what we witness during the 1910s is exactly the dynamic constitution of one such *assemblage,* pivoting around the movie screen.

Furthermore, this shift of the cinema screen from a technological appliance to a cultural and actual dispositive allows us to highlight another aspect. As Giorgio Agamben pointed out, a dispositive is always a tool for managing wider economic dynamics.[22] In this case, the screen as a hypnotic-cinematographic dispositive inaugurates the confluence and synergy of at least three economic systems: an economy of *space and attention* (the screen as a *topological* component), an economy of light and other such *flows of energy* (the screen as an *operating* component), and an economy of *trust and belief* (the screen as an *epistemic* component). Consequently, around the idea of the screen as a dispositive there begins to emerge—no longer

faisceau lumineux de la projection, comme un vol de moucherons dans le rayon d'un phare. Dès que la lanterne s'allume, les moucherons humains accourent et s'immobilisent. Cette fascination impérieuse qui affaiblit singulièrement le libre arbitre et le sens critique des spectateurs [...] *plonge le sujet dans un état physique assez voisin de l'hypnose'.* Vuillermoz, p. 224. However, just a few years later, we see a diverse group of writers describe cinema's hypnotic effect quite differently: Carlo Mierendorff ('In these catacombs [...] everyone presses forward, toward that mighty, flickering square eye that conjures, threatens, and mesmerizes.' Mierendorff, p. 427); Alfred Döblin ('[The little man, or the little woman] flocks to the movie theatres. [...] There, in the pitch-dark, low room, a square screen as tall as a man shimmers over a giant audience, over a mass that this white eye spellbinds with its vacant stare.' Döblin, pp. 1-3); and Jean Epstein ('I will never find the way to say how much I love American close-ups! Point blank. A head suddenly appears on screen and drama, now face to face, seems to address me personally and swells with an extraordinary intensity. I am hypnotized.' Epstein, pp. 235-236). All these writers decidedly emphasize the key role of the screen. Nevertheless, the *topos* of the light beam as a means of hypnotic induction never entirely disappears; see, for instance, about sixty years later, Roland Barthes: 'In that opaque cube, one light: the film, the screen? Yes, of course. But also (especially?), visible and unperceived, that dancing cone which pierces the darkness like a laser beam. [...] As in the old hypnotic experiments, we are fascinated—without seeing it head on—by this shining site, motionless and dancing.' Barthes, p. 347.

21   Casetti, pp. 80-110.

22   Agamben, pp. 1-24. In this book, following the current English translation of Foucault's works, the French term 'dispositif' has been translated as 'apparatus'.

10.9:   Roger Corman (b.1926), Frame enlargement from *The Undead*, 1957.

as a metaphorical overlapping but through a synecdochical shifting—the very idea of *cinema as a dispositive.*

Finally, a dispositive is also a form of cultural memory, one that extends its dynamic structure over time. It is no surprise, then, to see the metaphor of the hand-as-screen returning throughout the whole history of cinematic representations of hypnosis, at least until the 1980s. Accordingly, I conclude with an example that takes place thirty-four years after *Schatten*. In 1957, interest in hypnosis was very much alive in American cinema, following the success of such films as *The Search for Bridey Murphy* (Noel Langley, 1956), *I've Lived Before* (Richard Bartlett, 1956), and *The Three Faces of Eve* (Nunnally Johnson, 1957). Roger Corman exploited this trend by producing the film *The Undead* (1957); at the beginning of the movie, a physician (Richard Garland) induces deep hypnosis in a sex worker (Pamela Duncan) by placing his open hand before her eyes and intoning a long speech about hallucinatory images surfacing on his palm. (Figure 10.9)

Clearly, the distance in time has not weakened but has rather enriched the range of references and suggestions related to this gesture: the creation of a sphere of isolation and intimacy, the production of visionary experiences, the control and the power of the hypnotist over the subject. The hand-as-screen is still, after many years, an excessive surface, an *uncanny* site. Not only does this site negotiate the resurfacing of images, it also hosts the emergence of the Imaginary itself.[23]

Works Cited

Agamben, Giorgio. *What is an Apparatus? and Other Essays*. Translated by David Kishik and Stefan Pedatella. Palo Alto: Stanford University Press, 2009.

Albera, François and Maria Tortajada, eds. *Cine-Dispositives: Essays in Epistemology Across Media*. Amsterdam: Amsterdam University Press, 2015.

Alovisio, Silvio. *L'occhio sensibile. Cinema e scienze della mente nell'italia del primo Novecento. Con un'antologia di testi d'epoca*. Torino: Kaplan, 2013.

André, Emmanuelle. *Le choc du sujet: De l'hystérie au cinéma XIX-XXI siècle*. Rennes: Presses Universitaires de Rennes, 2011.

Andriopoulos, Stefan. *Possessed: Hypnotic Crimes, Corporate Fiction, and the Invention of Cinema*. Chicago: University of Chicago Press, 2008.

Askari, Kaveh. '*Trilby*'s Community of Sensation.' In *Visual Delights II: Exhibitions and Receptions*, edited by Vanessa Toulmine and Simon Popple, pp. 60-72. Eastleigh, UK: John Libbey Publishing, 2005.

Avezzù, Giorgio. 'Intersections between Showing and Concealment in the History of the Concept of Screen.' In *Screens: From Materiality to Spectatorship—A Historical and Theoretical Reassessment*, edited by Dominique Chateau and José Moure, pp. 29-41. Amsterdam: Amsterdam University Press, 2016.

Barthes, Roland. *The Rustle of Language*. Translated by Richard Howard. Berkeley: University of California Press, 1989.

Bellour, Raymond. *Le Corps du cinéma: Hypnoses, émotions, animalités*. Paris: POL Traffic, 2009.

Berton, Mireille. *Le corps nerveux des spectateurs: Cinéma et sciences du psychisme autour de 1900*. Lausanne: L'Age d'Homme, 2015.

Blassnigg, Martha, Gustav Deutsch, and Hanna Schimek. *Light, Image, Imagination*. Amsterdam: Amsterdam University Press, 2013.

Carroy, Jacqueline. *Hypnose, suggestion et psychologie: L'invention des sujets*. Paris: Presses Universitaires de France, 1991.

Casetti, Francesco. *The Lumière Galaxy: Seven Key Words for the Cinema to Come*. New York: Columbia University Press, 2015.

---

23 'Hypnosis has something positively uncanny [and] the characteristic of uncanniness suggests something old and familiar that has undergone repression.' Freud, 1949, p. 95.

Chateau, Dominique and José Moure. *Screens: From Materiality to Spectatorship—A Historical and Theoretical Reassessment*. Amsterdam: Amsterdam University Press, 2016.

Crabtree, Adam. *From Mesmer to Freud: Magnetic Sleep and the Roots of Psychological Healing*. New Haven, CT: Yale University Press, 1993.

Crary, Jonathan. *Suspensions of Perception: Attention, Spectacle and Modern Culture*. Cambridge, MA: MIT Press, 1999.

Didi-Huberman, Georges. *The Invention of Hysteria: Charcot and the Photographic Iconography of the Salpêtrière*. Translated by Alisa Hartz. Cambridge, MA: MIT Press, 2003.

Döblin, Alfred. 'The Theatre of the Little People' (1909), translated by Lance W. Garmer. In *German Essays on Film*, edited by Richard W. McCormick and Alison Guenther-Pal, pp. 1-3. New York: Continuum, 2004.

Ellenberger, Henri F. *The Discovery of the Unconscious: The History and Evolution of Dynamic Psychiatry*. New York: Basic Books, 1970.

Epstein, Jean. 'Magnification' (1921), translated by Stuart Liebman. In *French Film Theory and Criticism: A History/Anthology, Vol. 1: 1907-1929*, edited by Richard Abel, pp. 235-236. Princeton: Princeton University Press, 1988.

Eugeni, Ruggero. *La relazione di incanto: Studi su cinema e ipnosi*. Milano: Vita e Pensiero, 2002.

———. 'The Phantom of the Relationship, the Poverty of Cinema and the Excesses of Hypnosis.' In 'Dead Ends/Impasses', edited by Leonardo Quaresima, special issue, *Cinema & Cie, International Film Studies Journal* 2 (spring 2003): 47-53.

———. 'Voce, scena, suggestione in *Trilby*: La donna ipnotizzata dal romanzo di George du Maurier ai film di Maurice Tourneur e Archie Mayo (1894-1931).' In *Scena madre. Donne personaggi e interpreti della realtà. Studi per Annamaria Cascetta*, edited by Roberta Carpani, Laura Peja, and Laura Aimo, pp. 417-426. Milano: Vita e Pensiero, 2014.

Forrest, Derek. *Hypnotism: A History*. London: Penguin, 2000.

Freud, Sigmund. *Group Psychology and the Analysis of the Ego*. Translated by James Strachey. London: Hogarth Press, 1949.

———. 'Charcot' (1893). In *The Standard Edition of the Complete Psychological Works of Sigmund Freud*, vol. 3, edited and translated by James Strachey, pp. 7-23. London: Hogarth Press, 1962.

Gauld, Alan. *A History of Hypnotism*. Cambridge, UK: Cambridge University Press, 1992.

Gordon, Rae Beth. *Why the French Love Jerry Lewis: From Cabaret to Early Cinema*. Palo Alto: Stanford University Press, 2001.

Gunning, Tom. *The Films of Fritz Lang: Allegories of Vision and Modernity*. London: BFI, 2001.

Huhtamo, Erkki. 'Elements of Screenology: Toward an Archaeology of the Screen.'
    ICONICS: International Studies of Modern Image, Tokyo, vol. 7 (2004): 31-82.
———. 'Messages on the Wall—An Archaeology of Public Media Displays.' In *The
    Urban Screen Reader*, edited by Scott McQuire, Meredith Martin, and Sabine
    Niederer, pp. 15-28. Amsterdam: Institute of Network Cultures, 2009.
———. 'Screen Tests: Why Do We Need an Archaeology of the Screen?' *Cinema
    Journal* 51.2, (2012): 144-148.
Killen, Andreas. 'The Scene of the Crime: Psychiatric Discourses on the Film Audi-
    ence in Early Twentieth Century Germany.' In *Film 1900: Technology, Perception,
    Culture*, edited by Annemone Ligensa and Klaus Kreimeier, pp. 153-172. New
    Barnet: John Libbey, 2015.
Kittler, Friedrich. 'Dracula's Legacy.' In *Literature, Media, Information Systems:
    Essays*, edited by John Johnston, pp. 50-84. New York: Routledge, 1997.
Manovich, Lev. *The Language of New Media*. Cambridge, MA: MIT Press, 2001.
Mayer, Andreas. *Sites of the Unconscious: Hypnosis and the Emergence of the
    Psychoanalytic Setting*. Chicago: University of Chicago Press, 2013.
Mierendorff, Carlo. 'If I Only Had the Cinema!' (1920), translated by Jeffrey Timon.
    In *The Promise of Cinema: German Film Theory 1907-1933*, edited by Anton Kaes,
    Nicholas Baer, and Michael Cowan, pp. 426-432. Oakland, CA: University of
    California Press, 2016.
Mitchell, W.J.T. 'Screening nature (and the nature of the screen).' *New Review of
    Film and Television Studies* 13.3 (2015): 231-246.
Monroe, John Warne. *Laboratories of Faith: Mesmerism, Spiritism and Occultism
    in Modern France*. Ithaca: Cornell University Press, 2008.
Musser, Charles. 'Toward a History of Screen Practice.' *Quarterly Review of Film
    Studies* 9.1 (1984): 59-69.
———. *The Emergence of Cinema: The American Screen to 1907*. London and New
    York: Simon & Schuster, 1990.
Natale, Simone. *Supernatural Entertainments: Victorian Spiritualism and the Rise
    of Modern Media Culture*. University Park, PA: Pennsylvania State University
    Press, 2016.
Peters, John Durham. *Speaking into the Air: A History of the Idea of Communication*.
    Chicago: University of Chicago Press, 1999.
Richer, Paul and Gilles de la Tourette. 'Hypnotisme', in *Dictionnaire Encyclopédique
    des Sciences Médicales*, edited by Amédée Dechambre and Léon Lereboullet,
    quatrième série, Tome XV, pp. 67-132. Paris: Masson – Asselin et Houzeau, 1889.
Rogers, Kenneth. *The Attention Complex: Media, Archeology, Method*. New York:
    Palgrave MacMillan, 2014.
Ronetti, Alessandra. 'Les pratiques de suggestion dans 'Le peintre néo-impression-
    iste' (1910) d'Émile Cohl.' In *Cinema, sogno e allucinazione dale origini agli anni*

Venti, edited by Silvio Alovisio and Mireille Berton, Special Issue of *Immagine. Note di storia del cinema*, n. 18, 2018, pp. 116.

Roussillon, René. *Du baquet de Mesmer au "baquet" de S. Freud. Une archéologie du cadre et de la pratique*. Paris: Presses Universitaires de France, 1992.

Schweinitz, Jörg. 'Immersion as Hypnosis: The Evolution of a Theoretical and Cinematic Stereotype in Silent Cinema.' In *In The Very Beginning, At The Very End: On the History of Film Theories*, edited by Leonardo Quaresima and Valentina Re, pp. 39-44. Udine: Forum, 2010.

Väliaho, Pasi. *Mapping the Moving Image: Gesture, Thought and Cinema Circa 1900*. Amsterdam: Amsterdam University Press, 2010.

Vuillermoz, Émile. 'Routine' (1918). In *Le temps du cinéma: Émile Vuillermoz père de la critique cinématographique*, edited by Pascal Manuel Heu, pp. 224-226. Paris: L'Harmattan, 2003.

Weingart, Brigitte. 'Contact at a Distance: The Topology of Fascination.' In *Rethinking Emotion: Interiority and Exteriority in Premodern, Modern, and Contemporary Thought*, edited by Rüdiger Campe and Julia Weber, pp. 72-100. Berlin and Boston, De Gruyter, 2014.

William, Paul. 'Screens.' In *Encyclopedia of Early Cinema*, edited by Richard Abel, pp. 830-834. London and New York: Routledge, 2005.

Zielinski, Siegfried. 'Designing and Revealing: Some Aspects of a Genealogy of Projection.' In *Light, Image, Imagination*, edited by Martha Blassnigg, Gustav Deutsch, and Hanna Schimek, pp. 151-179. Amsterdam: Amsterdam University Press, 2013.

About the Author

Ruggero Eugeni is professor of media semiotics at Università Cattolica del Sacro Cuore in Milan. His interests are focused on the living media experience as defined both in historical-sociological terms and from a phenomenological-neurocognitive perspective. On this basis, he is currently developing historical and theoretical research on filmic representations of hypnotism as metaphors for the cinematic dispositive and its experiential, cultural, and political implications. His leading works are 'Film, sapere, società. Per un'analisi sociosemiotica del testo cinematografico' [*Film, Culture, Society. For a Sociosemiotic Analysis of the Film*] (Milano, 1999), 'La relazione d'incanto. Studi su cinema e ipnosi' [*The Enchanted Relationship. Studies on Film and Hypnotism*] (Milano, 2002). His most recent monographic work is 'Semiotica dei media. Le forme dell'esperienza' [*Media semiotics. Forms of Experience*] (Rome, 2010).

Several of Eugeni's articles, papers, and preprints in English are available at http://ruggeroeugeni.com.

11. Material. Human. Divine. Notes on the Vertical Screen

Noam M. Elcott

Abstract

Taking cues from architecture, painting, and experimental cinema, Noam Elcott maps three distinct paradigms for the format of the vertical screen. Portraiture—the erect human figure or face—may be understood as the eponymous and paradigmatic form of this vertical format. Vertical screens also align with the celluloid strips that run vertically through nearly all projectors, whose properties were interrogated by postwar avant-gardes and have taken on renewed urgency in light of celluloid's impending obsolescence. Finally, the luminous verticality of stained glass windows helped define the Gothic order, which provided a model for avant-garde experiments in light and space for a century or more, and which have suddenly returned to centre stage in contemporary art. Elcott's three distinct paradigms map a centuries-long encounter with vertical screens that resonate unexpectedly yet unambiguously in the present.

Keywords: Format, Media Archaeology, Contemporary Art, Installation, Phantasmagoria

Past prisms present

Screens For Looking at Abstraction (2011-), a multi-part installation by Josiah McElheny, encapsulates the whole history of abstract cinema. Selections from the canon and margins of abstract film—projected upside-down, backwards, and in reverse—are refracted horizontally, vertically, or prismatically across a series of mirrors and screens to form new kaleidoscopic configurations. (Figure 11.1) These visual symphonies immediately conjure the iridescent images produced on Sir David Brewster's kaleidoscope

Buckley, C., R. Campe, F. Casetti (eds.), *Screen Genealogies. From Optical Device to Environmental Medium*. Amsterdam: Amsterdam University Press, 2019

DOI 10.5117/9789463729000_CH11

(patented in 1817), A. Wallace Rimington's Colour Organ (patented in 1895), Alexander B. Hector's Apparatus for Creating Colour Music (patented in 1921), the lumia of Thomas Wilfred (to which I will return), and hosts of other commercial, scientific, and artistic ventures. One quickly recalls the abstract films of Walter Ruttmann and Hans Richter (in the 1920s), Len Lye (beginning in the 1930s), and Stan Brakhage (in the later part of his career), as well as the Whitney brothers' pioneering use of analogue computers (beginning in the late 1950s) and Douglas Trumbull's adaption of the slit-scan technique for the Star Gate sequence in *2001: A Space Odyssey* (Stanley Kubrick, 1968). The multiplied, folded, and expanded screens point, in turn, to the proliferation of screens in the *Farblichtmusik* performances of Oskar Fischinger and Alexander Laszlo (in the 1920s), the Expanded Cinema of Stan VanDerBeek, Robert Whitman, and others from the 1960s and 1970s as well as myriad recent film and video installations. More than any single reference, however, *Screens For Looking at Abstraction* encapsulates the history of abstract film because the installation's parts are literally devices for viewing the history of abstract film. McElheny lets others program the films. But the operations he mandates—films must be projected upside-down, backwards, and in reverse; and then refracted further by angled mirrors—render virtually any footage abstract. Accordingly, the whole history of film is mobilized for the experience of abstraction. Generations earlier, the inveterate Dadaist Man Ray bricolaged a functionally identical apparatus for his personal use: 'I go to the movies without choosing the program, without even looking at the posters. I go to the theatres that have the comfortable seats. [...] I invented a prism system that I adapted on to my glasses: this way, I watch black and white films that bore me in colours and in abstract images.'[1] For Man Ray and McElheny, abstraction inheres not only in the works but also and above all in their exhibition. For Man Ray and his circle, the operative element was lenses. For McElheny and our generation, the operative element is screens.

It is time we looked at cinema not through a different lens but on a different screen: the vertical screen. More than any other force in recent years, the vertical screen has changed our orientation to cinema, whether mass-produced or avant-garde, industrial or artistic, contemporary or historical. A single technological device—the smartphone—has made vertical screens ubiquitous. But their origins and reverberations run much deeper and have only begun to be charted. This is a brief and schematic overview of vertical screens.

---

1   Man Ray, p. 45.

11.1:   Josiah McElheny (b.1966), *Screens for Looking at Abstraction*, 2012. Aluminum, low-iron mirror, projection cloth, film transferred to video (variable program), video projectors with stands, wood, metal hardware; three parts, overall dimensions variable. © Josiah McElheny.

Tall screens, buried histories

A century ago, new screens were still reliant on new lenses. In late 1926, the French astronomer and inventor Henri Chrétien applied for a patent for an anamorphic lens, called the Hypergonar, in the hopes of advancing early efforts in colour and stereoscopic (or 3D) cinema.[2] These efforts appear to have gone nowhere. But as is so often the case in the history of technology, an invention patented for one application proved to be the solution for an altogether different problem. The catalyst was Abel Gance's 1927 cinematic epic *Napoléon*. For the dramatic conclusion of the film, Gance employed a triple-projector system known as Polyvision in which three traditional cameras and projectors were interlocked to produce vast panoramas and highly choreographed triptychs across a 4:1, super-widescreen field. Inspired by Gance, Chrétien repurposed his Hypergonar anamorphic lens toward a new cinematic experience: not widescreen but rather a cinematic cross

2   Belton, pp. 40-43.

that could accommodate 1.33:1 at its centre (for conventional scenes), 2.66:1 widescreen (for panoramas), and 1:2.66 'tall-screen' suitable, according to Chrétien's patent application, for the interiors and façades of churches, among other scenes. (Figure 11.2) Understood as an added attraction rather than as a standard format, a number of directors, not least Claude Autant-Lara, mobilized the Hypergonar anamorphic lens to produce films with widescreen and 'tall-screen' sequences, a feat accomplished using two projectors outfitted with anamorphic lenses mounted horizontally and vertically.[3] In the late 1920s, 'tall-screen' cinema was technologically no less viable than widescreen cinema. Yet given the choice between tall-screen cinema and widescreen cinema, professionals and publics resoundingly chose sound cinema. Chrétien's Hypergonar anamorphic lens was quickly abandoned and forgotten until its 1952 re-discovery and rebranding as Cinemascope.

Twice buried in the history of Cinemascope lies a history of the vertical screen. It is a history previously consigned to failed technological experiments and other antiquarian anecdotes. Today, however, it is the history of the present. Spurred by the vertical video captured and played on smartphones, YouTube, Facebook, and other leading video portals have recently enabled full-screen vertical video. For billions of users, vertical video is now a normative format.[4] And yet, vertical cinema is at once new and ancient. Whether on canvas or on the iPhone, vertical orientation is known as portrait format. The cinematic incunabula of Muybridge and Marey were often oriented vertically, as were the slits or mirrors of phenakistoscopes, zoetropes, praxinoscopes, and other nineteenth-century 'pre-cinematic' optical toys—not least because they took their measure from the erect human. And there is no question that the social practice of portraiture—codified as an aesthetic genre centuries or millennia ago—gets us closer to vertical cinema than does the iPhone. As Gilles Deleuze famously remarked: 'Technology is [...] social before it is technical.'[5] But the social practice of portraiture does not get us close enough. For the screen—whatever its orientation—has no essence, no apodictic form, no timeless ideal. Instead—and here is the wager that undergirds the speculations to come—if screens have no essence, they nonetheless manifest clear propensities, such that certain types of screens promote and

---

3   Decades later, Disney retrofit *Fantasia* with a variable aspect ratio projection system to stretch the animated sequences to 2:1 widescreen, while the live-action sequences retained their 1.33 format. See Wasserman, pp. 14-15.

4   See Manjoo, 2015.

5   Deleuze, pp. 39-40.

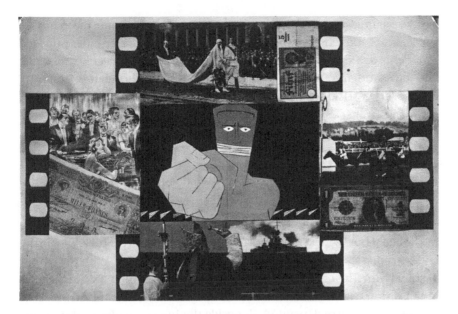

11.2:   Claude Autant-Lara (1901–2000), Collaged mockup for *Construire un Feu* (1928–30).
Courtesy John Belton.

inhibit certain types of images in specific types of locations. Screens have
no essence, but neither is their deployment merely a product of chance.[6]

What follows is a series of speculations on the broader, longer cultural
associations and technical implementations of the vertical screen. I will draw
on recent and comparatively archaic instances of vertical cinema in an effort
to map three distinct paradigms for the vertical screen. Portraiture—that is,
the erect human figure or face—is surely the eponymous and paradigmatic
form of the vertical format. I will return to the question of portraiture in
the middle of this essay, albeit mediated through the ghostly scrim of the
phantasmagoria. I will also examine two additional paradigms. On the
one hand, vertical screens align with the celluloid strips that run vertically
through nearly all projectors. For the last fifty years, verticality hinted at
film's otherwise invisible material support, whose properties were interrogated by postwar avant-gardes and have taken on renewed urgency in

6   For nuanced reflections on the arbitrary and the more fundamental non-mimetic elements
of images—such as frames, rectangularity, left/right and up/down—see Meyer Schapiro's 'On
Some Problems in the Semiotics of Visual Art'. Alas, Schapiro's comments on orientation are
limited to the commonplace that 'We live more in the horizontal dimension than the vertical'
and, ultimately, that 'I shall pass over the role of proportions and shape of the field, which is a
vast problem'. Schapiro, 1972, pp. 13 and 15.

light of celluloid's impending obsolescence. On the other hand, the luminous verticality of stained glass windows helped define the Gothic order, provided a model for avant-garde experiments in light and space for a century or more, and have suddenly returned to centre stage in art world debates. In short: I will explore vertical screens and vertical cinema in relation to three distinct paradigms: material, human, and divine. Although hardly exhaustive, these three *topoi* will map a centuries-long encounter with vertical screens that resonates unexpectedly but unambiguously in the present.

Eisenstein's dynamic square

In the late 1920s, widescreen and 'tall-screen' cinema were technologically feasible, practically implemented, and vigorously debated. With the advent of sound film, the 1.33:1 aspect ratio that lorded over cinema since the days of Edison and the Lumières came under pressure. Sound-on-film—that is, an optical soundtrack printed alongside the image—colonized precious celluloid real estate and reduced the already squat 1.33 ratio to a mere 1.18, an all-but-square format. (Fritz Lang's *M* [1931] is perhaps the most famous film released in this aspect ratio.) At the same time, directors and technicians frequently championed but rarely realized ever wider formats. Many of these aesthetic and technical reflections were recounted in a special issue of *The Journal of the Society of Motion Picture Engineers*, a Hollywood-based association, published in January 1930. Representatives from the scientific bureau of Bausch & Lomb Optical Co. or Bell and Howell Camera Co. affirmed widescreen for reasons 'artistic, technical, and economic' as well as 'psychological, metaphysical, and physiological'.[7] The affirmation of horizontality was nothing less than axiomatic.[8] And yet it was in this milieu—specifically, at a September 1930 meeting organized by the Technicians Branch of the Academy of Motion Picture Arts and Sciences in Hollywood—that the great Soviet director and contrarian Sergei Eisenstein staged his intervention into the proper proportions of the film screen.

The talk was soon published in the important English-language film journal *Close-Up*. Rather than champion widescreen cinema and accept as

7   Howell and Dubray, pp. 82, 60, and passim.
8   Just a few years ago, an ultimately futile campaign against vertical video spawned countless YouTube videos, many of which capture the axiomatic adherence to cinematic horizontality as well as the earlier scientific papers—and with much more hilarity. See, for example, 'Vertical Video Syndrome' at https://youtu.be/Bt9zSfinwFA.

axiomatic the horizontality of the screen, Eisenstein marshalled the brewing debate to question the basic assumptions that had governed cinematic proportions for more than three decades. Physiologically, economically, and, above all, aesthetically, the horizontal screen, according to Eisenstein, was little more than a residue of the theatrical origins of cinema. Film images were horizontal because stages—and paintings modelled after stages—were horizontal. Eisenstein, to the contrary, embraced 'the hymn of the male, the strong, the virile, active *vertical* composition!'9 Lest he offend the sensitive listener, Eisenstein did not elaborate at length on 'the dark phallic and sexual ancestry of the vertical shape as a symbol of growth, strength or power'. Rather, and in concert with Freud's *Civilization and its Discontents*, published the same year, he rehearsed humanity's evolution from worms, creeping on their stomachs, to four-legged animals, only to become 'something like mankind from the moment when we hoisted ourselves to our hind legs and assumed the vertical position'. Man then 'marked in vertical milestones each step in his progress to a higher level of social, cultural or intellectual development': Indian lingams, Egyptian obelisks, Trajan's column, the Christian cross, the Gothic arch, the Eiffel Tower, and, in his own time, the ultimate sublimated phalluses, armies of skyscrapers, rows of chimneys, and trellises of oil-pumps. But here, at the height of his vertical psalm, Eisenstein's argument took a surprising turn:

> By now, surely, you will have deduced that my suggestion for the optical frame of the supreme and most synthetic of all arts [the cinema] [...] is that it must be vertical.
> Not at all.
> For in the heart of the super-industrialised American, or the busily self-industrialising Russian, there still remains a nostalgia for infinite horizons, fields, plains and deserts. [...] This nostalgia cries out for horizontal space. [...]
> So neither the horizontal nor the vertical proportions of the screen *alone* is ideal for it.
> [...]
> What is it that, by readjustment, can in equal degree be made the figure for both the vertical and horizontal tendencies of a picture?
> The battlefield for such a struggle is easily found – *it is the square* [...]
> The 'dynamic' square screen.10

9   Eisenstein, p. 207.
10   Ibid., pp. 208-209.

Parenthetically but potently, Eisenstein specifically rejected the vertical proportions attained by masking the right and left sections of the frame—as seen, for example throughout Lotte Reiniger's animated silhouette fairytale *Cinderella* (1922) or *The Holy Mountain* (1926), a mountain film by Arnold Fanck, starring Leni Riefenstahl. For Eisenstein, 'The *vertical spirit* can never be attained this way: first, because the occupied space comparative to the horizontal masked space will never be interpreted as something *axially opposed to it*, but always *as part* of the latter and, second, because in *never surpassing the height* that is bound to the horizontal dominant, it will never impress as an opposite space axis – the one of uprightness.'[11] Thus, Eisenstein abandoned the vertical screen, teeming with the dark phallic and sexual ancestry of the vertical shape, in favour of the more dialectical and dynamic square screen—which he failed to act on all the same. Indeed, neither Eisenstein nor his Hollywood technician audience nor any other major forces in cinema succeeded in promulgating a screen much different from the 1.33:1 ratio established by Thomas Edison's deputy, W.K.L. Dickson, in 1892. A year after Eisenstein's speech was published, the Academy of Motion Picture Arts and Sciences adopted the so-called Academy ratio of 1.375:1. The dynamic square, the erect phallus, and the nostalgia for infinite horizontal fields would remain, for decades, unrequited dreams.

Materiality

Nearly 85 years after Chrétien proposed 35mm anamorphic vertical cinema, Tacita Dean inadvertently landed on precisely the same procedure. A maker of beautiful, haunting, and above all melancholic works in film and other media, Dean received the final Unilever commission for the Tate Modern's cavernous Turbine Hall—a long, narrow, and exceptionally tall exhibition space. The shape of the project, quite literally, appeared to her instantly:

> I wanted to try and make a portrait format anamorphic film with the lens I normally use to stretch my film into a double-width landscape format. I wondered what would happen if I turned the lens 90 degrees and stretched the image from top to bottom instead of from left and right: make a portrait format film for a portrait format space?[12]

11   Ibid., p. 209.
12   Dean, p. 16.

From the beginning, then, Dean aligned the vertical format with portraiture and a portrait format space. But a central question remained unanswered: a film portrait of what? 'I realized', she said, 'I was making an ideogram and, unbeknown to me, the portrait I'd been struggling to recognise for so long was a portrait of film itself'.[13] Dean jettisoned nearly all post-production and all digital effects in favour of antiquated modes of in-camera editing using glass matte painting, multiple exposures, and masks—in particular, the iconic sprocket holes visible on the left and right of every vertical frame—to create an iridescent film that captured the unique qualities of film. She then projected the looped film vertically onto a 13-meter high monolith. Thus, the history of the 2011 work aptly titled: *FILM.* (Figure 11.3)

Dean's vertical cinema piece is silently shot through with a materialist— and feminist—history of film, above all works of structural and materialist filmmakers in the U.S. and Europe, such as *Film in Which There Appear Edge Lettering, Sprocket Holes, Dirt Particles, Etc.* (1966), by George Landow (now known as Owen Land), or Malcolm Le Grice's *Little Dog for Roger* (1967), a 16mm film whose primary content is an old home movie shot on 9.5mm, a film gauge famous for its central sprocket hole and which, by the late 1960s, was rapidly approaching obsolescence. In other words, these were precisely the preoccupations of Dean.[14]

Annabel Nicolson—Le Grice's student and Dean's future mentor—advanced this aesthetic with a distinctly feminist edge in a number of formative works from the early 1970s. In her film *Slides* (1971), for example, Nicolson ran the celluloid through a sewing machine, wove it with thread, collaged shreds of photographic transparencies and filmstrips directly on the celluloid, and pulled it by hand through a Debrie step printer. And in her classic Expanded Cinema piece, *Reel Time* (1973), she ran film through a sewing machine and a projector, puncturing and eventually destroying the film. Although these films maintain traditional aspect ratios, the verticality of the filmstrip produces the unambiguously dominant axis. This verticality is precisely not aligned with the male, the virile, and the phallic, as Eisenstein suggested, but with women's work—editing as sewing—as announced already in Vertov's epoch-making film, *Man with a Movie Camera* (1929), whose eponymous cameraman (Mikhail Kaufman, Vertov's brother) must

13   Ibid., p. 28.
14   The material substrate of film is frequently confused with its essence or ontology. As P. Adams Sitney and Malcolm Le Grice recognized decades ago in their essay 'Narrative Illusion vs. Structural Realism', this argument often boils down to warmed over Greenbergianism misapplied to cinema. Le Grice and Sitney, p. 145. On the historically variable—rather than ontologically stable—roles played by celluloid in avant-garde art and film, see Elcott, 2008.

11.3:   Tacita Dean (b.1965), FILM, 2011. 35mm color and black and white portrait format anamorphic film with hand-tinted sequences, silent, 11 minutes, continuous loop. Installation view: The Unilever Series: Tacita Dean, FILM. 11 October 2011 – 11 March 2012, Turbine Hall, Tate Modern. Photo © Tate. Courtesy: The Artist and Marian Goodman Gallery New York/Paris; Frith Street Gallery, London.

yield to the film's editor (Elizaveta Svilova, Vertov's wife) whenever the material celluloid enters the picture. As contemporary artist and theorist Hito Steyerl has argued: 'In the age of reproduction, Vertov's famous man with the movie camera has been replaced by a woman at an editing table, baby on her lap, a twenty-four-hour shift ahead of her.'[15]

In the context of vertical cinema proper, however, an even more immediate analogue comes to mind: the films and installations or 'locational' films of Paul Sharits. In *S:TREAM:S:S:ECTION:S:ECTION:S:S:ECTIONED* (1970), Sharits superimposed multiple shots of streaming water and then slowly overlaid these camera images with scratches that run the length of the celluloid, thereby foregrounding the materiality of the filmstrip and that of the screen. As Rosalind Krauss argued at the time: 'For film, the world of experience—all photographic experience—is trapped between these two parallel flatnesses', the screen and the filmstrip. The dramatization of this fact is the basis for Sharits's film.[16] We might augment Krauss's account with the equally vital recognition that the world of experience—all cinematic experience—is also caught between the horizontality of the screen and the verticality of the strip, which becomes the basis of the film's development as the live-action stream of water slowly gives way to vertical scratches that course down the celluloid or, as Sharits explained, 'A conceptual lap dissolve from "water currents" to "film strip current"'. The underlying tension between vertical filmstrips and horizontal aspect ratio is brought to a boil in his 1982 locational film titled *3rd Degree*. The installation includes three projectors rigged with mirrors so that they throw vertical images. The content of the images is of a filmstrip being run through an optical printer, sprocket holes and all. These filmstrips, in turn, depict the face of a woman, who appears to be threatened with a match. The filmed filmstrips advance haltingly, sometimes stopping before the lamp so long that the celluloid boils and burns, thus the titles of the installation—*3rd Degree*—and of the single-screen version, *Bad Burns*. The film of the burning filmstrips is subsequently run through the optical printer, creating two and then three generations of filmstrips whose recursive logic is matched only by their material precariousness and violence. In *3rd Degree*, the vertical image and physical filmstrip would be aligned unambiguously except that Sharits has flipped the images on their sides through mirrored projection so that the depicted filmstrips and their plainly visible sprocket holes now advance horizontally. Instead of a one-to-one correspondence between image and

15   Steyerl, p. 184.
16   Krauss, p. 101.

11.4:   Paul Sharits (1943–1993), 3rd Degree, 1982. 16 mm, color, sound, 24fps. Duration: looped films 7 1/2 min each. Courtesy the Paul Sharits Estate and Greene Naftali, New York.

material support, Sharits choreographs a recursivity of doubt that envelops the original footage, the three generations of film, their vertical projection, and, ultimately, the viewer's place therein. (Figure 11.4)

This tension between vertical filmstrips and horizontal aspect ratio is even more pronounced in Sharits's *Frozen Film Frames* series (from the 1970s), in which he suspended strips of celluloid between sheets of Plexiglas such that the strips maintain their vertical flow but often take on proportions like 55 in. by 41.61 in., that is, precisely 1.33:1. (Figure 11.5) The *Frozen Film Frames* were an elaboration of Peter Kubelka's earlier installation of *Arnulf Rainer* (1960), where the celluloid strips were mounted horizontally on the wall. Jennifer West has recently added her own version to this historical series in 'film quilts' like *Magic Lantern Film Quilt Underwater Anamorphic Moon* (2015), comprised of 35mm and 70mm filmstrips, and measuring 52 in. by 40 in. or 1.3:1. Unlike Sharits or Kubelka, however, West's celluloid strips undergo alchemical transformations induced by nail polish, ink, Axe body spray, lavender mist air freshener, skateboard tire marks, Ho-Hos, melon juice, lipstick, and numerous other material interventions by West and her often anonymous collaborators (such as London skateboarders). Such physical

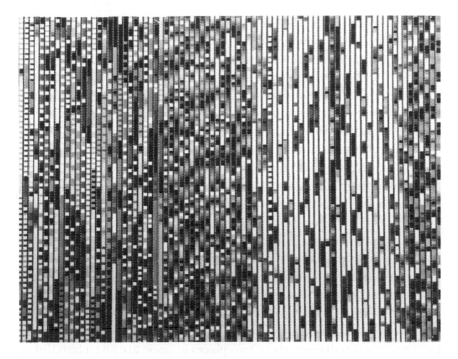

11.5:   Paul Sharits (1943–1993), Untitled (Frozen Film Frame), c.1971-76. 16mm film strips and Plexiglas, 41 1/2 x 55 x 1/4 inches overall 105.4 x 139.7 x .6 cm. Courtesy the Paul Sharits Estate and Greene Naftali, New York.

transmogrifications most famously recall the camera-less films of Stan Brakhage. More importantly, they evoke the pickled, stir-fried, deep-fried, and other cooking-based films by Tony Conrad, which, as Branden Joseph has demonstrated, were part and parcel of a broader reckoning between materialist and feminist practices, that is, between filmmaking and homemaking.[17] Where Conrad's cooking confronts 'timeless' gender norms, West's nail polish, Axe body spray, and lipstick encounter their perennial construction.

Human/ghost

From the eighteenth-century spectacular attraction perfected by Étienne-Gaspard Robertson through Gary Hill's 1992 Documenta video installation *Tall Ships*, phantasmagorias have effected an assembly of bodies and images

17   See Joseph, 2012.

in real time and space.[18] In Robertson's phantasmagoria, spectators were immersed in darkness and ghoulish figures were projected onto translucent screens or clouds of smoke such that they appeared to occupy the same space as the spectators. (Figure 10.6) In Hill's *Tall Ships*, spectators were immersed in darkness and forlorn figures were projected onto invisible black walls such that they appeared to occupy the same space as the spectators. In these and other phantasmagorias, images are not distant visions (like those proffered in the cinema), nor are they circumscribed pictures (like those enclosed in frames or television sets); instead, they appear to abandon their material supports and enter our world. Stripped of the derisive connotations prevalent already in nineteenth-century discourse and concentrated to toxic intensity by Adorno and others in the twentieth century, phantasmagoria—or, more precisely, the phantasmagoric *dispositif*—simply and directly describes the (perceived) assembly of bodies and images in real time and space. The phenomenon is a mainstay of live and recorded audio.[19] And it is sweeping the world under the erroneous rubric of holography. Tupac Shakur, Michael Jackson, Chief Keef, and the French communist politician Jean-Luc Mélénchon, who used the technique to campaign simultaneously in two places at once, are just a handful of the figures recently resurrected or teleported 'holographically', that is, by means of the nineteenth-century technology called Pepper's Ghost (and originally designated 'the Dircksian Phantasmagoria'). Similarly, the innumerable devices hawking 'augmented reality'—such as Microsoft's HoloLens and Google Glass—speak to the contemporary obsession with a world suffused with living images. Even as the histories of art and film are littered with phantasmagoria—from Bernini's *Ecstasy of Saint Teresa* (1647-1652) through Ken Jacobs's decades-long pursuit of 3D cinema—the upsurge in recent decades is pronounced. Robert Whitman's *Shower* (1964), Gary Hill's *Tall Ships* (1992), Diller-Scofidio's 1998 ballet *EJM*, Fiona Tan's *Correction* (2004), Rodney Graham's *Torqued Chandelier Release* (2005), Bill Viola's *Ocean Without a Shore* (2007), Richard Maxwell's *Ads* (2010), and Carrie Mae Weems's *Lincoln, Lonnie, and Me* (2012) are just several of the countless major and minor works best understood neither as paintings or sculptures nor as cinematic films or theatrical dramas but rather as phantasmagorias. Each work engenders the sensation that the image

18   For a more extensive discussion of phantasmagoria, treated separately from the question of verticality, see Elcott, 2016.

19   See Sterne, pp. 110-131. The greatest artistic practitioners of phantasmagoric sound today are surely Janet Cardiff and George Bures Miller. See Uroskie, pp. 1-3.

11.6:   Étienne-Gaspard Robertson (1763–1837). Frontispiece from *Mémoires récréatifs, scientifiques et anecdotiques*. (1831–1833).

may be real or, at the very least, that 'the images have been freed into the materiality of real time and space'.[20] Among the few elements shared by these utterly disparate works is the vertical screen.

Exemplary—in its technical implementation, if not its aesthetic and philosophical pretensions—is Viola's *Ocean Without a Shore*: a high-definition video triptych installed in the Church of San Gallo as part of the 2007 Venice Biennale. Three enormous plasma screens mounted vertically and three pairs of stereo speakers were inserted into the church's three altars. From the dark depths of the screen—or is it a deep recession in space?—grainy black and white figures approach a nearly imperceptible threshold that, upon contact, reveals itself as a wall of water that visually rhymes with the plasma screen. In slow motion, the actors cross the water/ plasma threshold, emerge in high-definition colour, and enter not the Land of Oz but the Church of San Gallo, that is, the very space we occupy, only to return to the grainy darkness from which they issued. (Figure 11.7) *Ocean Without a Shore* rehearses the history of video installation—from the grainy black-and-white figures who approached the viewer and retreated into the darkness of Hill's *Tall Ships* through the recent turn to high production values—only to arrive back at phantasmagoria as it was practiced in the eighteenth century. Robertson famously installed his phantasmagoria in a

20   Cooke, p. 18.

11.7:   Bill Viola (b.1951), *Ocean Without a Shore*, 2007. High-definition color video triptych, two 65-in. flat panel screens, one 103-in. screen mounted vertically; six loudspeakers (three pairs, stereo sound). Room dimensions: 14 ft 9 in. x 21 ft 4 in. x 34 ft 5 in. (4.5 x 6.5 x 10.5 m). Continuously running Performers: Luis Accinelli, Helena Ballent, Melina Bielefelt, Eugenia Care, Carlos Cervantes, Liisa Cohen, Addie Daddio, Jay Donahue, Howard Ferguson, Weba Garretson, Tamara Gorski, Darrow Igus, Page Leong, Richard Neil, Oguri, Larry Omaha, Kira Perov, Jean Rhodes, Chuck Roseberry, Lenny Steinburg, Julia Vera, Bill Viola, Blake Viola, Ellis Williams. Photo: Thierry Bal. © Bill Viola.

Capuchin convent where he projected moving vertical figures in colour, like the Bloody Nun or the recently departed, onto invisible screens suspended in the darkness. Like the original phantasmagoria and *Tall Ships*, *Ocean Without a Shore* is a meditation on life and death: the title derives from the Andalusian Sufi mystic Ibn Arabi, who wrote that 'the Self is an ocean without a shore'.

But phantasmagoria need not get mired in ponderous metaphysics and extravagant pyrotechnics. Indeed, phantasmagoric configurations also undergird some of the most critically attuned film and video installations of the last fifty years, such as the work of Anthony McCall. Beginning with his now-canonical *Line Describing a Cone* (1973), McCall's solid light films comprise the projection of two-dimensional geometric forms through a misty and darkened space such that the beam of light is perceptible as a three-dimensional, immaterial sculpture. As McCall himself declared in a searing 1974 statement, the solid light films negated core aspects of the cinematic apparatus (virtual time and space, spectatorial immobility, and the frontal screen) in favour of real time, real space, and ambulatory and omnidirectional spectatorship.[21] He and others understood the work in largely negative terms. But in the longer history of cinema, the solid light films were and remain unambiguously phantasmagoric: projections on smoke in darkened spaces that assemble humans and images. As Gunnar Schmidt argues, McCall's *Line Describing a Cone* is 'a new combination of modern abstraction and premodern theatricality'.[22] The perfect circle formed at the climax of *Line Describing a Cone* is oriented neither vertically nor horizontally. But other major pieces from the period—*Long Film for Four Projectors* (1974) or *Long Film for Ambient Light* (1975)—forcefully prioritize vertical blades of light or vertical screens. Given the proclivity of the phantasmagoric for the vertical, it is no surprise that McCall's recent work has introduced vertical projection down from the ceiling. Titles like *Breath* (2004) and *Coupling* (2009) allude to abstract, surrogate bodies that rise ten metres high, occupy our space, and in turn are occupied by our bodies. (Figure 11.8)

The verticality of these works exceeds the imperatives of portraiture. And yet verticality cannot be divorced from its generic past. The opposition between the horizontal landscape and the vertical portrait dates back at least to the Renaissance and likely to the late Medieval distinction between icon and narrative (or *imago* and *historia*). In so much as cinema has been a vehicle for narrative, it has remained horizontal. The vertical video formats suddenly available to billions of amateurs only solidifies—by mass consensus—the seemingly eternal link between verticality and portraiture. We might hazard that the turn to verticality stems from or even effects a shift from narrative to image, from *then and there* to *here and now*; in short, from diegesis to mimesis, telling to showing. Whereas the horizontal format frames a stage, the vertical format makes certain claims to immediate presence, ghostly absence, or, most accurately, ghostly presence.

Divine

McCall's vertical pieces have induced heavenly resonances for lay and professional audiences alike. (The fact that *Between You and I* [2006] has been exhibited in several decommissioned churches has only encouraged the associations—despite McCall's repeated disavowals.) Chrétien's patent application singled out the interiors and façades of churches. And

---

21   See McCall, 2003.
22   Schmidt, p. 27.

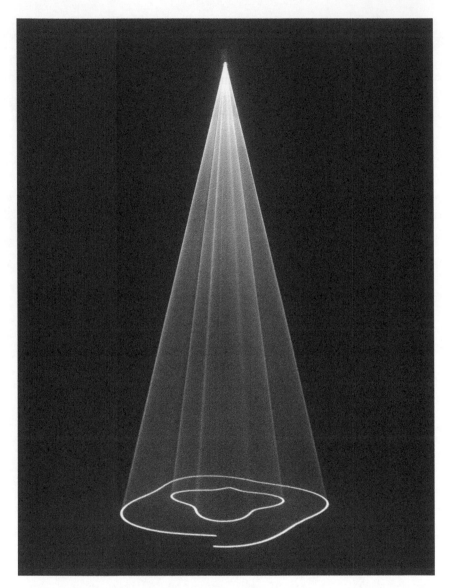

11.8:   Anthony McCall (b.1946), *Coupling*, 2009. Video projector, computer, QuickTime Movie file, haze machine, 16 minutes. Courtesy: The artist and Sean Kelly, New York.

when Sonic Acts commissioned films for a custom 1:2.35 Cinemascope screen as part of their Vertical Cinema project (2013), they first projected them in the Klangraum Krems Minoriten Church. There is no escaping it. Vertical luminous images conjure the divine and, more precisely, evoke the earliest instance of abstract, luminous vertical screens: stained glass windows.[23] Like countless other avant-gardists, László Moholy-Nagy espoused a 'new culture of light' and embraced screens of every size and shape. In his epoch-making treatise *Painting, Photography, Film* (1925/27), Moholy-Nagy traced his experiments in the direct manipulation of light back through the abstract films of Walter Ruttmann, Viking Eggeling, and Hans Richter; the colour organ performances of Thomas Wilfred and Alexander Scriabin; early efforts by Newton and his student Pater Castel; and finally, as the ur-scene of so much Bauhaus thought and practice, the lustrous Medieval cathedral and its stained glass windows.[24] Herbert Molderings has rightly described Moholy-Nagy's aesthetic as a 'secularized light cosmogony'.[25]

Stained glass is an essential reference point because it is the oldest and most consistent instance of vertically oriented luminous screens, a tradition that runs more or less continuously from Suger's Saint-Denis cathedral in the twelfth century to De Stijl impresario Theo van Doesburg's stained glass windows, like *Composition IV* (1917), and Gerhard Richter's monumental stained glass window for the south transept of the Cologne Cathedral (2007), which makes explicit the link between backlit pixelated computer screens and panes of stained glass. But the link between vertical stained glass and vertical media screens had been made definitively already in *Chartres Bleu* (1983-1986), the most famous work by West Coast Conceptualist artist Paul Kos. Kos's radiant installation reconstructs a 27-pane stained glass window in the choir ambulatory of the Chartres Cathedral using 27 television monitors turned on their sides, that is, oriented vertically. (Figure 11.9) The choice of window was dictated not by the Biblical narrative or the beauty of the design but by the proportions of each pane of glass: 3:4 or 1:1.33, the aspect ratio of standard definition video turned on its side.[26] Each monitor plays a 12-minute video loop that reconstructs—via 35mm transparencies—a 24-hour cycle. The 'anagogical manner' promulgated by Suger, Abbot of Saint Denis—that is, the ascent from the material to the immaterial world[27]—is here braided and looped: darkness cedes to light and Gospel is birthed from the void, only for the luminosity to reach an intensity so fierce that it

23   The proportions or aspect ratios of paintings have proven irresistible catnip to big data analysts. Thus far, the conclusions tend to confirm commonplace knowledge. See, for example, Trott's 'Aspect Ratios in Art' (2015) and Roeder's 'A Nerd's Guide to the 2,229 Paintings at MoMA' (2015).

24   Moholy-Nagy, pp. 18-19.

25   Molderings, p. 14.

26   Kos and Phillips, p. 145.

27   Suger, pp. 63-65.

11.9:   Paul Kos (b.1942), *Chartres Bleu*, 27 channel video installation. Edition 1 of 3.
Permanently installed at di Rosa Art Preserve, Napa California. Photo: Courtesy of Paul
Kos, Anglim/Gilbert Gallery, San Francisco and Galerie George -Philippe and Nathalie
Valois, Paris.

obliterates the image and yields a pile of blue screens at once transcendent
and opaque. The loop returns to darkness and begins the cycle anew.

For the interwar and post-WWII avant-gardes, the single most important
practitioner of the art of light may very well have been Thomas Wilfred.[28]
The Danish-born, Parisian-trained American artist founded 'lumia', the art
of light, in the early decades of the twentieth century and constructed its

28   For an overview, see Stein, 1971.

primary instrument, a colour organ dubbed the Clavilux ('light keyboard'), in 1919. (Figure 11.10) Moholy-Nagy referenced the work as early as 1922, and Wilfred has continued to inspire (but also disappoint) avant-garde and mainstream artists and filmmakers like Ken Jacobs, James Turrell, and Terrence Malick through the present. Wilfred's lumia enjoyed widespread success in the 1920s and 1930s. He toured with conductor Leopold Stokowski and the Philadelphia Orchestra in a series of concerts in 1926, presaging Stokowski's more famous turn in Disney's *Fantasia* (1940). Wilfred fell into partial obscurity in the 1940s and 1950s (though he was exhibited alongside Jackson Pollock and Mark Rothko at MoMA's *Fifteen Americans* show [1952]). And he saw a brief revival in the 1960s, including the *Lumia Suite, Opus 158* (1963-1964), a major MoMA commission that resulted in what was perhaps the first looped light or film display on long-term exhibition in a major art museum.

Wilfred's lumia pieces can be likened rhapsodically to undulating curtains of light or diaphanous clouds of colour. For better or for worse, their closest mainstream analogue today are screensavers. Like most practitioners of visual music (a term Wilfred resisted), Wilfred was stirred by higher powers, be it theosophic knowledge of the divine or the sidereal firmament. He envisioned 'a major fine art' whose origins and foundation are to be found in the starry skies, 'apart from earthly phenomena and the human body'.[29] The theosophic and celestial rhetoric resounded in titles like *Ascending Forms* or *Fourth Study in Rising Forms* (both 1954), but his relation to verticality was ultimately more practical, as is evidenced in a series of works straightforwardly titled *Vertical Sequence I-III* (1935-1941). Most relevant for a history of vertical screens, Wilfred, like Eisenstein, recognized the limitations of the traditional and expanded horizontal formats. He contrasted lumia to Cinerama and Cinemascope: 'Both of these employ "panoramic" screens [...] and both yield impressive illusions of depth. Such screen proportions, however, would not serve in lumia because so many of the lumia compositions depend on the vertical dimension for effectiveness.'[30] Wilfred emphatically addressed these technical limitations as soon as he shifted his emphasis from concert performances to home and gallery installations. In his first Home Clavilux models, known as the Clavilux Junior (1930), the duo-stacked walnut cabinets stored a 100-watt moving lamp, hand-painted glass disks, and other equipment on the bottom

29   Wilfred, 1969, pp. 252-253.
30   See Wilfred's unpublished manuscript *Lumia, The Art of Light* (1945-1947), excerpted in Stein, 67.

11.10:   Thomas Wilfred (1889–1968), *Clavilux Junior*, 1930. Carol and Eugene Epstein
         Collection.

and a vertical screen on top. A substantial number of opuses similarly
utilized vertical screens, including *Counterpoint in Space (Opus 146)* (1956),
Multidimensional (1957), *Sequence in Space* (1965), and *Untitled (Opus 161)*
(1966). (Figure 11.11) The first of these included stained-glass pieces rather
than gel-based paint on the revolving colour record inside the machine,
thus establishing a direct techno-material connection to vertical church
windows. The last was made for a vertical screen 32 in. by 51 in., but it gained
its widest audience as part of Terrence Malick's *Tree of Life* (2011)—a major

motion picture otherwise suffused with 'organic' special effects created by Douglas Trumbull and others using fluorescent dyes, paints, CO_2, milk, flares, and a Phantom camera shooting at 1,000 fps, which function almost independent of the pompous narrative and voiceovers. Here, to commence the creation of the universe, Wilfred's vertical cloud of colour stands in for nothing less than divine light.

Wilfred was not, however, an evangelist for vertical screens. Like Eisenstein before him, he gravitated toward a dynamic square or squat rectangle that enabled horizontal and vertical forms. MoMA's *Lumia Suite*, for example, is rear-projected onto an 8 ft. by 6 ft. screen, that is, in traditional 4:3 or 1.33:1. But the piece comprises three 12-minute cycles or movements: horizontal, vertical, and elliptical. Similarly, Wilfred produced the first Home Lumia Instruments (1935-1936) in horizontal and vertical models (with sides measuring 16 and 20 inches in either direction).

And so we return to McElheny's seven *Screens For Looking at Abstraction* to find a pervasive but also contradictory embrace of the vertical. (Figure 11.1) The artist and his interlocutors categorically understand the work as 'sculptural screens' or simply as 'sculptures'.[31] (A better analogy may be to painted altarpieces with open wings.) As sculptures, they are resoundingly vertical. With the exception of *Screens For Looking at Abstraction Nos. 3* and *6*, the proportions of the seven screens range from a near square 1:1.08 (*No. 4* and *No. 7*) to a towering 1:1.83 (*No. 5*)—physical ratios that are markedly elongated phenomenologically through the real (rather than perceived) depth of the angled screens.[32] But these sculptures are not only sculptures. They are also 'machines', in McElheny's evocative analogy to a video arcade, machines that are 'some kind of portal or entry to someplace else'.[33] This 'someplace else' is often resolutely horizontal. Nowhere is the tension between sculptural verticality and virtual horizontality more pronounced than in *Screen No. 1*. An 84 in. by 96 in. screen flanked by two mirrors (facing each other and perpendicular to the screen), *Screen No. 1* creates an infinitely regressive horizontal image whose aspect ratio is 1:∞. The physical sculpture is vertical; the virtual image is boundlessly horizontal.

At the core of McElheny's *Screens For Looking at Abstraction* is neither the materiality of the screen nor the virtuality of the image but their mutual

31 McEhleny, Herrmann, and Trodd, p. 75.
32 These measures do not take into account the pressure mounted vertical armature, whose dimensions vary with the space but always raise the screens off the ground and soar far above their width.
33 McEhleny, Herrmann, and Trodd, p. 80. Early video arcade games, not least Pac-Man (1980), are another instance of pervasive vertical screens.

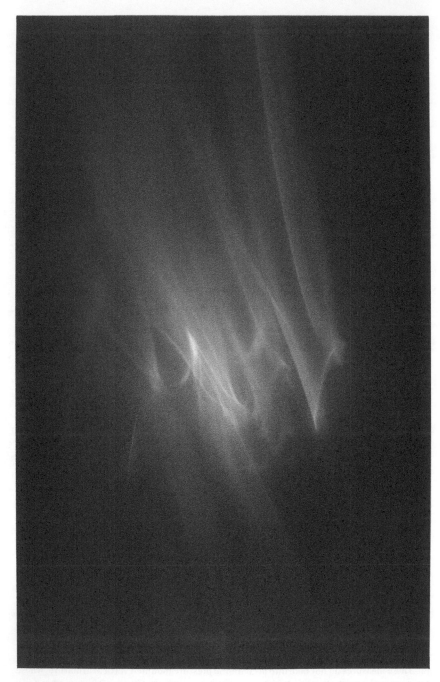

11.11:   Thomas Wilfred (1889–1968), *Untitled (Opus 161)*, 1966. Digital still image of an analog time-based Lumia work. Carol and Eugene Epstein Collection.

dependence. Each screen poses an optical riddle and demands scrutiny and study. And yet even when the riddle is 'solved' and the virtual image is mapped onto the material screen, the visual pleasure does not abate. For the kaleidoscopic regime of images harbours no standstill where contemplation can wholly master the conflation of sculpture and image. The industrialization and standardization of the vertical screen is, no doubt, epoch-making. But the towering verticality of *Screen No. 5* is of no greater consequence than the squareness of *Screens Nos. 4* and *7* or the diamond-like reflections of *Screen No. 6*. As Eisenstein understood generations ago, the ultimate aim cannot be to replace or even augment the axiom of horizontal narrative with the axiom of vertical portraiture—be it of celluloid or iPhones, humans or ghosts, spirits or gods. No Chrétien cross to augment a squarish centre with wide and 'tall' screens. No iPhones to switch between portrait and landscape. Rather than an agenda, McElheny's *Screens For Looking at Abstraction* advance a recognition: there is no image without its material screen and no screen without its virtual image and no cinema without the confluence of the two.

Works Cited

Belton, John. *Widescreen Cinema*. Cambridge, MA: Harvard University Press, 1992.

Cooke, Lynne. 'Gary Hill: "Who am I but a figure of speech?"' *Parkett* no. 34 (1992): 16-27.

Dean, Tacita. 'FILM.' In *Film: Tacita Dean*, edited by Nicholas Cullinan, The Unilever Series. London: Tate Publishing, 2011.

Deleuze, Gilles. *Foucault*. Translated by Seán Hand. Minneapolis: University of Minnesota Press, 1988.

Eisenstein, Sergei. 'The Dynamic Square.' In *Selected Works, vol. 1: Writings 1922-1934*, edited by Michael R. Taylor. London: BFI, 1991.

Elcott, Noam M. 'Darkened Rooms: A Genealogy of Avant-Garde Filmstrips from Man Ray to the London Film-Makers' Co-op and Back Again.' *Grey Room* 30 (2008): 6-37.

———. 'The Phantasmagoric Dispositif: An Assembly of Bodies and Images in Real Time and Space.' *Grey Room* 62 (2016): 42-71.

Glove and Boots. 'Vertical Video Syndrome.' YouTube, 5 June 2012. https://youtu.be/Bt9zSf1nwFA. Accessed on 12 November 2018.

Howell, A.S. and J.A. Dubray. 'Some Practical Aspects of and Recommendations on Wide Film Standards.' *Journal of the Society of Motion Picture Engineers* XIV, no. 1 (1930): 59-84.

Joseph, Branden W. *The Roh and the Cooked*. Berlin: August Verlag, 2012.

Kos, Paul and Glenn Phillips. 'Paul Kos.' In *California Video: Artists and Histories*, edited by Glenn Phillips, pp. 142-145. Los Angeles: Getty Research Institute, 2008.

Krauss, Rosalind. 'Paul Sharits.' *Film Culture* no. 65-66 (1978): 103-108.

Le Grice, Malcolm and P. Adams Sitney. 'Narrative Illusion vs. Structural Realism.' In *Experimental Cinema in the Digital Age*, edited by Malcolm LeGrice, pp. 134-152. London: BFI, 2001.

Man Ray. 'Tous les films que j'ai réalisés...' *Études cinématographiques* no. 38-39 (1965): 43-46.

Manjoo, Farhad. 'Vertical Video on the Small Screen? Not a Crime.' *The New York Times*, 12 August 2015.

McCall, Anthony. '*Line Describing a Cone* and Related Films.' *October* no. 103 (2003): 42-62.

McEhleny, Josiah. 'Josiah McEhleny in Conversation with Daniel F. Herrmann and Tamara Trodd.' In *Josiah McElheny: The Past was a Mirage I'd Left Far Behind*, edited by Daniel F. Herrmann, pp. 75-85. London: Whitechapel Gallery, 2012.

Moholy-Nagy, László. *Malerei Fotografie Film*. Edited by Hans M. Wingler. Berlin: Gebr. Mann Verlag, 1927; reprinted 1986.

Molderings, Herbert. 'Lichtjahre eines Lebens: Das Fotogramm in der Ästhetik Laszlo Moholy-Nagys.' In *Laszlo Moholy-Nagy: Fotogramme 1922-1943*, edited by Renate Heyne, Floris M. Neusüss, and Herbert Molderings, pp. 8-17. München: Schirmer-Mosel, 1995.

Roeder, Oliver. 'A Nerd's Guide To The 2,229 Paintings At MoMA.' *FiveThirtyEight* (blog). 28 August, 2015. http://www.fivethirtyeight.com/features/a-nerds-guide-to-the-2229-paintings-at-moma. Accessed on 12 November 2018.

Schapiro, Meyer. 'On Some Problems in the Semiotics of Visual Art: Field and Vehicle in Image-Signs.' *Simiolus* 6, no. 1 (1972-1973): 9-19.

Schmidt, Gunnar. *Weiche Displays: Projektionen auf Rauch, Wolken und Nebel*. Berlin: Verlag Klaus Wagenbach, 2011.

Stein, Donna. *Thomas Wilfred: Lumia*. Washington, DC: Corcoran Gallery of Art, 1971.

Sterne, Jonathan. 'Space within Space: Artificial Reverb and the Detachable Echo.' *Grey Room* 60 (2015): 110-131.

Steyerl, Hito. *The Wretched of the Screen*. E-flux. Berlin: Sternberg Press, 2012.

Suger, the Abbot of St. Denis. *Abbot Suger on the Abbey Church of St.-Denis and its Art Treasures*. Translated by Erwin Panofsky. Second edition. Princeton: Princeton University Press, 1979.

Trott, Michael. 'Aspect Ratios in Art: What Is Better Than Being Golden?' *Wolfram* (blog). 18 November, 2015. http://blog.wolfram.com/2015/11/18/aspect-ratios-in-art-what-is-better-than-being-golden-being-plastic-rooted-or-just-rational-investigating-aspect-ratios-of-old-vs-modern-paintings/. Accessed on 12 November 2018.

Uroskie, Andrew V. *Between the Black Box and the White Cube: Expanded Cinema and Postwar Art*. Chicago: University of Chicago Press, 2014.

Wasserman, Norman. 'Special Projection Process Give *Fantasia* New Look.' *International Projectionist* (March 1956): 14-15.

Wilfred, Thomas. 'Light and the Artist.' In *Total Theatre*, edited by E.T. Kirby, pp. 252-264. New York: E.P. Dutton & Co., 1969.

About the Author

Noam M. Elcott is associate professor of Modern and Contemporary Art and Media at Columbia University. His research focuses on Europe and North America, with an emphasis on interwar art, photography, and film. Elcott is the author of *Artificial Darkness: A History of Modern Art and Media* (2016). He is currently at work on *Art in the First Screen Age: László Moholy-Nagy and the Cinefication of the Arts*, which traverses interwar painting, architecture, photography, film, theatre, and exhibition design in the age of cinema. Elcott is an editor of the journal *Grey Room*, which covers architecture, art, media, and politics. His articles have appeared in leading journals like *October* and *Aperture*.

Acknowledgments

This collection emerged from the initiative "Genealogy of the Excessive Screen" that the three editors developed and led in the years 2015-2018. The initiative started in 2015 with the seminar, "The Resurfacing of the Screen," funded by the Whitney Humanities Center (WHC) at Yale University. We extend our gratitude to Gary Tomlinson, director of the WHC for making this initial event possible, and for hosting many of the subsequent seminar meetings. We also thank the participants of the initial seminar for their stimulating contributions: Carol Armstrong; Giuliana Bruno; Mauro Carbone; Beatriz Colomina; Tom Conley; Ruggero Eugeni; Bernard Siegert; Anthony Vidler; Laura Wexler; and John Williams. The initiative grew over the following years thanks to a Andrew W. Mellon Foundation Sawyer Seminar grant, which made possible a lecture series on screen practices, two booklets with the Yale Gallery and the Yale Center for the British Arts, and a seminar taught by Francesco Casetti and Bernard Geoghegan. We are indebted to the speakers and respondents who made the seminar such an rewarding intellectual adventure: Dudley Andrew, Tim Barringer, Marijeta Bozovic, Rizvana Bradley, Rey Chow, Keller Easterling, Noam M. Elcott, Juliet Fleming, Kurt W. Forster, Yuriko Furuhata, Tom Gunning, Brian Kane, Gundula Kreuzer, Kathryn Lofton, Phillippe-Alain Michaud, W.J.T. Mitchell, Paul North, Keely Orgeman, John Durham Peters, Brigitte Peucker, Antonio Somaini, Barbara Stafford, Jocelyn Szczepaniak-Gillece, and Katie Trumpener. We also thank our team of graduate students for the extraordinary support they provided: Regina Karl, Anna Schechtman, Andrew Vielkind, and Swagato Chakravorty. The project found warm support from Yale's museums. We thank Jock Reynolds and Pamela Franks of Yale University's Art Gallery, and Amy Meyers from Yale's Center for British Arts for welcoming the project into their institutions. From the beginning and throughout the project we were grateful for the support of Tamar Gendler, Dean of the Faculty of Arts and Sciences, and Amy Hungerford, Dean of Humanities. We are very thankful for the work of Mal Ahern, who copy-edited and commented on the texts, and Theodossis Issaias, who researched and secured rights for the book's illustrations.

Index

Printed and bound by CPI Group (UK) Ltd, Croydon, CR0 4YY

27/10/2024

14580699-0002